Reaction Formations: Dialogism, Ideology, and Capitalist Culture

Studies in Critical Social Sciences Book Series

Haymarket Books is proud to be working with Brill Academic Publishers (www.brill.nl) to republish the *Studies in Critical Social Sciences* book series in paperback editions. This peer-reviewed book series offers insights into our current reality by exploring the content and consequences of power relationships under capitalism, and by considering the spaces of opposition and resistance to these changes that have been defining our new age. Our full catalog of *SCSS* volumes can be viewed at https://www.haymarketbooks.org/series_collections/4-studies-in-critical-social-sciences.

Series Editor
David Fasenfest (SOAS University of London)

Editorial Board
Eduardo Bonilla-Silva (Duke University)
Chris Chase-Dunn (University of California–Riverside)
William Carroll (University of Victoria)
Raewyn Connell (University of Sydney)
Kimberlé W. Crenshaw (University of California–LA and Columbia University)
Heidi Gottfried (Wayne State University)
Karin Gottschall (University of Bremen)
Alfredo Saad Filho (King's College London)
Chizuko Ueno (University of Tokyo)
Sylvia Walby (Lancaster University)
Raju Das (York University)

Reaction Formations: Dialogism, Ideology, and Capitalist Culture

The Creation of the Modern Unconscious

JONATHAN HALL

Haymarket Books
Chicago, IL

First published in 2019 by Brill Academic Publishers, The Netherlands.
© 2019 Koninklijke Brill NV, Leiden, The Netherlands

Published in paperback in 2020 by
Haymarket Books
P.O. Box 180165
Chicago, IL 60618
773-583-7884
www.haymarketbooks.org

ISBN: 978-1-64259-196-5

Distributed to the trade in the US through Consortium Book Sales and Distribution (www.cbsd.com) and internationally through Ingram Publisher Services International (www.ingramcontent.com).

This book was published with the generous support of Lannan Foundation and Wallace Action Fund.

Special discounts are available for bulk purchases by organizations and institutions. Please call 773-583-7884 or email info@haymarketbooks.org for more information.

Cover design by Jamie Kerry and Ragina Johnson.

Printed in United States.

10 9 8 7 6 5 4 3 2 1

Library of Congress Cataloging-in-Publication Data is available.

Contents

Acknowledgements IX

Introduction 1

1 Dialogism: the Potential for Change and for Resistance to Change 8
  1 The Sources of "Becoming" in Philosophical Idealism 10
  2 "Becoming" as Socio-linguistic Event 13
  3 Towards a Historical Account of the Unconscious? 16
  4 From Literary Dialogism to Dialectical "Becoming" 21
  5 "Speech Genres" and Creativity 24
  6 Anticipation and Prevention: the Problem of Temporality 27
  7 Conclusion 33

2 The Fissured Modern Subject: Paradox versus "Becoming" in Dostoevsky's *Notes from Underground* 36
  1 Dialogical "Becoming" or Frozen Dialectic? 38
  2 The Ethics of Capitalism 45
  3 The Internal Catastrophe 48
  4 The Prison House of Paradox 52
  5 A Modern Liar's Paradox 54
  6 An Unconscious within Hyperconsciousness? 61
  7 Revolutionary Dreams or Literary Nostalgia? 66
  8 Dialogism Violated 69
  9 Literature and the Social Unconscious 79

3 Rethinking Ideology as a Field of Dialogical Conflict 82
  1 Bakhtin's Developmental Model 82
  2 The Authority Concealed in the Utterance 85
  3 The Idea of a Single Ideology Is Itself Ideological 90
  4 Ideological Conflict and the Production of the Unconscious 92
  5 The Dialectics of Repression 95
  6 Interpellation Revisited 98
  7 The Relationship of Dialogism and Dialectics 101

4 A Contradictory Symbiosis Is Born: the Rival Ideologies of the Market and the State under Capitalism 105
  1 The Rival Myths of Nature in Bourgeois Ideology 107
  2 The Capitalist Double-bind and the Displacement of Guilt 114

3 Social Contradiction Internalised   116
  4 Loyalty versus Law: a Buried History   117
  5 Market Addressivity: Capitalism without Guilt?   119
  6 The Market's Need for Permanent Non-satisfaction   123
  7 Conclusion   126

5 **Captivating the Unruly Subject: Ideology in Early Modern Europe**   127
  1 Monetarisation and the Crisis of Identity   130
  2 The Symbolic Divinisation of the State   138
  3 Royal Charisma: a Concealed Contradiction in the Baroque Spectacle   141
  4 The "Theatricality" of Power?   144
  5 Capturing the Will to Believe   148
  6 The Solar Theatricality of Absolutism in Shakespeare's Henriad   151
  7 From Solar Absolutism to "Charismatic" Seduction   155
  8 Carnival and Charisma: the Concealed Connection   158
  9 Carnival and Dialectics   161
  10 Anticipation, Prevention, and Unconscious Guilt   164

6 **Repairing the Universe: Mysticism as Loss and Longing**   167
  1 The Reactionary Activist: a Serious Quijote?   172
  2 Textual Authority: from Desire to Method   179
  3 Transverberation: the Divine Word Reincarnated   185
  4 Conclusion: from Mysticism to "Modernity"   197

7 **Baroque Incompletion, the Captivated Subject, and the Humour of *Don Quijote***   199
  1 Theatrical Addressivity   203
  2 The Comic Counter-discourse   204
  3 Capturing the Spectator's Desire   207
  4 Baroque Incompletion   210
  5 The Aesthetics of "Becoming" versus Timeless Form   212
  6 A Comic Great Theatre of the World   215
  7 The Captivated Reader   219
  8 Competitive Desire   225
  9 Charisma and Competitive Envy   229
  10 The Captivated Quixotic Critic   235

8 The Dialectics of Laughter and Anxiety 239
 1 Carnival Enters into History 243
 2 Laughter and Religious Conflict 248
 3 The "Risibility" of the Lower Other in Classical Aesthetics 250
 4 Laughter and Unconscious Anxiety: the Emergent Modernity of Hobbes' Theory of Laughter 253
 5 Modernising Hobbes' Dialectic 259
 6 Playing with Breakdown: a Structural or a Dialogical Model of Laughter? 261

Conclusion 271

Bibliography 275
Name Index 282
Subject Index 285

Acknowledgements

I would like to express my thanks to my friends and colleagues, particularly Craig Brandist, Jeremy Tambling, Ackbar Abbas, and Galin Tihanov for their unstinting support and for many hours of interesting discussions, some of which have produced an answering echo in this book. In his capacity as director of the Bakhtin Centre at the University of Sheffield, Craig Brandist has been especially generous in extending his hospitality to enable me to participate in its programme of lectures and discussions. I am also very grateful for the support over several years of its founding director, David Shepherd. I have benefitted from the lively discussions at a number of the series of International Bakhtin Conferences initiated by Clive Thomson and held at various locations across the world. These have provided me with many friendships, and with the memorable differences of opinion, which they have enabled me to grapple with. I hope that they will continue to do so. The reader will judge for herself if these exchanges have been fruitful. The test here is not whether my explorations are conclusive, although I hope that they are provocative, but whether they open up a useable potential for further questions. Here, paradoxically, I would leave the last word to Mikhaïl Mikhaïlovich Bakhtin who wrote that the "last word" is never spoken.

Introduction

"But I hear *voices* in everything and dialogic relations among them"
M.M. BAKHTIN[1]

∴

The twin concepts of "monologism" and "dialogism" were first put forward in the 1920s and 1930s by the Russian philosopher and critic, Mikhaïl Bakhtin and his Marxist co-thinker, Valentin Voloshinov. Some critical debate has focused on the relative contributions of Bakhtin and Voloshinov but, despite their divergences, these co-thinkers developed along broadly similar lines the apparently simple concept of the "dialogical" nature of all language. They extended their concept of dialogism to include the silent language of "inner speech" which we normally call thought. In this respect, their thinking coincides very closely with the developmental psychology of their compatriot, Lev Vygotsky, although there is no evidence of any direct influence. The purpose of this book is to explore the possibilities which these concepts offer for a historical understanding of the subjective aspects of the conflicts and crises engendered by the culture of capitalism.

The investigations of the "Bakhtin Circle", as it has come to be called, could best be summed up as pursuing the consequences of considering language as primarily dialogical in nature. This means that they give primacy to the "utterance" which is always addressed to another, who is either a real or an anticipated addressee, rather than to any putative underlying linguistic system or structure. Chapter One discusses this anti-systemic account of language. At first Bakhtin argued that dialogism was the unique stylistic creation of Dostoevsky, which he contrasted with the "monologism" of other novelists, meaning the overall dominance of the author's viewpoint in their work. But later he extended the concept of dialogical interactivity to the language of the novel as a literary genre, and later still to all the other non-literary genres, including the scientific, sociological, and philosophical genres.

With this evolution in Bakhtin's theory of language, dialogism became for him and Voloshinov the condition of possibility for changes in human consciousness. Throughout this development, Bakhtin's insistence on the dialogical nature of language in general retained his ethical concern with the

---

1 Bakhtin 1986, p. 169.

individual's "answerability" or "responsibility" (*otvetsvennost'*) to others. Whether at the individual or at the socio-historical level, the constitutive dialogical relationship with others puts every individual human subject, and every social group, in a position of potential "outsideness" (*vnehakhodimost'*) in relation to the discourses through which they have already developed and continue to think and respond to those others. Here Bakhtin adopted and adapted the concept of "becoming" from Ernst Cassirer's *Philosophy of Symbolic Forms*, and indirectly from Cassirer's own assimilation of Wilhelm von Humboldt's ideas on language as creative *energeia*. Cassirer was moving at that time towards Hegelian ideas on the historical development of the forms of consciousness, and Bakhtin and Voloshinov responded to that trend.[2] But the specific contribution of both Bakhtin and Voloshinov was to argue that it is the dialogical nature of language which gives all human subjectivity the potential for openness to change or, in Cassirer's terms the capacity for "becoming". By now, however, the contrast between monologism and dialogism itself shifts. They become reformulated as two interlinked but opposing principles within all language. Monologism is no longer an alternative mode of discourse to dialogism but its active resistance, dialogically engaged despite itself.

In his introduction to his book on Dostoevsky, Bakhtin quotes Anatoly Lunacharsky's essay (1929) on the "Plurality of Voices" in Dostoevsky's work. That leading Marxist theoretician agreed with Bakhtin's analysis, and with his argument that this Dostoevskian plurality of "voices" was made possible by the catastrophic and belated irruption of capitalism into Russian society.[3] Lunacharsky also argued that the destructive social and psychological "splintering" caused by this development repeated the similar upheaval caused by early capitalism in Shakespeare's England. Both catastrophes provided the conditions which favoured the development of the two writers' creativity. In his late essay (1961) entitled "Towards a Reworking of the Dostoevsky book",[4] Bakhtin reiterated this view that the sudden arrival of capitalism in Russia had provided the historical conditions of possibility for Dostoevsky's creative insights. However, there is a significant paradox in the fact that Bakhtin first developed his views on the dialogical nature of human consciousness largely in response to his reading of Dostoevsky. This paradox comes to the forefront of Bakhtin's own critical discourse because the capacity for "becoming" only appears negatively in Dostoevsky's major works. It is not simply absent (Bakhtin is right

---

2 Hamlin and Krois 2004, pp. 99–116; Brandist 1997, pp. 20–27; Tihanov 1998, pp. 596–621; Lähteenmäki 2002, pp. 193–204.
3 Lunacharsky 1965.
4 Bakhtin 1984, Appendix 2.

to detect it there), but it is only present as a potential which is actively prevented from development by the characters' hyper-conscious resistance to it. In analysing this conflicted "inward dialogism" as a scene of "catastrophe", Bakhtin gives particularly close attention to *Notes from Underground*, whose first-person narrator-protagonist he calls an "ideologist" whereas Dostoevsky calls him a "paradoxalist". For my argument this detail is significant because paradox formulates contradictions rhetorically without any space for transformation or "becoming", whether dialogical or dialectical. In Chapter Two I follow Bakhtin's insights closely but critically, to explore how this narrator-hero's internalised conflict with his addressees, including the anticipated responses of his absent readers, provides a way of understanding how the unconscious is produced out of intensified dialogical conflict when there is no process leading to change. My reading of Dostoevsky's famous novella extends Bakhtin's own insights beyond some of his presuppositions. But it also provides the starting point and paradigm for Chapter Three on ideology. Although ideology is usually theorised in various ways as a unified structure, it is better seen as a non-unifiable field of struggle between rival discourses, each of which pursues its own dominant singularity whether the rivalry with others is consciously acknowledged or not.

The concept of "reaction formations", which provides the title for this book, rests on the proposition that every would-be dominant discourse is inwardly fissured by its continuing dialogical conflicts, and by those out of which it has arisen historically. Here I make three general points: Firstly, no discourse can ever be truly monological. Althusser's concept of the constitution of subjects through *interpellation* is still useful, but only if its structuralism is replaced by Bakhtin's concept of dialogical *addressivity*. Voloshinov's *Marxism and the Philosophy of Language* [1929][5] argues that every would-be dominant ideology is always dialogically engaged with its rival discourses in a historical struggle for dominance, whether by appropriating them into itself or by silencing them. But in either case the inescapability of the dialogical relationship means that hegemony, to use Antonio Gramsci's term for linguistic and cultural dominance, is always inwardly fissured because it is always contested. The second point follows: not only is complete monological dominance an unachievable goal, but its pursuit is in effect a reactive desire to regress to an imaginary prior state of uncontested harmony where the rival discourses would not yet exist. Psychoanalysis knows this reactive drive as narcissism, but it can be a shared collective phenomenon as well as an individual one. This brings up the third point, which is developed in Chapter Four. There I consider the specific nature

---

5   Voloshinov 1973.

of capitalist ideology, namely its historical provenance from within the contradictory symbiosis of the territorial nation-state and the unprecedented power of the market. In short, with the advent of capitalism, not only is the ideology of the dominant class contested by the social forces which it struggles to maintain in subordination, but it is itself inwardly fissured between the demands of the market and the need for state control.

A cultural history of the dynamic changes brought into existence by capitalism would be inadequate without taking account of its equally dynamic resistances to its own potential for revolutionary transformation. This book explores the inner contradictions of this ideology, born out of the very processes of historical change which it brought into being even as it struggled to arrest them. Capitalist ideology has never been a controlling structure, however entrenched this monological assumption has become in much contemporary theory. As a field of rival discourses struggling for dominance, it has sometimes been marked by passionate aspirations and/or desperate defensiveness. That is why I pay attention to the symbolic and discursive struggles through which the hegemonic ideologies of the Church and State in early modern Europe sought to negate the threat of change, by representing the proliferation of the threatening new discourses as a return to "Chaos", "the Flood", and/or "diabolical" disorder. These were the various imaginary absences of order which constituted the widespread anxiety, or even concealed paranoia, of the early modern "Culture of the Baroque" in Western Europe.[6] The theatricalised displays by those in power, or by those organising the spectacles on their behalf, did not actually constitute that power as some have maintained,[7] but nor were they merely empty. Their flamboyant displays of the uninterrupted "presence" of power should be understood by us now as symptomatic responses which functioned to negate the anxieties haunting the ruling order (or barely contained disorder) of the early modern European states. This theatricality was above all a form of dialogical *addressivity*. It was aimed at eliciting a response, of enthusiasm or at least acquiescence, from its potentially rebellious addressees. Insofar as the self-display was successful, it also provided the rulers with the reassuring narcissism characteristic of Absolutist reaction. Indeed, the rulers may have been more effectively captivated than their subjects.

There is a long history here, in the course of which the rulers of the centralising nation states in Western Europe usurped for themselves the older but weakening universal claim of Christendom, while claiming to represent its

---

6 Antonio Maravall, *The Culture of the Baroque: analysis of a historical structure* [1975], Minnesota and Manchester U.P. 1986.

7 Cf. Greenblatt 1988; Tennenhouse 1986.

continuing presence on earth. From this characteristically Baroque theatricality and its spectacular constructions of a quasi-divine monarchical presence at the centre of the emergent nation state, our modern "imagined community"[8] has inherited its own spectacular strategies of re-enchantment. These national spectacles addressed to the population are still quite familiar. When Karl Marx called religious belief the "heart of a heartless world" and "soul of a soulless situation",[9] his paradoxes summarised a collective psychology: the imaginary "heart" negates the real "heartlessness", and the imaginary "soul" compensates for its absence. But in order to achieve these effects in the modern "disenchanted" world brought into being by capitalism, the rulers of the early modern states had to usurp for themselves the enchantments of the vanishing aura of the old sacred centre. In the early modern period, the ruling class rituals previously enacted in the sight of God, became spectacles addressed to the populace. The emotional force of this state-centred re-enchantment still sustains many subjects' loyalty to the "imagined community". Without it, the nation-states system would perhaps not continue for very long.

Chapter Six, "Repairing the Universe: Mysticism as Loss and Longing" takes up Michel de Certeau's analysis of the "mystical moment" in the sixteenth and seventeenth centuries. It was an attempt to rescue the universe itself from the fragmentation and loss of transcendental meaning which de Certeau himself invokes, and which Max Weber (echoing Schiller) famously called the "disenchantment of the world".[10] De Certeau borrows the threat of fragmentation from Lacanian psychoanalysis, and he identifies it as the source of the subject's compulsion to overcome it in order to restore the unity of the universe itself. This anxiety could be described as the experience of an existential crisis at the heart of the early modern "Culture of the Baroque". But the real historical condition of possibility for this sense of fragmentation was the vast expansion of the social forces brought into being by emergent capitalism, and the accompanying proliferation of incompatible discourses which we call the Renaissance. This was undeniably a momentous liberation from the narrow constraints of earlier modes of understanding, but it brought with it the counter-active desire to rediscover and reaffirm the absent or disappearing unity. The "Baroque" culture of feverish interpretation was aimed at unveiling the real but absent "totality", and it was carried over into the modern world.

---

8   Anderson 1983. Anderson attributes this unifying imagination to the power of "print capitalism" which favoured the emergence of a single national language.
9   Marx 1977, p. 64.
10 Weber 1965.

The imaginary restoration of the universe to its real but absent unity in the face of the proliferation of "deceptive" appearances made the desiring subject the agent of this rescue. Chapter Seven discusses Cervantes' Don Quijote as the captivated hero of this contemporary drive to restore the absent order, with himself as its imaginary agent. He fashions himself by identifying with the epic heroes of the past, recycled by the new capitalist presses in the form of the proliferating novels of chivalry to meet the demands of the new mass market. But the comic nature of Cervantes' work raises a difficult question: who or what is the object of the reader's laughter? Is it the deviant "madman" who can be mocked satirically from a position of apparently untroubled ideological security, or is it the dominant reactionary ideology itself masked behind a thin veil of displacements and misrecognition? The first kind of laughter is conservative, and it is powerful because it is ultimately reassuring, while the second gives the reader the potential for critical "outsideness". This carries the possibility of a change in consciousness, but it can never be completely free of the subject's anxious defence of the established ways of thinking.

In Chapter Eight, I take the inwardly embattled nature of modern subjectivity in an apparently different direction, in order to approach the closely related topic which Bakhtin himself sought to elucidate in his well-known *Rabelais and his World*,[11] namely the possibility of understanding laughter in relation to history. The epigraph to his book quotes the nineteenth-century Russian radical, Alexander Herzen: "It would be extremely interesting to write the [or 'a'] history of laughter". Clearly, to write a single history would be unmanageable, but the real question is: How is it possible even to conceive of laughter historically? Bakhtin sometimes refers to it as a form of consciousness, but laughter is not a form. Nor is it an idea or doctrine. It is a bodily response to an address to the subject, which is usually linguistic but is quite often visual and/or gestural. Laughter has great significance for Bakhtin because it is both intersubjective and a living proof of the interconnection between the mind and the body. His positive argument in his book on Rabelais is quite well known: the popular laughter of the Carnival, and its pre-Christian antecedents, liberated humanity from its millennial "fear of the sacred, of prohibitions, of the past, of power".[12] This popular resistance through laughter desublimated all the spiritual and transcendental pretensions of ruling class ideology in the name of the "grotesque" lower body, shared by all. The scene of this symbolic levelling was not only the public square where it was enacted; it was above all the inner scene of the participants' subjectivity. In short, it was not the external forms

---

11   Bakhtin [1965] 1968.
12   Bakhtin *ibid.*, p. 94.

INTRODUCTION   7

of political or social oppression which were overthrown by Carnival laughter (that very rarely happened), but the repression normally exercised over the revellers' desire to rebel through their internalised fear and respect for established social forms.

However, this introduces the problem of the ambivalent nature of laughter itself. Many critics of Bakhtin's positive assessments of the collective festivities have noted that the objects of its mocking laughter were often supposedly inferior scapegoats, such as foreigners, witches, stereotypical Jews, insubordinate women and many other candidates for punishment, subordination, or exclusion. Using Mauron's theory of laughter as the overcoming of potential anxiety (*le renversement d'une situation angoissante*),[13] I argue that the self-aggrandising mockery of the scapegoat protects the mocking subject from conscious recognition of the real social causes of the anxiety to which his laughter is a response. In this scenario, the subject's unconscious displacement of anxiety into mocking laughter directed against his lower "risible" targets also protects the dominant ideology from that subject's possible critique and rebellion. Nonetheless, it can happen that the comic utterance or visual display gives its addressees a genuinely dialogical position of critical "outsideness" which enables them to recognise and mock the dominant ideology itself. When this occurs, laughter liberates the laughing subject from his/her/their unquestioning internalisation of social or intellectual norms, and from the anxieties of fear or of guilt through which those "mind-forg'd manacles" (William Blake) maintain their hold and prevent rebellion. In short, laughter can indeed open a way towards "becoming" through the subject's liberation into new ways of thinking and feeling. Bakhtin made that argument for Carnival laughter when it was incorporated into the historically developing culture of the Renaissance. But he also showed how the possibilities in that collective laughter were closed down by the forces of centralism.

A historical approach to laughter requires a dialogical understanding of its ambivalent relationship to the anxieties from which it provides release. Here too dialogism provides an indispensable tool for understanding ourselves historically. The capacity for laughter shows that we are not merely imprisoned by nature or by our cultural conditioning; we are potentially capable of surpassing that conditioning, and of changing ourselves in the process.

---

13   Mauron 1964.

CHAPTER 1

Dialogism: the Potential for Change and for Resistance to Change

Dialogue is generally understood as it is defined by the Oxford English Dictionary: "a conversation between two or more persons: a colloquy". This commonsense view is largely unaffected by the influential linguistics founded by Ferdinand de Saussure, which focuses on a shared system of signs as the precondition for every act of communication between speaker and recipient. Saussure's approach made the system primary in two senses. Firstly, of course, the shared system actually precedes the communication between individual speakers which it makes possible. Secondly (and more controversially) it is only this prior system that should be the object of a properly scientific "semiology", to use Saussure's own term. Bakhtin and Voloshinov by no means challenge the usefulness of the idea of a system of language, but they focus critically on the concept of a science which abstracts the system of language (Saussure's *langue*) to give it priority over its realization in speech acts. For Saussure, these speech acts belong to the domain of the history of any given language, which he designated as a distinct and purely secondary *linguistique de la parole*. In contrast with this by now familiar distinction between *langue* and *parole*, which separates the "synchronic" study of language from its "diachronic" histories, Bakhtin and Voloshinov insisted on the primacy of the dialogic "utterance" (*vyskazyvanie*). For them, the cost of Saussure's abstraction was that it overlooked the historical nature of the structures brought into being and continuously modified by the dynamic creativity of the acts of communication. Through these unending dialogical modifications, utterances create new possibilities of meaning, instead of simply conforming to those permitted by a pre-existing system. From a Bakhtinian perspective, systemic linguistics is a product of deductive rationality, since it is only through a critical analysis of actual utterances that the hypothetical underlying system is rationally deduced by the theorist. This has its own validity for descriptive purposes, but it by no means grants the system a transcendent existence outside time and process.

An important work from the Bakhtin Circle was Valentin Voloshinov's *Marxism and the Philosophy of Language*.[1] Despite certain limitations to be

---

1 Voloshinov [1929] 1973.

discussed later, this has retained its significance amidst current debates, largely because of its challenge to the proto-structuralism of Saussurean linguistics, which provided the dominant model for the "linguistic turn" in the social sciences of the 1920s and 1930s. There is no denying the wide-ranging and fruitful influence of this turn, but it brought with it an ahistorical reification in the form of a putative transcendent structure underlying all language and thought, which may not have been intended by Saussure himself. For some thinkers of the time this antecedent structure was unique to particular societies, or to ethnic groups defined by their language, and therefore it tended to merge into ethnic nationalism. For others it was, and still is, a universally shared structure of the human mind, ultimately grounded in the biological structure of the brain. Noam Chomsky, for example writes:

> The study of language falls naturally within human biology. The language faculty, which somehow evolved in human prehistory, makes possible the amazing feat of language learning, while inevitably setting limits on the kinds of language that can be acquired in the normal way.[2]

On the following page in the same work we find a paradox: "humans may develop their capacities without limit, but never escaping certain objective bounds set by their biological nature". Since these limitless capacities are linguistic (in this context), what are the "objective bounds" set by biology? Or, if there are indeed "objective bounds", why should we suppose that they are set by biology (currently, genetic codes) rather than, say, the forms previously achieved by thinking and communicating human beings at any particular historical juncture, or in any specific cultural context? These limits are by definition provisional, even if they last over long periods of time. Bakhtin consistently resisted the systemic definition of language propounded by Saussure and his successors, partly because he rejected the determinist view which Fredric Jameson has called the "prison house of language",[3] and partly because he insisted that the study of language should focus on the inherent creativity of the "utterance" and the human capacity for change or "becoming" (*stanovlenie*). These two positions are closely linked. Where Saussure had assigned the study of utterances to the secondary "diachronic" field, Bakhtin and his co-thinkers restored the utterance, and with it the diachronic perspective itself, to the central position from which they believed that both had been dislodged by Saussure's claim

---

2   Chomsky 1975, p. 123.
3   Jameson 1972.

that only the underlying system, or *langue*, could be the proper object of the new "synchronic" science.

1 The Sources of "Becoming" in Philosophical Idealism

In developing their views on the creativity of language, Bakhtin and Voloshinov drew extensively on Ernst Cassirer's *Philosophy of Symbolic Forms*.[4] Their indebtedness to a leading twentieth-century idealist philosopher clearly calls for critical assessment, if any credence can be given to the claim for their contribution to a materialist view of history, particularly in the case of the Marxist Voloshinov who translated three sections of the first volume of Cassirer's work into Russian. Cassirer is still celebrated as an outstanding historian of ideas and art, even by those who criticise his idealist premises. For him the human being is a "symbolic animal" (*animal symbolicum*), which significantly reformulates the more familiar dualism of Aristotle's "social animal" (*zoon politikon*). Nowadays, thanks largely to the influence of Jacques Lacan, we have become accustomed to thinking of the "symbolic order" of language as a structure, albeit an unstable one because of its reliance on the shifting signifiers which constitute it. But Cassirer is a reminder of another, currently unfashionable tradition for which language is not only constitutive of consciousness but is also an agency of historical transformation ("becoming"). Cassirer's overall argument is that all human experience is mediated through the "symbolic forms" (including language) which human beings have created for themselves in the course of their socio-historical development. These mediating "symbolic forms" make the reflexive consciousness of human beings possible, and their historical development enables and shapes its expansion. The crucial point is the ability of human beings to reflect upon their own symbolic modes of understanding. This means that a history of knowledge, up to and including modern science, must be more than a positivist record of the accumulated knowledge of its objects. It must also be a historical anthropology of the changing "symbolic forms" through which those objects have become conceptualized by human understanding (and, it should be added, by human practices). Cassirer's cultural anthropology may appear somewhat Eurocentric, but that is largely because of its tendency to universalize a single "consciousness in general". In an

---

4 Cassirer [1923; 1925; 1929] 1955; 1957. Brian Poole has revealed that some pages of Bakhtin's work on Rabelais are copied verbatim from Cassirer's *The Individual and the Cosmos in Renaissance Philosophy*: cf. Poole 1998, pp. 542–4.

informative essay on Voloshinov and Cassirer, Mika Lähteenmäki points out where Cassirer differs significantly from Voloshinov and Bakhtin:

> It seems that Cassirer is mostly interested in how "consciousness in general" comes to grips with reality and what are the universal forms that underlie our knowledge of reality, which means that his account simply brackets out considerations of intersubjective aspects of language and its formation. Voloshinov, by contrast, starts from the role language plays in social interaction and argues that language is first and foremost a social phenomenon. This means that signs and meanings are created intersubjectively and emerge in the process of social interaction between different consciousnesses.[5]

Cassirer's *longue durée* history is concerned with the development of the different modes of symbolic abstraction which are the pre-requisite for all human understanding, from the minimal level of abstraction brought into being by the totemic forms of mythical consciousness, followed by the higher levels of abstraction enabled by religious consciousness, which then lay the basis for modern scientific forms of enquiry with their reliance on mathematical abstraction. Cassirer's concern with the process of "becoming" led him to affirm that every developmental phase involves a higher degree of abstraction by the different "symbolic forms" through which knowledge is pursued.

In some of his later work, published posthumously as Volume Four of his *Philosophy of Symbolic Forms*, Cassirer emphasised Wilhelm von Humboldt's view of language as an agency of "becoming", thanks to the creativity of the "speech act". In the passage below he reiterates Humboldt's idea of language as dynamic *energeia*, rather than static *ergon*, to argue that his own concept of "becoming" should be understood as a transcendence of the dualist impasse of *Lebensphilosophie*. This so-called "philosophy of life" conceived of the symbolic forms of culture as impediments which, although originally created by the "living" dynamism of language, then congeal into structures, effectively preventing their own further "becoming". (Henri Bergson is probably the best known exponent of this philosophy). Cassirer turns back to Humboldt to surmount this dualist impasse:

> Perhaps the clearest example of this confronts us in the structure of language. Of course here too one normally makes a distinction between the creative process of language as such and the forms that are thereby

---
5 Lähteenmäki, 2002, p. 202.

created, and in this distinction we take note of the form, of how the synthetic structure and grammatical "categories" of language not infrequently stand opposed to the living movement of language so as to restrict and inhibit it. *But this external dualism is refuted again and again as soon as we conceive of language in Humboldt's sense, not as an ergon, but as an energeia, not merely as something that has become what it is, but which is continuously shaping itself.* [....] The individual speech act does not hereby take place when the speaker merely reaches into a world of completely finished forms from which a selection has to be made but which otherwise must be treated as given, like a minted coin. *The speech act is never in this sense an act of mere assimilation; rather it is, in however small a way, a creative act, an act of shaping and reshaping* [emphases added].[6]

In a more recent work, José Medina also endorses this apparently outdated Romantic tradition going back to Humboldt, but without referring to Cassirer:

According to Humboldt, it is essential for an adequate understanding of language that we recognize that the web of language is being perpetually recreated in speech, that is, continuously extended, altered, and reconfigured in our linguistic performances and practices. As he famously put it, language is first and foremost *energeia*, not *ergon*, an activity, not a product. There are indeed products of our linguistic activities, but these tentative and ever-changing fruits of our practices are webs that we weave as we go and can never amount to a finished and complete system.[7]

Medina adds that this Romantic "expressive tradition inaugurated a *dialogism* that underscores the social dimension of language and the impact of discursive practices in the constitution of human communities". This is where Bakhtin and Voloshinov adapted Cassirer's argument. They posited their own concept of social dialogism as the dynamic principle which is the condition of possibility for creativity and "becoming" (*stanovlenie*). For them, every utterance is essentially a dialogical address to another (present or imagined), but it has also been formed on the basis of the past utterances of others. So social dialogism gives every subject the potential for reflection upon the already created forms

---

6 Cassirer (posthumous vol. 4) 1996, pp. 15–16. The "minted coin" probably refers to Saussure's metaphor for the sign, whose value is determined by the system of differences which is language.
7 Medina 2005, pp. 44–45. Medina writes that this Romantic "expressive tradition inaugurated a *dialogism* that underscores the social dimension of language and the impact of discursive practices in the constitution of human communities".

of his/her own thought from a position of "outsideness" (*vnenakhodimost'*), and this reflexive ability enables the human subject to escape from merely conditioned repetition into the creativity of "becoming". However, this creativity cannot exist outside a struggle against already established forms, and the social relations which they support or justify. So from the standpoint of those established forms, the struggle for "becoming" must appear destructive. Cassirer's holistic argument on the constant creativity of all language realized in individual speech acts overlooks this difference: if every speech act is indeed "a creative act, an act of shaping and reshaping", what would be the difference between the "creative act" which gives rise to something historically new, and the "creativity" which reiterates the already known and therefore maintains an already instituted structure? There are good grounds here for thinking that Bakhtin's and Voloshinov's concept of "monologism" significantly reformulates the static *ergon* which Cassirer simply refutes (on the grounds that language is by definition always *energeia*), because in their own critical practice they treat "monologism" too as *energeia*. It is not a merely static form "that has become what it is" but a dynamic activity which resists the potential for further "becoming" within the field of sociolinguistic conflicts. This has wider implications for understanding ideology as dialogical *agon*, which I will explore more fully in Chapter 3.

2 "Becoming" as Socio-linguistic Event

The major difference between Bakhtin and Voloshinov is their relationship to Marxism. Bakhtin himself was not a Marxist, and he frequently criticized Hegelian dialectics as the antithesis of dialogism, on the grounds that it organised all differences into a single teleology which inevitably prepared for the famous higher synthesis. For him, therefore, dialectics was a "monological" theory, even if its all-inclusive "totality" would only be fully realized at the end of history when all "becoming" would cease. As a Marxist, Voloshinov did not preserve this antithesis between the openness of dialogism to an always-undisclosed future and the ultimate closure anticipated in advance by dialectics. For him dialogism could enable new non-dogmatic possibilities for extending Marxist thought in a field largely ignored by it, namely the philosophy of language. But this difference between the two thinkers is not clear-cut because Bakhtin himself often used Marxist terminology, particularly in his writings on the novel in the 1930s and 1940s. In these essays there is a strong neo-Hegelian influence (as there is in Cassirer too) which was part of his critical engagement with Georg Lukács who had emerged as an important influence in the Soviet Union.[8] The American scholar Gary Saul Morson, who is himself no friend of Marxism, acknowledges Voloshinov's own creative contribution, and suggests that there was a genuinely two-way dialogical exchange between these co-thinkers and close friends.[9]

In his *Marxism and the Philosophy of Language*, Voloshinov criticised the rational "objectivism" of the early structuralism of Saussurean linguistics, but he also criticised the trend in linguistics which he identified as its formal opposite, the "subjectivism" of the idealist Romantic school of thought, running from Humboldt through to Croce and Vossler. This demands more attention than it is usually accorded. A noteworthy exception is Patrick Sériot, the Slavicist scholar who, in his introduction to his jointly authored Franco-Russian edition, strongly criticizes Voloshinov for his excessive closeness to the German Romantic tradition.[10] Be that as it may, Voloshinov differentiates himself from the Romantic school by rejecting their view that only *individual* creativity, prototypically that of the exceptional poetic genius, is the source of all innovation. He dismissively sums up Vossler's aesthetic individualism: "everything that becomes a fact of grammar had once been a fact of style".[11] For the same reason he criticizes Simmel's "philosophy of life", saying that it fails because of its attribution of creativity to the individual genius isolated from the social process. This division is metaphysical for Voloshinov because it sets up an insuperable "fixed antinomy" between the creative "living" individual personality and the dead immobility of objective culture. The theoretical failure of this fixed antinomy is that it fails to grasp the "vital *dialectical* contradiction" between the psyche of every subject and the objective ideology in which he/she exists:

> For Simmel, an irreconcilable discrepancy exists between the psyche and ideology: he does not know the sign of [*as?*] a form of reality common to both psyche and ideology. Moreover, though a sociologist, he utterly fails to appreciate the thoroughgoing social nature of the reality of ideology, as well as the reality of the psyche. Both the one and the other kind of reality are, after all, a refraction of one and the same socioeconomic existence. As a result, the vital dialectical contradiction between the psyche and existence assumes for Simmel the shape of an inert, fixed antinomy – a

---

8   Cf. Tihanov 2000; Skidelsky 2008; Krois 1987.
9   Morson and Emerson 1989, pp. 3 and 47–48; Brandist 2000.
10 Sériot in Volochinov 2010, pp. 13–93.
11 Voloshinov 1973, p. 51.

"tragedy", and he endeavours in vain to surmount that antinomy by resorting to a metaphysically colored dynamics of the life process.[12]

Voloshinov argues that this "fixed antinomy" merely reproduces in theory the familiar Romantic tragedy of the isolated poetic genius in conflict with the social order. But, although both Bakhtin and Voloshinov rejected the "tragedy" of Romantic individualism pitted against the overwhelming system, the antinomy persists for them at the level of social discourses as the underlying conflict between the potential for evolutionary or revolutionary "becoming" on the one hand, and the monological stasis persistently sought by the dominant social order on the other. In this respect the influence of Cassirer is a continuing factor in their thought, even when they invoke other philosophical influences, including Marxism.

In general, the philosophies gathered under the term *Lebensphilosophie* conceptualise the contradiction between creative change and static form (or *energeia* versus *ergon*) as a permanent struggle between "life" and culture, in which the cultural forms inevitably freeze the creative energy which originally produced them. That is why Cassirer rejected its dualism. There were many variations of this constitutive contradiction, which Simmel called "tragic". They run from the agon of Apollo and Dionysos in the early Nietzsche's *Birth of Tragedy* through to Bergson's *élan vital* which struggles against repetitive mechanism and life-threatening incrustation. The Bakhtin scholar Galin Tihanov argues that Bakhtin's account of the sociolinguistic basis of the novel is weakened by his reliance on this same repetitive transhistorical metaphysics in the form of a permanent opposition between centrifugal and centripetal forces. However, it is significant that in Tihanov's critical observation the concept of "living" energy versus dead or mechanical stasis becomes a rivalry of "two contradictory forces":

> The way in which the novel could become the host for different and, at times, antagonistic pictures of the world is reconstructed by Bakhtin with constant reference to an evidently metaphysical necessity. At each stage of human history, two contradictory forces are at work: a centripetal one busily creates the unity and the centralization of the verbal-ideological world and canonizes ideological systems, while a centrifugal one seeks to

---

12 *Ibid.*, p. 40. My suggested "as" in brackets simply makes the English coherent. The Russian is "on ne znaet znaka obshchei i dlya psikhiki i dlya ideologii formoi deistvitel'nosti", [Leningrad 1930, p. 44].

erode this process. Bakhtin never attaches a clearly defined social group or class to either force, any more than he presents the concrete historical dynamics of this conflict, and this makes for the metaphysical resonance of his account.[13]

Tihanov includes here Voloshinov's concept of "life ideology" (*zhiznennaia ideologia*) which in effect transports the concept of "life" from the realm of natural forces onto the terrain of social discourses. Consequently "life ideology" is more spontaneous (closer to "life") than the more coherently organised discourses of "official ideology". This underlying contrast may well have its origins in the metaphysical dualism of *Lebensphilosophie* but it is not as far as it may seem from Antonio Gramsci's Marxist view that the dominant ideology in class society is a more integrated form of consciousness, and that this coherence helps to sustains its "hegemony". Mere force alone cannot explain or sustain ideological dominance, and that is why Gramsci's concept of "hegemony" extends the Marxist theory of class dominance to the field of socio-linguistics, which is where his own intellectual formation began. But Gramsci introduced an important political dialectic which inverts the values of *Lebensphilosophie*. For him, the masses have to *rise above* their spontaneous "lived" forms of consciousness in order to challenge the hegemonic ideology, because it is their own lack of a coherent ideology which keeps them divided, unaware of their own historical potential, and therefore subordinate. Hopefully, aided by the efforts of "organic" intellectuals (and by a revolutionary movement or party), they would be able to achieve for themselves the coherence of a conscious alternative culture, capable of overcoming and replacing the hegemony of the contemporary ruling class in Italy and elsewhere.[14]

3 Towards a Historical Account of the Unconscious?

For Marxism the forces of transformation are not a permanent feature of nature or "life" but of historically specific forms of socioeconomic organisation. In the modern world, it is not the force of "living life" but the capitalist mode

---

13 Tihanov 1998, p. 46.
14 Ives 2004. In Gramsci's view, the Italian ruling classes (unlike the other major national bourgeoisies in Europe), had signally failed to achieve national integration. Therefore the historic task of national unification fell to the leadership of the working class. Ives [p. 73] explains this difference between Bakhtin and Gramsci: "Bakhtin is absorbed with Stalin's centralization of everything involving culture and language. Gramsci is preoccupied with the disorganization and chaos of a working-class movement that ended in defeat".

of production which has introduced unceasing transformations into human relations and the corresponding forms of consciousness. Indeed, for any historian, Marxist or not, significant change cannot be anything but social, while it is the realm of nature which is relatively constant. But when it is a matter of a social discourse which at first supported the expansion of "becoming" and then resisted it, there may be a considerable degree of convergence with Marxism. This contradictory process can be identified as the ideological struggle of the bourgeoisie, firstly to establish its hegemonic position (in the name of universal "nature"), and then later to maintain it. And if, in this second historical phase of reactive consolidation, the forces which it struggles to control are conceptualised as arising "from below" (whether as Gramsci's spontaneous ideology or as Voloshinov's *zhiznennaia ideologiia*), then this interaction between the "natural" and the "social" may well be compatible with a Marxist account of ideology, despite the transhistorical metaphysics noted by Galin Tihanov.

The Hegelian heritage becomes important here, because the widespread "linguistic turn" in the human sciences in the 1920s and 1930s was a way of reconceiving how the otherwise unreflective or spontaneous natural forces in every human being become socialised through the symbolization which gives form and meaning to every subject's experience of the world. In effect, the old static polarity of nature *versus* culture gets rewritten as a foundational dialectic, providing an account of how the social "second nature" of Aristotle's *zoon politikon* actually comes into being. The old fixed antinomy between nature and culture, or body and mind, is overcome, to be resituated within the sociality that is language, or more generally "the symbolic order" (which can include imagery). This structure preserves, but in a transmuted form, the natural forces or "instincts" which the moment of *aufhebung* (sublation) has cancelled out by including them in the higher stage of development. But, unlike Cassirer's philosophy of "becoming" with its ongoing historical development of the *animal symbolicum*, the structuralist version of this single-step founding narrative does not allow for any subsequent developmental stages of "becoming" in history. Nonetheless, it depends upon a key dialectical moment, because the natural state is not simply left behind. It is transformed as it is subsumed into the "symbolic order" of culture, and this is conceived as the trajectory followed by every human subject in formation. Jacques Lacan conceives of this as the induction of the non-speaking *infans* into the "symbolic order". In his account, the structure of the linguistic "symbolic order" is marked by its unstable relationship with its own unruly signifiers through which the natural biological drives have become human desires. Broadly speaking, for Freud, particularly as he has been interpreted by Lacan, the unconscious is founded here, at the dawn of the social, when the natural "instincts" are no longer merely natural but have always already become human desires.

These structuralist presuppositions would be put into question if one could show the production of the unconscious *within* history, rather than at its dawn, through the repressive activity of the various would-be monological reaction formations brought into being by historical conflict. This is a large topic, which I will pursue in Chapter 3, where I am concerned with the essentially conflictual nature of ideology. But it remains the case that the politically conservative Lacan is the major theoretician who relates the "symbolic order" of language to the unconscious. In an uncharacteristically clear passage (except for an obscurity in the second sentence in the paragraph below), Lacan explains his famous statement that "the unconscious is structured like a language" (*comme un langage*) by recourse to the structural anthropology of Lévi-Strauss. Like Cassirer in this respect, Lévi-Strauss also saw totemism as the original basis of the symbolic order. Lacan's argument locates the emergence of its meaning-creating structures even prior to any subsequent socio-historical dynamics:

> Before any experience, before any individual deduction, even before those collective experiences that may be related only to social needs are inscribed in it, something organizes this field, inscribes its initial lines of force. This is the function that Claude Lévi-Strauss shows us to be the truth of the totemic function, and which reduces its appearance [*sic*] – the primary classificatory function.[15]

The syntax of the last sentence is confusing, but the main argument seems clear enough. The "primary classificatory function" has always existed, even prior to the manifest totemic structures which it brought into being. And it still persists. Our modern knowledge of this primary function was first reached by Lévi-Strauss who reduced the historically higher complexities to the basic binary operation which generated them. Lacan then uses this reductive logic of Lévi-Strauss' structural anthropology to advance his own version of the way nature becomes organised into meaningful "signifiers":

---

15   Lacan 1987, p. 20. The original French text is no clearer: "C'est la fonction que Claude Lévi-Strauss nous montre être la vérité de la fonction totémique, *et qui en réduit l'apparence* – *la fonction classificatoire primaire*", Seuil, Paris 1973, p. 28. Lacan appears to use *réduire* (from *reducere* "to take back or refer a thing to its origins" – OED) as synonymous with *déduire*. If Lacan had actually said "déduit" rather than "réduit", it might have been clearer. Thus: "Lévi-Strauss ... who deduces the primary classifying function from its appearance".

Before strictly human relations are established, certain relations have already been determined. They are taken from whatever nature may offer as supports, supports that are arranged in themes of opposition. Nature provides – I must use the word – signifiers, and these signifiers organize human relations in a creative way, providing them with structures and shaping them.[16]

For Lacan, the pre-social "combinatory operation" transforms arbitrarily selected natural objects "in a creative way", by organizing them into signifying binary oppositions. In so doing, it founds all social order and the subjects within it. Here Lacan claims that his own focus on the "pre-subjective" organisation of the signifiers into the binary oppositions which constitute the symbolic order itself, guarantees the scientific status of psychoanalysis:

In our time, in the historical period that has seen the formation of a science that may be termed human, but which must be distinguished from any kind of psycho-sociology, namely linguistics, whose model is the combinatory operation, functioning spontaneously, of itself, in a pre-subjective way – it is this linguistic structure that gives its status to the unconscious. It is this structure, in any case, that assures us that there is, beneath the term unconscious, something definable, accessible, objectifiable.[17]

The Lacanian readings of Freud can be summed up as extraordinarily complex investigations of the ways in which the subject's unconscious is dominated by the play of the signifiers through which his/her no longer "natural" drives have always already been organized into human desires. Essentially, Lacan criticises the old but persistent binary opposition of nature and culture, on the grounds that the so-called "natural" drives or instincts can only be found already subsumed by the combinatory play of signifiers which constitute them as human desires. Later Lacan turned from this "creative" basis behind Lévi-Strauss' anthropological structures to the timeless principles of geometrical abstraction, in order to map the structure of the unconscious topologically in terms of the relationship of the "symbolic" order to the "imaginary" and to the "real" (which resists symbolization). In contrast to these structural delineations of the unconscious, the Bakhtin Circle remained largely focused on the socio-linguistics of consciousness and on the potential of dialogism to account for historical

---

16   Lacan, *op.cit.*
17   *Ibid.*

changes in consciousness (becoming). The concept of an unconscious is mostly (but not always) eschewed.

The starting point for Bakhtin's dialogical theory of the relationship of consciousness to language is to be found in his early philosophical critique of Kantian ethics. In place of an ethics grounded in individual consciousness, Bakhtin posited his concept of the self as fully constituted through its relationship with others. It may not be new to learn that man has a "second nature" which makes him a "social animal" (to borrow Aristotle's terms), but Bakhtin's philosophy is more interesting than the recycling of such established ideas. It asserts that even our intimate self-conscious perception of ourselves depends upon seeing ourselves from a position of "outsideness", that is from a position made available to us by our relationship with others, which Bakhtin describes as being like a "gift" functioning as a social bond. This view rests upon his essentially beneficent conception of our relationship of dependency upon others, whereby even our sense of our own self-completion depends upon being seen by them, and seeing them see us, since otherwise we could not see ourselves from outside as whole beings. (By contrast, for Lacan this self-completion is the visual "lure" [*leurre*] which constitutes the drive for unmediated autonomy known as narcissism). Bakhtin's positive account was part of his turn away from Kant's concept of ethical duty, grounded in the transcendental "categorical imperative" within each individual, towards a theory of ethical responsibility or "answerability" (*otvetsvennost'*) to others, grounded in a relationship of social mutuality. He later came to conceive of this inter-subjectivity in terms of linguistic dialogism. Our species' conscious existence through the dialogism of language confirms that no man is an island. This shared existence is not just formulated as a utopian ideal for some unspecified future (or as a dystopian dread of individual submersion) but is grounded in the very social nature of our being in speech and thought. It is, so to speak, an existential necessity immanent to our social being, and is not just an injunction from an abstract moral "ought" or absent God. But the problem is that this ethics depends rather uncritically upon the concept of the relationship between individual and society as both constant and essentially supportive, whereas the concept of dialogism also reveals the constitutive nature of historical conflict and social division. The conflictual discourses also operate "dialogically" to construct not only hostile external relations between subjects (whether individuals or groups), but also the fissured inner disposition of every individual subject within our divided, conflictual, and sometimes fragmented societies.

My argument is therefore not a global defense of the implausibly benign version of all dialogism which has become widespread in Bakhtinian studies. It is rather that Bakhtin's and Voloshinov's ideas on the dialogical nature of language and consciousness, which they conceived as an open-ended process of "becoming", calls for critical reassessment. The key point is that Bakhtin's monologism is a discursive attempt (in short, a desire) by a caste or a class, to establish or maintain its dominance over its rivals, but it is by that very fact inescapably dialogical. Even when Gramsci's hegemony may seem achieved, it can never be absolute, since the silenced dialogism remains its historical condition of possibility and is still operative. Whether the subject in question is an individual or a social group, s/he (or it) is the scene of this continuing but occluded conflict. This means that within any dominant ideology there is always a continuing struggle to arrest the very process of "becoming" which dialogism brings with it. I will return to this in subsequent chapters but to put it briefly here: Bakhtin's and Voloshinov's arguments on "inner dialogism" as the necessary condition for human consciousness, ineluctably point beyond their own theory of the social nature of consciousness towards a not yet fully articulated theory of the social and historical *production of an unconscious*. Any individual or social group seeking "monological" dominance must not only subordinate or silence its rivals, but must also deny its own reciprocal relationship of dependency upon them. And since the complete elimination of the dialogical engagement of self and others is an impossibility (being for Bakhtin and Voloshinov the very condition for consciousness itself), the pursuit of hegemony must have recourse to that oblique form of simultaneous acknowledgement and negation of the discourse of "the other" which Jacques Lacan has called "misrecognition" (*méconnaissance*).[18] Another way of putting this is to say that any subject captivated by the desire for unchallengeable (absolute) dominance must struggle to forget, or disregard, precisely those constitutive relationships which cannot be completely forgotten or disregarded. That is the essence of Bakhtin's reading of Dostoevsky's *Notes from Underground*, which I will explore in the next chapter. But the broader consequence, to be pursued in the following chapters, is that a historical approach to unconscious formations becomes possible, provided that attention is paid to the reactive activities of monologism. Ideology should not be conceived as a really existing structure, as it usually is, but as the unachievable goal of a social struggle for that unchallengeable dominance.

4 From Literary Dialogism to Dialectical "Becoming"

Bakhtin first developed his concept of the dialogical nature of consciousness as a response to the works of Dostoevsky. But in his writings of the 1930s, Bakhtin extended the concept of dialogism from Dostoevsky's works to the novel in

---

18   Lacan 1966, p. 165.

general. For example, in his later essay "Discourse in the Novel" (1934–35), he examined the dialogism of Tolstoy, his former example of an arch-monologist. But this is not just a critical reappraisal of Tolstoy. It is a redefinition and further development of the concept of dialogism. Not only does it become the property of the novel as a literary genre, but as the latter interacts with the other genres it also undermines their previously unchallenged monological representations of the world, in a process which he calls the "novelisation of the other genres". By this he means that the novel played an active role in the social "process of 'becoming'" by undermining the closed universe and single-valued outlook of the established genres:

> Of particular interest are those eras when the novel becomes the dominant genre. All literature is the caught up in the process of "becoming", and in a special kind of "generic criticism". This occurred several times in the Hellenic period, again during the late Middle Ages and Renaissance, but with special force and clarity beginning in the second half of the eighteenth century. In an era when the novel reigns supreme, almost all the remaining genres are to a greater or lesser extent "novelised".... Those genres that stubbornly preserve their old canonic nature begin to appear stylised. In general any strict adherence to a genre begins to feel like a stylization, a stylization taken to the point of parody, despite the artistic intent of the author.[19]

In these essays of the 1930s and 1940s, this transformative capacity of the "polyphonic" language of the novel acquires a marked neo-Hegelian force, despite Bakhtin's opposition to Hegelian versions of history. Thanks to the dominance of the novel over all other genres, literature becomes a discursive reorganisation of consciousness which permits both the writer and the reader to adopt a new critical "outsideness" vis-à-vis all the other socially established discourses out of which the work is made:

> In the novel, literary language possesses an organ for perceving the heterodox nature of its own speech. Heteroglossia-in-itself becomes, in the novel and thanks to the novel, heteroglossia-for-itself; languages are implicated *in* each other and begin to exist *for* each other (similar to exchanges in a dialogue). It is precisely thanks to the novel that languages are able to illuminate each other mutually; literary language becomes

---

19 Bakhtin 1981, pp. 5–6

a dialogue of languages that both know about and understand each other.[20]

Moreover, not only does this element of self-reflexivity make the novel a privileged genre, widening the privilege accorded to Dostoevsky alone in the previous study, but the novel also becomes an agency of a cultural transformation which extends far beyond the confines of literary discourse. By now the novel is for Bakhtin the medium *par excellence* for the historical expansion of human self-consciousness. In "Epic and Novel", he pursues this historical transformation in terms of a crisis or "disintegration" which is productive because it gives rise to a higher form of consciousness. The heroes of novels develop a self-consciousness that is split between the self as definable object and a self-awareness that is no longer defined because it contains new possibilities for "becoming":

> The epic wholeness of an individual disintegrates in a novel [in other ways as well]. A crucial tension develops between the external and the internal man, and as a result the subjectivity of the individual becomes an object of experimentation and representation – and first of all on the humorous familiarizing plane. Co-ordination breaks down between the various aspects: man for himself alone and man in the eyes of others. The disintegration of the integrity that an individual had possessed in the epic (and in tragedy) combines in the novel with the necessary preparatory steps toward a new, complex wholeness on a higher level of human development.[21]

The starting point for this theory of dynamic change is still neo-Kantian, in the sense summed up by Michel Foucault in *The Order of Things* when he points to Kant's striking paradox as the key to the divided nature of modern subjectivity:

> Man appears in his ambiguous position as an object of knowledge and as a subject that knows: enslaved sovereign, observed spectator.[22]

---

20   *Ibid.*, p. 400.
21   Bakhtin *op. cit.* pp. 37–38.
22   Cited in Sass 1994, p. 51. Foucault's paradox provides the title for a whole chapter within Sass' general argument that schizophrenia is not produced out of regression to primitive levels of consciousness but out of modern hyperrationality, alienation from physical reality, and the "mind's perverse self-apotheosis". Sass does not mention Dostoevsky's *Notes from Underground* but this "perverse self-apotheosis" is central to the underground hero's self-consciousness. See Chapter 2.

But in Bakhtin's essays of the 1930s and 1940s this static paradox is transformed theoretically into a dialectical process of "becoming". The novel is now for him the bearer of historically new possibilities for reflexive self-awareness because it incorporates all the other pre-existing social discourses into itself, and this inclusion introduces a productive crisis into their previously separate, self-enclosed, "monological" certainties. The consequent "disintegration" of the prior forms of consciousness (such as the epic) is positively creative because it gives rise to more complex forms of self-consciousness at a "higher level of human development". In these essays Bakhtin assigns to the intervention of the novel the historical sublation of the forms of consciousness which Gramsci assigns to political intervention. The "disintegration" of the forms inherited from the past is also similar to Lunacharsky's "splintering" of consciousness discussed in the Introduction. It is the destructive aspect of dialectical creativity in its progress towards higher integration. But, as I will show in Chapter 2, Bakhtin's work on Dostoevsky provides a very significant counter-example to this positive dialectics. His reading of *Notes from Underground* shows very clearly that it is paradox, not dialectics, which is the key to Dostoevsky's exploration of a crisis for which there is no "becoming" or "higher level of human development".

5 "Speech Genres" and Creativity

By the time he came to write "The Problem of Speech Genres",[23] Bakhtin had moved beyond the exclusive privileging of literature, and especially the novel, as the bringer of reflexive consciousness and creative transformation. Now, for him all language is a field of communicative and creative activity which consists of a whole range of "speech genres" or "genres of discourse" (*rechevye zhanry*). He opens with a statement that every utterance is unique but is formed out of a general typology of genres:

> Each separate utterance is individual, of course, but each sphere in which language is used develops its own *relatively stable types* of these utterances. These we may call *speech genres* [original emphases].[24]

---

23 Written in 1952–3, but not published till 1979 in his *Estetika slovesnogo tvorchestva*, Iskusstvo, Moscow 1979. For English translation see Bakhtin 1986.
24 Bakhtin 1986, p. 60.

He gives a short list of such genres which are, however, "so diverse because they differ depending on the situation, social position, and personal interrelations of the participants in the communication".[25] They also have their own ways of negotiating hierarchies or close intimacies through shifts in intonation and style. Moreover, like the literary genres too, they are subject to irony and parodic repetition. We might conclude that the concept of "speech genres" should be replaced by the more commonsense ideas of linguistic performance or stylistic registers, particularly as Bakhtin concedes that, "no list of speech genres yet exists, or even a principle on which such a list might be based".[26] A genre which cannot be classified or defined might seem to be a candidate for non-existence. But his key point is that, although these genres may be too open-ended and flexible to be classified, linguistic creativity depends upon their prior assimilation by the subject who has learnt to use them in creating every speech act. So the "speech genres" are best understood as historically created expectations which carry the authority of past uses but are also open to "free creative reformulation":

> The majority of these genres are subject to free creative reformulation (like artistic genres, and some, perhaps, to a greater degree). But to use a genre freely and creatively is not the same as to create a genre from the beginning: genres must be fully mastered in order to be manipulated freely.[27]

By now Bakhtin has come to identify literature as just one of the complex forms of reflexive "secondary speech genres" characteristic of dynamically changing societies, even though the novel continues to be the most important for him. All of these "secondary genres" perform the transformational activity which he had attributed earlier to the novel alone:

> Secondary (complex) speech genres – novels, dramas, all kinds of scientific research, major genres of commentary, and so forth – arise in more complex and comparatively highly developed and organized cultural communication (primarily written) that is artistic, scientific, sociopolitical, and so on. During the process of their formation, they absorb and digest various primary (simple) genres that have taken form in unmediated [*sic*] speech communion. These primary genres are altered and assume

---

25   *Ibid.*
26   *Op. cit.*, p. 80.
27   *Ibid.*, p. 80.

a special character when they enter into complex ones. They lose their immediate relation to actual reality and to the real utterances of others. For example, rejoinders of everyday dialogue or letters found in a novel retain their form and their everyday significance only on the plane of the novel's content. They enter into actual reality only via the novel as a whole, that is, as a literary-artistic event and not as everyday life.[28]

Here Bakhtin retains a distinction between the "literary artistic event" and "everyday life", but his overall argument gives a dynamic consciousness-changing capacity to all of the "secondary genres", especially literature. By incorporating the more immediate "primary genres" circulating in society, the complex "secondary genres" react with them and transform them. This transformative response by the "secondary genres" to the "primary genres" out of which they are made is in effect a process of aesthetic sublation which makes self-reflexivity possible. When Bakhtin argues that "the rejoinders of everyday dialogue ... enter reality only via the novel as a whole, that is, as a literary-artistic event and not as everyday life", the crucial point is not so much the distinction between the form of the novel and the "speech genres", which he considers "unmediated" until they are aesthetically transformed, but rather that these transformed genres do not remain enclosed in the aesthetic work. They in turn "enter actual reality" thanks to the novel (through the acts of writing and reading, presumably).

This view attributes to the novel a particularly important historical role in enabling a transformative coming-to-consciousness, but it has implications that are not fully explored. If we grant that the form-giving activity of the novel (and the other "secondary genres") enables reflexive consciousness to emerge out of the relatively unreflective or spontaneous "primary speech genres" circulating in society, how are we to understand this process of transition to higher awareness? Here I would make a provisional suggestion. Against the ultimately conservative dictum that literary language merely re-iterates the already known but in an aesthetically pleasing form, as in Alexander Pope's elegant neo-classical formulation: "What oft was thought but ne'er so well expressed", Bakhtin's dialogical version of the transformative aesthetics of literature implies something much more interesting, but unfortunately less amenable to elegant compression. This view of literary discourse is that it makes perceptible what was not consciously thought, and indeed could not be thought until it was "well expressed", *but which was nonetheless there,* inchoate but available for thought (perhaps even demanding recognition) in the heterogeneous

---

28   *Op. cit.,* p. 62.

social discourses which are both the material of the literary work and its object of reflexive critical attention. In effect this is a dialectical version of literary "outsideness", and it implies the prior existence of a concealed or not yet realized potential in the "primary speech genres" circulating in society. The literary work makes that potential available to consciousness. So the creative process of coming to a new understanding is also a process of discovery and recognition of that previously unrealized potential.

6 Anticipation and Prevention: the Problem of Temporality

Bakhtin and Voloshinov go beyond the usual idea of dialogue as reciprocal communication between autonomous subjects, because they argue that the dialogical nature of "inner speech" is made possible by the active presence of the speech of others within the thought processes of any given individual. The constitution of the speaking and thinking individual on the basis of Voloshinov's "interindividual territory" of the linguistic sign[29] means that this "interindividual territory" is necessarily *intra-individual* as well. Clearly, this calls into question the psychological unity of the "individual" subject of speech or thought. However, their concept of interindividual "addressivity" as the basis of intra-individual "inner speech", and therefore of individual consciousness, becomes complicated by Bakhtin's further argument that any speaker or writer silently anticipates his/her addressee's possible future responses in the act of shaping his/her own utterance. This means that the addressee is not necessarily an external other. The addressee is always an imagined position of potential response, constructed provisionally by the speaker within the process of forming his thought, whether that thought is then externally articulated as an "utterance" or not. Bakhtin explores this anticipatory aspect of "inner dialogism" in his relatively late *Problems of Speech Genres* but it gives rise to problems that are not completely resolved.

In this essay Bakhtin reiterates his argument on the essentially dialogical nature of any "utterance". He insists that there is one defining quality of all utterances, namely that they are always directed to an addressee:

> An essential (constitutive) marker of the utterance is its quality of being directed to someone, its *addressivity* ["ego *obrashchennost'* k komu-libo, ego *adresovannost'*".] (original emphases).[30]

---

29   Voloshinov 1973, p. 12.
30   Bakhtin 1986, p. 95 [*Estetika slovesnogo tvorchestva* p. 275].

Bakhtin's term, "directedness" (*obrashchennost'*) is synonymous with "addressivity" (*adresovannost'*). The somewhat strange use of these abstract nouns, in both English and Russian, makes the point that "addressivity" is a defining quality of every utterance, not merely a pragmatic use to which an utterance may or may not be put. Bakhtin emphatically repeats this point:

> Thus addressivity, the quality of turning to someone is a constitutive feature of the utterance; without it the utterance does not and cannot exist.[31]

There is an aspect to "addressivity" which distinguishes it quite significantly from the essentially pragmatic theories of rhetoric to which it is obviously very close. Craig Brandist points out that Bakhtin and Voloshinov were influenced by the Swiss linguist Anton Marty's "act-based theory of linguistic meaning".[32] For Marty the speech act is not primarily the expression of the inward psychology of the producer of the utterance, as it was for Romantic expressivism. It is directed towards a recipient and is aimed at triggering (*auslösen*) either a judgement or an emotion. Marty's anti-expressivist argument could justly be described as an expanded rhetorical theory of the speech act, somewhat like the later speech act theories of Austin and Searle:

> The announcement of one's own psychic life is not the only, nor the primary, thing which is intended in deliberate speaking. That which is primarily intended is much rather a certain influencing or controlling of the alien psychic life of the hearer. Deliberate speaking is a special kind of acting, whose proper goal is to call forth certain psychic phenomena in other beings

But there is a complicating factor in Marty's "deliberate speaking":

> In relation to this intention, the announcement of processes within oneself appears merely as a side-effect [*párergon*].[33]

---

31   *Op cit.*, p. 99. The Russian text makes it clear that "addressivity" is not even just "*an* essential ... marker of the utterance", as the English indefinite article suggests, but *its* defining quality (*obrashchennost', adresovannost' vyskazyvaniya est' ego konstitutivnaya osobennost'...*), *Estetika slovesnogo tvorchestva*, p. 279.
32   Brandist, 2004, p. 100. Derived from the anti-Kantian theory of Brentano, Marty's approach was taken up by Voloshinov and provided some of the ground for his critique of Romantic expressivism.
33   *Ibid.*

The argument that the main intentional activity of "deliberate speaking" (i.e rhetoric) is aimed at "influencing or controlling" the psyche of the addressee is clear enough. But the dismissal of the processes within the active producer of such "deliberate speaking", by identifying them as the unintended "side-effect" (*párergon*, or "supplement") of the main activity, brackets off the very problem which Bakhtin's work does most to elucidate. As Brandist observes, in Marty's theory "the [speech] act's anticipated reception became a constitutive moment of the act itself".[34] So there is a loop-back effect upon the enunciating and thinking subject after all. The problem which is elided here is bound up with the temporal nature of the "dialogical" relationship between speaker and addressee. It is worth comparing Marty's "deliberate speaking", which he calls above "a special kind of acting", with Bakhtin's reformulation of this as the production of specific forms of "internal dramatism" (*vnutrenii dramatizm*) within the utterance. Here the concept of anticipation plays a major role, and its inner effect upon the utterance is not bracketed off:

> Accounting for the addressee and anticipating his responsive reaction are frequently multifaceted processes that introduce unique internal dramatism into the utterance (in certain kinds of everyday dialogue, in letters, and in autobiographical and confessional genres).[35]

Since every utterance is already shaped by the anticipated responses of its addressee(s), anticipation is central to Bakhtin's concept of consciousness itself as essentially dialogical:

> [But] from the very beginning, the utterance is constructed while taking into account *possible responsive reactions*, for whose sake, in essence, it is actually created. As we know, the role of *others* for whom the utterance is constructed is extremely great. We have already said that the role of these others, *for whom my thought becomes actual thought for the first time* (*and thus for my own self as well*) is not that of passive listeners, but of active participants in speech communication. From the very beginning, the speaker expects a response from them, an active responsive understanding. The entire utterance is constructed, as it were, in anticipation of encountering this response [emphases added].[36]

---

34   *Ibid.*
35   Bakhtin 1986, p. 96.
36   *Op cit.*, p. 94.

Anticipation here has an important aspect which distinguishes it from the rhetorical term *prolepsis* which it closely resembles. Unlike the rhetorical term, it does not focus our attention upon the devices required for the speaker (or writer) to achieve control over the responses of an external addressee. It names, rather, the thinking subject's open alertness to *possible responses* that have not yet occurred and may never occur. Although Bakhtin affirms the active role of the addressees in the dialogical communication, the intersubjective communication in question may not actually take place. Indeed, there may not be an actual addressee, but only an imagined possible response. When Bakhtin writes that through the anticipated response of the addressees "my thought becomes actual thought for the first time" this is a theory of the thinking subject's dialogical engagement without certainty. What anticipation shares with the rhetoric of *prolepsis* is intentionality, but when this is redefined by Bakhtin as an orientation towards the "*possible responsive reactions*" of others, dialogism provides a space for desire, anxiety, and internalised struggle because, unlike the traditions of rhetoric, it acknowledges a real difference between an anticipated range of "possible responses", and an actual response which may or may not occur. Moreover, even when there is an actual external dialogue, the speaker's expectations are necessarily provisional, because they are constantly open to the possibility of new unexpected rejoinders and points of departure. In short, they allow a certain temporality to come into play, in the form of an orientation towards a not yet disclosed future.

Bakhtin's argument on "inward dialogism" shows that since anticipation shapes not only the verbal act but also the thought even prior to any external articulation, it seeks to bridge inwardly the gap between the utterance and any possible response. At the same time that temporal gap is tacitly acknowledged in the very act of seeking to overcome it through anticipation. That is how it constitutes a space of desire in the individual subject for a particular response on the part of any possible addressee. But it may also be an anxious desire to prevent or forestall the responses which it anticipates. This inescapably uncertain nature of anticipation is not fully assessed by Bakhtin. He continues to treat the dialogical relationship as though it were fully constituted by an actual two-way interaction, without giving adequate consideration to the temporality of anticipation as a disturbing factor. Nonetheless, even in his earlier essay "Discourse in the Novel", Bakhtin had evoked the internal pressure of anticipation:

> [But] this does not exhaust the internal dialogism of the word. It encounters an alien word not only in the object itself: every word is directed towards an *answer* and cannot escape the profound influence of the answering word that it anticipates……

> ... Forming itself in an atmosphere of the already spoken, the word is at the same time determined (*opredelyaetsya*) by that which has not yet been said but which is needed and in fact anticipated by the answering word.[37]

So the anticipated response has a profound influence on the form, tone, style, and even the strategic silences, of the utterance itself. Moreover, the subject's anticipation of possible responses conditions his thinking itself, not just prior to its verbal externalization but even in the absence of an external addressee.

Bakhtin's insistence that the utterance is always an address to some other, or plural others, is the basis for his theory of the way in which those others' *possible* responses are already anticipated by the speaker (or writer) who includes them in the very formation of his thought, even in the absence of its external utterance. So the anticipated responses are his imaginary constructs, even though they may be formed on the basis of his past personal encounters and/or the collective social experience which he has internalised (through the "speech genres"). This inner attitude towards a response that has not yet occurred can vary in kind and intensity. Sometimes it is relatively trivial. A speaker's or a writer's expectations may be fulfilled or not, without dire consequences. He/she may be relaxed about the response to come, or even genuinely interested in the new or unexpected response which the dialogical "event" might disclose. In the latter case, the dialogical utterance is exploratory, and even experimental. But occasionally, the stakes are stacked quite differently, and the speaker's emotional investments, in the form of a desire for a particular response or an anxious desire to prevent it, can be very intense. "Anticipation" is a term which recurs frequently in Bakhtin's formulations of the concept of *addressivity*. Its link to temporality, and to the imagined status of the addressee, plays a key role in his own critical practice. For example in his reading of Dostoevsky's *Notes from Underground*, the underground hero's proleptic desire to control an outcome (the response of the other) constitutes the crisis-ridden "inner dialogism" of his would-be monological address to his various interlocutors. I will consider this more closely in Chapter 2. But in "The Problem of Speech Genres" Bakhtin cites his own experience as writer and speaker to discuss the role of anticipation:

---

37   Bakhtin 1981, p. 280. The English "determined" is probably too strong. The Russian *opredelit'* means "to determine" or "to define", but in the reflexive form used here, the emphasis on causality is less pronounced. The Oxford Russian-English Dictionary gives its range of meanings: "To be formed; to take shape; to be determined".

> When constructing my utterance, I try actively to determine [*aktivno opredelit'*] this response; on the other hand, I try to anticipate it, so this anticipated response, in turn, exerts an active influence on my utterance (I parry objections that I foresee, I make all kinds of provisos, and so forth).[38]

His "I" here is a generalised "I", because this is not primarily a confessional utterance but a theoretical citing of the personal to make the general point. Despite the fact that dialogical relations are frequently taken by commentators, and by Bakhtin himself, as the basis for a social ethics of responsibility (*otvetstvennost'*), this discussion of anticipation makes it clear why the relationship of a speaker's utterance to the anticipated responses of others is not necessarily benign. The dialogical engagement can sometimes take the form of a struggle in which the others being addressed are not just necessary partners enabling the utterance to exist, but may be at the same time internalised antagonists to be overcome. Whatever its genre-based indebtedness to past utterances, the struggle for mastery always takes place in a present for which the future is at stake. Essentially, this is the argument which is spelt out in very striking terms, in his essay of the 1930s, "Discourse in the Novel". In that essay, the capacity to formulate one's own thoughts involves a struggle against others' prior possession of the "word":

> The word in language is half someone else's. It becomes "one's own" only when the speaker populates it with his own intention, his own accent, when he appropriates the word, adapting it to his own semantic and expressive intention. Prior to this moment of appropriation, the word does not exist in a neutral and impersonal language (it is not, after all, out of dictionaries that the speaker gets his words!), but rather it exists in other people's mouths in other people's contexts, serving other people's intentions: it is from there that one must take the word, and make it one's own. And not all words for just anyone submit equally easily to this appropriation, to this seizure and transformation into private property.[39]

---

38 Bakhtin 1986, p. 95. I have departed from McGee's translation of the original *ya starayus' ego predvoskhitit'* ("I try to anticipate it" i.e. the other's response) which he renders as: "I try to act in accordance with the response I anticipate". But, *pace* McGee, the only act in this context is the attempt to "actively determine" (*aktivno opredelit'*) the other's response. This is a speech act theory, but one that is transported onto the psychology of the speaking subject.

39 Bakhtin 1981, p. 293.

The speaker's or writer's engagement in a social struggle against all others' intentions in order to make the utterance his own "private property" is surprising and perhaps rather playful. Private property, like "the word in language" is still a social form. But Bakhtin goes on to make the main point, which is that many utterances produced by others remain implacably alien to the individual speaker's intentions, refusing expropriation:

> Language is not a neutral medium that passes freely and easily into the private property of the speaker's intentions; it is populated – overpopulated – with the intentions of others. Expropriating it, forcing it to submit to one's own intentions and accents, is a difficult and complicated process.[40]

Property and expropriation are metaphors for the inward power struggle which Bakhtin is describing here. Language remains "overpopulated ... with the intentions of others" (i.e. it is multi-voiced or, in Bakhtin's terms, "polyphonic"). The speaker (or writer) is indeed indebted to the prior utterances of others, but to speak or think in his "own" voice he is engaged in an endless competitive struggle to subordinate them to his own intentions.

7 Conclusion

The mutual implication of self and other in Bakhtin's and Voloshinov's theory of the dialogical nature of language, and of human consciousness in general, is often explained by recourse to a spatial metaphor. Accordingly, individual consciousness comes into existence on the "borderline between oneself and the other".[41] As Voloshinov puts it:

> A word is a bridge thrown between myself and another. If one end of the bridge depends on me, then the other depends on my addressee. A word is territory shared by both addresser and addressee, by the speaker and his interlocutor.[42]

This spatial metaphor of the shared territory is indisputably useful, but it diverts attention away from anticipation. Bakhtin's thought requires the gap between

---

40   Ibid.
41   Op cit., p. 291.
42   Voloshinov 1973, p. 86.

speaker and addressee *both* to persist as a feature of communication between separate external entities *and* to be bridged on a frontier that is internal to the speaker's consciousness. But when the speaker's or thinker's "inner dialogism" is a scene of hostile struggle against the anticipated responses of others, the consequence is an attempt to arrest the process of "becoming" which dialogism makes possible. This introduces the temporal factor of anticipation discussed above, but in the form of a negation or prevention of change. Of course, in the sphere of purely external communication between self and others, time cannot be suppressed, and it is within this non-subjectivised time and space that the external addressee always has the freedom to respond in ways unanticipated by the subject. But that is why a speaker's monological drive to dominate the addressee through the anticipation of all his/her possible responses within his own utterance is actually an attempt to negate temporality. This attempt is generally doomed to failure, for, if it were successful, there could be no such thing as creativity or "becoming". There could only be the frozen co-existence of two or more "voices" or discursive positions, not only on the external scene but within the single subject, too. That is to say, there could be no "event" in Bakhtin's sense of the word. As some commentators have noted, Bakhtin plays on the Russian for "event", *sobytie*, which etymologically denotes "co-being", to suggest that the meaningful linguistic event is necessarily an encounter between at least two voices or viewpoints. In her introduction to her translation of *The Problems of Dostoevky's Poetics*, Caryl Emerson writes:

> *Sobytie* (event) and its adjective *sobytiinyi* (full of event potential) are crucial terms in Bakhtin. At their root lies the Russian word for "existence" or "being" (*bytie*), and, – although the etymology here can be disputed – *so-bytie* can be read in both its ordinary meaning of 'event', and in a more literal meaning as 'co-existing, co-being, shared existence or being *with* another'. An event can occur only among interacting consciounesses; there can be no isolated or solipsistic events.[43]

But an important point too is that this co-existence is not reducible to the sum of the engaging parties, because an event occurs in time and it engenders something new. In this uniqueness, it is more than the "co-being" of its constituent voices. That is why the "event" is not just a prolongation of the past into the present but the dynamic formation of a potentially different future. That potential is the threat which monologism seeks to prevent. When the subject seeks to dominate and control the addressee's anticipated response,

---

43 Bakhtin 1984, p.6 footnote *a*.

he is also seeking his own permanence by arresting the potential for change in himself too. In my reading of Bakhtin's interpretation of Dostoevsky's *Notes from Underground*, I will argue that "solipsistic events" may well be impossible, as Caryl Emerson argues in her preface, but they cannot be considered simply absent from Dostoevsky's novella or from Bakhtin's reading of it. While complete solipsism is impossible, it can certainly exist as the (unachievable) goal of desire. There is a paradox here, which is closely related to the anticipation and prevention of "becoming" in Dostoevsky's representation of crisis. My extended reading of this paradoxical discourse in the next chapter will provide a starting point for moving on to consider ideology more generally as embattled *addressivity*, dialogically engaged despite itself in its struggle for timeless monological dominance.

CHAPTER 2

The Fissured Modern Subject: Paradox versus "Becoming" in Dostoevsky's *Notes from Underground*

Bakhtin's *Problems of Dostoevsky's Art* (1929) was his first literary study, and its importance for him is clearly shown by his return to it to produce his revised version, *Problems of Dostoevsky's Poetics*, published in 1963. But in the interim, Bakhtin's own interest had shifted from describing the aesthetic form of Dostoevsky's novels to their dialogical discourse. In the opening pages, Bakhtin enters into dialogue with other critics, many of whom had been struck by Dostoevsky's "multi-voiced" novels. The striking autonomy of their characters was sometimes compared with Shakespeare because of both authors' effacement of any clear unifying authorial overview. Among these critics was Otto Kaus, for whom this multiplicity of co-existing viewpoints reflected the way in which the belated arrival of capitalism in Russia had broken down the previous self-sufficiency of the various "social, cultural, and ideological" planes of existence there. Bakhtin agreed with Kaus' view that this cultural shock provided the historical conditions of possibility for Dostoevsky's multi-voiced or "polyphonic" novel:

> The polyphonic novel could indeed have been realized only in the capitalist era. The most favourable soil for it was moreover precisely in Russia where capitalism set in almost catastrophically, and where it came upon an untouched multitude of diverse worlds and social groups which had not been weakened in their individual isolation, as in the West, by the gradual encroachment of capitalism.[1]

For Kaus this cataclysmic event was also unifying because it "jolted these worlds and wove them into its own contradictory evolving unity".[2] But Bakhtin rejected his idea of a developmental "evolving unity" in Dostoevsky's works. He even partly endorsed the view of Anatoly Lunacharsky, the Commissar for Enlightenment, who wrote that "the internal splintering [*rasscheplenie*] of Dostoevsky's consciousness" reflected the social "splintering of young Russian

---

1 Bakhtin 1984, pp. 19–20.
2 *Ibid,.* p. 19.

capitalist society".[3] He also quotes Lunacharsky's arguement that capitalism provided the historical conditions of possibility for the creativity of Shakespeare and Dostoevsky:

> What were the social factors reflected in Shakespeare's polyphonism? Why, of course, in the last analysis, precisely those we find in Dostoevsky. That colourful Renaissance, broken up into a myriad of sparkling shards, which had given birth to Shakespeare and his contemporaries was, of course, the result of the stormy irruption of capitalism into the comparative calm of medieval England. Here, as in Dostoevsky's Russia, a gigantic breakup was getting under way. The same gigantic shifts were taking place and the same unexpected collisions between traditions of social life and systems of thought which had previously had no real contact with one another.[4]

For Bakhtin too the catastrophic arrival of capitalism provided "the most favourable soil" for Dostoevsky's creativity. But he argued that even Shakespeare's dramatic form could never achieve the polyphonic multiplicity of intersecting but unmerged viewpoints to be found in the Dostoevskian novel. Fortunately, he did not maintain this contentious downplaying of dialogism in drama which borders on absurdity. But the stronger point in his argument is his insistence that all consciousness is constituted dialogically. Therefore even the apparently single-voiced utterance is internally multi-voiced, and this inward plurality is the general condition explored by Dostoevsky. But if the internalised voices which constitute human consciousness are locked into irreconcilable conflict, that is because so is society at that historical moment. Bakhtin's insights into the dialogical language of Dostoevsky's novels raise this very problem for his own philosophical connection between dialogism and "becoming", which he derived from Cassirer (see Chapter 1). This problematic relationship emerges with particular sharpness in Dostoevsky's *Notes from Underground*, which anticipates his major novels, because Bakhtin himself shows that all "becoming" or potential for change is fiercely resisted within every utterance of its first-person narrator/protagonist. In this chapter I will show that the potential for "becoming" is not simply absent from this novella's inwardly fissured discourse; on the contrary, it is present but actively negated.

---

3   *Ibid.*, p. 34.
4   Lunacharsky 1965, p. 111; Bakhtin *op. cit.*, p. 33.

1 Dialogical "Becoming" or Frozen Dialectic?

Notes from Underground first appeared in two parts in 1864, in the first two issues of *The Epoch*, which Fyodor Dostoevsky edited with his brother. In a footnote appended to the title the editor explains that, while the underground man is certainly a fictional character, he is nonetheless a typical representative of contemporary man:

> If we take into consideration the conditions that have shaped our society, people like the writer not only may, but must, exist in that society. I have tried to present to the public in a more striking form than is usual a character belonging to the very recent past, a representative figure from a generation still surviving.[5]

The narrative closes with the same editor's statement that this "paradoxalist" could in principle go on talking/writing forever, so he is intervening to stop him. These two framing comments suggest that there is a significant link between the "representative figure" of the "underground man" (as this nameless figure is usually called) and his paradoxical discourse. Bakhtin describes him as an "ideologist" because of his polemical stance towards all others, but Dostoevsky himself calls him a "paradoxalist". In this chapter I will focus on the way paradox not only characterizes the underground man's utterances but conditions his total behaviour.

In the opening section of his *Problems of Dostoevsky's Poetics* Bakhtin makes the point that dialogism constitutes the self-consciousness of the Dostoevskian hero in general:

> A character's self-consciousness in Dostoevsky is thoroughly dialogized: in its every aspect it is turned outward, intensely addressing itself, to another, [to] a third person [*k sebe, k drugomu, k tret'emu*]. Outside this living addressivity toward itself and toward the other [or plural "others": *k drugim*] it does not exist, even for itself.[6]

However, Bakhtin shows that the first-person narrator and protagonist of *Notes from Underground* constantly struggles to assert that non-existent autonomy through his polemical dialogue with all his addressees. These include

---

5 Dostoevsky 1972, p. 13
6 Bakhtin 1984, p. 251. Bakhtin himself emphasizes this plurality of "others" (*ibid.*, p. 253). I discuss this in "The Ethics of Capitalism" section (*infra*).

his imagined listeners or readers. In resisting their power to "finalize" him by passing judgment on him, he asserts his autonomy, but this assertion is inherently paradoxical, given his dialogical dependence on those others without whom his self-consciousness "does not exist, even for itself". Bakhtin's acute reading of this novella shows that it by no means exemplifies dialogism in the ethically positive manner propounded in his philosophy. On the contrary, it gives only negative support to his ethics by representing dialogical relations perpetually transformed into scenes of crisis under the influence of the underground man's attempted assertions of dominance. Moreover, his dialogical relationship with others condemns this narrator-protagonist to a humiliating recognition of his failure to be absolutely dominant. The self here is *aut Caesar aut nihil* or, as Raskol'nikov was to put it in *Crime and Punishment*, either a Napoleon or a louse.

For Bakhtin the dialogical relationship with others opens the human subject up to the potential for change, and for different possible futures. These are the key ideas discussed in Chapter 1. To understand Bakhtin's link between dialogism and "becoming" (*stanovlenie*) is to understand how self-conscious subjects come into existence and are capable of change in time. But here there is no process of "becoming", dialectical or dialogical. Instead there is an essentially static situation which could be called a frozen dialectic, because it allows for no development beyond the polar opposition of self to other taken to destructive extremes.[7] In his criticism of several Hegelian readings of Dostoevsky's works, Bakhtin writes that "Each novel [by Dostoevsky] presents an opposition, which is never cancelled out dialectically, of many consciousnesses", and he compares this timeless structure with "the formally polyphonic world of Dante". But even within this apparently positive aesthetic evaluation he sounds a negative note because he adds: "At best each [novel] could form, as in Dante's world a static figure ... but this static figure would resemble a congealed event [*kak by zastyvshee sobytie*]".[8]

This futureless "event" problematises the link between dialogism and "becoming". Bakhtin even argues that Dostoevsky's works in general are characterised by an absence of "becoming", so what is the effect of this absence on the "inner dialogism" which enables self-consciousness to exist but precludes any development? In my reading of *Notes from Underground* I will offer a critical extension of Bakhtin's insights to argue two interconnected points. The first is

---

7   My suggested "frozen dialectic" is borrowed from the conservative Spanish critic Joaquín Casalduero (Casalduero 1949). He describes the radical antitheses in Baroque literature as *una dialéctica congelada*.

8   Bakhtin 1984, p. 26.

that the underground man's attempted monologism is an active denial of dialogism in pursuit of his proclaimed autonomy, which he feels to be threatened by his dialogical engagement with others. That is to say, in his case at least, monologism is not an alternative mode of discourse to dialogism but its active negation, dialogically engaged with others despite his denial. The second point follows: this active negation produces what can only be called a preventive repression of this narrator-cum-protagonist's own potential for "becoming", meaning the very possibility of actually becoming other to the present self to which he clings. My turn to the psychoanalytical concept of repression takes Bakhtin's argument in a direction which is not his own. But I will argue shortly that Bakhtin's reading calls for a reformulated non-Freudian version of repression. As an imagined anticipation, the possibility of change may be experienced by the subject as either a promise or as a threat, or indeed as both simultaneously. That is to say, it can be desired and feared at the same time. The underground man exemplifies that contradiction without resolving it.

The underground hero's self-narration opens with three apparently blunt statements: "I am a sick man, I am a spiteful man. I am an unattractive man". Bakhtin begins his interpretation by focusing on their rhetorical intensification, but it is in the breaks between them that he detects the unsaid which conditions this hero's rhetoric:

> The ellipsis and the abrupt change of tone after it are significant. The hero began in a somewhat plaintive tone "I am a sick man", but was immediately enraged by that tone: it looked as though he were complaining and needed sympathy, as if he were seeking that sympathy in another person, as if he needed another person! And then there occurs an abrupt dialogic turnaround, one of those typical breaks in accent so characteristic of the whole style of the "Notes", as if the hero wants to say: You perhaps were led to believe from my first word that I am seeking your sympathy, so take this: I am a spiteful man. I am an unpleasant man.[9]

Bakhtin's key point is that this "gradual increase in negative tone" is motivated both by a desire "to spite the other", who is the reader in this instance, and by the contrary desire to demonstrate his independence from him. But this paradoxical display of aggressive indifference means that his utterance finds itself "under the influence of the other's anticipated reaction".[10] As I point out in Chapter 1, anticipation is integral to the very concept of "inner dialogism".

---

9   Bakhtin *op. cit.*, p. 228.
10 *Ibid.*

Here Bakhtin goes on to show that this hero's "internal polemic with the other" is at first concealed, but then it breaks out more overtly in his utterance, sometimes even in the form of direct quotations attributed to the others whom he is addressing. These others are a series of listeners or readers (the recurrent "gentlemen" of his sarcastic mode of address) whose responses are anticipated in his attempt to demonstrate that he stands outside or beyond whatever versions of himself that they (or we, his actual readers) may construct. The point that Bakhtin makes about this opening is that the underground man addresses these anticipated others in order to demonstrate to them, and therefore to himself, that he does not need them. But this attempt continually fails to achieve its goal, because it makes him all too conscious of his need for his addressees.

At the same time, however, Bakhtin writes that the underground man's internalisation of everyone else's actual or potential words about himself releases him into a freedom from external definitions:

> But he also knows that all these definitions, prejudiced as well as objective, rest in his hands and he cannot finalize them precisely because he himself perceives them; he can go beyond their limits and make them inadequate. He knows that he has the *final word* and he seeks at whatever cost to retain for himself this final word about himself, the word of his self-consciousness, in order to become in it that which he is not. His consciousness of self lives by its unfinalizability, by its unclosedness and its indeterminacy (original emphasis).[11]

Bakhtin affirms that dialogically open self-consciousness is a trait of all the major characters in Dostoevsky's works, including *Notes from Underground*, and that this self-consciousness confers a capacity for positive self-transformation:

> They all acutely sense their unfinalizability, their capacity to outgrow, as it were, from within and to render *untrue* any externalization and finalizing definition of them. As long as a person is alive he lives by the fact that he is not yet finalized, that he has not yet uttered his ultimate word (original emphasis).[12]

But here what the underground man "knows", namely that in the field of self-consciousness "he has the final word [about himself]", is actually an illusion, since by anticipating others' definitions he proves to them and to himself, that

---

11   *Ibid.*, p. 53.
12   *Ibid.*, p. 59.

such a final self-defining word cannot exist. No-one can have it. That is why, in his discussion of the so-called "loophole" (*lazeika*, a term used by the underground man himself), Bakhtin says that the character has the "penultimate word", not the final one. On the other hand, in the first passage quoted above we are told something significantly different, namely that he "seeks to retain for himself" that impossible final self-defining word. In Bakhtin's own commentary there is an unmarked shift towards a theory of desire for an object that can only exist as an imaginary goal. The language of desire for an unattainable imaginary object suggests the problematics of an unconscious (and its controlling power over the conscious subject), rather than a truly free developing consciousness. Bakhtin does not advance any such psychoanalytical arguments, but he does observe that the underground man is locked into endless competition for that imaginary self-possession, and that it takes the form of his anxious anticipation of any challenge to it. He writes that the underground man "tries to outguess and outwit all possible definitions of his personality others might offer"[13] and he adds that this is a trait which he shares with all of Dostoevsky's principal heroes:

> Dostoevsky's hero always seeks to destroy that framework of *other people's* words about him that might finalize and deaden him. Sometimes this struggle becomes an important and tragic motif in the character's life (as, for example, with Nastasya Filipovna) [original emphasis].[14]

This general truth of the Dostoevskian hero is summed up by Bakhtin as a consequence of the dialogical constitution of individual personality: "A man never coincides with himself".[15] That is what makes him free, not only in the sense that he cannot be determined by others' definitions but also, far more significantly, even by those which he advances himself in his unending internalised dialogue with them. And that is the real issue: the competitive nature of the hero's desire for autonomous superiority becomes a vehicle for its opposite, namely an inescapable enslavement to "the other". In Bakhtin's reading, the hero's struggle with others to demonstrate his freedom actually locks him into the endless dialectic which some critics have explicitly identified as the Hegelian dialectic of the master and the slave.[16]

---

13   *Ibid.*
14   *Ibid.* Nastasya Filipovna Barashkova is the tragic heroine of *The Idiot*.
15   *Ibid.*
16   Tsvetan Todorov writes: "This logic, which is never formulated but is endlessly represented … is the logic of the master and the slave, or, in Dostoevsky's own terms,'scorn' and 'humiliation'. Far from showing gratuitousness, irrationality, or spontaneity, the behaviour

This hero's enslavement arises because his desire for autonomous mastery can only be complete if that mastery is recognised by them, but this leads immediately to an unwelcome recognition of his dependence on them. In this context, Bakhtin writes that he is not actually free, since the "style of the tale" which he tells is "under the powerful all-determining influence of other people's words".[17] The result is what Caryl Emerson translates as the "vicious circle". The Russian is *durnaya beskonechnost'*, which is the term from Hegel's *Phenomenology of Spirit* usually rendered into English as "bad infinity",[18] i.e. roughly, endless repetition without change. Bakhtin writes that the undergound man's anticipation is marked by a striving for autonomy, but this striving in fact traps him:

> Such anticipation is marked by one peculiar structural trait: it tends [or "strives": *stremitsya*] towards a vicious circle [*k durnoi beskonechnosti*]. The tendency [*tendentsiya*] of these anticipations can be reduced to the necessity to retain for oneself the final word. This final word must express the hero's full independence from the views and words of the other person, his complete indifference to the other's opinion and the other's evaluation. What he fears most of all is that people might think that he is repenting before someone, that he is asking someone's forgiveness, that he is reconciling himself to someone else's judgment or evaluation, that his self-affirmation is somehow in need of affirmation and recognition by another. And it is in this direction that he anticipates the other's response. But precisely in this act of anticipating the other's response and in responding to it he again demonstrates to the other (and to himself) his own dependence on this other. He *fears* that the other might think that he *fears* the other's opinion [original emphases]. But through this fear he immediately demonstrates his own dependence on the other's consciousness, his own inability to be at peace with his own definition of self. With his refutation, he confirms precisely what he wishes to refute, and he knows it. Hence the inescapable circle [*bezvykhodnyi krug*] in which the hero's self-consciousness and discourse are trapped ...[19]

---

of the underground man, as René Girard has already pointed out, is obedient to a very precise schema": Todorov 1972, p. 24 (my translation). Todorov's reference is to Girard's *Deceit, Desire and the Novel* [1961] 1966.

17 Bakhtin 1984, p. 229.
18 I am indebted to Galin Tihanov for this observation.
19 Bakhtin 1984, pp. 229–230. For the Russian references, Bakhtin 1972, pp. 394–395.

This is an extremely acute analysis of the determined nature of this character's drive to establish his autonomy *against* the very dialogism which makes his self-conscious life and utterance possible. It also incorporates Hegel's definition of human desire as the desire for recognition by another, but in the inverted form of a psychological negation. Bakhtin does not invoke Hegel or desire here, but his acute analysis shows how this hero denies that he desires recognition, while constantly striving to achieve it, since he demands the recognition of his superiority by others in order to experience it himself. So the paradoxical drive for autonomous mastery endlessly reveals the very dependence which it seeks to deny. And Bakhtin makes a further point here: it is through this very denial of dependence that even the desire for recognition is transformed into hostility and fear (i.e. fear of the other's dominance). That is the essence of Bakhtin's analysis. However, it leaves an important question hanging: Is that feared "dependence", which is revealed to the underground man's consciousness through his defeated attempts to deny it, the ultimate truth of his relationship with others? Or is it not, on the contrary, produced out of the necessary failure of his competitive struggle for absolute mastery, and hence a distortion of self-other relations misrecognised as the inescapable truth? If so, this misrecognition (to borrow Lacan's term, *méconnaissance*) entails a willed overlooking or psychological negation of something that is known, even at the very heights of the consciousness which does not wish to know it.

Just prior to this passage, Bakhtin writes that in all this "extreme and acute internal dialogisation, there is literally not a single monologically firm, undissociated word".[20] The clear implication is that the underground man is locked into a struggle to utter precisely such a "monologically firm word". But what could Bakhtin have meant by calling it an "undissociated word"? This double negative needs to be unpacked. In Russian the positive *razlozhennoe* is derived from *razlozhit'* which, like the English "to dissociate" means to break down a substance into its components or to actively "decompose" it, as in chemistry. But in the reflexive form which is more pertinent here, *razlozhit'sya* means "to decompose, rot, decay" or figuratively "to become demoralized, to crack up, to go to pieces".[21] Bakhtin's double negative may be confusing, but his argument clearly indicates that, in the context of his "extreme and acute internal dialogisation", this hero's failure to utter even a single "undissociated word" means that his every word is internally broken up. Up until this point Bakhtin's main argument has been that the underground man's polemical attack on all others

---

20   Bakhtin 1984, p. 227; In Russian: "*ni odnogo monologicheski tverdogo, nerazlozhenogo slova*", Bakhtin 1972, p. 392.
21   The Oxford Russian-English Dictionary.

is a struggle for mastery, so any acknowledgement of dialogical mutuality must appear to him as an unacceptable acknowledgement of subordinate dependence. But the point which he makes here goes further: the underground man's failure to master those others within his own internally dialogized speech leads to its disintegration. So his inner speech breaks up into mutually hostile voices. This might well be considered a symptom of schizophrenia. His would-be monological self-affirmation constantly leads him towards an inner disintegration which is alternately narcissistic and paranoid in its defensive aggression against the insisting voices of others within the self. I will return shortly to this inward scene of "catastrophe", as Bakhtin calls it.

2   The Ethics of Capitalism

In Bakhtin's reading of the underground man's utterances, his anxiously defensive struggle not to be the object of another's discourse (his "word") is the obverse of his aggressive struggle to turn all others into objects of his own. Bakhtin's name for this competitive desire which seeks to negate the reciprocity of dialogical relations in its pursuit of mastery, is monologism. Its effect is to seek a reification of others as "the other" in pursuit of an unachievable absolute domination. In reality, those others are plural, but he reifies them as "the other". Bakhtin notes this characteristic reifying abstraction in the underground man's solipsistic utterance, by pointing out how it leads him to transform the world of real others into the binary opposition of two camps: I and "the other":

> He reduces all people to a single common denominator – "the other". School friends, fellow civil servants, his servant Apollon, the woman who has fallen in love with him, and even the creator of the world order with whom he polemicizes, all are reduced to this category by the Underground Man, and his primary reaction to them is as "others" in relation to himself.[22]

This reduction of dialogical relations to the generalized abstraction of the binary self/other opposition is a familiar intellectual move nowadays. And its validity is widely accepted. All others become the Lacanian "big Other" which is, potentially at least, a paranoid construction imposed on the world. But I would argue that its competitive drive for discursive dominance can be re-expressed

---

22   Bakhtin 1984, p. 253.

in equally familiar socio-economic terms. The inner logic of competition (its "ideal" or absolute form, so to speak) demands that each competitor must seek absolute dominion, either through the elimination of all rivals or through their subordination to the would-be dominant self. After all, the ultimate goal of every competitor is monopoly, not the continuation of competitive relationships. To fail to follow this imperative is to lay oneself open to attack by all the other competitors. There can only be winners or losers (masters or subordinates). So the subjective counterpart of this Hobbesian war of all against all is the aggressive/defensive ego seeking to become the centre of its "own" world, in a solipsist drive for which all others (including "the creator of the world"!) would be either eliminated or subordinated adjuncts of the self.

This argument, which sees monologism as the discursive equivalent of monopoly, may appear to impose a political perspective quite alien to Bakhtin's ethical concerns. But in his "Notes towards a Reworking of the Dostoevsky book" (1961),[23] the question of Dostoevsky's relationship to the rapid emergence of capitalism in Russia, which Bakhtin had already invoked in the opening pages of the Dostoevsky book, is given a new significance. Bakhtin introduces this social perspective by re-affirming his familiar view that Dostoevsky's dialogism testifies to "the impossibility of the existence of a single consciousness", because consciousness "takes place on the *boundary* between one's own and someone else's consciousness, on the *threshold* [original emphases]". Bakhtin continues:

> Thus does Dostoevsky confront all decadent and idealistic (individualistic) culture, the culture of essential and inescapable solitude. He asserts the impossibility of solitude. The very being of man (both external and internal) is the *deepest communion. To be* means *to communicate....* To be means to be for another, and through the other, for oneself. A person has no internal sovereign territory, he is wholly and always on the boundary; looking inside himself, he looks *into the eyes of another* or *with the eyes of another* [original emphases].[24]

But while solitude may well be an "impossibility", as the above passage states, Bakhtin argues that it is in effect a really existing impossibility. That is to say, it is produced by a particular social form, which he calls "the culture of essential

---

23   *Op. cit.* Appendix II, pp. 283–302.
24   *Ibid.,* p. 287.

and inescapable solitude", and which he then identifies specifically as the culture of capitalism:

> Capitalism created the conditions for a special type of inescapably solitary consciousness. Dostoevsky exposes all the falsity (*lozhnost'*) of this consciousness as it moves in its vicious circle.
>
> Hence the depiction of the sufferings, humiliations, and *lack of recognition* of man in class society. Recognition has been taken away from him, his name has been taken away. He has been driven into forced solitude, which the unsubmissive strive to transform into *proud solitude* [original emphases].[25]

The self-validation bestowed by mutual recognition is removed from "man in class society", and this engenders either submissive subordination or else a reactive affirmation of "proud solitude". But this second reaction of proud self-affirmation is not really an alternative to humiliating submission; it is rather the defensive-aggressive reaction of the individual "driven into forced solitude" by the culture of capitalism. These observations on Dostoevsky's work were actually published later than his *Problems of Dostoevsky's Poetics*, but even in his earlier reading of *Notes from Underground* Bakhtin had already shown how the underground man's affirmation of "proud solitude" is a refusal of mutual recognition. Bakhtin refers to the "impossibility of solitude", which I have labelled above a "really existing impossibility". By this paradox I mean that the solipsist aspiration is real, in the sense of having an effective social existence, but its goal is unachievable. The deceptive lure of complete mastery, to become sole master of the universe, leads ineluctably to the subject's sense of his failure to achieve it. Bakhtin specifically defines the scene of this desire as the competitive culture of capitalism. Dostoevsky's confrontation with this culture, which fosters the solipsist desire for autonomous mastery as though it were an achievable goal, consists in his exploration of its baleful effects. This is not a matter of a merely utopian exposition of the ethical superiority of the dialogical mutuality which this culture negates (which in Dostoevsky's case would mean a Christian apologia for such an alternative), but of uncovering the link between its outward competitive aggression and its inner self-destructive drives. This is where the novelist takes over from the combative journalist and ideologist.

---

25   *Ibid.*, p.288.

3   The Internal Catastrophe

In the Introduction to her English translation, Caryl Emerson notes that Bakhtin specifically rules out a Hegelian schema of progression, calling it a monological mode of understanding.[26] This observation is undeniably correct. For example, Bakhtin writes that, "the unified, dialectically evolving spirit, understood in Hegelian terms, can give rise to nothing but a philosophical monologue".[27] But Emerson skates over Bakhtin's assessment of the negative side of this absence of any "dialectical evolution of the spirit" in Dostoevsky's novels. In the same section of his book, Bakhtin himself goes on to note that there is blindness as well as insight in "Dostoevsky's visualizing power", as it remained "locked in place at the moment that diversity revealed itself":

> Dostoevsky's extraordinary capacity for seeing everything in coexistence and interaction is his greatest strength, *but his greatest weakness as well* [emphasis added]. It made him deaf and dumb to a great many essential things; many aspects of reality could not enter his artistic field of vision. But on the other hand this capacity sharpened, and to an extreme degree, his perception in the cross-section of a given moment, and permitted him to see many and varied things where others saw one and the same thing. Where others saw a single thought, he was able to find and feel out two thoughts, a bifurcation; where others saw a single quality, he discovered in it the presence of a second and contradictory quality. Everything that seemed simple became, in his world, complex and multistructured. In every voice he could hear two contending voices, in every expression a crack, and the readiness to go over immediately to another contradictory expression; in every gesture he detected confidence and lack of confidence simultaneously; he perceived the profound ambiguity, even multiple ambiguity, of every phenomenon. But none of these contradictions and bifurcations ever became dialectical, they were never set in motion along a temporal path or in an evolving sequence ...[28]

On the positive side, Bakhtin praises Dostoevsky's ability to detect what was "complex and multistructured" behind apparent unity, and to uncover the "profound ambiguity, even multiple ambiguity, of every phenomenon". Bakhtin's insight into Dostoevsky's novelistic discourse is truly illuminating. But what is

---

26   *Ibid.*, introduction, p. xxxii.
27   *Ibid.*, p. 26.
28   *Ibid.*, p. 30.

excluded from Dostoevsky's acute perception is the temporality of "becoming". Bakhtin notes quite clearly that this absence finds expression only as a fissure or "crack", with no possible temporal outcome or resolution. There is only the possibility of sudden reversal ("the readiness to go over immediately to another contradictory expression") or the co-existence of contradictory attitudes within the split subject, whose every gesture displays "confidence and lack of confidence simultaneously".

In his "Notes towards a re-working of the Dostoevsky book", Bakhtin identifies the spiritual and psychological crisis represented in Dostoevsky's work as "the problem of catastrophe". With this term he finally confronts theoretically the fate of dialogism when there is no "becoming". Instead of even the triumphant finalization promised by Hegelianism, there is catastrophe:

> Catastrophe is not finalization. It is the culmination, in collision and struggle, of points of view (of equally privileged consciousnesses, each with its own world). Catastrophe does not give these points of view resolution, but on the contrary reveals their incapability of resolution under earthly conditions; catastrophe sweeps them all away without having resolved them. Catastrophe is the opposite of triumph and apotheosis. By its very essence it is denied even elements of catharsis.[29]

Catastrophe is "the opposite of triumph and apotheosis" in the precise sense that it too is a case of dialogism, but it occurs when the participants are locked into conflict without the crucial element of mutual transformation and "becoming" ("under earthly conditions", at least). It would best be described as a clash of monologisms forced into irreconcilable confrontation. This completely reverses quite a lot of Bakhtin's own statements like the general assertion that the authorial stance towards the hero in his novels is "one that affirms the independence, internal freedom, unfinalizability, and indeterminacy of the hero".[30] While these are indeed the ethical values that inform Dostoevsky's writing, the actual representation of his heroes' consciousness provides extremely negative examples of the "internal freedom" bestowed by dialogical interaction. "Catastrophe" is a much better description of this intensely monologised dialogism, which is bereft of all "becoming" or transformation within the heightened consciousness of his major heroes. To put the matter clearly, bi-polarity, or the logic of mutual exclusion, is the negative achievement of monologism as it distorts the mutual interdependence

---

29   *Ibid.*, p. 298 (Appendix 2).
30   *Ibid.*, p. 63.

which enables transformations to occur. By turning dialogical relations into a single bi-polarity, it freezes its own potential for change. The consequence, however, is not the desired transcendental ego or God-like dominance but the explosive inward confrontation which characterises the widely acknowledged hyperconscious lucidity of the Dostoevskian hero, and his agile capacity for paradox. Seen in this way, even the capacity for rational paradox appears more as a symptom of madness than of control. It barely conceals within its display of discursive control an inward catastrophe which consists of irreconcilable contradictions.

Bakhtin's formulation of the Dostoevskian heroes' response within this frozen temporality is extraordinarily interesting. Their hyperconsciousness, which resists process and change, engenders what he goes on to describe paradoxically as a willed forgetting. He argues that, since the plot in a Dostoevsky novel is not a revelatory process of new possibilities, like the plot of a *Bildungsroman* for example, it enters the consciousness of the Dostoevskian hero as a series of explosive events. At these moments, there is no development. Instead, the catastrophe discloses a reality which was already known but overlooked:

> That internal ideological struggle which the hero wages is a struggle for a choice among already available semantic possibilities, whose quantity remains almost unchanged throughout the entire novel. The motifs "I didn't know that", "I didn't see that", "that was revealed to me later", are absent from Dostoevsky's world. His hero knows and sees everything from the beginning. That is why it is so common for heroes (or for a narrator speaking about a hero) to announce, after a catastrophe, that they had known and foreseen everything in advance.... It is true, as we shall soon see, that *the hero very often hides from himself what he knows, and pretends to himself that he does not see what is in fact constantly before his very eyes*. But in such cases this characteristic trait stands out all the more sharply [emphasis added].[31]

This paradoxical mental act by the hero, hiding from his own knowledge and sight things that are already known and seen, is a good working definition of the unconscious produced by negation. Bakhtin links this struggle amidst mutually exclusive "semantic possibilities" to an unbearable hyperconsciousness for which a significant time of becoming does not exist, and to the absence of any plot which would bring new knowledge, new realisations, and consequent changes in the self too. In this respect, the Dostoevskian heroes' hyperconsciousness is remarkably similar to Freud's view of the *unconscious*

---

31 Bakhtin 1984, p. 239.

which "knows no time".³² The common feature is not the mere absence of the consciousness of time but its repression. For all their lucidity, these heroes' knowledge in advance of the imminent catastrophe (which is also immanent) cannot liberate them into a capacity for acting or being otherwise. They cannot become other. They anticipate the catastrophic event because they are hyperconscious, but they can only "announce" that it had to happen after it has happened (thus fully acknowledging it only retrospectively). This monological freezing of self-other encounters, transforming their potential for change into mutual exclusives, is the cultural disaster which Dostoevsky explores at the level of his heroes' psychology.

Freud invokes just such a binary logic in the notorious Dora case to describe the production of unconscious thinking through active negation:

> Contrary thoughts are always closely connected with each other and are often paired off in such a way that the one thought is excessively intensely conscious while its counterpart is repressed and unconscious. This relation between the two thoughts is an effect of the process of repression. For repression is often achieved by means of an excessive reinforcement of the thought contrary to the one which is to be repressed. This process I shall call *reactive* reinforcement, and the thought which asserts itself exaggeratedly in consciousness and (in the same way as a prejudice) cannot be removed I call a *reactive thought* [original emphases].³³

This bi-polarity accounts for unconscious thought as the product of hyperconscious awareness, "the thought which asserts itself exaggeratedly in consciousness", rather than as the residue of primitive, pre-social urges persisting beneath rational or civilised consciousness. What Freud calls the "relations between two thoughts" brought about by "the process of repression" is clearly a dynamic relationship within a single consciousness. It is dialectical insofar as it produces a third term, namely the unconscious "counterpart" of the dominant thought. But it is, so to speak, a regressive dialectic, in the sense that it does not produce a moment of "becoming" or transformation. If the subject

---

32 Freud 2005a.
33 Freud 2005b, p. 89. Feminist critics, in particular, have argued that Freud does not register the way in which his own emphatic interpretation of Dora's account of her relationships with her governess, her father, and Herr K, imposes a patriarchal interpretation upon Dora's words, in collaboration with her father's unspoken wishes. Cf. Bernheimer and Kahane 1985. But, although Freud's unconscious blindness in this respect seems undeniable, his lucidity on the repressive nature of such "excessively intensely conscious" thoughts actually provides the key to his own blindness.

is indeed captured here, the regression is not really a surrender to a putative primal force controlling his consciousness from beneath his own threshold of awareness, as in so many "Freudian" explanations (sometimes from Freud himself, admittedly). It is rather a matter of being trapped by what Dostoevsky's underground hero himself theorises in the early section of *Notes from Underground* as the "laws of heightened consciousness" (*zakony sil'neishnego soznaniya*). Dostoevsky's use of the superlative form of *sil'niy* (strong) for this "heightened" consciousness indicates an activity of the will, comparable to that of Nietzsche's superman. His "strong consciousness" is close in meaning to the French *esprit fort*, which designates an intellect (or wit) superior to religious prejudices and, by extension, all conventionally accepted norms. But, while much of the underground hero's polemic is aimed at showing that heightened consciousness (exemplified by himself) is subject to his will alone, and is not determined by any rational, scientific, or natural laws, he also maintains in the course of his argument that there are indeed "laws" which set limits to that very "heightened consciousness". In his struggle to elucidate them, he has recourse to the endless paradoxes through which he displays his verbal mastery. But it turns out constantly that this "paradoxalist", as Dostoevsky calls him, is not so much the master of his paradoxes as their slave. They are actually symptoms of his inner crisis, and when he deploys them to account for his own behavior, they signify the very opposite of mastery, namely his subordination to the "laws of heightened consciousness". These controlling laws are not rational or scientific laws but the laws of his desire.

4   The Prison House of Paradox

Much of the underground hero's polemic in the first part of the *Notes* is aimed at the determinist theories of human nature which supported the various forms of progressive politics at the time. The reason why the Crystal Palace figures so prominently in this polemic is that it represented the fulfillment of aspirations to rationality, transparency, and control, whether these were the achievement of capitalist development, as in the case of the London exhibition itself, or whether they were the goal of utopian socialism, as in the theories of Fourier. The underground man treats all these ideas as the expression of an illusory desire to change human nature in accordance with the rational, mathematically calculable nature of man's true interests. He measures this goal against the paradoxical reality of human desires which, from the standpoint of reason must appear perverse. He emphasizes that human desire, quite unlike the activities of the anthill, is a process whose goal is desired but is also dreaded and must never be reached. Man, he says, may indeed love creating things and building roads etc., but he also loves chaos and destruction. The basis for this paradoxical assertion is that the love of destruction is certainly perverse but it has one positive feature: it prevents the feared arrival at the termination of the desiring process which is life itself.[34] That is why his unending polemic with those who would "finalize" him (to use Bakhtin's term) is also a manifestation of his own perverse desire.

Paradox is central to the underground hero's formulation of the "laws of heightened consciousness" and his endless attempts to explain them to others and to himself. In his concluding remarks at the end of the tale, Dostoevsky as quasi-fictitious editor writes that there was in fact no conclusion to the utterances of this "paradoxalist", so he is imposing one. But my further reason for preferring "paradox", rather than ambivalence, to describe the underground man's utterances is that paradox formulates binary oppositions rhetorically, in timeless stasis. So it is opposed to both dialogical "becoming" and dialectical transformation. The Oxford English Dictionary is useful in providing a highly paradoxical definition of the word itself. Firstly, it is "a statement contrary to received opinion or belief, sometimes with favourable, sometimes with unfavourable connotation". But the second definition goes further and points to a more significant equivocation in paradox itself:

> A statement *seemingly* self-contradictory or absurd, though possibly well-founded or essentially true, 1569. b) Often applied to a proposition that is *actually* self-contradictory and so essentially absurd or false, 1570 (emphases added).

In his dialogical struggle with his imagined others (listeners or readers) whose judgment he anxiously anticipates, the underground hero operates across this division. He generally attributes to these addressees the second of the above judgments of himself, namely that his words are "absurd" or "false". Such a response from them (or us) would annihilate him, reducing him to being a mere object of contempt or ridicule within their superior discourse. Or rather, it would so reduce him unless he can prove to them that his self-contradictions should be perceived as intentional. In that case, even his "absurdity" would not be really absurd but a surface appearance, concealing a deeper coherence which only a perceptive intelligence like his own could discern. Consequently, to speak in paradoxes would be to utter deeper truths through a necessary oracular indirection. So is he speaking (or writing) from a position

---

34 Dostoevsky 1972, pp. 40–41.

that is "actually self-contradictory", or from one that is only "seemingly self-contradictory"? In the latter case, he would have turned the tables on those who try to dismiss him as "absurd or false", because intentional contradictions must indicate a controlling intention.

5   A Modern Liar's Paradox

If intentional "falsehood" means lying, it would be the falsehood of the liar who knows the truth in order to be able to lie. The successful liar, after all, is the master of appearances because he knows the truth behind them. Friedrich Nietzsche wrote to Overbeck (February 23rd 1887) that his recent discovery of *Notes from Underground* gave him extraordinary joy, and in *The Twilight of the Idols* (1888) he added that Dostoevsky was "the only psychologist, incidentally, from whom I had something to learn"[35] (despite his contempt for Dostoevsky's Christian beliefs). And in his *Genealogy of Morals* Nietzsche gives a very pertinent expression to his insistence that the liar must know the truth in order to be able to lie, because for him it was precisely the capacity for strong self-knowledge that had been lost to modern consciousness:

> Our educated people of today, our "good" people do not tell lies – that is true; but it is *not* to their credit. A real lie, a genuine, resolute "honest" lie (on whose value one should consult Plato) would be something far too potent and severe for them; it would demand of them what one *may* not demand of them, that they should open their eyes to themselves, that they should know how to distinguish "true" and "false" in themselves. All they are capable of is a *dishonest* lie (original emphases).[36]

Nietzsche identifies this modern loss of the capacity for truth, and therefore for real ("honest") lying, as a defining cultural crisis:

> The most distinctive feature of modern souls and modern books is not lying, but their inveterate *innocence* in moralistic mendaciousness. To have to re-discover this "innocence" everywhere – this constitutes perhaps the most disgusting job among all the precarious tasks a psychologist has to

---

35   Nietzsche 1973, p. 549.
36   Nietzsche 1989, p. 137.

tackle today; it is part of *our* great danger – it is a path that may lead precisely *us* toward great nausea (original emphases).[37]

In effect Nietzsche re-deploys the classical liar's paradox in terms of a historical decline. But his enthusiastic response to Dostoevsky's novella does not mean that the underground man actually represents a masterful exception to modern degeneracy, where the knowable boundary between truth and falsehood has collapsed (in Nietzsche's view and perhaps in Dostoevsky's too). It is rather that he struggles constantly to display the self-knowledge of the proto-Nietzschean superman in order to demonstrate that superiority to the herd of his conformist contemporaries, and to himself.

From the outset this hero's affirmation of freedom, which he conceives as an autonomous independence from others' anticipated definitions, is associated with the promise of mastery through lying about himself. For example, early in the work he withdraws his own opening definition of himself as "spiteful", by saying that he was lying. But then he reaffirms its truth in the very next sentence:

> I was lying just now when I said that I was a spiteful civil servant. I lied out of spite.[38]

Here both his lying and his spitefulness are jointly flaunted and withdrawn: his act of lying is attributed to the spite which he then says is a lie. Like the example of the Cretan liar who says that all Cretans lie, and is therefore not lying at the moment when he says that he is, he confronts the reader, his imagined listeners, and even himself, with the paradoxical nature of his own speech. But, unlike the purely logical conundrum of the classical liar's paradox, this paradox is psychologically motivated by "spite" directed at the addressee of his own speech act. Towards the end of the first part of the novella, there is an extreme example of the liar's paradox, when he casts a retrospective glance over his entire utterance up to that point, and says that it is all lies. But this is a willfully simplifying judgment because it too contains a "loophole" (*lazeika*), which enables him to concede that actually he may not have been lying, after all:

> It would be better if I believed even a small part of everything I have written here. I swear, gentlemen, I don't believe a word, not a single word, of

---

37 *Ibid.*
38 Dostoevsky 1972, p. 16.

all I have scribbled down! That is, I do perhaps believe it, but at the same time, I don't know why, I feel or suspect, that I'm lying like a trooper.[39]

This contradictory statement finally provokes the fictional "gentlemen" who are his imagined addressees, to burst out in fury, denouncing his endless duplicity and describing him as a coward and a liar. This infuriated attack has a very interesting conclusion, because what these anticipated others call his cowardly *inability* to tell the truth is identified by the very same term which Bakhtin re-accentuates as the hero's *freedom* never to utter his "final word" (*poslednee slovo*):

> ...... There is truth in you, but no virtue; out of the pettiest vanity you carry your truth to market to be exposed to scorn and shame ... You really do want to say something, but you keep your last word hidden [*pryachete vashe poslednee slovo*], because you haven't the resolution to speak it, only cowardly impudence. You pride yourself on your intellectual power, but you do nothing but vacillate, because although your brain works, your heart is clouded with depravity, and without a pure heart there can be no full, correct understanding. And you are so importunate, so thrusting, so full of airs and graces! Lies, lies, all lies!.[40]

But the underground hero immediately counter-attacks by reminding them that, despite the quotation marks identifying this angry judgment as an external other's denunciation, this furious attack is his own "literary" creation:

> Of course, I have just this minute invented all these words of yours. They also come from under the ground. I have been listening to these words of yours through a chink for forty years. I made them up myself, I have nothing else to think about. It is not to be wondered at if they were got by heart and have acquired a literary form.[41]

He flaunts his mastery over his addressees, by asserting in effect that they are his literary creation. This is a verbal act for which we would have to coin another paradoxical term: "triumphant solipsism". But even here, immediately shadowing this declaration of authorial mastery, there is an admission of the dialogism which enables his authorship to exist: "I have been listening to these

---

39 *Ibid.*, p. 44.
40 *Ibid.*, p. 44.
41 *Ibid.*, pp. 44–5.

words of yours through a chink for forty years". This contradictory stance leads him into an exploration of the insoluble paradox inherent in his monological claim to authorship over his "own" utterance, because it cannot be truly his own if it depends upon his addressees.

There is another logic at work in this recourse to the liar's paradox. While it is true that he often mocks his readers' inability to grasp the truth behind his paradoxical formulations in order to demonstrate his autonomous superiority, he also confesses an alternative truth which makes this lying very problematical. That is because it dissolves the very concept of the single controlling self who would be capable of lying, and therefore of mastery (since the successful liar is effectively in control of himself and his addressees). He explains that, however spitefully he may have behaved towards others, all his actions, including his speech acts, were always a willful denial of all the other potentialities (he calls them "elements") boiling away within himself and even demanding outward expression or enactment:

> I was simply playing a game with the officer and my other callers; in reality I could never make myself malevolent. I was always conscious of many elements showing the directly opposite tendency. I felt them positively swarming inside me, these elements. I knew they had swarmed there all my life, asking to be let out, but I wouldn't let them out, I wouldn't, I wouldn't. They tormented me shamefully; they drove me into convulsions and – in the end they bored me, oh how they bored me! You think that now I'm making some sort of confession to you, asking your forgiveness, don't you? ... I'm sure you do ... But I assure you it's all the same to me if you do think so.[42]

He refers to his verbal acts as "a game", and later he will say the same thing about his treatment of the prostitute Liza. Of course, it is possible to retort (in that later context too) that the will to make oneself malevolent is perhaps yet another manifestation of malevolence, and therefore it is not "a game". So there is a "sort of confession" here, after all. But in this passage the underground man is making another point, namely that, being aware of all the contradictory "elements" swarming within himself despite his efforts to deny them, he could never really *be* a solid single character and could only role-play without true conviction (it was only a "game"). Since role-playing too is a form of lying (controlling appearances to conceal a truth), the liar or actor who unmasks himself reveals something else.

---

42   *Ibid.*, p. 16.

It is not that these appearances are merely false. That would be too simple. It is rather that they are an attempt to *be* something through a willful denial of all the inner tendencies which contradict his display of mastery. Bakhtin's ethical philosophy gives such multiplicity within the self a positive inflection, by identifying it as the truthfulness of all "personality" (*lichnost'*), grounded in social "polyphony" and openness to the mobility of "becoming". But when the underground man confronts his own inner multiplicity, he affirms the value of the unmediated singularity which he sees outside himself in the supposedly "normal" men of fixed character. For him, their normality consists in the fact that their appearance and their being seem to coincide. On the one hand, he despises these men of fixed character for their stupidity, and he clearly projects this objectifying fixity onto everyone, thus identifying himself as their observing superior. But on the other hand, this observing satirist also voices his envy of their capacity to be something, however stupid. He lists such men, and his list is even extended beyond the envied men of action to include anyone who can be something, even passively but in an untroubled way in accordance with their undivided nature (like the man who takes pride in being a connoisseur of Château Lafitte). But here too he acknowledges his dependence upon the judgmental gaze of those others, when he adds that the desired gratification of being something would actually consist in being recognized and described by them:

> Oh, if only it was out of laziness that I do nothing! Lord, how much I should respect myself then! I should respect myself because I had something inside me, even if it was only laziness; I should have at any rate one positive quality of which I could be sure. Question: what is he? Answer: a lazy man; and it really would be very pleasant to hear that said of me. It would mean being positively defined. It would mean that there was something that *could* be said of me. "A lazy man" – that is a name, a calling; it's positively a career. Don't laugh, it's true.[43]

There is a comic note here, which the hero himself concedes when he insists on its seriousness: "Don't laugh, it's true". Earlier he has explained that even if he calls himself a mouse, in contrast to the envied real men of action, the truth of the matter is that he could not even be an insect. In short, he is threatened by the persuasion that he cannot *be* anything at all. Following the same logic, he could not even be a liar, because he is too inwardly divided and does not occupy the position of undisturbed (Nietzschean) mastery over self and others

---

43   *Ibid.*, p. 28

which lying promises. But those despised others can nonetheless bestow upon him that desired fullness of being through their act of recognition. If to be a lazy man is to be recognized and described as such by others, as he says, then the same solicitation for recognition would apply to being a liar. The crucial point is that the dialogical constitution of identity means that to be a definable character is to be recognized and described as such by others. So, even when he imputes to others the judgment that he is a liar and a coward, through such self-denigration via the external gaze and judgment of others he is also seeking a stable identity. Even though it comes at the price of the most humiliating acknowledgement of dependence on those whom he despises, it brings with it the gratifications of the recognition which bestows being.

This "paradoxalist" cites perversity itself as proof of the independence of the human will when it confronts any boundary, physical or moral, which would define its limits. Perversity is invoked to demonstrate the human capacity to step over any given boundary. In this sense it anticipates the theme of "stepping over" or transgression (*prestuplenie*) in *Crime and Punishment* (*Prestuplenie i nakazanie*), and other later novels. Despite being a burden and a "sickness", and despite his arguments that it shapes the desires of this "comical creature" (mankind), this capacity for transgression is also given an elite status when he contrasts it with the other kinds of men, who are completely untroubled by it. Those others are his healthy "spontaneous people and men of action". He says that they act and think within the prescribed boundaries of the laws of nature and, by the same token, within the impulses of their own nature. Moreover they are positively content to think and act within such boundaries, because they take them to be simply given, and therefore they do not challenge them or their defining hold.[44] His metaphor for such protective containment within the laws of nature is "the wall", which is a provocative insult to a man like himself since it would simplify and define him. By contrast with hyperconscious mental transgressives like himself, his so-called "normal man" simply follows his own impulses without even being aware of the way in which he is externally conditioned. He gives this undivided creature a French label taken from Rousseau, the *homme de la nature et de la vérité*. Taken together with the generic singular which groups all such people into a single category, this source

---

44 Raskolnikov shares this contempt for the ordinary. And yet, as the detective Porfiry observes after reading his brilliant article on the exceptional Napoleonic being, it is precisely this intellectual identification with Napoleon which makes him rather typical. Contemporary intellectuals all imagine themselves as Napoleon, he says. Stendhal's Julien Sorel is a famous literary example of the fascination of the Napoleonic legend for an earlier generation. We learn from Sudir Hazareesingh 2004, that in the 1840s more French madmen took themselves for the returning Napoleon than for any other figure except Jesus Christ.

already casts a shadow of doubt, suggesting that these other "natural" people are a philosophical fiction embraced by the underground hero because, in contrasting himself with them, he seeks to frame them in this reifying omniscient way.

However, the most striking paradoxical feature of this reductive definition of all others is that, while they are constructed by him as objects of his superior intellectual contempt, they are also objects of his intense envy. Doubling his affirmation of his own superiority is his simultaneous envy of these simplified objects of his own discourse. They are "stupid", certainly, but "as their mother nature intended". They are what men ought to be, and are therefore not internally divided and conscious of that division, like the "developed" man of sick but "heightened consciouness", who is the nineteenth-century intellectual represented in his own text by the underground man himself. Alternative expressions for this enviable "stupidity" could be "wholeness", "integrity", or "authenticity". These are certainly not his own terms, but they serve to pinpoint the nature of his discontent with himself for lacking that unmediated reality of being which he attributes to them. Echoing Hamlet, he reproaches himself for being "a coward and a slave" incapable of action. Consequently he envies those same despised primitives which he sees in his fellow human beings. For him they have even become an ego ideal and an object of envy. This envy is the dialectical counterpart of his contempt. It is the countervailing desire, to close the gap, to be with them and to be like them (in this sense it is a demand for equality), but this desire is in direct conflict with his competitive affirmation of superiority which he demands that they recognize. So the monological desire to dominate others by objectifying them, and by taking up a position of satirical superiority, is doubled by a regressive desire to abandon the protective barriers of this would-be dominant self, in order to recapture the more authentic mode of being possessed by his envied primitives.

Here my reading differs from that of Joseph Frank. For him these natural "men of action" are the followers of Chernyshevky's determinist theory of human nature, which they reduce to "the blank nullity of the laws of nature".[45] It is true that these determinist laws could not account for the contradictory perversity embodied in the underground man, who cites himself as their counterexample. Frank identifies these natural men as the contemporary radicals who are the real objects of Dostoevsky's satire which shows them to be blinded by their stupdity: "It is only the impenetrable obtuseness of the radical men of action that prevents them from seeing the underground man as their mirror

---

45   Frank 2010, p. 420.

THE FISSURED MODERN SUBJECT 61

image".⁴⁶ But, *pace* Frank, if they are obtuse and impenetrable, in what sense could they be his "mirror image"? The true insight of Dostoevsky's novella lies far beyond Frank's satirical realism. Not only is it possible to be envious of fictions (like the Underground Man), but envy is *always* based on a fictional construction projected onto others. When they are rivals, they become the imaginary "other" who possesses the fullness of being which the self lacks.⁴⁷

6 An Unconscious within Hyperconsciousness?

While the underground man frequently deploys his paradoxes in a rhetorically ostentatious manner, in pursuit of his desire to demonstrate that his own self-understanding lies beyond any finalizing judgement which another could make (as Bakhtin's analysis shows), there are significant occasions when he recognizes that he is rather more a slave of these paradoxical "laws of heightened consciousness" than their master. Early in the work, he poses a rhetorical question:

> Tell me this: why is it that it always had to happen, as if on purpose [*kak narochno*], that in those moments, yes, in those very same moments, when I was most capable of recognizing all the subtleties of "the highest and the best", as we used to say, I could not only fail to recognize them, but could actually do such ugly, repulsive things as ... well, such things, in short, as perhaps everybody does, but which always happened to me, as if on purpose, when I was most conscious that I ought not to do them? [....] But the chief feature of all this was that it was not accidental, but as if it had to be so. It was as if it was my normal condition, not a disease or a festering sore in me, so that finally I lost even the desire to struggle against the spell. I ended by almost believing (or perhaps fully believing) that this was my normal state [emphases added].⁴⁸

The most striking point in this self-narration is that out of the heightened consciousness itself a certain alien control begins to emerge. He cannot fully

---

46   *Ibid.*, p. 421.
47   Lacan labels this object of desire the *objet petit a*, which is located in the "Other", and is the cause of envy. Cf. Lacan 1987, p. 116. In his essay on the "mirror phase" he explains that the child sees in the mirror an image of completion which he lacks, and this is the source of his aggressive drive to overcome his lack by identifying with that image: Lacan 1966, pp. 93–94.
48   Dostoevsky 1972, p. 18.

explain it, but he is not simply unconscious of it. It is like another intentionality or purpose, he says, which at first asserted its dominion over his will to fight against it until, with time, he finally accepted its superior alien power as part of his normal condition.

At this point, the narrative account of his past turns into a present struggle to explain why these "laws of heightened consciousness" are indeed "laws". They preclude the very possibility of changing oneself, or even of desiring to change oneself, because "there is perhaps nothing to change into" [*i peredelyvat'sya-to, mozhet byt', ne vo chto*].[49] The desire for change requires an anticipated future state in which the desiring subject can provisionally believe. In its absence, the desire collapses and boredom ensues. Romantic *ennui* takes a new form here. It is no longer just the response by a rebellious poetic sensibility to the surrounding social conformity, or to the discursive power of the *cliché* which safeguards that hated conformity through empty repetition, as in Flaubert and many post-Romantics after him.[50] It is rather a resignation to the way in which his own prized mental detachment has trapped him too into the endless circle of repetition, because his desire for "becoming" has lost its object.[51]

The end of Part 1 is marked by an intensification of the struggle to demonstrate that, unlike everyone else, he is capable of telling the complete truth about himself. But this struggle takes place within his solipsist project: "Confessions of the sort that I intend to begin setting forth do not get printed or

---

49   I have departed from the Penguin translator's version: "it wasn't worthwhile to change", which seems to substitute a commonsensical misreading for a rather more enigmatic statement. Who or what is the missing model that he could not become? Is it the self-aggrandising Napoleonic figure of his romantic dreams, alternately repudiated and embraced, or the Christ whom Dostoevsky initially wrote in as the solution to Part 1 but never restored, even when the censorship would have permitted it?

50   As Flaubert revolted against his own Romanticism after *La Tentation de Saint Antoine*, he still retained the Romantics' horror at the emptiness of mere repetition. Clearly expressed in his late *Dictionnaire des Idées Reçues* and *Bouvard et Pécuchet*, the deadening power of repetition was the dominant theme of *L'Education Sentimentale* and *Madame Bovary*. Newness or originality may have been unavailable socially or politically, but it could still be won aesthetically through the author's ironic engagement with the discourse of the triumphant enemy and its power to empty lives of meaning. Flaubert's irony in these novels is, in its own way, a supreme example of dialogical struggle, operating within the commonplace language of the world in order to destroy the overpowering conformism of its *clichés*.

51   In his *Arcades Project*, Walter Benjamin wrote that "we are bored when we don't know what we are waiting for", adding that "boredom is the threshold to great deeds" (p. 105). This is the threshold which the underground man cannot cross; he merely dreams of it constantly.

offered to others to read".⁵² Citing Heine's opinion that Rousseau lied about himself in his *Confessions*, he asserts that Heine was right, but only because he "was talking of men making public confessions" whereas "I, however, am writing for myself alone". So solipsism is for him the condition for knowing and telling the truth. This is partly undercut by our knowledge as real readers that we are reading a published book. But that is not the main issue. The underground man is actually pursuing a very Bakhtinian question. If a book is an "utterance" which anticipates at least one addressee, what is an utterance which denies that anticipation? Having denied that he will have any readers, the underground man confronts what Bakhtin identifies as the more fundamental point, namely the dialogical nature of every utterance including his own, irrespective of his denial:

> And here is the problem that puzzles me: why, in fact, do I address you as "gentlemen", and speak to you just as if I was genuinely speaking to readers?⁵³

In *The Legend of Freud*, Sam Weber quotes Freud himself on how he does not write for others, even if their recognition is indeed gratifying, "but nevertheless we write in the first place for ourselves, following an inner impulse". Weber comments that this shows a deluded Freud, quite unlike the theorist of the unconscious:

> And yet Freud's entire theoretical effort to articulate the importance of the unconscious belies the clear-cut distinction between 'inner impulse' or gratification, and 'other people'. If the unconscious means anything whatsoever, it is that the relation of self and others, inner and outer, cannot be grasped as an interval between polar opposites but rather as an irreducible dislocation of the subject *in which the other inhabits the self as its condition of possibility* [emphasis added].⁵⁴

The underground man's utterance is conditioned by the same solipsist delusion, but also by his struggle to explain it to himself and to his imagined readers. Having affirmed the non-existence of actual readers in order to be able to tell the truth about himself, he is puzzled to find that he needs them anyway. His conclusion to this solipsist conundrum is: "If I write as if I were addressing

---

52   Dostoevsky 1972, p. 45.
53   *Ibid.*
54   Weber S. 1982, pp. 32–3.

an audience, it is only for show and because it makes it easier for me to write. It is a form, nothing else: I shall never have any readers".[55]

This claim to eliminate his addressees in pursuit of an empty form (*odna pustaya forma*) is itself questioned as the underground man imputes to his imagined readers a series of questions concerning the purpose of writing at all if it is not for readers. He could just run his memories through his head, they suggest. He admits the cogency of these arguments in favour of complete solipsism, but he then tentatively justifies the idea of writing as a means of achieving control over the many painful memories in his head. The ultimate aim of this control, however, is to separate himself from them. Writing about the particular memory which will become the basis of his narrative in Part 2, he stresses that it has a will of its own, refusing to be separated from him, so that his answer to the question as to why he should write for himself alone is that it will establish his authority over himself, allowing him to gain mastery over the memory that is tormenting him. His justification for this self-dividing activity starts with a rather comical combination of ethical and aesthetic motives, before turning frankly psychological:

> [Exactly, but] on paper it will be somehow more impressive. There is something awe-inspiring about it, one sits more severely in judgement over oneself, one's style is enhanced. Besides perhaps I shall really get relief from writing it down.[56]

His psychological motive for writing is to gain release from the oppressive and clinging power of the old memory, as though repeating it aesthetically would somehow lessen its hold on him. In the passage below, I include in brackets the original repetition of *otvyazat'sya* (literally: "to unbind itself" from me, or "myself" from it) to show that Dostoevsky carefully registers this division as the scene of an inward struggle:

> Now, for example, I am particularly oppressed by one ancient memory. It sprang clearly into my mind the other day, and since then has remained with me like a tiresome tune that keeps on nagging at one [*kotoriy ne khochet otvyazat'sya*]. And yet one must get rid of it [*nadobno ot nego otvyazat'sya*]. I have hundreds of memories like it; but from time to time one of the hundreds becomes prominent and oppresses me. For some

---

55   Dostoevsky 1972, p. 45.
56   *Ibid.*, p. 46.

reason I believe that if I write it down I shall get rid of it [*ono i otvyazhet-sya*]. Why not try?⁵⁷

The repeated use of the reflexive *otvyazat'sya* oscillates between the memory's refusal "to unbind *itself*" from the hero in the first instance, and the hero's desire to "to unbind *myself* from it [*ot nego*]" in the second. This involves an internal battle of wills between "I" and "it". And then, in the third instance, he hopes that when it is written down the memory "will unbind itself". This internal struggle is the basis of his whole act of narration which is Part 2, culminating in his encounter with the prostitute, Liza. Having emphasized that the memory clings to him with a will of its own, he tells us that it arose directly out of a sense impression. It is like a negative version of Proust's famous madeleine and cup of tea: the bodily sensation repeats a past one, recalling the associated memory to consciousness:

> It is snowing just now, in wet, dingy swirling flakes. It was snowing yesterday too, and the day before as well. I think it was the sleet that reminded me of this incident that now refuses to let me alone. So let this be a story apropos of falling sleet.⁵⁸

The reader later re-encounters this falling sleet, as the underground man rushes off in a frenzied pursuit of his male companions after an excruciating dinner together, only to encounter Liza in their place. There seem to be more than sufficient grounds to describe the underground man's narration as an attempt to deal with what Freud calls the return of the repressed. The memory has not been consciously recalled, but has returned under its own volition, summoned only by a sensual perception, but one loaded with associated meanings which are a threat to the would-be controlling ego. But if so, this is not a talking cure, or a "working through" in writing, in the Freudian sense. Although his writing is an attempt to deal symbolically with the pain of this obsessive memory which "refuses to unbind itself", the project which he sets himself is an attempt at control by getting rid of it. This means (paradoxically, as ever) attempting to return the memory to oblivion through conscious aesthetic organisation. The actual consequence, however, is not liberation but compulsive repetition.

It may seem far-fetched to present the underground man's confession in Part 2 as a failed "talking cure" because his very lucidity would seem to make any reference to the unconscious seem out of place. Indeed, he even identifies

---

57   Ibid.
58   Ibid.

his own writing as a struggle against the unconscious, although this is not formulated in Freudian terms, of course, but as the need to avoid self-deception (lying to oneself). Lying, considered as the deception of others, implies a knowledge of the truth which is consciously concealed. But beneath this concealment is the problem of the concealment of an intimate truth from oneself, and it is here that writing will become a test of the capacity for truth, which he understands as a will to confront it (even if he conceals it from others):

> In every man's remembrances, there are things that he will not reveal to everybody, but only to his friends. There are other things that he will not reveal even to his friends, but only to himself, and then only under a pledge of secrecy. Finally, there are some things that a man is afraid to reveal even to himself, and any honest man accumulates a pretty fair number of such things. That is to say, the more respectable a man is, the more of them he has. At least, only a little time ago I made up my mind to recall some of my former adventures, but up till now I have only skirted round them, with, indeed, some uneasiness. But now, when I am not only remembering, but have decided to write them down, now I want to test whether it is possible to be completely open with oneself and not be afraid of the whole truth.[59]

Towards the end of his tale he states that his "story" (*povest'*) is also a "confession" (*ispoved'*), but this will to confessional truth does not release him from his embattled monological attempt to deny the dialogical relationships at the basis of his personality. Instead of the potential for change and "becoming", the narrative is dominated by paradox and compulsive repetition.

7 Revolutionary Dreams or Literary Nostalgia?

Marshall Berman in *All that is solid melts into air* argues that, as a member of the "raznochintsy" (men of various ranks) who had emerged as a significant social force in the 1860s, the underground man is in incipiently revolutionary conflict with the constricting hierarchy of his contemporary Russia.[60] This positive reading can be textually supported, and Berman's historical placing of it in terms of the developing revolutionary consciousness in nineteenth-century Russia is illuminating. But it is one-sided because it rests on a complete

---

59   *Ibid.*, p. 45.
60   Berman 1983.

absence of any reference to his intense relationship with his former schoolfriends, his masterful servant Apollon, and above all, Liza. To this list we have to add the embattled dialogue with his addressees, whether we consider these to be listeners or readers. In all of these cases, his feeling that his superiority is under threat fuels his desire to assert it. Yet it is also undeniable that he seeks equality and above all "recognition", as Berman argues, at least in the fantasies which he half-heartedly attempts to re-enact.

These fantasies are largely derived from his reading of Romantic literature, particularly German and French, which he mocks for its pretentiousness, non-Russianness, and idealist escapism. He mocks the Russian devotees of Schiller who do not allow their dreams of "the good and the beautiful" to interfere with their official positions and their perks within the official hierarchy. As always, his mockery is also directed at himself even though he has left the civil service, thanks to a small inheritance. Despite this economic independence, he remains trapped mentally within the wider social hierarchy where his fate is not to be acknowledged by his superiors who now proliferate everywhere. This widens the field of the competitive individualism fuelling his resentment, which Berman sees as prefiguring the great positive affirmations of popular presence on the city streets from 1875 through to the Revolution of 1905. He dreams of duelling with those who do not recognize his existence (or perhaps refuse to recognize it), like the arrogant officer whom he vainly seeks to confront on the Nevsky Prospect. Duelling, a foreign literary affectation, can only take place between equals, which is why he acknowledges its impossibility in his situation, while still mocking himself for desiring it. He explains that he would even prefer to be thrashed by one of these superiors, and thrown out of a bar window, rather than being casually moved aside like an unacknowledged object, which is what actually happens. He would at least be acknowledged by them, and would therefore *be*. Even an insult implies a fleeting recognition of equality incompatible with the principle of hierarchy, where the subordinate is unnoticed and therefore feels annihilated. It is precisely this logic of hierarchy which Zverkov, the rival whose recognition he is seeking, throws back in his face when he offers an apology for offending him:

"I am asking you to be friends, Zverkov. I offended you, but ... "
"Offended me? You? Offended *me*? Let me tell you, my dear sir, that you could never in any circumstances offend *me*".[61]

---

61 Dostoevsky 1972, p. 80.

Here it is very clear why his Romantic literary dreams of duelling, modelled on Pushkin and Lermontov, are liable to swift transformations into dreamt embraces and expressions of brotherly love. Duelling involves a recognition of equality, but only between aristocratic enemies, and if equality were to be recognised, fraternity would easily follow.

Such are his Romantic dreams, inherited from an identifiable revolutionary tradition now lost and distorted, in which liberty for a brief moment was felt to be compatible with equality and fraternity. But these Romantic dreams are not only in conflict with the rigidly hierarchical Russian social system. The underground man is not only a representative of the Russian *raznochintsy*, as Berman rightly asserts, but also of a whole trend in European culture after the failed revolutions of 1848. Even in France itself the revolutionary aspiration to *liberté, égalité, fraternité* had long been replaced by the modern bourgeois ideal of "a career open to all talents without distinction of birth". This formulation was Napoleon's own promise, addressed to every individual within his imperial state bureaucracy. Instead of the collective overthrow of the existing power structures, this new imperial version of freedom offered to the individual the possibility of rising within the re-established social hierarchy. Nowadays this equality is called "equal opportunity" or, in Britain especially, the level playing field. An alternative metaphor is Benjamin Disraeli's "greasy pole". In any case, it is a powerful institutional discourse which produces the individualised desire for the freedom of self-fulfilment instead of the old revolutionary aspiration to equality and social transformation. The underground man satirises his own outmoded Romantic dreams for their bookishness and their "lying" relationship to his ego-centric desires. He mocks himself for dreaming of being a Napoleonic figure who overcomes the forces of the Pope before celebrating his victory on Lake Como, and for being simultaneously a modern Hamlet incapable of action because of his precious hyperconsciousness. As he well knows, even if his dreams have become ridiculous, they are rather more Napoleonic than generously Quixotic. They are a reaction against his sense of his inferiority in status, in physical appearance, and above all in other people's estimation. His response is to seek to reverse this position vis-à-vis those others, but always within the hierarchy of prestige to which he remains intensely loyal despite his own failure to be dominant. Where the revolutionary tradition had dreamt of altering the power relations themselves by abolishing hierarchy in the name of liberty, equality, and fraternity, the underground man only entertains such dreams when he feels himself to be in an inferior position. When equality threatens, he seeks to re-assert his individual liberty through domination. He is a very modern bourgeois subject, captivated by competitive individualism but also by nostalgia for the equality and fraternity which he actually repudiates.

An early instance of his response to the threat of equality is his bullying of the school companion who offers friendship, but the major instance is Liza, who offers love.

8   Dialogism Violated

Having received the final rebuff from Zverkov, after a grotesque dinner party in which he had been seeking everyone's recognition of his superiority from a position of resentful inferiority posing as indifference, the underground man desperately rushes off after him and his companions to a brothel. But even then he still cannot decide whether he is seeking brotherly love or self-affirmation through revenge:

> "I'll go *there*", I shrieked. "Either they shall kneel before me, embracing my knees and begging for friendship, or … or, I'll give Zverkov a slap in the face!"[62]

When he gets there, these male companions and rivals for pride of place have disappeared. They are replaced by Liza. His encounter with this young prostitute occurs at the end of the intensifying series of encounters which structure his whole narrative. But even more significant than her place at the culmination is the fact, attested at the beginning of Part 2, that she is the primary cause of the involuntary memory which his narrative struggles vainly to control.

On first seeing Liza, the narrator reports that he was struck by a certain wondering innocence in her gaze, and by how different she was from the companions whom she was replacing. But this quality promised potential victimhood: "Something foul seemed to sting me; I went straight to her … "[63] As he goes to Liza, the underground man sees himself in the mirror, and what gratifies him is that the mirror shows him the image of himself that he thinks she must be seeing:

> I caught sight of myself in a mirror. My agitated face seemed to me repulsive in the extreme: pale, vicious, mean, with tangled hair. 'All right, I'm glad of it' I thought, 'I'm glad to seem repulsive to her; I like that …'[64]

---

[62]   *Ibid.*, p. 80.
[63]   *Ibid.*, p. 85.
[64]   *Ibid.*

This is a supreme example of the underground man's inversion of what Bakhtin celebrates in his early ethical writing as the self-completion bestowed by the gaze of the other. The desecration of his own image offers the gratification of sadistic mastery over the other, since her submission to this depraved thing that he sees as though through her eyes, will be her absolute humiliation at his hands. This aggressive drive to sadistic mastery involves self-abasement. But its gratification also consists in his sense of being acknowledged, even in the form of being judged as depraved by her. What immediately follows is the blank of the chapter break, so that the sexual act itself is negatively present in his narration as a joint obliteration of both self and other from consciousness. This narrative strategy is repeated later in his own house, when he again has recourse to the sexual act in order to escape from his own humiliation by insulting her. These gaps in the narration are more significant than the observance of conventional decency by Dostoevsky. The silence itself signifies. In the sexual act he has sought either domination or, failing that, the joint obliteration of both self and other. So the logic of *aut Caesar aut nihil* governs his sexuality too, transforming it into a death drive. But the consciousness to which he returns after this momentary obliteration is already familiar. Seeing himself as an alien object under her judgmental gaze, he turns back from self-annihilation to resentment:

> My head was full of fumes. Something seemed to be hovering over me, nagging at me, rousing and disturbing me. Anger and misery seethed up in me again, seeking an outlet. Suddenly, beside me, I saw two eyes, open, regarding me with curiosity and fixed attention. Their look was coldly indifferent, sullen, like something utterly alien; it irked me.[65]

With this return to consciousness and resentment under her gaze, he becomes aware that he has exchanged no words with her up until then. Only then does he initiate a dialogue, as a response to the crushing power of her gaze. When he finally starts the dialogue, he finds self-defensiveness and resistance on her part to his invasive intimacy. But as he elicits more information about her life, he breaks down this resistance, earns her trust, and begins to find pleasure in seducing her. This verbal seduction does not have sexual intercourse as its goal, since the crude power of money has already provided that. It is a spiritual seduction in pursuit of a more essential dominance. But the complexity of his relationship to his own motives emerges fully when he tells her of exactly the same sense of disgust which he reports to the readers as his inner response to

---

65 *Ibid.*, p. 86.

THE FISSURED MODERN SUBJECT

her gaze. However, in his address to her, it assumes a different accentuation and meaning:

> "After all, people drink because they're unhappy; well, I'm here because I'm unhappy. Well, tell me, what's good about this? After all, you and I ... came together ... just now, and we didn't speak a word to one another the whole time, and afterwards you began to stare at me like a wild thing; and so did I at you. Is that love? Is that the way two human beings ought to come into contact? It's ugly, that's what it is!"
>
> "Yes!" she agreed sharply and quickly. I was astonished by the swiftness of that *yes*.... So the same thought had perhaps been running through her head too, a short time before, when she was watching me? So even she was capable of some ideas? ... "Damn it, how very interesting that we should be *akin*!" I thought, almost rubbing my hands.[66]

At first, he has established a dialogue with her to break away from the power of her dominant gaze, and her response is so immediate that it surprises him. But then, at this very moment of a truly dialogical mutual recognition (they are "akin"!), he reports another response on his part. This will violate her in a way far worse than the sexual violation which he has just denounced. It is worse in the sense that it violates the intimacy which the dialogue has initiated, because in his own mind he has already started to treat her as a manipulable object, repudiating the mutual recognition at the very moment when it emerges.

As his speech to Liza gets more controlled and authorial, he starts with his own background as an orphan, links it to her loss of family and future prospects, and draws on his literary language with its recognisable sources, in order to gain a fuller hold on her inner emotions. In this he succeeds, but at first she expresses her response by remarking that he talks like a book. Given his contemptuous dismissal of his own Romantic dreams, he reports that this appeared to him at the time as an insulting rejection, but as present narrator he now understands the defensiveness in her that he was blind to then:

> I didn't understand that the mockery was deliberately assumed, like a mask; it was the last subterfuge of the kind usual with shy and pure-minded people, whose hearts are subjected to coarse and insistent probing, whose pride will not let them yield until the last moment, and who are afraid to express their feelings. The very timidity with which she ventured on her mockery, the several attempts before she succeeded in

---

66   *Ibid.*, p. 91.

> making herself express it, ought to have enabled me to guess. But I did not guess, and my heart brimmed over with spite.
>
> "Just you wait!" I thought.[67]

As a result of her unintended insult, which he only now as present narrator recognizes retrospectively as his own projection onto her words, he pulls out all the stops in his literary address, aimed at manipulating her by depicting the horror and degradation of her future life as a prostitute. He succeeds, but then he is appalled by his very authorial success in reducing her to absolute despair, and this leads him to resolve the situation by magnanimously inviting her to come to his house. This magnanimity is itself an imitation of literary sources, which he immediately regrets, thus repudiating the very response in himself which has led him to make it. Many have observed that the whole episode which follows is a parodic reversal of a similar episode in Chernyshevky's novel *What is to be done?*, and, even more specifically, of the tale of the rescue and redemption of a prostitute in the fragment of the poem by Nekrassov, which serves as his epigraph to Part 2.[68] The underground man himself is all too aware that he is imitating literature, but Liza finally does turn up at his house, enacting in his life the very literary scene which he has mocked. In response to this event, he introduces two further lines from the Nekrassov poem as a mocking prologue to his narration of Liza's second appearance:

> Enter now then, bold and free,
> Be mistress of my house and me
>
> Then we should begin living happily ever after, travelling abroad etc., etc. In short the whole dream would get extremely low and common, and I would end by jeering at myself.[69]

It is important not to simplify the deployment of literary parody here, and throughout the whole novella. Many critics read the parody as Dostoevsky's mocking rejection of Romanticism. For René Girard, for example, such passages show Dostoevsky's novelistic (*romanesque*) debunking of the romantic (*romantique*), in accordance with his own major thesis on the vocation of the novel since *Don Quijote*.[70] The assumption that this is just an example of

---

67   *Ibid.*, pp. 95–6.
68   This fragment from the Nekrassov poem is inexplicably absent from the Penguin translation, though its sequel appears later.
69   *Ibid.*, p. 107.
70   This is summed up in the original French title, *Mensonge romantique, vérité romanesque*.

Dostoevsky's mockery tends to simplify his admiration for Nekrassov, and even respect for Chernyshevsky despite their ideological differences.[71] But the main point is that such criticism is thoroughly monological, in the sense intended by Bakhtin, because it attributes the parodic intent to Dostoevsky's authorial voice alone, which would reduce the character to the level of an object of the author's satirical mockery.[72] In fact, the parody of literary Romanticism (including its Napoleonic echoes) is transferred to the divided consciousness of the underground man himself, as he rejects and mocks his own dreams. They may be "lies" but they are also integral to himself, and to jeer at them, as he says, is to be "jeering at myself". He is his own fierce critic and satirist. But, at the same time, the one thing which truly disturbs him is that, even as he denounces his words for their lying "literary" insincerity, he is acutely aware that they are also sincere. As he makes every effort to move Liza to tears, he reports being overwhelmed and feeling a lump rising in his throat. This even modifies his earlier reported feeling that the seduction is just a "game" and a bid for power. Now it has become something else. Just as he cannot be the complete liar, he cannot be the complete manipulator:

> I simply couldn't get myself straightened out. Something was working and seething in my soul, incessantly and painfully. I returned home, utterly shattered. It was as though I had a crime on my conscience.[73]

His sense of guilt arises from his violation of Liza, but also from his recognition that he would do the same again, if she were to come. This anticipation means that the encounter with her has not been a transient event but the manifestation of a repetitive response in himself which he recognises. He dreaded her coming, he says, because it would mean that he would have to live up again to his own literary posturing. As he reflects on this, he mocks himself for the "lying mask" that he would have to put on in front of her. But at this point, he once again recoils against himself. There was, after all, a truth within his lies although they remain lies:

> But when I reached this point in my thoughts, I burst out: "Why dishonest? What is there dishonest about it? What I said yesterday was quite

---

71 Berman points out that Dostoevsky was a lone voice in defending the imprisoned Chernyshevsky against his detractors, despite his fundamental disagreement with him: *op. cit.*, p. 220.

72 Similarly, Joseph Frank reads the *Notes from Underground* as essentially satirical and quite different from the later great novels.

73 Dostoevsky 1972, pp. 104–5.

sincere. I remember feeling genuinely moved. I really wanted to arouse her noblest emotions ... If I made her cry, that was a good thing. I was producing a wholesome effect ..."

But all the same I could not make my mind easy.[74]

When Liza finally does appear at his house, it is in the midst of one of his humiliating conflicts with his servant Apollon. The latter asserts his mastery over his master by maintaining an impenetrable calm in the face of the underground man's futile attempts to assert his control. Apollon's refusal to respond as his master demands puts the servant in a position of dominance. To the underground man he appears alternately as a lower thing-like block to be scorned, and a superior manipulative silent other, to be feared and resented. So this recently emancipated serf constantly demonstrates to the Master his dependence on the Slave. Once again Liza provides a focus for the pent-up resentment arising from his failure to be master in his own house. This displacement takes the form of a "real fit of hysteria" which is both genuine and contrived like all his self-display:

> "Water, give me some water – over there!" I muttered feebly, conscious, however, that I could quite well do without water, or feeble mutterings, either. I was *putting on an act*, as they call it, to preserve the decencies, even though my hysteria was genuine enough.[75]

This posturing, which is also "genuine enough" (i.e. not just a lie), rapidly develops into an attack on her for believing his words. He now denounces them to her face as being cynical manipulative lies:

> It was power, power, power, I wanted then, the fascination of the game; I wanted to get your tears, your humiliation, your hysterics.[76]

This diatribe then develops into a full-scale denunciation of his own cowardice, egotism, and lying pretenses at being a hero and her saviour, and it ends up with the inevitability of his being even more resentful against her for listening to him:

---

74   *Ibid.*, p. 105.
75   *Ibid.*, p. 114.
76   *Ibid.*, pp. 115–6.

> Do you understand how much I shall hate you for being here and hearing me tell you all this? After all, a man doesn't talk like this more than once in a lifetime, and then only if he's hysterical! ... What more do you want? Why are you still here, tormenting me, after all that, why don't you go?[77]

Having failed to dominate her, he seeks to cast her out. But the entanglement of self and other has become so intimate by now that his attack on her and his attack on himself are indistinguishable. As he says, his attempt to elicit a show of "hysterics" from her has in fact led to him becoming "hysterical". Sexual Master and Slave have changed places. But Liza's actual response to his speech is to disregard its entire dialectic of insult, revenge, and self-humiliation, and to recognize only the shared unhappiness. It is an immediate response of spontaneous love, but it gives rise to yet another "hysterical" collapse on his part, and as the moment passes, he sees himself yet again as a humiliated object under the power of her gaze. This humiliation sets off the old hyperconscious dialectic again, *but he confesses that he still does not really understand it*:

> But all the same, these hysterics could not go on for ever. And now (I am telling the sickening truth) as I lay down on the sofa, flat, with my face buried in my cheap leather cushions, I began little by little, as if from afar, unwillingly but uncontrollably to feel that it would be terribly awkward to raise my head and look Liza in the eyes. *What was I ashamed of? I don't know, but I was ashamed.* The idea came also into my overwrought mind that our roles had definitely been reversed, she was the heroine and I was just such another crushed and degraded creature as she had been that night – four days before ...[emphasis added].[78]

The repeated and explicit reference to hysteria reinforces his own point about the reversal of roles, because in the nineteenth century hysteria was still taken to be a womanly complaint. In seeking to induce "hysterics" in her, he has in fact produced them in himself. But even as present narrator looking back, this reversal still comes as a shock which he struggles to understand:

> *My God, surely I didn't envy her even then, did I?*
> I don't know, I still can't make up my mind, but then, of course, I was still less able to understand it than I am now. [emphasis added][79]

---

77   Ibid., p. 117.
78   Ibid., p. 118.
79   Ibid.

Again he confesses that he still does not understand his envy, even though he consciously recognizes it. Such is the nature of the unconscious detected by Dostoevsky within this "heightened consciousness". In order to reverse the dreaded reversal of the positions of Master and Slave, and in response to his envy at her superiority (comparable to his envy of the "normal men" whom he considers his inferiors), he again re-asserts his mastery through the act of sexual aggression which, once again, marks the chapter break.

After narrating his shameful and insulting dismissal of Liza by attempting to pay her five rubles for her services (which she silently refuses by leaving them on the table), he confesses the pain and regret that this memory still causes him. But he consoles himself with a reflection on the "benefits of insult and hatred" which he hopes to have installed in her by this brutal act. He will have educated her, he says, into becoming a higher conscious being like himself, and then he justifies this corruption by challenging the reader to say which is best: "cheap happiness or lofty suffering?" The clear implication is that by rejecting the "cheap happiness" offered by Liza, he has opted for the "lofty suffering" of the isolated Romantic poet, and has offered it to her. This grotesque version of himself as alienated poetic sensibility completes the parody of Nekrassov's and Chernyshevsky's tales of redemption. Instead of the commonplace nineteenth-century literary *topos* of the salvation of a prostitute, which casts the hero as moral master and redeemer, the underground man's confessional tale tells of his potential redemption *by* a prostitute. This reversal makes it completely unacceptable to this anti-hero. Later, the epilogue of *Crime and Punishment* relates Raskol'nikov's redemption in Siberia by another victimised prostitute, Sonya Marmeladova. In that context it is not mocked, but throughout the main body of the novel it is as fiercely resisted by the would-be Napoleonic hero of that novel as by the underground man.

The only significant change brought about by his past experiences, and now assimilated into his present discourse, is that his sense of separation and distance from others ("I am alone and they are everyone") is attributed to his youth ("This shows that I was still very young").[80] But as present narrator and polemicist, he now presents his alienation as a shared modern condition, for which he characteristically claims to be the exceptionally lucid spokesman:

> We are so unused to living that we often feel something like loathing for "real life" [*"zhivaya zhizn'"*] and so cannot bear to be reminded of it. We

---

80   This time difference is missed by René Girard who makes this statement of alienated loneliness a definitive sign of the character's ridiculous Romanticism, scornfully mocked as lies by Dostoevsky but not by the narrating character himself, cf. Girard 1976, pp. 260–262.

have really gone so far as to think of "real life" as toil, almost as servitude, and we are all agreed for our part, that it is better in books.[81]

He goes on to denounce the desire for independence by recourse to a paradox which may well reflect Dostoevsky's own recoil against the Romantic rebellion of his pre-Siberian days:

> And what is it that we sometimes scratch about for, what do we cry for, what do we beg for? We don't know ourselves. And it would be worse for us if our stupid whims were indulged. Just try giving us, for example, as much independence as possible, untie the hands of any one of us, loosen our bonds, and we ... I assure you we should all immediately beg to go back under discipline.[82]

Here again the important issue is not the easily detectable coincidence between his ideas and those of Dostoevsky as he turned back to Tsarism and Orthodoxy, but the way they operate within the underground man's utterance. This passage reiterates his constant refrain concerning the perversity of human desire: if it happens to achieve its apparent objective (liberation), it will turn back to desire the repression which originally provoked it as a desire because, as he has said earlier, man is a "comical creature" who dreads the final accomplishment of his desires. That fulfilment would be their death.

At the same time this passage is also an assault upon the defenses of his imagined/anticipated listeners whose rejection is immediately framed in his own speech. He has these imagined listeners respond to his assault:

> "Talk about yourself alone [you say], and your underground miseries, don't dare speak of 'all of us'!"[83]

But then, his reply to this attack by his addressees, which he has in fact anticipated in order to include it in his own utterance, is to deny that "with that allness" he is seeking to defend himself:

---

81 Dostoevsky 1972, p. 122.
82 *Ibid.*
83 Dostoevsky 1972, pp. 122–3. The original Russian is "*Govorite, deskat', pro sebya odnogo ...*" I have departed from the Penguin translation's use of the indicative in the first part ("You are talking only about yourself ...") before it switches to the imperative for the second clause only. For readers not familiar with Russian, *deskat'* is a colloquial particle indicating reported speech. Hence one might insert "you say", as in the square brackets above. It makes the internal dialogism more palpable.

> Excuse me, gentlemen, I am not trying to excuse myself with that *all-ness*. As for what concerns me personally, after all I have only carried to a logical conclusion what you yourselves didn't dare to take more than half-way; and you supposed your cowardice was common sense, and comforted yourselves with the self-deception. So perhaps I turn out to be more alive than you [*eshche "zhivee" vas vykhozhu*]. Look harder! After all, we don't even know where "real life" is lived nowadays, or what it is, what name it goes by.[84]

Here he claims that in speaking of his isolation and detachment from "life", he is neither confessing nor glorifying an individual idiosyncrasy, both of which would set him apart, but is actually the unacknowledged spokesman for them all, uttering truths which they are unwilling to face about themselves. In short he is typical, but (true to form) he is also uniquely perceptive because he knows these shared truths to which everyone else is blind, either through stupidity or cowardice. Because of his higher consciousness, he says, he may turn out to be more "more alive" than them. This claim repeats, albeit with a different accentuation, Dostoevsky's opening quasi-editorial statement that he has taken a "representative figure" and presented it to the public "in a more striking form than is usual". The underground man aggressively asserts this very point. He is "more alive" than everyone else because he is aware of what they conceal, while they are represented in his discourse as denying that he does speak for their concealed truth. The question as to whether he really is alone, as he thought in his youth, or like everyone else, as he affirms now, is left open. But, as I have argued earlier by quoting Bakhtin on the essential "solitude" of capitalist culture, it is precisely in his defensive/aggressive isolation that he may indeed resemble everyone else. His attempt to put an objectifying framework around those others, while denying their ability to impose such a reductive framework around himself, is the competitive basis of his endless circle of paradoxes. Yet, concealed within his aggressive affirmation of his superiority above others, which is intensified by his paranoid fear of their ability to do the same to him, there is also the contrary impulse to affirm his resemblance to them. That is to say, in his aggressive polemical claim to know what they conceal about themselves, there is nonetheless a compulsion to re-establish a

---

84   *Ibid.*, p. 123. The Penguin translation omits the original text's quotation marks around "more alive" (*"zhivee"*), although it rightly retains them around "real life". These are important because they make the inner dialogism explicit. The underground man is quoting another's value-laden words while distancing himself from them. This is particularly significant when those words are closely identified with Dostoevsky's own beliefs.

connection with them and to break out of his superior solitude. But the only language available to this isolated individual is the language of competitive self-affirmation and its fearful denial of the power of "the other". In short, the language of defensive aggression contains its opposite, namely the language of love, brotherhood, or equality, which it simultaneously deforms and vehemently rejects. It is with the emergence of this paradox that Dostoevsky's novella reaches its open-ended conclusion in which nothing is concluded. Yet something important is explored.

9 Literature and the Social Unconscious

In claiming to speak for others, the underground man asserts his power as an author with true insight into his addressees, thus turning them into objects of his discourse, however much they protest and resist. His authorial claim to superior insight is supported by his equally emphatic assertion that he knows them intimately. He has watched them, listened to them through a chink in his underground space, and can therefore anticipate their every response. So his introspective ego-centrism (with all its paranoid dialectic of aggression and self-defense) is also the dialogical basis of his authorial claim to know them all better than they know themselves. Such is the nature of authorship, and this fictional hero may perhaps be confessing obliquely for Dostoevsky.

Bakhtin is right to dismiss the applicability of the concepts of unconscious motivation in a Freudian or Jungian sense. That would constitute an authorial framing of motives hidden from the character's own self-consciousness. In Bakhtin's terms, it would be a monological claim by an author who would be putting himself on a higher level of understanding from that consciously "lived" by his hero. But this does not necessarily eliminate the validity of some concept of the unconscious if we consider literary discourse itself as a dialogical engagement with the multiple discourses which have come to be called "the social text" in which we all exist. Certainly, the unconscious is not a structure which defines and delimits the representation of the underground man as a character, for there is nothing in his own conduct and thought which escapes his self-conscious scrutiny, even though he still cannot fully understand what he knows. But what about his claim to insight into his readers, based upon his insight into himself?

These readers occupy an ambiguous space and temporality, because they are cast as both listeners to his spoken utterance and readers of his written text. In this aspect as readers, they are closer to us, but as his listeners they respond more immediately to his utterance. In both aspects, however, they are this narrator-hero's imaginary constructs, produced out of his acts of anxious anticipation. It is the mediating space occupied by his imagined listeners/readers that counts here, because through them we too are being seductively or aggressively addressed and interrogated. Do we share these addressees' various framing judgements of the underground man, as they distance themselves from him and belittle him in their acts of critical judgement, or do we partly identify with him, in an act of recognition which would mean acquiescing to his claim to a revelatory insight into us which we did not have before reading his words? *Notes from Underground* ends with this narrator's direct claim to understand a shared truth which his addressees do not have the courage or insight to acknowledge. This claim is dialogically addressed to us, in the sense that we are as free as the fictional listeners/readers to reject it, thereby reducing him to being an object of our own superior critical insight. But his fictional addressees' dismissive contempt ("talk about yourself ... don't dare say 'all of us'") can likewise be read as an act of psychological distancing and negation on their part (and ours, if we share their reaction), exactly mirroring this hero's pattern of defensive aggression. If that resemblance is admitted, then his authorial claim to know us better than we have known ourselves prior to reading his words, must also be admitted as worthy of consideration.

In Chapter 1, I point out that Bakhtin's dialogical account of literary discourse is that as the "primary" utterances circulating in society are incorporated into it, they become dialogized and capable of the higher level of self-reflexivity made possible by the "outsideness" which dialogism brings with it. This gives literature a cognitive and innovative potential which transcends the mere repetitiveness of Alexander Pope's neo-classical formulation: "what oft was thought but ne'er so well expressed". The ending of *Notes from Underground* makes this claim in its dialogical address to its addressees. The underground man, who is the fictional author makes a claim to reveal what is not consciously thought by his addressees but potentially available for thought in those addressees themselves. However, every reader has the freedom to acknowledge it or reject it. If the literary "utterance" is properly understood as a provocative or seductive address to the reader, what it demands from that addressee is not just an interpretation of its own complexities (real though those may be), but an answering response in Bakhtin's sense, leading to the reader's re-interpretation of his/her own self-understanding, including of course the self-other relations within which he/she exists. And here is the key to Dostoevsky's dialogism. Insofar as this fictionalized author's address to us engenders a self-critical exploration and re-evaluation on our part, it brings into our consciousness possibilities for self-understanding which have not been acknowledged, and may even be resisted. The fact that the underground man's anticipated fictional readers resist and reject his insights does not mean that actual readers will reject them. It is this version of literature which emerges as Dostoevsky's insight into the writer's activity. When the underground man says to his resisting addressees: "I may turn out to be 'more alive' than you", a claim is being made for literature. In unveiling his own inner contradictions, this fictionalized author makes a plausible claim to lay bare what normal readers conceal from themselves. The social unconscious is made available to consciousness through the literary work's dialogical address to the reader.

CHAPTER 3

Rethinking Ideology as a Field of Dialogical Conflict

1   Bakhtin's Developmental Model

Bakhtin argues that the dialogical encounter is the basis of consciousness, because the "word of another" or plural others does not remain a purely external utterance but becomes an integral part of the subject's "inner speech". That is why the dialogical encounter is the basis of childhood speech development. He writes that we have all learnt the grammatical and lexical forms of our native language through the process of responding to the utterances addressed to us:

> We know our native language – its lexical composition and grammatical structure – not from dictionaries and grammars but from concrete utterances that we hear and that we ourselves reproduce in live speech communication with people around us. We assimilate forms of language only in forms of utterances and in conjunction with these forms. The forms of language and the typical forms of utterances, that is, speech genres [*rechevyie zhanry*], enter our experience and our consciousness together, and in close connection with one another. To learn to speak means to learn to construct utterances (because we speak in utterances and not in individual sentences, and, of course, not in individual words).[1]

This dialogical account of speech development reformulates the argument made earlier by Voloshinov in his *Marxism and the Philosophy of Language* (1929) where he writes that the child's assimilation of both sign and structure simultaneously through dialogue is quite the opposite of the process followed by the adult learner of a foreign language. The latter learns the lexical items and the rules of their combination separately. He then awkwardly strings the items together in a grammatically correct syntagmatic chain according to the rules which he has learnt, but he can still only produce a chain of "signals" which is not yet a combination of signs. It is only when the learner can produce dialogical responses that he or she becomes capable of producing signs. The

---

1   Bakhtin 1986, p. 78.

ability to formulate utterances by responding to the utterances of others is the precondition for the creativity of language in use.[2]

The Bakhtin scholar and translator, Caryl Emerson points out that this echoes very closely the ideas of their compatriot and contemporary, L.S. Vygotsky, whose *Thought and Language* strongly criticised Piaget's structuralist version of development.[3] Piaget, at that time at least, considered that the phenomenon of "egocentric speech" (the developmental phase when young children talk aloud to themselves) pre-exists the child's full "socialisation". But Vygotsky criticised this very term:

> We prefer to use the term *communicative* for the form of speech that Piaget calls *socialized* as though it had been something else before becoming social."[4]

This is not a mere quibble over terms:

> The development of thought is, to Piaget, a story of the gradual socialization of deeply intimate, personal, autistic mental states. Even social speech is represented as following, not preceding, egocentric speech.[5]

Vygotsky's counter-argument is that "the primary function of speech, in both children and adults, is communication, social contact":

> From our point of view, the two forms, communicative and egocentric, are both social, though their functions differ. Egocentric speech emerges when the child transfers social, collaborative forms of behavior to the sphere of inner-personal psychic functions.[6]

Therefore, his developmental schema reverses Piaget's. It is: "first social, then egocentric, then [silenced] inner speech" (*ibid*). At the same time, however, this reversal is perfectly in accordance with Piaget's own observation that "arguments between children give rise to the beginnings of logical reflection" (*ibid*). Common to Bakhtin, Voloshinov, and Vygotsky is the view that external dialogism is the basis for internal development. This supports their shared view that

---

2 Voloshinov 1973, p. 69.
3 Emerson 1983, pp. 245–263.
4 Vygotsky, 1962, p. 19.
5 *Ibid.*
6 *Ibid.*

individuality is not a quasi-natural autonomy subsequently subjected to socialization through the language system. On the contrary, individuality is itself the outcome of a prolonged social development of increasing differentiation and complexity. And the source of this increasing complexity, which enables individuality, creativity, and 'the beginnings of logical reflection' to emerge and develop, is the increasing range of dialogical encounters. For all three thinkers, then, the fundamental externality of the sign means that it is intersubjective before becoming intra-subjective, when it becomes the substance of "inner speech". When Bakhtin and Voloshinov turn to the dynamics of childhood speech development, their point is that all language abilities are the outcome of essentially social processes of dialogical addressivity and response.

Vygotsky also notes explicitly that "inner speech", in both child and adult, is characterised by abbreviation. The thinking individual does not go through the time-bound syntagmatic association required by external articulation. Nor, of course, does s/he repeat inwardly all the preceding dialogical encounters in the history of her/his language which have shaped the meanings of the signs that s/he uses. This point is obvious enough. But it is important, because the difference between the abbreviated nature of inner speech and its external articulation as an utterance means that, while consciousness is the outcome of the myriad of past dialogical encounters in both individual and collective histories (which Bakhtin called 'great time'), it is also produced by synthetic abstraction from them. This provides a way of understanding the process which assimilates the overwhelming multiplicity of utterances into the generalising formal abstractions from the particular which are necessary for both consciousness and communication. Vygotsky points out that the development of the capacity for linguistic abstraction requires a necessary erasure or 'forgetting' of particulars. For example, even the ability to name a particular barking and hairy animal a "dog" requires a capacity for abstraction which is the outcome of prior development. These symbolic abstractions from the particular might be said to constitute a linguistic system, but they do not require the prior existence of a single transcendent system, like that proposed by Saussurean linguistics to account for the otherwise unsystematisable acts of *parole*.

This developmental schema makes dialogism the source of "becoming". But it leaves out the point that the internalization of the speech of others also creates a field of internalized conflict with those others. In Chapter 2 I have shown how Bakhtin's theory of consciousness as dialogical becomes a theory of the dialogical production of the social unconscious, thanks to his encounter with the resistance to "becoming" which he uncovers in the intense dialogism of Dostoevsky's "underground man".

2   The Authority Concealed in the Utterance

Ken Hirschkop makes an important contribution to this problematic when he observes that the fundamentally intersubjective nature of the utterance means that "the varying degrees and kinds of authority" within it have to be recognised by the addressee:

> All utterances come to us from elsewhere, but they may come endowed with varying degrees and kinds of authority. Whether it is the patriarchal and maternal authority of parents who teach you to speak, the expert or professional authority which runs through language in social and cultural institutions, or the political authority manifest in the speech of leaders, power and authority are intrinsic to the meanings grasped by the subjects of language. A communicating person who could not recognize the authority of particular utterances, and gauge the changes in response these would dictate, would be an inept member of a linguistic community. Saussure imagines that speakers face a language of more or less authoritative or habitual forms, but in fact speakers have to recognize authority – or claims to authority – whenever they understand utterances. The fundamental feature of intersubjectivity does not remain outside language proper, but is reflected in the style of the utterances of those speaking and responding.[7]

This multiplicity of authorities is extremely useful. But the act of recognising 'the authority of particular utterances' remains rather ambiguous. Our early development of language abilities through dialogical engagement shows that we do not simply learn to 'recognise' the authority of the speaker in order to conform to his expectations. Not only do we learn to conceal and to lie as well as to communicate with others, but we also learn to play with the utterance itself, in the form of jokes, rhymes, rhythmic repetitions, metaphorical displacements, and fictional constructions of every sort. This shows a significant development of creative 'outsideness' (*vnenakhodimost'*) in all language users, not just literary creators. Dialogism is manifest in every addressee's capacity to criticize or to respond to an utterance in ways unanticipated by the speaker, without being merely 'inept', as Hirschkop puts it. Recognition here is even inseparable from an 'irresponsible' non-conformism or defiance of authority, because defiance is still a dialogical response, of course. But the subject's

---

7   Hirschkop 1999, p. 19.

defiance of that linguistic authority may not be a conscious act. The degree of the subject's autonomy from his/her internalized authorities is certainly individually and socially variable, but conformism can never be absolute. Moreover, whether the internalized authorities are defied or obeyed, they have always been created historically.[8]

One important consequence of Bakhtin's proposition that we learn our language from the authority of the utterances addressed to us, as Ken Hirschkop notes, is that we are informed about the world, physical or spiritual, at the same time as we assimilate the structures of our language. Initially, then, there is no significant gap between the knowledge of the world that we receive from others and the utterances in which we receive it. In this respect, the utterances addressed to us might even be said to constitute the world for us by organizing its multiple significations. In the early stages of our coming to consciousness, they exercise an authority which cannot be questioned. But Bakhtin's concept of dialogical "becoming" (*stanovlenie*) through the "speech genres" means that the subject soon learns to manipulate them creatively, and this ability to play with language testifies to the degree of "outsideness" and potential freedom achieved by any particular speaker.

There is a further consequence in taking notice of the authority concealed within utterances, namely that there could be no such thing as a purely factual or "constative" statement, which Speech Act theories generally contrast with performative acts. Even the most unchallengeably banal statement is a speech act which carries an implicit authority. The authority concealed within the factual statement is always there, even when the banality is presented as a self-evident truth. In the utterance there can be no self-evident truths because even if a truth is accepted as self-evident by the addressee, why is it being stated? And this questioning "why?" may give rise to further possible queries: such as, 'why now?' and 'why to me, or to them?' etc. Taking the context of an utterance into account, which we all do in practice, means that even when a speaker or writer presents a statement as simply an axiomatic truth, the addressee can only understand it in the context of the reasons for its utterance. If these

---

8 In the glossary at the end of the four essays published as *The Dialogic Imagination*, Michael Holquist comments on Bakhtin's use of 'the word': 'The Russian word *slovo* covers much more territory than its English equivalent, signifying both an individual word and a method of using words [cf. the Greek *logos*] that presumes a type of authority': Bakhtin 1981, p. 247. However, he also makes a categorical distinction between Bakhtin's "authoritative word", which one merely reiterates, and the "internally persuasive" word. Masking one's inner thoughts in Stalinist Russia must have made a lot of sense (like Catholic "equivocation" in Protestant England), but Holquist's distinction blurs the point that one person's "authoritative word" is another's "inwardly persuasive" one.

are not clear, s/he has to look for its unstated or concealed motives. Such an awareness of the speech act as an assertion of authority opens it up to different possible interpretations. Any addressee may be deceived or persuaded by a particular utterance, of course, but on the other hand s/he may feel able to decipher the conscious or unconscious intention as the true meaning behind the ostensible meaning. This decipherment can be mistaken, and can even lead to paranoid misinterpretations. Nonetheless, this practical hermeneutics of suspicion is an activity shared by all language users, not just sophisticated theorists. It depends on an alertness to the unsaid which is sometimes genuinely revealing.

But here the issue becomes more complex. The unsaid is not just a question of a speaker's individual intentions, conscious or not. The addressee may not even be suspicious about a speaker's motives, but simply alert to the range of the possible meanings of an utterance, irrespective of whether the speaker is consciously or unconsciously concealing his personal motives. In that case, to recognize the authoritative presuppositions underpinning ostensibly factual statements (assertions of the way things are) is to confront the power of the ideological *addressivity* within the utterance, whose source is no longer the individual sender but the social authority which he too has assimilated. It should be added that many authoritative statements are not banal, even if they present themselves as unquestionable. Challenging them from a position of "outsideness" can be difficult, and occasionally dangerous. It can also be 'mad', if madness is understood as deviation from accepted social norms. Of course, the concealment of authority within descriptive statements is usually unimportant, but it comes to the forefront whenever there is a conflict of descriptions, such as is common in political debates, religious disputes, philosophical controversies, family conflicts, divorces, judicial proceedings etc. This is because all "constative" or factual statements are made from positions of authority, and so a dispute over the real meaning of the facts, even when they are mutually agreed to be true, is always a conflict of authorities as well. Whether socially established knowledge circulates in the form of constative statements (assertions of the way things are) or in the form of normative quasi-imperatives (how to do things, how to speak or behave 'properly', and even what to think or believe), it is always within utterances whose producers occupy or have assumed a position of authority. But those producers of utterances are not the sources of the knowledge in question. They are agents who relay it through their use of the "speech genres" at their disposal. They may sometimes modify it creatively, but even then what is important is that they either endorse its authority, giving it legitimacy through agreement and approval, or else they may question it from a standpoint made possible by the existence of other rival authorities.

The Marxist theoretician Jean-Jacques Lecercle borrows from Deleuze and Guattari's anti-structuralist *Thousand Plateaux* the idea that the *mot d'ordre* is an inescapable aspect of all speech acts. This enables him to explore the presence of the authoritative imperative concealed within every speech act, including those utterances which speech act theory would normally call constative. The usual English translation of *mot d'ordre* is 'slogan', but the translator of Deleuze and Guattari's work has opted for a neologism: an 'order-word'. The justification for coining this rather outlandish expression is that it retains the notion of an implicit authority, just as the normal English word 'order' can describe either a structure or a command.[9] According to Lecercle, the *mot d'ordre* is a term which 'does not designate a type of utterance but an aspect of every utterance, just as the illocutionary force, for the Anglo-Saxon pragmatic linguists, is to be found not only in the speech acts which explicitly exercise a force, as in an insult, but is a component of every speech act'.[10] In support of this, he quotes the following passage from Deleuze and Guattari's *Thousand Plateaux*:

> We call *order-words* [*mots d'ordre*], not a particular category of explicit statements (for example, in the imperative), but the relation of every word or every statement to implicit presuppositions, in other words, to speech acts that are, and can only be, accomplished in the statement. Order-words do not concern commands only [*ne renvoient pas seulement à des commandements*], but every act that is linked to statements by a 'social obligation'. Every statement displays this link, directly or indirectly.... The only possible definition of language is the set of all order-words, implicit presuppositions, or speech acts current in a language at a given moment.[11]

For my argument, the important point is the internalization of these multiple concealed imperatives by the addressee. As we learn more in the form of

---

9   The English equivalent of *mot d'ordre* is 'slogan', but this English term carries implications of collective self-exhortation, while being also an assault on the outsider, rather than conveying the more instrumental *addressivity* of the French term. There is a buried history here, revealed by the etymology of 'slogan'. It is derived from the Gaelic *sluagh-ghairm* [host – cry] which, taken into English, denoted at first an Irish or Highlander battle cry (OED). No doubt the English were often enough the external addressees. The French term, by contrast, reveals its provenance from an organised military hierarchy. Lecercle discusses Lenin's *mots d'ordre*, as do Deleuze and Guattari. The Russian for slogan is *lozung*, which is a military term borrowed from German. Originally it meant a 'pass-word'.
10 Lecercle, 2004, p. 123 (my translation).
11 Deleuze and Guattari 1988, p. 79.

utterances or "speech acts" (behind which is the far longer "chain" of utterances which have constituted the implicit presuppositions of the culture in its present state), we also assimilate a whole series of authoritative positions. These usually differ, according to the matter of instruction or information (how to do things, what to think about other beings, whether animate or inanimate, how to address elders, equals, and various others, how to behave properly within assigned gender roles etc.), but such differences are not usually perceived as conflictual by the subject being so 'informed'.[12] In most cases, conflict is only a latent potentiality. This means that truly disturbing conflicts between authoritative positions can only arise in complex societies, when an accommodating coherence (or better, a still undeveloped and therefore unperceived contradiction between implicit imperatives), previously understood without question as the way things are (an ontology), is perceived to be breaking down into rival claims to authority.[13] It is even insufficient to theorise this situation as a breakdown in "order", which can then itself become a lost object of nostalgic desire for ontological certainty, like Lukács' integrated "epic" world. The subjectively perceived loss of such integration is not really produced by a Spenglerian social and cultural entropy ('Things fall apart/ The centre cannot hold', as Yeats put it) but rather by a socio-historical development into a higher level of complexity consisting of rival discourses and a consequent conflict of authorities, each with its competing claims to the truth. At such times of heightened conflict, at least some of the combatants will inevitably see themselves as restorers of the single order of things against the "deluge" or "chaos" caused by the disruptive presence of alien 'voices' or "abnormal" viewpoints within the new situation.[14] This is Bakhtinian monologism in action. It should be understood as a reactive attempt at the restoration of the disappearing single order. But that single order is itself an imaginary lost object of nostalgic desire, created in response to the proliferation of rival authorities.[15] It is, in short, a reaction formation.

Viewed within this historical dynamic, the very existence of critics or potential revolutionaries, who seek to replace the old ways of thinking and behaving, depends on their own prior achievement of a high degree of

---

12   The etymology of this word is surprisingly revealing. We are not just informed about facts, as in modern 'information'; we are *inwardly formed* by the utterances conveying those 'facts'.
13   Since epistemology involves both doubt and rivalry, it seems to arise as a philosophical preoccupation from the collapse of an unquestioned ontology.
14   A good example of this, in Western culture, is the fate of universal Christendom in the face of Renaissance rationality and science on the one hand, and the Protestant challenge to the Roman centre on the other.
15   This desire is central to the discourses of mysticism discussed in Chapter 6.

"outsideness". Otherwise they would not be capable of distancing themselves from the authority of their formerly unquestioned beliefs and practices. In short, both sides in the developing conflictual complex objectify their opponents by framing them conceptually, and by placing themselves outside that frame in a new position of authority. In such socially polarising situations, the opponents' utterances are construed as an "ideology" in the sense that their beliefs and claims to authority are encompassed, understood, and rejected, from the new hard-won position of "outsideness" where the authority of the rival version of the truth now takes its stand. In this respect, Louis Althusser was partly right when he wrote ironically that ideology is what other people have. An ideology, then, might be provisionally defined as the objectified and framed version of an opponent's thought, including his values and associated practices. It would be the product of a radically polarising society, in which the claim to detect an ideology implicitly or explicitly makes a competitive claim to authority grounded in truth, from which the other's limitations or untruths (not necessarily conscious lies) can be seen for what they are. Understood in this way, Bakhtinian "outsideness" is the condition of possibility for the activity of framing others' versions of reality, in order to name them as an 'ideology'. However, that objectification of others' discourse is quite the opposite of the positive assimilation of "the other's word" which provides the dialogical basis of "becoming" and transformation in Bakhtin's theory.

3   The Idea of a Single Ideology Is Itself Ideological

The concept of "ideology" arose out of the radical rationalism prior to the bourgeois revolution in France at the end of the eighteenth century. Coined by Destutt de Tracy, the term was at first a proposal for a science to investigate how ideas are formed in the human mind on the basis of Locke's sensationalism refined by Condillac. This approach persists in a modified form, and sometimes with fruitful results, in some Marxist or *marxisant* histories which distinguish the study of ideology from the history of ideas. Ideology is understood here as the historically shifting forms of social consciousness which, by responding to the changes in social and economic relations, allow certain specific ideas to come into existence, or even make them necessary. In effect, this denies the idealist proposition that ideas could really have an autonomous history. As practiced by English Marxist historians like Christopher Hill, Victor Kiernan, Roy Pascal *et al.*, it articulated the history of religious dissent and the emergence of modern scientific ideas in relation to economic and social developments, and especially in relation to the formation of the State, modern classes, competitive individualism, and so forth.[16] Here, ideology is only the focus of attention insofar as all ideas are conceived in their dynamic relationship with developments in both the 'economic base' itself and the forms of consciousness which such social relations of production have made possible, or even necessary. One of the striking aspects of this historical school's attention to ideology in the early modern period in England is their denial that there was such a thing as a single bourgeois ideology, since the class itself developed in contradictory and shifting relationships with the other classes and with its own expanding economic power. Consequently, ideology remains a semi-autonomous object of study, and not necessarily a unified one. There is little attempt to abstract it as an object to be studied in its own right. Indeed that is arguably a positive point, since ideology does not really exist as a separate object, even if it can be constructed by the theorist who (to borrow Hegel's metaphor) detects its operations behind the backs of its conscious agents.

In these hands, ideology has become an object of enquiry in its widely accepted modern senses as either a body of interconnected ideas or, more subtly, the structures of coherence holding such a body together. This coherence is sometimes assumed to be consciously held by its subjects (corresponding more or less to a world-view), but mostly, in a more sophisticated form, it is theorised as an absent structure underlying and conditioning the beliefs, ideas, and practices of its subjects in a way not consciously perceived by them. In both senses, however, ideology is a term which names a singularity perceived from outside. This objectifying frame of understanding imposes a unity upon alien others, which can itself become the object of either militant ideological critique or relatively disinterested historical enquiry. In detecting this coherence, we may well be right in various ways, but it is nonetheless a coherence which we construct mentally and then propose to our own addressees (co-religionaries, fellow thinkers, those we seek to persuade, or even ourselves whenever we repudiate all resemblances with the alien other). If it is seen in this way, as the discursive product of a polarising society, ideology can be redefined further. No longer just the specific contents identified and unified by the external observer's mental framing of others (i.e. the 'alien' world-outlook), nor even the frame itself (as in structuralist versions of the underlying unity), it can now be understood as the activity of framing, which means raising the observing subject to a transcendent position from which the unifying frame is constructed. Seen in this way, then, ideology is monologism in action, covertly engaged with rival discourses while claiming for itself a privileged position of detachment above the fray. The structuralist critique prevalent in the 1970s and

---

16 Cf. Parker 2008.

1980s with its claim to "scientific" transcendence was, perhaps unintentionally, a variant of this monologising activity.

But even if an ideology is redescribed as a covert dialogical engagement with others, which produces its own illusory singularity through the very act of framing them from a position of "outsideness", that does not mean that it can really be separated from its own ideational contents. That would mean abstracting it from its participation in the ongoing historically specific conflicts and collaborations, and to treat it as though it were simply a "will to power" indifferent to the contents of the ideas which it combats by re-describing them. Clearly, the contrary is the case: an ideology always operates through a range of propositions about the way things are (constative affirmations of its version of the truth) precisely because of its basis in a dialogical competition with others' rival versions whose authority it seeks to overcome, either by assimilating them into a subordinate position or by eliminating them.

4 Ideological Conflict and the Production of the Unconscious

Jean-Jacques Lecercle writes that 'Voloshinov attributes linguistic creativity ... to the ideological contents of the speech acts produced in the dialogical exchange', rather than to Chomsky's structuralist 'rule-governed creativity'.[17] Lecercle's insistence on the "creativity" of dialogism at the level of its propositional contents is very important. But Voloshinov's version of ideology as embattled *addressivity* also introduces a concept of repression, even though he avoids the word 'repression', probably because of its Freudian associations. There is a negative 'linguistic creativity' in Voloshinov's thinking, which is detectable in his theory of the active production of metaphorical 'refractions', metonymic displacements, and significant silences. This brings his insights close to Freud's version of the unconscious, particularly as it is reformulated in linguistic terms by Lacan. But Voloshinov does not set out to propound a theory of the unconscious. I will argue that it emerges as a necessary consequence

---

17   Lecercle 2004, p. 109: 'Volochinov attribue la créativité linguistique ... non à l'utilisation des règles, mais aux contenus idéologiques des actes de parole émis dans l'interlocution'. What is less persuasive is Lecercle's affirmation that Voloshinov's concept of dialogical creativity is compatible with Althusser's 'interpellation which calls the subject into being (*interpellation des locuteurs en sujets*)' on the grounds that 'every interpellation calls forth a counter-interpellation' (*ibid.*). This concept of a 'counter-interpellation' is impeccably dialectical but it is not Althusserian, as he admits on p. 191. He states that it is inspired by Freud's 'counter-cathexis' and Judith Butler's readings of Althusserian ideology in *Excitable Speech* and *The Psychic Life of Power* (1997), *ibid.*, p. 192.

of the dialogical struggle for dominant singularity, which is the main focus of his Marxist argument.

Voloshinov often uses the word "ideology" (*ideologiia*) rather loosely in the broadly accepted sense as a body or structure of interconnected ideas held in common by a single group or class (a usage shared by Leninism, too, it should be added). This lays him open to the charge of excessive focus on the individual as an integrated member of his group, with a consequent downplaying of discursive conflict. The Slavicist and Bakhtin scholar, Patrick Sériot, makes this accusation. He argues that in Voloshinov's thought, the dialogue with the other, whether the latter is actual or potential, merely introduces into the definition of the individual an exteriority which is entirely free of the notion of class or any other conflict:

> Voloshinov's only concern is to show how exteriority intrudes into interiority, and to recognise that an utterance [*énoncé*] is always made by taking an interlocutor into account, whether the latter is present or potential. But the field of this exteriority is not differentiated, and it is only invoked to effect a weakening of the frontiers between outer and inner speech [*parole*]. There can be no question of any discursive conflicts.[18]

It is true that Voloshinov, like Bakhtin (and Vygotsky as well), is concerned with showing that individuality is formed on the basis of collective dialogism, whatever the particular nature of the group concerned. But there are moments when Voloshinov understands the dominant "official ideology" like Bakhtin, as a monological discourse struggling for control within the field of dialogical signs which are the actual basis of all consciousness. He identifies the ideological struggle in question as one between opposing 'social value judgements'. This means that they are always specific and are not reducible to a contentless will to power. But the dialogical nature of this struggle also means that its monological goal is never a fully achievable state, even when it may appear to be. Although it seeks a final state of assured dominance, it cannot actually eliminate the underlying dialogism which is its historical condition of possibility. This dialogical understanding of linguistic dominance, which is close to Gramsci's 'hegemony', raises key issues.[19] Voloshinov defines the 'ideological

---

18 Zbinden and Henking 2005, p. 214 (my translation).
19 Cf. Ives 2004; Gardiner 1992. Both provide illuminating discussions of the political dimensions of Bakhtin's and Voloshinov's thought on language and consciousness. But the potential in Bakhtinian thought for a reconsideration of the unconscious as historically produced is not addressed.

sign' as the scene of a struggle for unity, for class dominance, and for ahistorical universal validity. He theorises this 'striving' for dominance in terms of a specifically Marxist dialectic of the class struggle. Under the conditions of historical struggle the 'vital and mutable' dialogical sign reveals its other aspect as a 'refracting and distorting medium':

> The very same thing that makes the ideological sign vital and mutable is also, however, that which makes it a refracting and distorting medium. The ruling class strives to impart a supraclass, eternal character to the ideological sign, to extinguish [*pogasit'*] or drive inwards [*zagnat' vnutr*] the struggle between social value judgements which occurs within it, to make the sign uniaccentual.[20]

This version of monologism (uniaccentuality), not as a fully achieved discursive and conceptual dominance but as a struggle for either extinction or concealment, is very important. It turns out that the actual outcome of this struggle for uniaccentual and unchallengeable dominance is not the extinction or inward silencing of the opposing 'social value judgements' sought by the ruling class, but an effect of refraction and distortion in the very signs through which the hegemonic discourse seeks such 'uniaccentuality'. This must surely imply the social production of an unconscious within the ongoing historical struggle, although that is definitely not a line of thought consistently pursued by Bakhtin or Voloshinov. Nonetheless, even in the above statement, Voloshinov's version of monologism contains an argument that goes beyond the purely external conditions of class struggle and its corresponding clash of consciously held views of the world. It also rules out any idea of the ruling ideology as an achieved structure, since it conceives of such a 'supraclass, eternal character' as the always deferred goal of the embattled aspiration 'to make the sign uniaccentual'. Meanwhile, the actual effect of this struggle is to make the linguistic sign a 'refracting and distorting medium'.

The inwardness of the oppositional discourses, whose extinction Voloshinov theorises as the discursive aim of ruling class ideology in pursuit of its own "uniaccentuality" (monologism), is not the same as his and Bakhtin's usual concept of the inwardness of the sign. In general, their concept of this silent "inwardness" means that it is continuous with the sign's external existence, both being the site of dialogical encounters. As Voloshinov observes: "Every sign *as* sign is social, and this is no less true for the inner sign than for the outer

---

20 Voloshinov 1973, p. 23.

sign".[21] This continuity across the difference between inner and outer speech is grounded in the dialogical nature of the sign, and it provides the link between individual consciousness and social communication. In short, it is simply the given nature of the sign as such in Bakhtin's and Voloshinov's dialogical theory of consciousness. But that is precisely why "extinguishing" an oppositional discourse (i.e. achieving total victory over it), or "driving it inwards" in the sense of imposing a silence, would be much more than a simple denial of external expression. It would amount to driving it completely from consciousness. And, since such a monological state of consciousness is impossible (consciousness being dependent on dialogical engagements), it is identified as a desired goal, not as an achieved result.[22] One does not have to be an orthodox Freudian to observe that any discourse which is driven inwards in this second sense, is "repressed" or prevented from direct expression, but is not actually obliterated.[23] It continues to exist within the imposed redirection, identified here by Voloshinov as refraction and distortion. Consequently, at moments of crisis, it can return within and against the very consciousness that seeks to negate it.

5   The Dialectics of Repression

All of this by no means contradicts Marx's well-known statement in *The German Ideology* that 'the ideas of the ruling class are in every epoch the ruling ideas'. But Marx has no theory of language to explore the dynamic set out by Voloshinov. In Marx's argument, dominance is achieved through the ownership of the material means of production, and he states that "generally speaking" this ownership includes the means of mental production:

> The ideas of the ruling class are in every epoch the ruling ideas, i.e. the class which is the ruling material force of society is at the same time its ruling intellectual force. The class which has the means of material production at its disposal, has control at the same time over the means of mental production, so that thereby, generally speaking, the ideas of those who lack the means of mental production are subject to it. The ruling ideas are nothing more than the ideal expression of the dominant

---

21 *Ibid.*, p. 34.
22 In Chapter 2 I have argued that Dostoevsky's Underground Man is the hero, or anti-hero, of this struggle.
23 Freud's metaphor of the unconscious as a conquered city comes close to this perspective. The city of repressed or silenced discourses causes disturbances and can even rebel.

material relationships, the dominant material relationships grasped as ideas; hence of the relationships which make the one class the ruling one, therefore, the ideas of its dominance. The individuals composing the ruling class possess among other things consciousness, and therefore think. In so far therefore, as they rule as a class and determine the extent and compass of an epoch, it is self-evident that they do this in its whole range, hence among other things rule also as thinkers, as producers of ideas, and regulate the production and distribution of the ideas of their age: thus their ideas are the ruling ideas of their epoch.[24]

Marx certainly does not intend to argue for the unchallengeability of the "ruling ideas", but the unresolved problem is that since "generally speaking" ideological dominance (defined as "control … over the means of mental production") is equated with ownership of the "means of material production", there is little room for a theory of challenge or resistance from outside that control. By contrast, Voloshinov's theory of the social struggle which continually takes place within discourse, draws attention to the unending, mostly silenced struggle through which the ruling ideas maintain themselves in their dominant, apparently unchallengeable position. In the course of this dialogical struggle between the dominant and the subordinated discourses, the latter only find oblique expression through the effects of refraction and distortion imposed on them by the dominant discourse. Nonetheless, this essentially dialogical encounter does enable the different strands of meaning to co-exist within the sign, even under conditions when they have become incompatible. The Freudian analysis of the unconscious, particularly after Lacan, relies on the mutability of the metaphor, understood as a signifier with more than one signified, but a dialogical view of this would be that metaphors are signs in which multiple discourses coincide, sometimes in conflict.

For Freud, the return of the repressed always takes place in the forms of refraction or substitution, which he calls 'displacement" (or its closely related form of disguise: "condensation"), since otherwise it would not be able to elude the vigilance of the repressing agency, which is what Freud's "censor" is. He discusses these essentially rhetorical strategies as the means whereby the repressed contents of the unconscious achieve a limited measure of expression. They assume the disguise of metaphors and metonymic substitutions in order to evade the ever-vigilant internal censor. In this formulation, the active initiative is entirely on the side of the repressed contents. They achieve a measure of expression by recourse to a whole series of metaphorical or metonymic

---

24   Marx 1977, p. 176.

disguises, which it is the task of the analyst to decipher in order to reconstruct the patient's repressed unconscious desire. But if Freudian thinking on "displacement" and "condensation" is reconsidered as the outcome of an inward dialogical encounter in which a discourse struggles to impose its dominance or to maintain it, these rhetorical strategies actually assume a double guise. The corollary to Freud's thesis, which would be necessary from the point of view of dialogical analysis, is that "displacement" and "condensation" are effects produced by the dominant discourse itself in its struggle for control.

Here Voloshinov's view of ideology as ongoing embattled *addressivity*, seeking (but never fully achieving) absolute dominance, comes into its own. It means that the rhetorical strategies outlined by Freud should really be considered as negotiations between the drive towards dominance and the aspirations constrained by it into postures of concealed resistance. The repressive discourse can only remain dominant on condition that it negotiates ("dialogically" one has to say) with the challenge "from below", that is to say, from those others which it struggles to designate as 'lower'. This is significant because Voloshinov's conception of the ideological sign as a "refracting and distorting medium", whose "vital mutability" permits expression to opposing discourses but only through the deviations which he identifies as refraction and distortion, is not as far as it might appear from the Freudian or Lacanian concept of "displacement" through metaphor or metonymic substitution. But in Voloshinov's reformulation, as the dominant discourse seeks to become monological it actively produces the unconscious, because the unconscious is that area of aspirations or desires which cannot be completely silenced or obliterated, and are therefore subjected to the refractions of preventive repression.

Moreover, these repressed desires are mediated through discourses whose resistance is anxiously anticipated by the dominant discourse, which therefore tries to prevent them, in the full sense of the word, from becoming conscious intentions. The Oxford English Dictionary definition of "prevention" is helpful here. Its primary meaning is anticipation, but its secondary more familiar meaning introduces the key paradox: prevention is that form of anticipation which tries to ensure that the anticipated event does not occur, as in 'preventive medicine', or indeed any other preventive measures. These anticipatory measures include the law, which exists in order to prevent an event by forbidding it. Of course, when these acts of preventive anticipation are (or seem to be) purely external, they are easily understood because they operate in an intersubjective social space. But internalised (intra-subjective) prevention is inescapably paradoxical (see Chapter 2). There the anticipated "event" (Bakhtin's dialogical *sobytie*) is prevented from becoming fully realised within the conscious self. That does not mean that the inward dialogical event is totally obliterated. It exists, but only as a possibility or potential which is anxiously anticipated by the dominant discourse in order that it should not occur.

6 Interpellation Revisited

If ideology is understood in Bakhtinian terms as *addressivity* from a position of authority, as Ken Hirschkop argues (see *infra*) it is close to Althusser's concept of *interpellation*, but for Althusser that authority is not subject to contestation by the addressee. He explains that *interpellation*, usually translated as 'hailing' someone, elicits instantaneous and unreflective self-recognition by the "interpellated" subject. His use of the standard French term, *interpellation*, includes one of its important connotations: that of a subject being stopped by the police, who are the agents of the very State of which s/he is 'always already' a subject. Althusser describes his own narrative exposition of this action by the so-called Ideological State Apparatuses as his 'little theoretical theatre'. This sometimes unnoticed metaphor allows him to make a significant revision to his own theoretical narration, because for him *interpellation* is not an event or process which takes place in time. In theatrical time, events are presumed to fall under the control of structure, so Althusser is able to withdraw their temporal nature because, he writes, the subject is 'always already' constituted by *interpellation*. The concealed truth of ideology (in the singular) is that it is an unchallengeable 'omni-historical' structure underpinning the various ideologies (in the plural) which have succeeded each other in history and will continue to do so. These specific ideologies are historically contingent, but concealed within them is their transcendental structural necessity. They are the means whereby the State ensures the reproduction of the social relations of production. Althusser even writes that, 'ideology is eternal, exactly like the unconscious'.[25] This is a formulation which is clearly indebted to Lacan's statement that the unconscious is 'structured like a language',[26] although in a later addendum Althusser reduced this eternity to the vast timespan of the historical existence of classes (hence his later distinction between 'eternal' and 'omni-historical'). By contrast, the many ideologies which have co-existed or succeeded each other within the changeability of human history are necessarily deluded forms of consciousness, because they all conceal the true

---

25   Althusser 1971, p. 152.
26   It is 'structuré comme un langage', which is not exactly the same as Saussure's concept. For Saussure structure is the property of 'la langue' which is conceptually distinct from the all-inclusive 'langage'.

'omni-historical' nature of ideology (in the singular), except from the theorist who can dissociate its transcendental reality from its historical appearances.

Althusser's 'little theoretical theatre' bears an extraordinarily close resemblance to the Baroque Great Theatre of the World. I will consider this historical antecedent later. Here it is sufficient to note that the metaphor of the Great Theatre of the World enjoined an essential distinction between the theatrical 'appearances' on the worldly stage, which are the source of sensual deceptions and intellectual delusions, and the permanent truths which only religious discernment could grasp. In the case of Althusser's theatrical metaphor, God is theoretically dispensed with, but the permanent order persists in the form of the concealed 'omni-historical' transcendental necessity for illusions. This is the truth which the theorist alone can grasp because his science, like the theology of yore, places him beyond the worldly illusions which succeed each other on the stage of history.

In her *Psychic Life of Power*,[27] Judith Butler mounts an apology for Althusser but she rightly points to the Christian metaphysic supporting his definition of ideology and the *interpellation* which calls its subjects into being:

> Although Althusser explicitly introduces 'the Church' merely as an example of ideological interpellation, it appears that ideology in his terms cannot be thought except through the metaphorics of religious authority.[28]

She explains that Althusser's use of religious examples (Saint Paul and Pascal in particular) actually goes beyond merely illustrating the nature of ideology:

> To illustrate the power of ideology to constitute subjects, Althusser has recourse to the example of the divine voice that names, and in naming brings its subjects into being. In claiming that social ideology operates in an analogous way, Althusser inadvertently assimilates social interpellation to the divine performative. The example of ideology thus assumes the status of a paradigm for thinking ideology as such, whereby the inevitable structures of ideology are established textually through religious metaphor: the authority of the 'voice' of ideology, the 'voice' of interpellation is figured as a voice almost impossible to refuse.[29]

---

27 Butler 1997.
28 *Op. cit.*, p. 109.
29 Ibid., p. 110.

To this we should add that in Althusser's account of subject formation there is, strictly speaking, no need for the concept of *interpellation*, since its purpose is always already achieved. His 'figure' of the theatre is quite unlike the *addressivity* theorized by Bakhtin and Voloshinov. For them, this concept presupposes an addressee whose potential resistance is anticipated in the very act of addressing him/her or them. So even though an address to the subject from a position of authority is indeed an *interpellation*, provided that we understand it as a bid for dominance, it is not a redundant concept, as it is in Althusser's theory. Its quality as an 'event' (in Bakhtin's sense) presupposes an addressee who could rebel, object, compromise, or otherwise evade its influence. In sum, when Althusser derives from his reading of Lacan the thesis that ideology "is eternal, exactly like the unconscious", he formulates it as the hidden but necessary structure subtending all its various appearances in history. Voloshinov, by contrast with Althussers' *interpellation*, views ideological addressivity as the activity of an embattled discourse which seeks to impose its monological singularity, but through an unavoidable dialogical engagement with all those rival discourses which it struggles to subordinate or to maintain in subordination. In the course of this struggle to make the rival discourses unthinkable (unconscious) it engenders the variety of metaphorical displacements or 'refractions' discussed above. So insofar as it achieves a measure of success (which can never be complete), it creates an unconscious in its addressees. Consequently ideology is not like the unconscious, conceived as the structural basis for all its subjects' necessarily deluded self-understanding. On the contrary, it seeks to cause a forgetting or repudiation of alternative possibilities in its addressees.[30]

As every dominant discourse or "hegemony" is subject to historical change, and cultural variance, so is the unconscious which it creates. But it is important to grasp that the addressees of this dominant discourse include the members of the ruling classes too. The hegemonic ideology which seems to secure their unchallengeable dominance is certainly reassuring to them, but this narcissism is not produced by a conscious intentionality on their part. For them too, the possibility of alternatives is made to appear unthinkable, until these negated possibilities actually occur on the historical scene. In this respect, Voloshinov's version of the dominant ideology as dialogically engaged in an

---

30   Michel Pêcheux 1982, p. 114, seems to come close to this position in his footnote: 'The term 'forgetting' here does not mean the loss of something once known, as when one speaks of a 'loss of memory', but the occlusion of the cause of the subject inside its very effect'. Such an occlusion might be explained as an effect of the preventive anticipation which Voloshinov helps us to grasp. But, in comparison, Pêcheux's 'occlusion of the cause of the subject in its effect' appears mystifying.

ongoing struggle to defend its embattled hegemony might well be said to put Althusser back on his feet.

7 The Relationship of Dialogism and Dialectics

Voloshinov makes a further point in his discussion of ideology as a discursive *agon*, rather than as a transcendental structure, and it is one which raises an interesting and unresolved issue concerning the relationship between dialogism and dialectics. Even if one grants the point that they are not mutually exclusive concepts (and a number of anti-Marxist Bakhtin scholars claim that they are), it does not follow that they are essentially the same. Voloshinov, however, tends to treat them as interchangeable terms:

> In actual fact, each living ideological sign has two faces, like Janus. Any current curse word can become a word of praise, any current truth must inevitably sound to many other people as the greatest lie. This *inner dialectic quality* of the sign [original emphasis] comes out fully in the open only in times of social crises or revolutionary changes. In the ordinary conditions of life, the contradiction embedded in every ideological sign cannot emerge fully because the ideological sign in an established, dominant ideology is always somewhat reactionary and tries, as it were, to stabilize the preceding factor in the dialectical flux of the social generative process [*sotsial'nogo stanovleniya*], so accentuating yesterday's truth to make it appear today's. And this is what is responsible for the refracting and distorting peculiarity of the ideological sign within the dominant ideology.[31]

His argument here states that historical moments of social crisis are also times when the monologising and stabilising force of ideology can be seen for what it is, namely a discourse in the service of political reaction. For him, the moment of historical crisis is a moment of revolutionary clarification. That is because at such moments the social struggle over meanings, which has been "driven inwards" or partially silenced through being subjected by the dominant ideology to "a refracting and distorting peculiarity", now re-emerges "fully in the open". At such moments of de-repression or unveiling, the buried "inner dialectical

---

31 Voloshinov 1973, pp. 23–24. The translation of *stanovlenie* ('becoming') as 'generative process' tends to obscure Voloshinov's reliance on this key concept, whose partial compatibility with Marxism is discussed in my Chapter 1.

quality of the sign' becomes overt, and by the same token, perceptible at the conscious level. Voloshinov's invocation of social dialectics in the context of the sign needs to be treated with respect, because it is by no means a recourse to orthodox narratives of historical inevitability. But I will argue that it also needs to be treated with caution.

At an earlier stage in his argument, he has carefully established the ideological neutrality of the linguistic sign and, consequently, its capacity to accomodate differing strands of meaning. The key point here is the crucial role of the "social *multiaccentuality* of the sign" by which it "maintains its vitality and dynamism and the capacity for further development" (*ibid*). This argument is perfectly consistent with the theory of the many-sided dialogical engagements which Bakhtin calls "polyphony" and which both thinkers identify as the condition of possibility for transformation or "becoming" (*stanovlenie*). But such a view is not the same as defining the sign in terms of a bi-polarity, "like Janus", and then going on to identify the emergence of that bi-polarity as the moment of truth when its normally buried "inner dialectic" is revealed. It is at least equally possible, and I would say more persuasive, to argue that these moments of truth are not moments of revelation or unveiling of a linguistic "inner dialectic", but are actually the effects on the social discourses caused by an intensifying social conflict to which the discourses respond. On this view, it is the intensifying social conflict which polarises the normal multiaccentuality of the sign into a single structure of binary opposition, whether this then yields to a higher resolution, as in Hegel, or not. If this is so, the only way to make coherent sense of Voloshinov's shift from the multiplicity of social "voices" to the binary opposition of the dialectic is to recognise that, even on his own account, the bi-polar logic of the dialectical opposition-within-unity is not actually the concealed truth of all sociolinguistic relations waiting to be revealed at moments of crisis. On the contrary, bi-polarity is a special or exceptional case of normal dialogical relations. It arises when the polarisation of the "social multiaccentuality of the sign" into the form of a single binary opposition actually does express, albeit still in a mediated way, the real state of affairs in a society heading towards intensified conflict, and even potential civil war. This moment of polarisation is not one of a revelation of the supposedly timeless truth of the nature of the sign (its "inner dialectical quality") but one of intensified simplification, as the "polyphonic" is reduced to the binary opposition within a real historical process of social polarisation whose effects are felt everywhere, both within the psyche and on the external scene. That does not mean that the detection of the social dialectic is false. Far from it. It is simply to point out that it is reached through an understanding of historical development which does not identify it with the nature of language as such. Historical dialectics does not refer us to a universal law of language finally emerging into the light of day under the pressure of events, but rather to a historically specific state of emergency in extra-discursive social relations. And it is this reality which engenders the narrowing of dialogical relations into an embattled unity of contraries in discourse too.

A state of emergency may give rise to potentially revolutionary moments which may indeed be theoretically grasped as such, as Voloshinov says. Even in such cases, however, it is not the moment of crisis *per se* which reveals its buried dialectic, but a critical consciousness responding to it and identifying it as a revolutionary moment. In other words revolutionary moments do not announce themselves directly to consciousness under the pressure of events, and certainly not in an uncontested fashion. Actually, the Leninist thesis on the need for leadership by a theoretically conscious revolutionary party is based precisely on this point.[32] As Voloshinov writes in the passage quoted above, the openness of the sign to opposing evaluations means that, 'any current truth must inevitably sound to many other people as the greatest lie'. By definition, any moment of revolutionary crisis must also be one of reaction and consolidation. Therefore it will inevitably be marked by a proliferation of all sorts of displacements and misrecognitions. So there is no guarantee that the moment of crisis itself would lead to clarification rather than to intensified tendencies to refraction and negation. Rather the opposite. The potential for a revolutionary clarification of new possibilities, which might transform both the individual self and the social order, must inevitably be accompanied by a reaction towards a defensive paranoid resistance to change, and there is even no reason why this contradiction should not be installed within the same individual subject or social group. But here I would add a final point which is the real stake in the larger project of this book. This can be summed up as follows:

A state of emergency can be very prolonged, and such an apparently static prolongation can all too easily be misrecognised as structural permanence. The overall argument of this book is that the culture of capitalism itself should be reconsidered as a historically prolonged "state of emergency", and its repressive denial of its own transformative potential is an inescapable ideological aspect of its normal existence. This denial is self-defensive, and it explains why its compulsive re-inventions of the timeless "sacred" traditions, which it constantly betrays in pursuit of its economic imperatives ('all that is sacred is profaned', as the *Communist Manifesto* puts it), are actually necessary to its political continuation. These restorations of 'the sacred' condemn the subjects of the modern bourgeois order to the various nostalgias or "false memory

---

32 Cf. Lenin 1961, p. 347–530.

syndromes" which are actually that order's saving illusions, frequently through kitschy restorations of "all that is sacred". Max Weber's argument on the 'disenchantment' of the modernizing world at the hands of the instrumental rationalism of bourgeois society has much to be said for it, but it needs to be doubled by an examination of the processes of re-enchantment, and even of the contrived divinisation of the state and its powerholders. I will consider this more closely in Chapter 5, which considers the *addressivity* of the spectacle in the formation of the State. As Eric Hobsbawn and Terence Ranger point out, the "invention of tradition" relies heavily on visual imagery and public display, as well as verbal discourse, to support the "imagined community" which is described rather too benignly by Benedict Anderson in his book which bears that title.[33] In other words, the visual imagery, whether static or theatricalized, should be understood as an address aimed at captivating the spectating subject. In the modern world these spectacular restorations have become the 'heart of a heartless world', largely replacing the central role vacated by religious ritual. Misrecognition is central to these ideological restorations. They should be understood as an active *addressivity* engaged in ongoing symbolic struggles for continued existence.

Finally, dispensing with the transcendental structural basis of ideology means that there is no need to insist on its singularity or unified coherence. I return to this issue in the next chapter, in order to consider the conflictual symbiosis of the relationship between the state and the market, which is specific to capitalism. This symbiosis underpins the internally contradictory *addressivity* through which this rather unsystematic "system" attempts to captivate its subjects' emotional support, or at least their acquiescence.

---

33   Hobsbawm and Ranger 1983; Anderson 1983.

CHAPTER 4

A Contradictory Symbiosis Is Born: the Rival Ideologies of the Market and the State under Capitalism

> The Duke cannot deny the course of law,
> For the commodity that strangers have
> With us in Venice, if it be denied,
> Will much impeach the justice of the state,
> Since that the trade and profit of the city
> Consisteth of all nations.
> *(The Merchant of Venice*, 3. iv. 26ff)

∙∙∙

Shakespeare's comedy resolves this contradiction, but purely symbolically, when the merchant capitalist's junior venturing partner marries the landed aristocratic heiress of neighbouring Belmont.[1]

∙∙

The contradiction between the sovereign power of the state and the demands of the international market may appear to be new in the light of the current crisis in the nation states system caused by the flows of globalised capital. But, although it may well have reached its apogee nowadays, this contradictory symbiosis has constituted the capitalist "order" (or disorder) ever since its early beginnings. In his classic *Civilising Process* [1939],[2] Norbert Elias argued that the generalised "monetarisation of society" in Western Europe provided the taxes which increased monarchical power over its feudal rivals, financed it against its foreign rivals, and enabled it to maintain standing armies, as well as navies to project its new mercantile power overseas. At the same time, the emergent monetary power itself needed the centralised state which it financed (and indebted). It needed the state bureaucracies and their abstract legal codification

---

1 See Hall 1995 Chapter 3, *A Future for Capitalism*.
2 Elias 1982.

which largely replaced the myriads of different local feudal rights and obligations. This abstract legality, backed by force, was imposed over the expanded tracts of territory (and later over the extra-territorial sea-lanes). Despite all its historical mutations, this contradictory symbiosis of the international market and the territorial state is still with us.

Markets have existed for millennia without necessarily coming into a conflictual relationship with the various forms of state or proto-state organisation. Ellen M. Woods points out in *The Origin of Capitalism*[3] that under all pre-capitalist modes of production markets simply offered the opportunity to buy cheap in one place and sell dear in another. She criticises many others, including fellow Marxists, for failing to recognise the crucial point that "the market became capitalist when it became compulsory".[4] Increasing monetary power was not the decisive initiating factor, although it certainly did provide the necessary preconditions: "While the accumulation of wealth was obviously a necessary condition of capitalism, it was far from being sufficient or decisive".[5] She argues that, unlike the long-established systems of political coercion for the extraction of surplus value, especially taxation, the new system of economic compulsion arose for the first time in sixteenth-century England, with its system of variable market-dependent rents payable to the landlords by their tenant farmers. The latter were quite different from the small peasant producers. They owned nothing but their labour power, while the landowners found a new advantage in increasing their productivity, and subsequently that of the other small producers who became their waged employees:

> In the new agrarian relations, landlords increasingly derived rents from the commercial profits of capitalist tenants, while many small producers were dispossessed and became wage labourers. Marx regards this rural transformation as the *real* 'primitive accumulation' not because it created a critical mass of wealth but because these social property relations generated new economic imperatives, especially the compulsions of competition, a systematic need to develop the productive forces, leading to new laws of motion such as the world had never seen before.[6]

Ellen Wood points out that the capitalist development of productive forces included measures to "improve" the land itself in order to make it more profitable for the market. She emphasises that the new economic compulsions exercised by the emergent capitalist market were then expanded to coerce all

---

3 Wood 2017.
4 *Ibid.*, p. 12.
5 *Ibid.*, p. 36.
6 *Ibid.*, p. 37.

producers, even those in the still non-capitalist territories, to lower their prices in order to survive by competing at the national, international, and ultimately global level. She criticises those who see the economic developments introduced by the capitalist mode of production as merely liberating the productive forces from their feudal fetters (or from their non-European equivalents). Her principal target is their unacknowledged ahistoricism. However unintentionally, they see capitalism as endemic to human nature held in check by the various pre-capitalist social formations, and waiting to be released eventually by the advent of capitalism:

> In other words, in these accounts capitalism really has no beginning, and its development involves no real transition from one mode of production to a very different one. They tend to take capitalism for granted, to assume its latent existence from the dawn of history, and to 'explain' its development, at best, by describing how *obstacles* to its natural progression were removed in some places as distinct from others.[7]

In effect, although Ellen Wood does not say it bluntly, these accounts unwittingly endorse the ideology of the free market by seeing it as the expression of a natural human drive, only held in check by the state or earlier proto-state formations. But although she insists on the revolutionary global impact of the new capitalist mode of production, she concedes that the earlier bourgeois accumulation of wealth was indeed its necessary precondition. Her point is that the bourgeoisie as a class pre-existed capitalism and co-existed easily with the feudal and absolutist state formations, without being capitalist in any real sense.

1   The Rival Myths of Nature in Bourgeois Ideology

Descriptions of bourgeois ideology since the advent of capitalism are bound to be inadequate if no attention is paid to the market. With the historical development of capitalist relations, the market rapidly developed its own institutions. In the modern world, they not only organise production and the coercive need to compete in order to survive, as Ellen M. Wood points out; they also relay their own ideological *interpellations* (to borrow Althusser's term) in the form of apparently "constative" descriptions of the way things are, and the consequent need for every subject to conform and compete. Such descriptions convey the concealed imperatives, or Deleuzian "order-words" discussed in the previous chapter. These can be summarised: for example, "be free", "be your naturally

---

7   *Ibid.*, p. 28.

competitive self", "fulfil your own potential", and even "pursue your dreams/ desires" etc. In the modern world, this ideology is not only relayed through educational institutions and the family (Althusser's "Ideological State Apparatuses"), but also through works of fiction, newspapers, films, the "entertainment industry", and advertising in particular. The authority circulated by this ideological *addressivity* consists in making the compulsions produced by the capitalist economy appear as natural needs or desires which the subject spontaneously recognises in himself. Althusser theorised the subject's spontaneous self-recognition as the necessary form of deluded consciousness produced by the *interpellations* of state ideology, but it is matched, or rather mismatched, by the self-recognition produced by the *interpellations* (or Bakhtinian *addressivity*) of the capitalist market. There is a concealed double-bind in this ideological *addressivity* to which I will return.

Roland Barthes maintained in his *Mythologies* that myths always function ideologically to naturalise the social order: "We reach here the very principle of myth: it transforms history into nature".[8] In these essays which have had a great influence on much cultural theory, Barthes writes about the ways in which human nature is invoked in modern society as a mythical alibi for bourgeois norms. In his final essay he sets out to provide a structural analysis of the "second order" language of these modern mythologies. This has lost whatever plausibility it had at the time, because the structuralist analysis of myths covertly grants them a transhistorical existence even when it may seem to criticise them. But the more challenging point raised by Barthes' idea that modern myths mask bourgeois society's social and historical existence in the garb of eternal nature is that, unlike previous forms of social domination, bourgeois ideology does not affirm the continuity of the existing social order with the natural (or supernatural) order of things. On the contrary, it operates through a discourse of shifting binary oppositions, in which nature is made to appear as the antithesis of the social order. This is irrespective of whether it represents the social order as the source of repression and alienation from "natural" freedom ("man is born free but is everywhere in chains": Jean-Jacques Rousseau), or whether it represents that same "natural" freedom rooted in humanity's presocial origins as a potentially monstrous threat to civilisation.[9]

---

8 Barthes 1973, p. 129
9 One striking example is Barthes' analysis of the trial of Domenici, who is judged according to the psychological norms of the bourgeois novel. This produced the *midi* peasant as a preliterate "other" who was therefore naturally inclined to murder. But another often cited example is the *Paris Match* image of the black soldier saluting the French flag. This image gratifies the bourgeois viewer by offering the reassuring spectacle of difference overcome by the inclusion of the former "other" into the fraternity of the Republic. In the first example,

This second option still shapes common-sense discourse whenever we are told that warfare is the consequence of the irruption of the primitive into the civilized world, leading to a breakdown of "civilisation". The discourse of regression to unrestrained savagery, "feral" in its aggression (or sometimes "bestial" in its sensuality) is an ideological myth because it distracts attention from the modern production of "savagery" out of social competition, national or international, as though it were some irrational or even animal residue quite out of place in bourgeois civilisation. So the social production of competitive violence is occluded by its identification with "natural" disorder. The same can be said of the idea that madness is the outcome of regression to a primitive, pre-rational mode of being dominated by "natural" impulses. In these instances, the ideology of regression to the "natural", which circulates in everyday discourse, masks the production of disorder by our "advanced" state of civilization. The conflicts produced by capitalist civilisation are made to appear as instances of the permanent contradiction between nature and culture, instincts and reason etc., in which for better or for worse the natural appears as a remnant of prehistory. In the malign version, nature appears as the residue of primal violence whose return must be prevented at all costs. But in the benign version, whose provenance can be traced back to Rousseau's secularized version of our expulsion from Eden, this remnant appears as a fragment of the lost state of being repressed by the onset of civilisation. The point that the feared "chaos" or disorder can also be desired as de-repression or liberation, and even by the same individual subject, is a major insight of psychoanalysis, not to mention many works of literature. But that does not mean that it can really be traced back behind our historically created cultural contradictions to the constant mythical substratum of nature.

There have been plenty of apologists for the social order who have represented it as a necessary resistance against the violence of nature "red in tooth and claw" (Tennyson). Historically this is often linked to a reactionary trend running from Hobbes' universal *bellum omnium contra omnes* (war of all against all) to various Modernist thinkers of the twentieth century for whom classical order, both aesthetic and political, was a defence against the chaos fomented or unleashed by the Romantic cult of natural freedom. C.B. MacPherson's *Political Theory of Possessive Individualism*[10] argues from within a Marxist perspective that Hobbes' "war of all against all" was a metaphor which expressed

---

the "natural" is a threat, but in the second the threat is already overcome. Barthes does not comment on the racist subtext of this imperial taming of the "other", but the continuing loyalty of the black African must have been particularly reassuring in the light of the recent losses in Indochina and North Africa.

10   MacPherson 1962.

a historically new truth. That truth cannot be grasped by understanding the metaphor literally in terms of Hobbes' mythical pre-social state of nature as a state of war (often contrasted with the later benign versions of Locke and especially Rousseau), but by seeing it as Hobbes' way of conceptualising the effects of the newly emergent market forces of his day.

This conflation of nature with the market is not immediately apparent, because Hobbes' project was more directly and obviously concerned with formulating a rational alternative to the civil wars and the mayhem of religious controversies raging in his time. But MacPherson argues that we should understand how Hobbes deployed his concept in accordance with the rationalist procedures of the philosophy of his time. Hobbes carefully noted the effects of the destructive play of human passions, which he observed empirically in the behaviour of those around him, and he then proceeded to describe what would be the effect of the removal of *all* social constraints upon those passions. The theoretical remainder is what he called the state of nature, which he had extrapolated from the carefully observed social conditions around him.[11] MacPherson argues, therefore, that the historically new condition of possibility for Hobbes' theory to come into being, and to appear descriptively true, was the unprecedented power of market relations. Hobbes accurately perceived that the old fixed inequalities of the aristocratic hierarchy were being replaced by a new universally shared equality, which he called the "equality of insecurity". He even saw that as a consequence, the "estimation" of all values was becoming merely relative in a world in which each was valued in terms of his serviceability to others, and each was engaged in a struggle to command the power of others.[12] This means that the emergent power of the market was creating a new world of winners and losers, whose psychology was being formed in response to its intransigent demands. The new era of competitive "possessive individualism" was undermining the society based on acknowledged hierarchy and status, and in doing so it universalised the competitive aspiration to mastery.

Hobbes' rational deduction from this universal war of nature, namely the need for an Absolutist state to guarantee the security of each subject from all

---

11 David Hawkes in his *Ideology* alleges that the weakness in Hobbes' argument is his empiricism: this "leaves him vulnerable to the charge of deriving eternal verities about human nature from the specific, observable behaviour of people in his own particular society. Most notably he assumes that the predatory individualism of nascent capitalism reflects an ineradicable 'state of nature'": Hawkes 1996, p. 42. This inverts MacPherson's view that Hobbes' empirical observations give substance to his rationalism.
12 The older hierarchical sense of service as social and affective bond was giving way to a universal struggle to make others servants. The older bonds were already under strain in Shakespeare's time: cf. Schalkwyk Cambridge 2008.

the others, is well known. According to this argument, social harmony depends upon the self-interested rational capacity in these otherwise feral creatures to recognise the need for all to alienate their natural freedom perpetually and unconditionally in favour of their own rational construct, namely the "mortall God" of the Absolutist state. I would only add to MacPherson's interpretation, that this Hobbesian levelling of the relatively stable hierarchies of status society in favour of competitive market relations, which was the historical achievement of capitalism in the West before becoming global, by no means eliminates the principle of hierarchy. On the contrary, it naturalises it on a new basis. Marx and Engels' famous statement on the permanent revolutions introduced by capitalism: "All that is solid melts into air, all that is sacred is profaned" etc. seems indisputable. Even the old "mortall God" of the state itself is currently under threat. But this often leads us to overlook the fact that hierarchy is not actually abolished by this culture centred on universal competition, which is often misnamed "democratic" nowadays. Rather, it mutates into dynamic social aspiration and the corresponding psychological drive for domination misrecognised as "natural" (partly thanks to Hobbes).[13] As this socially constructed desire in response to market demands is reformulated in terms of universal human nature, the solipsist aspiration to eliminate or subordinate all others and become "his majesty the ego", in Freud's apt phrase for this goal of narcissistic desire, emerges as an endless social project in pursuit of its unachievable goal. But if the goal of solipsistic monopoly were actually achievable, it would put an end to the social dialogism in which even the unrestrained competitive individual must exist. In that sense, this socially engendered desire for absolute dominance is a death drive seeking its own extinction, just as the achievement of complete monopoly would (or will?) terminate the competition for dominance which capitalism requires.

Christopher Hill observed that, "Hobbes' state of nature is bourgeois society with the policeman removed".[14] Compared with MacPherson, there is a slight difference of emphasis here, because Hill points to the ruling classes' fear of the lower masses as the basis of Hobbesian ideology and its persistence into modernity. He draws a parallel with Calvin's version of natural man who lacks grace and therefore must be disciplined. By implication, since the majority lack the internal discipline bestowed by divine grace, the state must impose it to prevent unholy natural "chaos". Luther's views on the need to repress

---

13   Under the conditions of universal competition, each individual is enjoined not only to seek monopoly in the economic sphere but also Bakhtin's "monological" dominance over self and other in the psychological one (see Chapter 2).
14   Hill 1964, p. 234.

the rebellious German peasantry were similar. Christopher Hill's analysis of Hobbes' ideology may seem more obviously Marxist than MacPherson's work which defends a measure of historical truth in Hobbes' theory by seeing it in terms of his response to the historically new "possessive market society". But MacPherson also notes that Hobbes' focus on the emergence of competitive individualism sidesteps the issue of class. By this he meant that, while Hobbes acknowledged the existence of classes, he overlooked the possibility that the Sovereign called upon to supply the security absent from the state of universal war, might be the agency of a dominant class rather than just the rational choice of competitive individuals seeking security from each other under the law founded by contract. Of course, individual competition is not the same as the clash of mutually linked and opposed collective identities known as class war, so the argument that capitalism dissolved the fixed social bonds of pre-capitalist society, producing social atomization and "possessive individualism", without noting that it also produced the dynamically interrelated modern classes in the place of those earlier bonds, would be seriously one-sided, as MacPherson himself notes. Marx and Engels' own argument on this issue is that the bourgeoisie is only constituted as a class, rather than as a collection of competing individuals, through its dialectical struggle with its opponent class:

> The separate individuals form a class only in so far as they have to carry on a common battle against another class; otherwise they are on hostile terms with each other as competitors.[15]

The dominant class' fear of anarchical disruption from below, observed by Christopher Hill, is therefore accompanied by a mutual fear of the other competitors. That is why monopoly, which is the ultimate goal of every competitor, is also forbidden or deferred, at least as long as there is a state power willing and able to impose deferral and to earn loyalty from the potential losers for this protection from their rivals. This preservation of social cohesion, and the capitalist state's continuing rule against its own dissociative "natural" forces, makes the myth of the social contract central to the "rule of law" and the continuation of capitalism itself as a social formation. But we should add that with the full development of capitalism, the myth of "natural" competition becomes central in another sense. It not only defines the daily practices of bourgeois *homo economicus*, but also his self-understanding. That is to say, it constitutes his consciousness of both self and world, in the sense that it appears to define his essential, but never fully possessed, freedom.

---

15 Marx and Engels 1975, p. 70.

If this myth of natural competition is indeed central to the way in which the market economy *interpellates* its subjects (borrowing Althusser's term, but extending its *addressivity* beyond the institutions of the state), we can see that it provides the vocabulary for a familiar commonsense view in which all social conflicts are misrecognised as motivated by the supposedly natural aspirations of free individuals to become "top dog" or "master of the universe". This commonsense view constitutes the outlook of the dominant class, insofar as its members tend not to see themselves as a social class but as a number of winners operating in response to the demands of "the real world". The demands emanating from this real world are, of course, identical with those of the capitalist market. This makes them clear cases of *interpellation* in the sense proposed by Althusser, namely that they elicit the subject's apparently free self-recognition, but as a natural competitor in this instance and not only as an unquestioning subject of the state. They also conceal, within the utterances conveying their commonsense descriptions of the world, the same kind of command or imperative masked as a description of "the way things are" which I have discussed earlier in terms of Bakhtinian *addressivity* and of Deleuze and Guattari's "order-words" (*mots d'ordre*) concealed within apparently "constative" statements of fact. This ideological *addressivity* circulates in the dominant discourses of capitalist society, but always in contradiction with the state-centred discourses enjoining the subject's self-recognition in an assigned place, which Althusserian theorists of ideology emphasise.

The capitalist market's ideological production of this misrecognition is especially effective when it is internalised as the self-understanding of subjects who are not actually capitalist competitors. Insofar as it is successful (which is by no means always the case), it makes it possible for any collective challenge to the existing hierarchy to be misrecognised as the self-understanding of "losers", because losers are by definition unsuccessful competitors in the field of our "reality", and this reality is the only game in town, as they say. All collective aspirations are individualized by this ideological misrecognition, and all protests are made to appear as the expression of the natural resentment of "losers". The attribution of resentment to the "loser" arises from the universalisation of the psychology of individual competition. But whether the individual recognizes himself/herself as a successful competitor or as a failure, the aim of this market *addressivity* remains the same: it seeks to persuade its addressees to see themselves as naturally autonomous individuals in a field of universal competition. Its ideological function is to prevent, or at least disrupt, any conscious awareness of collective interests on the part of the opposing classes or other subordinate groups, because that would be a threat to the law of natural competition itself. (To take a classic example, trade union organization threatens free individual competition in the labour market). What MacPherson identifies as a gap in Hobbes' theory, namely that it overlooks the reality of the formation of classes and class conflict, can now be seen as an ideologically motivated blindness to a degree that was not yet the case in Hobbes' own time.

But there is a further point. Nowadays, the demand that the individual should recognize him/herself as a natural competitor means that the whole world must be understood as a global market, and this has actually become a tirelessly repeated refrain. Consequently, the nation state too is taken to be "naturally" locked into competition with other states. "There is no alternative", as the acronym TINA has it, to the untranscendable horizon of this version of the real. To call this universal natural competition "Hobbesian" misses the point that Hobbes' rationalist divinisation of the state as a "mortall god" made the state a controlling power which would prevent mutual destruction within each nation. But in the modern neo-liberal version, there is a revaluation of all values. The state itself becomes the agency for liberating "natural" competition on the international scene. As international competition intensifies, the ideology of competitive individualism mutates into competitive nationalism. The Marxist economic analysis of this intensifying international competition identifies its underlying cause as the falling rate of profit which is endemic to the capitalist mode of production. If that decline in profitability can no longer be overcome by increasing the rate of exploitation of the national working class (for whatever reasons), it must be overcome by competitive expansion to appropriate the surplus extracted by its rival foreign capitals. The role of the ideology of nationalism in concealing this social compulsion is almost self-evident. But the effectiveness of its persuasive power is by no means guaranteed.

2   The Capitalist Double-bind and the Displacement of Guilt

Taking the ideology of the market into account means recognising that capitalist ideology is itself profoundly self-contradictory. If there is an ongoing active *interpellation* or Bakhtinian *addressivity*, as I have argued by extending Voloshinov's theory, then it is also a split *addressivity* from the two sides of the fissured symbiosis which has long constituted the ideology of the capitalist social order/disorder, namely the free market and the nation state. This split *addressivity* is not unifying but potentially schizophrenic, and the contradictory injunctions or Deleuzian *mots d'ordre* concealed within its apparently neutral "constative" affirmations of fact, could even be summed up theoretically in the form of a Laingian double-bind: 1) "Be your naturally free self in competition with all equally free others, or else you will be dominated by them"; 2) "Do not act this out because that would destroy the only existing community and, ultimately, your own existence within it". Taken to extremes, this double-bind injunction could be put more bluntly still: 1) "Follow your natural desires" and 2) "Be guilty for destroying 'all that is sacred'".[16] Of course, the schizophrenic double-bind injunction is never seen consciously by its addressees for what it is, and no capitalist has ever been caught expressing guilt for his anti-national activities. Moreover when times are propitious, the contradiction is concealed behind a unifying ideological screen. At such times, the values of individual competition and acquisition are proclaimed as both natural to humankind and a social good, beneficial to the whole national community. But there have been other times, marked by economic crisis, political breakdown, and the eruption of passionate social conflicts. At such times the inner contradiction in the ruling ideology itself has threatened to emerge too clearly. Then the responsibility for the breakdown is displaced onto "guilty" scapegoats, in order to protect the dominant order/disorder itself from conscious criticism. In the past, these have usually been the mythical "Jewish" money men and/or the rootless "deracinated" cosmopolitans (nowadays the "liberal élite" or "citizens of nowhere"), both of whom could be made to bear the guilt for betraying the "imagined community" (Benedict Anderson) of the territorial nation state. Those times are always capable of returning, however distant they may appear at any particular juncture, because the capitalist nation state cannot exist outside the compulsions of the international market. Social crisis is always an occasion for the "return of the repressed" but this return is never a simple clarification of the concealed truth. It comes in the guise of "displacements" (Freud) and "misrecognition" (Lacan) which Voloshinov attributed to "the refracting and distorting peculiarity of the ideological sign within the dominant ideology",[17] discussed in the previous chapter. Antisemitism has been essential to the displacement mechanisms of the nation-based

---

16 The concept of the double-bind was first formulated in the 1960s "anti-psychiatry" of Laing in Britain and Bateson in the United States. It explained the symptoms of schizophrenia as the outcome of incompatible demands from a beloved authority figure (usually the mother) in a so-called dysfunctional family. Leaving aside certain disastrous clinical group exercises in de-repression, one unintended consequence was the demonisation of the patients' families, especially their mothers, as though they were the source rather than a relay for social injunctions. (For a critique see Sedgwick 1982.) Laing made these intra-family messages the source of all disturbance. So, contrary to his own proclaimed radical politics, he made the family central to the social order by casting the dysfunctional family as the source of all disorder.

17 Voloshinov 1973, pp. 23–24.

"order" of capitalism because it enables the ineluctable contradiction between the territorial nation state and international capital to be concealed by the projection of guilty responsibility onto the imaginary "Jew".

3   Social Contradiction Internalised

Understanding that capitalist ideology is inwardly fissured means understanding that the production of guilt (meaning the betrayal of loyalty) is inextricably bound to the market imperative to be free and to treat all others as competitive rivals. In principle, even the King, President, or any other revered figure would be just another rival. That is the logic of an unbridled free market. Although it is unthinkable by the loyal subject of the state, it is thought unconsciously, i.e. desired by "his majesty the ego", in Freud's apt term for this narcissistic drive. To put this in non-Freudian terms, within every "autonomous" and rationally self-interested bourgeois subject there is a competitive madman who would be King and master of his universe. Freud himself expressed this in the terms of his patriarchal family myth, according to which the son becomes a rival to the father, while nonetheless continuing to love him and to identify with him. Under these conditions, the imaginary identification with the father means taking his place, i.e. desiring to kill him in order to take his place. But this guilty desire has to be driven into the unconscious if the social structure is to continue. In Freud's earlier anthropological version of this conflict in *Totem and Taboo* (1912), which later became the basis of the "Oedipus complex", the rivalry with the primal father figure is not for the affections of the mother but for the possession of all the women of the "primal horde", hitherto monopolized by the father. His murder by the male sibling rivals leads to their acknowledgement of shared guilt and the totemic pact which founds the patriarchal social order under a mutually accepted law to forbid its recurrence. In Freud's anthropological narrative the rival male siblings devour their murdered father, jointly acknowledge their shared guilt, and disavow any repetition of that founding act of parricide. Left to themselves, their competitive drives would engender a regression to the endless mayhem of pre-social appetites. Freud's primal feast is in effect the scene of the founding social pact in which the natural "war of all against all" is renounced.

Freud observes, however, that this founding parricide does not need to have occurred historically for it to be psychologically true. To make sense of this I would argue that for Freud too, the real issue is not an ancient repressed memory but an *anticipation* which is also a repressive *prevention*, in the full sense of the word which I have discussed earlier. The return of the bourgeois myth of a founding pact, to contain "natural" competition by pre-emptively renouncing its goal, is almost unmissable. The only difference is that the rationality of the mythical social contract, theorized from Hobbes through to Locke and Rousseau, is replaced in Freud's narrative by the primal feast, derived from Darwin's speculation that primitive society was a "primal horde" ruled by a powerful male despot.[18] (In fact Hobbes too had argued that the endpoint of the lawless "war of all against all" would be cannibalism, since the winner would have an unrestrained right to everything, including the body of the loser). Hobbes' rationalist myth of the founding contract is replaced in Freud's version by the siblings' guilt, sustained by their continuing love for their murdered father. This guilt is the basis of the pact which prevents the enactment of parricidal/regicidal and fratricidal desires. So the potential future murders are prevented by "the Law".

4 Loyalty versus Law: a Buried History

Under Freudian influence, psychoanalytical discourse makes "the Law" an anthropological constant, like the guilty disavowal which it installs, without acknowledging that actual laws are historical institutions subject to change. But that overlooked history is not really eliminated. It has left a very significant linguistic trace of the process of modern subject formation. In early modern Europe, personal loyalty to the sovereign, which was often called "love", secured (or sought to secure) the subject's repudiation of the rebellion which would make him guilty if it were enacted or even consciously intended. To be truly effective, however, the repudiation itself had to be shielded from the consciousness of the loyal subject, for otherwise the rebellious intention would become too patent. So the repudiated desire became the latent guilty secret. Seen from a Freudian perspective, it is the parricidal/regicidal monster, always hovering on the brink of being unveiled within the otherwise loving and therefore "innocent" subject. But in the increasingly bureaucratic world of the modernizing state, subjective "loyalty" became dissociated from objective "legality", the latter being the written, abstract and impersonal form of the law, which demands only conformity, not love. Both of these terms have the same etymological root (*legalis*), but "loyal" is the much earlier term whose slow development from Latin in the feudal epoch can be traced philologically, while "legal" is the historically later term imported directly from classical Latin. This linguistic doubling was characteristic of the rationalizing and centralizing

---

18   Acknowledged by Freud himself. Cf. Freud [1922] 1959, Chapter 10.

institutions of the early modern European state.[19] The historical dissociation of the rational and juridical term *legal* from the earlier *loyal* has left this earlier term with all the subjective range of affects with which we are familiar. In modern discourse they have even become antithetical, testifying to the radical "dissociation of sensibility" identified by T.S. Eliot in the modern culture of the West (the "mind of Europe") which separated subjective feelings from impersonal rationality.[20] In the most obvious sense, legality is the basis of modern state power because it is backed by coercion, i.e. either by violence or by the implicit threat of violence. But in reality subjective "loyalty" is not weakened by this historical divorce from objective "legality". On the contrary, it is abstract "legality" which is weakened, because it is easily defied or circumvented whenever it is perceived as ineffective. By contrast, the objects commanding "loyalty" have a stronger hold on the subject and continue to be objects of love. That is why guilt is the hidden obverse of loyalty/love but not of legality. It depends upon the subject's repudiation of the desire to rebel (or, in Freudian terms, to kill the beloved Father), not merely upon refraining from it rationally as an illegal act.[21]

However, this historical dissociation of personal loyalty from abstract legality has left a gap which is sometimes filled by nostalgia for a "charismatic" leader who could be loved (and therefore betrayed too). Reactionary politics in our epoch has often made use of this nostalgic desire by contriving certain theatrical or spectacular reinventions of personal "charismatic" presence whenever the void at the centre of the modern bureaucratic state has become too patent. This theatricalised contrivance of a "charismatic" presence to address the unruly subjects of the nation state has its historical origins in early modernity, which I will discuss in Chapter 5. But, of course, in our time the preferred medium for mass *addressivity* has undergone technological change. At times of crisis in the twentieth century, the charismatic "leadership principle" replaced the patent emptiness of bourgeois legality in favour of personal loyalty, and its

---

19 According to the French *Dictionnaire Robert*, *légal* was a 14th century innovation but it functioned as an effective double for the older *loyal* until the 18th century. Similarly, the Oxford Dictionary places the emergence of *legal* in the 15th century. Spanish too makes a similar distinction between *leal* and *legal*.

20 Eliot 1951, pp. 281–291.

21 The chapters dealing with the trial for parricide in Dostoevsky's *Brothers Karamazov* turn upon the emptiness of legality which is identified with modernity and rationalism. In contrast with the guilty parricidal desire experienced (but not enacted) throughout the novel by Ivan, Mitya, and even the saintly Alyosha, only Smerdyakov is legally guilty of performing the forbidden act. Being incapable of love he is incapable of experiencing the restraint of guilt.

enthusiastic followers even celebrated its supposedly non-bourgeois archaism. In the current economic and political crisis, loyalty to a leader is once again replacing respect for legality.

5   Market Addressivity: Capitalism without Guilt?

While the state-centred social order still requires loyalty (and therefore guilt as the consequence of disloyalty), the market does not. For market relations, abstract legality is quite sufficient. Nonetheless, the market is a dominant institution like the state, and in the modern world it too has to address (Bakhtin) or "interpellate" (Althusser) its subjects in its efforts to control them. This is where Freud's nephew, Edward Bernays took Freud's arguments in a direction which discarded his "Oedipal" theory of guilt and repression. In his *Three Essays on the Theory of Sexuality* Freud had argued that human desire is not only the source of all creativity through "sublimation" but also that its "labile" or "polymorphous" capacity for displacements and substitutions is the source of all the so-called perversions. The immediate scandal lay in this desublimation, but the crucial aspect of Freud's theory for Bernays was the distinction between bodily needs and human desires. The former are biological, in the sense that they have to be satisfied or the organism dies. But the latter are always redirected through any number of metaphorical or metonymic substitutions, which are in principle endless. This principle of the infinite malleability of human desires was picked up at a propitious historical moment by Bernays, who transformed it into the founding principles and practices of modern advertising. He achieved this by separating the principle of the infinite malleability of desires from the social need for their repression. Clearly, to discard the social need for repression is to discard the requirement for guilt. This is not just a matter of theory, but also of practice. It explains why our contemporary sexual "liberation" has been so closely related to the requirements of the market (which does not mean that it always has to be, of course). But the question remains as to whether the triumphant market has really dispensed with the older social demand for guilt and the self-policing which it installs in the subject.

It hardly needs to be said that advertising is a supreme example of market *addressivity* or *interpellation* of subjects. The specific historical conjuncture for Bernays' appropriation of Freudian thought, and his dismissal of the social requirement for repression and guilt which Freudian thought entails, is very instructive. In the aftermath of the First World War, Bernays was impressed by Freud's *Massenpsychologie* (translated as "Group Psychology"), seeing it as a key to the manipulation and therefore mastery of the aforesaid masses. Much of Bernays' *Propaganda*, published in 1928, is very explicit on this power of the new experts to manipulate the masses.[22] During the war, he had been engaged in the largely successful attempt to manufacture support for America's participation in the war "to save democracy". But it was not really state control which interested him, let alone the original religious control denoted by the term, which comes from the Catholic Counter-Reformation's *Congregatio de Propaganda Fide*, ("Office for the Propagation of the Faith", founded in 1622).[23] What Bernays did share with Counter-Reformation ideology, however, was the desire to remould the subjectivity of its addressees in order to overcome a sociopolitical crisis. Bernays' post-war interest in the wider control over society by an unelected élite (which he equated with the normal need for order in democratic society) coincided with the looming crisis of industrial overproduction in the post-war situation in the United States. Unless the large majority of the producers, not yet identified as a group called "consumers", could be persuaded to buy what they did not need, the economic crisis could only deepen. This was the moment when Freud's theoretical distinction between needs, which humans share with animals, and human desires operating through the symbolic order of language and images unique to our species, became the basis of a new capitalist praxis. Hitherto advertising had largely proposed commodities as objects which were desirable because they corresponded to needs.[24] But Bernays' version of Freud promised the manipulation and prolongation of desires independent of needs on a grand scale, aimed at the preservation of an economic system and supported by a universal theory:

> It is chiefly the psychologists of the school of Freud who have pointed out that many of man's thoughts and actions are compensatory substitutes for desires which [he] has been obliged to suppress. A thing may be desired not for its intrinsic worth or usefulness, but because he has unconsciously come to see in it a symbol of something else, the desire for which he is ashamed to admit to himself. .... This general principle, that men are largely actuated by motives which they conceal from themselves, is as true of mass as of individual psychology. It is evident that the successful

---

22 Bernays 2005.
23 The *Collegium de Propaganda Fide* followed in 1627, for the education of missionary priests.
24 Admittedly, earlier debates over the trade in luxury goods, which clearly exceeded needs, provide an exception. But they were often marked by the view that luxuries catered to women, were essentially wasteful, and weakened the body politic. Rousseau certainly thought so.

propagandist must understand the true motives and not be content to accept the reasons which men give for what they do.[25]

In this passage, Bernays still subscribes in theory to Freud's concept of repression as the subject's concealment of the true object of desire from himself, and of his unconscious metaphorical substitution of that object by another one. But the concept of guilt is weakened to that of shame, which is more easily overcome. The *interpellations* of modern advertising are all too familiar by now, but their transformation of all commodities into objects of labile desire, whose widespread common feature is the sexual metaphor or metonymic association, is a historically remarkable phenomenon. It is supported by the construction of the addressee's self-image as someone who could gain access through consumption to this ever-receding and ever-renewed consummation. The metaphor has now become so universalized that absolutely anything desirable is "sexy", while sex itself appears in common discourse as an object that might be possessed or "had" by the consumer. Of course, it is an imaginary object which eludes the promised possession in order to reappear in a series of endlessly renewed guises. Sex, it might be said, now functions as an imaginary universal equivalent, almost like money. If there is still an unconscious operation here, it does not take the form of a "guilty" Freudian repression of sexuality. On the contrary, the subject is brought to identify with an ego-ideal imagined as free from all restraint and able to enjoy endlessly. He/she misrecognises the self in accordance with the demands of the newly dominant form of discursive control. This is commodity fetishism as the lynchpin of market *addressivity*. Fetishism is no longer just a matter of the theoretical obfuscation of the producer's actual relations to his products, as in Marx's classical formulations, even if these retain their validity.

Bernays developed the ideas for his book when he attended the post-War Versailles conference with the American delegation in 1919. As it happened, Max Weber attended the same momentous conference with the German delegation, shortly before his death. The moment is significant because it marks a historical shift in the theory and practice of capitalism. In his *Protestant Ethic and the Spirit of Capitalism* (1904–5), Weber had argued that the ascetic self-denial of Protestantism, particularly in its Calvinist and Puritan extremes which demanded the repression of all spontaneous and "natural" enjoyment (including consumption of the fruits of labour), was a necessary cultural precondition for the very secular business of the primitive accumulation of capital. This process required an ethical sense of duty to business as an end in itself.

---

25   Bernays, *op cit.*, p. 75.

For the Protestant ethic, moneymaking takes over from the earlier religious "calling" or "vocation", in an extraordinary revaluation of all values. But for the divine purpose in the world to be truly served (without hypocrisy, that is), there should be no hedonistic or ungodly enjoyment by the rich of the riches being accumulated. That enjoyment would be guilty. In this respect, therefore, Freud's "repressive hypothesis" (Foucault's term) operates on the same terrain as Max Weber's argument. Both are based on the infinite deferral of satisfaction required by the social order, but Freud identified it with the permanent necessity of the "reality principle" whereas Weber located it historically as a specific discourse wrenched out of its original theological framework. But Bernays' adaptation of Freud abolished the old repressive deferral, along with the guilt which it associated with immediate gratification. Liberation of desire from need, under the guidance of those specialists serving the needs of the market, became the order of the day. Perhaps the secular "pursuit of happiness", defined as a natural political right and "self-evident" truth, lent support to this market *addressivity*. Unlike Freud, Bernays in his somewhat propagandistic book in favour of propaganda (which others were coyly calling "public relations") does not give particular emphasis to sexuality. But this relative silence was strategic. For example, his practical and highly successful campaign to extend the tobacco market to women, who up until then had tended to regard smoking as both male and foul smelling, depended on confronting them with the desirable and seductive new film stars smoking on screen. He had also initiated this in collaboration with the Hollywood studios. This imaginary construction of an alternative life to be admired and imitated (which is still considered "cool" by many) was suggested to him by what he took to be the truth: namely his Freudian theories of women's unconscious desire for a substitute for the absent penis or, in Lacan's more persuasive terms, for the "phallic" empowerment which it represented. So the visible cigarette became the living proof of that liberation, and the beginning of an imaginary "empowerment" achieved through a purely symbolic reversal. It is possible but unlikely that Bernays himself was unaware of the orality of these "cool" gestures, seductively exchanged between the hero and heroine onscreen but actually addressed to the audience in a covert, and therefore more powerful seduction.

It might seem that the consumerist *interpellations* of modern advertising, aimed at the intensification of desires freed at last from traditional restraints and ultimately from those of guilt, are essentially different from the kind of *addressivity*, which I have traced back beyond Freud to Hobbes' concept of universal war and the consequent need for a strong state to restrain it. My argument has relied on MacPherson's identification of this universal war as a metaphor for the emergent power of the market coming into conflict with other social relations. To recapitulate that argument: the contradictory *addressivity*, from the market on the one hand and the state on the other, seeks to constrain the individual to recognize himself as "naturally" driven by competitive desires. These have to be controlled in order to fend off mutual destruction and to preserve the order of the state, but at the same time they also have to be unshackled in pursuit of the market's promise of freedom and self-realisation. But if this is granted, does the installation of consumer fetishism at the centre of the newer construction of desire really replace the older restraint of guilt imposed on competitive individualism?

6   The Market's Need for Permanent Non-satisfaction

In his *History of Sexuality*, volume 1, Michel Foucault is dismissive of the Freudian "repressive hypothesis", on the grounds that it underwrites the prevailing myth of our sexual liberation from "Victorian" repression. He criticises the view of the nineteenth century as an epoch of sexual repression by pointing to the endless pursuit of the hidden truth of sex in the scientific discourses of that time. But he does not extend this critique to the discourses of the market and their incitement of the equally endless pursuit of that absent object of desire through consumerism in the twentieth century. For him the discourses on sexuality which proliferated in the nineteenth century were a secular and scientific continuation of the Counter-Reformation and the Christian confessional/inquisitorial procedures for making the secrets of sexuality speak (which he calls their *mise en discours*). This whole tradition had passed from Christianity into the secular and rational *scientia sexualis*, which he contrasts with the erotic traditions of other cultures, including the pre-Christian West. This longstanding confessional "science" constituted sexuality as the hidden secret which had to be endlessly pursued but was always just beyond the limits of every discursive investigation through which it was sought. Foucault's argument emphasizes this secret as an object of desire pursued by a perverse and obsessive discourse:

> But this often stated theme, that sex is outside of discourse and that only the removing of an obstacle, the breaking of a secret, can clear the way leading to it, is precisely what needs to be examined. Does it not partake of the injunction by which discourse is provoked? Is it not with the aim of inciting people to speak of sex [*à en parler, et à toujours recommencer à en parler*] that it is made to mirror [*qu'on le fait miroiter*], at the outer limit of every actual discourse, something akin to a secret whose discovery is

imperative, a thing abusively reduced to silence, and at the same time difficult and necessary to divulge.[26]

I include the French in square brackets because the rather wooden English translation partly obscures the fact that Foucault is quite knowingly writing about the seduction controlling this confessional "science", as it pursues its unobtainable object of desire "over and over again" (the English version simply omits the phrase: *à en parler, et à toujours recommencer à en parler*). The translator's choice of "to mirror" for *miroiter* is similarly disastrous. *Miroiter* means to reflect light intermittently, but *faire miroiter* means to set up something as a seduction or entrapment. The *Robert* dictionary explains this expression by referring to the multiple lark mirrors which French hunters use to lure those high-flying birds down into the range of their guns. This is similar to Lacan's metaphor of the *leurre*, the illusory object which provokes a desire and sustains it by precluding its achievement. (The fulfillment of the desire would be its death, as it is for the larks). But Foucault's argument is not that this fleeting object of desire is a universal absence subtending and sustaining all language, as in Lacan's thinking. Rather, it is an object obsessively constructed and reconstructed by a particular discursive discipline in the service of a perverse will to truth (*la volonté de savoir*), which he considers characteristic of all post-classical Western culture. This pursuit is endlessly renewed but cannot ever achieve its goal, even now when there has been the widespread reversal of values and the proclamation that sex has finally been liberated from the enforced silence of its repression. For Foucault, there has been no such moment of truth in the modern world. On the contrary, there is just an intensification of its pursuit. Foucault inverts Freud's older concept of the "polymorphous perversity" of desires (which have to be repressed, according to Freud) and substitutes for them the "polymorphous techniques of power". These techniques not only control and channel desires but also incite and intensify them.[27] In principle this argument, namely that the discourse of sexuality produces its imaginary object, would appear to assign to modern advertising a prominent place among these manipulative and endlessly productive "polymorphous techniques", even though that is not the direction taken by Foucault's argument.

This modern desire for unattainable fulfillment is also a competitive desire produced by the needs of the capitalist market. Its individualism may be narcissistic in aspiration, but its competitive aspect makes it social, despite itself. It is constantly reinforced by the belief that others are rivals who possess the

---

26   Foucault 1978, pp. 34–35.
27   *Op. cit.*, p. 11.

imaginary object, and this socially backed persuasion gives the object itself an even greater appearance of reality. It must be real, it seems, because others have it. So the imaginary object of this desire is not just sex, which has become a metaphorical substitute for the ever-receding fulfilment promised by the discourse of consumerism. It is above all the selfhood which used to be conferred by status within a relatively stable social hierarchy, but has now been transformed by the discourse of the market into a property of the purchasable commodity. A few decades ago, the concern with status was more family-based and was summed up by the familiar phrase: "keeping up with the Joneses". Nowadays, "brand loyalty" confers status, and among the relatively dispossessed the cultivation of the addressees' self-image around the need to have the latest desired object (currently trainers or mobile phones) has led to extraordinary competitive violence in schools and streets. The objects in themselves are trivial, but the imaginary object is not. The market fosters the desire for a new self who could possess it, thus addressing the subject's discontent and potentially revolutionary desire for change, while redirecting it and ensuring its recontainment within competitive individualism.

However, the violent competitive individualism in this underclass is only half the story. The formation of gangs, in the absence of older and broader collective identities, tells the other half. Gangs, however "feral" or "mindless" they appear to the outsider, are also characterised by intense group loyalties, sometimes directed towards a temporary "charismatic" leader and often centred on a narrowly defined territory. Alongside the market-engendered individualism and its competitive violence, there is a counteractive almost unbreakable code of solidarity which forbids the treasonable betrayal of any members of the gang to the state agencies or other outsiders. There is a strong sense of loyalty here, and it is fiercely defended. Although there is a threat of real violence against those who may break the codes, this loyalty is not secured by violence alone. However perverse it may appear to outsiders, there is also a sense of potential guilt which sustains the precious bonds of loyalty. This so-called "gang culture" has replaced to a certain extent the older bonds of class-based or religious affiliations, but it also recreates in microcosm the affective bonds of the weakened or disappearing nation state. Perhaps that is what enables it to be glorified in much gangster fiction, for which loyalty and betrayal are nearly always major motifs. Clearly such fictions, addressed to the general public, speak obliquely to that public about itself. The "gang" is like the state with which it is in competition, and it too increases its authority, based on loyalty, from competitive rivalry with other gangs. At the same time, like the state it is threatened internally by competitive individualism and the disloyalty which goes with it.

7 Conclusion

The rival *interpellations* emanating from the market and the state do not produce the unified identities theorized by Althusser, because they produce desiring subjects. Despite his debt to Lacan, Althusser's account of ideology has no place for the discontented subject divided by desire. To be more accurate, however, one should say that the contemporary capitalist market addresses the already discontented subjects of the nation state, and that it even encourages their discontent with their subjection while channeling it for its own ends. The promise conveyed to its addressees through the discourse of modern advertising is not just the possibility of possessing the new object specified in any particular advertisement, but the possibility of becoming new, or accessing a new mode of being, by means of that possession. Hovering behind the material object which is obtainable through legal purchase or robbery, is the obscure object of desire constructed as a seductive lure by this discourse of persuasive information. As this essentially imaginary object is infinitely renewable, it serves the economic drive in capitalism towards permanent renewal without "becoming", that is to say, towards perpetual expansion but without any unwelcome political transformations. In short, the discontented subject's desire for "the new" (that old revolutionary cry of Romantic individualism) is addressed, and is even provoked nowadays on a mass scale, but only in order to be displaced into the purchase of novelties and the preservation of the same social order/disorder. That is how Freud's symbiosis: "Civilisation and its Discontents", is kept stable. From its very beginnings in the epoch of mercantile capitalism, the conflicting imperatives of the market and the state have always been combined symbiotically, in a unity which is conflictual but not dialectical. Together they form the contradictory ideologies and practices of that truly paradoxical entity, the capitalist nation state.

CHAPTER 5

Captivating the Unruly Subject: Ideology in Early Modern Europe

In the previous chapter I have argued that an ideology only exists as such within a field of conflict where rival discourses struggle for dominance, not only on the external social scene but necessarily (since this struggle is discursive) in the minds of all those being addressed by them. My second argument in that chapter was more specific to capitalist ideology: the dominant role of the market which emerged historically with mercantile capitalism, was and still is in contradiction with capitalism's need for control vested in the apparatus of the nation state.

However, this modernizing symbiosis of market and state did not simply replace the older contradictory symbiosis of monarchical and ecclesiastical powers. That remained in place, but within the historically new situation the centralizing state took upon itself, and even surreptitiously usurped, the divine authority relayed from God. From the point of view of the state, it is not enough to keep its subjects in subordination through violence or the threat of violence. They must also be captivated in the full sense of the word. The Oxford English Dictionary gives the primary meaning of "to captivate", dated 1526, as: "To make or hold captive", but its secondary meaning is more significant: "To subjugate (the mind)", and an even earlier instance, dated 1525, is "To enslave, fascinate, charm". Lacanian psychoanalysis calls the seductive power of the image *captation* to account for its capacity "to imprison the subject in a disabling fixation".[1] This chapter will examine how and to what extent the power to fascinate in order to exercise control was achieved by monarchical self-display in the context of early modern state formation.

José Antonio Maravall's influential *Culture of the Baroque* provides an illuminating historical analysis of the ideological struggles of the ruling classes in early modern Europe. This struggle was conducted through visible displays as well as verbal discourses, in order to sustain the dominant fiction of

---

1 Evans 1996, p. 20. Lacan's theory of the captivating power of the image is not a dialogical theory of *addressivity*. But in Chapter 6 I will reconsider his theory of the captivating lure of the painted image as a mode of *addressivity* in the context of the anxious desires provoked by the cultivation of incompletion in Baroque culture. Significantly, Lacan himself writes that the painted image functions like a linguistic sign.

the transcendental "theocratic state".[2] Maravall considers the culture of the Baroque to have been a pan-European phenomenon, lasting from the mid-sixteenth century to the end of the seventeenth, and he defines it as "a guided culture" (*una cultura dirigida*) under state control. But, despite the word "structure" in his title, he does not affirm the existence of a fully achieved cultural control, even in theocratic Spain and its empire. On the contrary, he shows how it struggled to assert its dominance, its unity, and its foundations in the universal cosmic order, in response to the new dissociative forces which it had to control. Maravall did not have at his disposal the concept of the unavoidably dialogical nature of all *addressivity*, even when it tries to exercise unidirectional dominance. Consequently there is no theoretical attention on his part to the ways in which the early modern state's displays of power were shaped inwardly by its anxious anticipation of its addressees' possible resistance. Nonetheless, he makes it quite clear that even in Spain, the dominant discourses of the sixteenth and seventeenth centuries were actually engaged in a struggle to impose and to maintain their dominance by deploying historically new forms of cultural control. Especially important is his extension of this would-be controlling cultural *addressivity* to include the public displays, the visual imagery, and the architecture for which the Baroque epoch is probably best known. He discusses all these symbolic forms in terms of a controlling address from the monarchical-cum-ecclesiastical centre to its new mass spectatorships. This must mean, I would emphasise, that these forms were constructed as though from such an imaginary centre by the various producers and reproducers of this mass-directed culture. The underlying concern of all these cultural productions, discursive and visual alike, was to affirm the timeless presence of the single transcendental order supposedly underpinning the "seignorial theocratic state", in the face of all the dissociative forces (social, economic, and intellectual) which were actually fragmenting it internally and threatening its dominance. Maravall's analysis provides a whole range of illuminating socio-historical insights into the barely contained dynamism within the visual displays and the verbal discourses of this period, which an earlier, conservative critic of Baroque literature in Spain had summed up as "a frozen dialectic" (*una dialéctica congelada*).[3]

Maravall's study focuses particularly on the culture of Spain from the mid-16th century to the late 17th century, but the historical implications are far wider. He insists that this embattled "culture of the Baroque" was not exclusively Iberian or Italian, as some have argued, nor was it just the artistic

---

2 Maravall 1986.
3 Casalduero 1949.

expression of the values of the Counter-Reformation. Furthermore it was not even a purely artistic or literary phenomenon. It was a European-wide phenomenon which arose from the clash between the expansive, exploratory, and innovative forces of Renaissance culture on the one hand, and the reactive reassertion of a whole range of would-be traditional forms of feudal rule on the other. These "reaction formations", as I call them, affirmed the enduring presence of the single universal sacred order behind its temporal political forms. Maravall's pan-European perspective is useful for grasping the cultural dynamics in territories quite other than Spain, like Protestant England or Absolutist France, where the socio-political outcomes were different. Despite their mutual political and religious rivalries, all these territories shared a common feature: namely that their would-be "monological" assertions of the timeless transcendental order supporting the state were made on a historically new, centralising, and modernising basis. The discrepancy between their displays of archaic forms of power on the one hand, and the new social and political forces which they were struggling to control by means of such displays on the other, is what made those displays modern. They were nostalgic rather than truly traditional.

When Maravall argues that the crisis besetting Spain was not essentially different from developments elsewhere in Europe, he provides a general formula for understanding this culture of intensifying inner contradictions and Spain's arrested development within it:

> The crisis of the seventeenth century cannot be understood in Spain without bearing in mind the broad European framework in which it unfolded, although in Spain its effects would turn out to be irredeemable for centuries. It was the spectacular and problematic breakdown of a society within which forces driving it towards change struggled with other, more powerful forces whose object was preservation. Wherever the resistance to these changes was greater, *although in no instance could things remain as they were*, the elements of the new society were not permitted to develop and all the factors of immobility become privileged [emphasis added].[4]

There are two important points here. The first is that within Maravall's "broad European framework", there were marked national differences within the overall process which some Marxists have called the "combined and uneven

---

4 Maravall 1986, p. 26.

development" of the capitalist nation states themselves.[5] This is not Maravall's theory, but his similarly synoptic view of this overall development in Western Europe at that time means that even Spain's almost legendary economic stagnation, in which "the factors of immobility become privileged", cannot be understood in terms of Spain's isolation from the inter-state rivalry which was eventually won by others. Spanish exceptionalism cannot explain the economic stagnation which had begun even before its apogee during the so-called Golden Age. The second point is that even in Spain itself the reactive resistance to change was not fully achievable in fact: "in no instance could things remain as they were". Despite themselves, the political and cultural forces seeking preservation and continuity in all these emergent nation states simply had to negotiate with the dangerous forces of change, if only in order to contain and control them.

This was therefore a scene of concealed dialogical engagements on many fronts. In Bakhtinian terms, it was genuinely "polyphonic" but this multi-voicedness was forced by necessity onto the emergent monologising centres. The discourses in support of the new state centralisms, and especially their accompanying spectacular strategies, were created in response to the potential threat from the newly mobile populations and their new psychological mobility, both of which were the consequences of the generalised "monetarization of society" theorized by Norbert Elias.[6] The outcome of this ideological *addressivity* from the imaginary centre was not a simple roll-back or restoration of traditions, but a radically new contradictory cultural formation, in which the centralising discourses struggled to assert the presence of a timeless order sanctified by tradition, within the very novelty of their actual practices of spectacular public display. Maravall describes the Baroque as a "gesticulating" culture of extremes, denoting by this term the emphatic assertions of a symbolic order that would actually have gone without saying if those societies had really been based in the continuities which they proclaimed.

1 Monetarisation and the Crisis of Identity

The wider cultural effects of the process of monetarisation amounted to an emerging threat to previously unquestioned hierarchies and established

---

[5] For a discussion of this formula, first advanced by Leon Trotsky in his polemic against the prevailing concept of autonomous national phases of development, see Anievas and Nişancioğlu 2015. These authors emphasise, perhaps excessively, the external factors behind the rise of capitalism in Western Europe.

[6] Elias 1982.

identities. The following lines by the conservative satirist Francisco de Quevedo, who prided himself on his ancient blood lineage, express his and others' anxiety over the dissolution of status by money:

> Pues es quien hace iguales
> al duque y al ganadero,
> poderoso caballero
> es don dinero.
> (*For it is he who equalizes/ the duke and the herder,/a powerful gentleman/ is sir money*)

These lines do not reflect the social situation, because the actual effect of Elias' "monetarization" at the time was increasing inequality, not the equalization of the duke and the herder lamented by Quevedo. But behind the threat to established social identities regretted in these lines, the poet is attacking the emergence of a newer and deeper threat; the power of "sir money" means that "all that is sacred" could now "melt into air", as Marx and Engels were to put it later. The public displays identified by Maravall were therefore forms of symbolic resistance to that immanent desacralisation. Max Weber's term for the threat to the hitherto sacred foundations of the social order is the "disenchantment of the world" at the hands of secular rationality. But, he should have added, that was precisely why the monarchical states had to contrive their effects of "re-enchantment" by raising the monarch to quasi-divine status. In other words, the spectacles mounted by the centralizing monarchies should be understood dialectically, not as the direct expression of continuing archaic beliefs but as a new mode of embattled ideological *addressivity* seeking to affirm the transcendental basis of the state in the minds of its potentially rebellious subjects. Although the quasi-divinity of the monarch could not be openly proclaimed, it still had to be understood as somehow present or incarnate in the royal body. The contrived sense of wonder, or *admiratio* in the terminology of the time, relied on affirming this divine "presence" in the face of the threat of its disappearance. But at the same time, the quasi-divinisation of the monarch implied what could rarely be stated directly, namely the monarch's rivalry with the authority of the "universal" Roman Catholic Church. There is a covert usurpation of the older sacred centre concealed within this spectacular divinisation of the state.

In England and elsewhere (including Spain), the process of "monetarisation" heralded the modern uprooted masses of mobile individuals, who somehow had to be recontained within a social discipline. In 16th- and 17th-century Spain the inflationary impact of gold plundered from the new American colonies exacerbated the impoverishment of rural communities, and intensified the population flows into the cities. A similar contradictory process is being repeated nowadays but on a global scale: not only are our modern nation states overwhelmed by population flows but they are also unable (and unwilling) to control the profitable flows of capital which are the root cause of the migrations. The paradoxical consequence of the triumphant expansion of Spanish imperialism into America was that its massive "monetarisation", in the form of imported sacred American gold melted down into exchangeable European quantities, led to uncontrollable domestic inflation. It also financed the monopolisation of land by the old feudal magnates. This increase of riches in the hands of the landed aristocracy, far from laying the basis for investment in new modes of production, ultimately contributed to financing the formation of Spain's more successful bourgeois rivals in Europe, reinforcing further its own uncompetitive "backwardness". In effect this was an early example of transnational "combined and uneven development", and it had internal national repercussions everywhere. In Catholic Spain, where the landed magnates and the Church retained their dominance, the ethic which favoured capital accumulation over consumption (Max Weber's thesis on Protestantism) failed to develop. But Spain was no less affected by the advent of capitalist monetarisation than its ultimately more successful rivals elsewhere in Europe. In the long run, they were the beneficiaries of the plundered riches of Spain's imperial expansion.

Maravall's insistence on viewing Spain in terms of the general effects of mercantile capitalism affecting the whole of Western Europe is clearly indebted to the work of the historian Fernand Braudel.[7] Braudel points out how the speculative buying of consumer goods in Seville, which enjoyed the monopoly of the American trade, ruined both the Spanish and the Spanish American economies. All consumer goods were snatched up at virtually any price, to be re-exported to the overseas Spanish possessions in exchange for gold. (Later, as production from the gold mines fell after 1560, it was replaced by silver from Potosí, whose extraction was enhanced by the new German method of amalgamation with mercury). The resultant inflation rapidly ruined the broader population, as well as the petty nobility who continued to live on collapsing rural rents. The socially familiar figure of the poor *hidalgo*, reduced to living on nothing but still continuing to maintain the appearances of past glory, was reflected in the literature of the time, for example in the first picaresque novel *Lazarillo de Tormes* (1543). Later, Cervantes' *ingenioso hidalgo* would seek to remedy this loss of status through his "ingenious" re-enactment of the nostalgic novels of

---

7 Braudel 1955.

chivalry. However, this emergent capitalism also tended to ruin the speculators themselves. Braudel quotes an aphorism by the contemporary Spanish observer, González de Cellorigo, on the new kind of poverty infecting Spain: "If she is poor, it is because she is rich". This recourse to paradox reflected the real situation, but it was also very characteristic of the Baroque style which easily lent itself to a religious way of understanding the otherwise incomprehensible, contradictory and uncontrollable reality of monetary power.

The intensifying economic and social crisis meant that the riches of the world were no longer just morally comprehensible snares and deceptive temptations, as in traditional Christian asceticism. Now the deceptive appearances seemed to have expanded their diabolical hold on everyday reality, leading to impoverishment for many and the inexplicable enrichment of a few. This contradictory social reality intensified the old ascetic view of the deceptive veil of life. So the Baroque sense of crisis, whose worldly causes were not fully understood, was grasped metaphysically by the defenders of the established order through the widespread metaphor of the Great Theatre of the World. The figuration of the world as a theatre of appearances was not entirely new, but was typically Baroque in the way that it deployed paradox as its central device. For the ideology of the Counter-Reformation in Spain, the deceptive appearances (*parecer*) were more triumphant than ever in the world, where they concealed the real transcendental being (*ser*) of the divine order. That is why the subjective experience of disillusionment with worldly appearances, and the consequent perception of universal emptiness (*vanitas* in the full sense of the word) were construed as the necessary spiritual preconditions for an encounter with the concealed truth. Any yielding to melancholy or despondency over the emptiness was an indication that the despairing soul was still clinging to worldly *vanitas*, and was therefore yielding to the principal temptation of the Devil in the test of faith confronting everyman. For this resurgent asceticism, the individual soul's response to the threat of emptiness becomes a crucial test: if the absent truth was grasped through a proper discarding of deceptions (*desengaño* in Spanish), then the surrounding darkness of emptiness and death would reveal itself as the veil concealing the eternal light. Through this metaphysical dialectic (which should be described as a dialectic of desire and anxiety seeking to overcome a void), the negatives of despair and disillusionment were transformed into vehicles for intensified religious faith and its affirmation of the continuing divine presence in the world. The threatening nothingness (*la nada*) was there to be overcome by faith. In much of the painting of the Baroque period, the darkness itself is represented as the source of the light.[8]

---

8 Cf. de la Flor 2002, pp. 77–120.

Despite their own rather Baroque flamboyance, Fernand Braudel's remarks on this cultural dialectic illuminate the intensity of this willed blindness to the surrounding reality, which was produced out of the contradiction between the new transformative power of mercantile capitalism on the one hand, and the absolute, transcendental refusal of its threat to the established hierarchy on the other:

> Under Philip II, Spain is less and less able to perceive the contradictions which grow more serious nonetheless. She escapes from the real. While her subjects are in revolt and her riches ruin her, she locks herself away in her interior castle.
>
> There is a sort of symbol in the fact that the Merchants' Exchange in Seville and the Escorial were designed by the same architect. On the one hand, the traffic of the global market which was overturning the world. On the other, the geometrically closed palace, modeled on the Castilian countryside, a convent and a cemetery, a place of study and of prayer, from where a political power struggled to hold back the march of time.[9]

The mere fact that the Seville Exchange (the *Casa Lonja de Mercaderes*) and the Escorial palace were designed by the same architect (Juan de Herrera, commissioned by Philip II himself) might be considered fortuitous. But the constitutive contradiction noted by Braudel between these symbiotically twinned institutional sources of social power, is not. Braudel's "symbol" unites contraries in a culturally defining paradox. The struggle between emergent capitalism, bearing a potential future capable of overturning the established order of things (a real historical "becoming"), and the reactive struggle of the theocratic state to *prevent* that future by arresting the "march of time", defines the inwardly split nature of the hegemonic ideology of this whole culture. But it was not merely static. Its reactive displays of power (and even its military-political exercise) were inevitably marked by their inward refusal to acknowledge the very disappearance of the substantial "presence" which they sought to prevent. In the next chapter I will consider how this anxious struggle against the "march of time" is a key to the intensified desire for restored plenitude, promised and occasionally satisfied by "mystical" experience.

In their *Social History of Spanish Literature*, Aguinaga, Puértolas, and Zavala point out the characteristic nature of another satirical poem by the reactionary Quevedo. This poem mocks the way that gold "is born and honoured by the flattering world in the Indies [America], before it returns to die in Spain, and

---

9 Braudel, 1955, pp. 50–51 (my translation).

is buried in Genoa".[10] For all its moralizing wit, it shows a typical failure (or perhaps refusal) to understand that the dead capital exported from Spain was not just buried in Genoese banks. It was invested outside Spain in the production of commodities, and in that form it was then returned to non-productive Spain, thus impoverishing that politically and militarily dominant country still further. Spain was the most powerful state at the time, and the only one with an empire in both America and continental Europe (unlike its mercantile imperial rival Portugal), but it did not develop a national bourgeoisie, except on its rebellious margins (particularly in Catalonia, and in the Netherlands which later became a nation state and a rival imperial power in its own right). When the Emperor Charles V relinquished the throne of Spain and the Empire to his son Philip II, Spain was virtually bankrupt, being heavily indebted to the foreign bankers who financed its imperial wars for the defense and expansion of Christendom. They were the winners of those wars. The monarchs of England and France were also similarly indebted, but not to the same extent.

The main issue for Maravall, however, is not the comparative economic backwardness of Spain and its continuing self-inflicted stagnation, but rather the *modernity* of the whole Western "culture of the Baroque". And one important key to this shared modernity is that Spain provides an early example of a modern urban "mass" society, where established local communities and the structures of social hierarchy were giving way to individual mobility, anonymity, and temporary associations of unstable urban crowds. These too were the social products of the general "monetarisation of society" which was driving the rural producers off the land. They possessed a certain temporary collective power but not yet the firm or lasting identity of an emergent class. In England, they were known as the "masterless men" and were considered dangerous because of that new absence of proprietary control. In both London and Madrid, the new urban crowds also provided the audiences for the theatres to whom, as Walter Cohen has argued, the new unifying national ideology was addressed in support of their respective monarchies.[11] For example, in many plays by Lope de Vega, of which *Fuenteovejuna* is just the best known, peasant rebellion in the countryside is represented as the consequence of feudal abuse, usually of a sexual nature (abuse of daughters or wives) so that honour in many such plays is always a political issue. For the feudal aristocracy, the male "code of honour" only applied to the blood nobility, but in these plays the King extends it downwards by recognizing the *honor* of the loyal "old Christian" peasantry.

---

10   Aguinaga *et al.* 1981, p. 284. Quevedo's poem runs: "Nace en las Indias honrado,/donde el mundo le acompaña;/ viene a morir a España,/y es en Génova enterrado".
11   Cohen 1985.

In *Fuenteovejuna*, King Ferdinand brings about the resolution as he rewards the loyalty of the erstwhile rebellious peasant subjects onstage, with whom the new audience offstage (composed largely of recently urbanised subjects) could easily identify. Lope brings in the King as a *deus ex machina*, but prior to that Royal appearance, the hero is the collective itself, as it resists the judicial torture designed to identify and isolate the individuals responsible for the anti-feudal revolt. Some later productions, in the Soviet Union and elsewhere, had no difficulty in lopping off the monarchical conclusion and overlooking the peasants' loud declamations of loyalty to the Catholic Monarchs as they rebel against their feudal oppressor.

Such Royalist *interpellations* of the new urban masses, whether through the public spectacles or through the actual theatres, were all the more remarkable in view of the recent social experiences and memories which they had to overcome. After all, the new imperial monarchy under Charles I (elected as the Holy Roman Emperor Charles V in 1517, and creator of the fearsome military *tercios*) had destroyed the *comunidades* at the battle of Villalar in 1521. The latters' insurrection in Castile in 1520 is considered by some to have been the first modern revolution. But Carlos Aguinaga and his co-authors point out that the leadership by this aspirant "Castilian bourgeoisie" was fatally divided between the exporters of wool based in Burgos, who quickly abandoned the cause, and the "emergent industrialists" of Segovia who remained rebellious to the end. They add that the violent suppression of the *comuneros* coincided with Cortés' capture of the Aztec capital, Tenochtitlán. So the founding of the overseas branch of the Empire coincided with the consolidation of the power of the aristocratic landed magnates at home, fixing its anti-bourgeois form for generations to come. The defeated *comuneros* included many *conversos* (forcibly converted Jews and Muslims) and this fact, according to Aguinaga and his fellow authors, explains "both their bourgeois and their anti-seignorial and anti-inquisitorial character".[12] Their suppression, followed by that of the *Germanías* (Brotherhoods) of Valencia, which these authors call "an undisguised class war",[13] laid the basis for the Spanish "Golden Age" (*Siglo de Oro*). This flattering term, borrowed from the already established nostalgic *topos* of classical literature, was first applied to the reign of Charles V in 1523 by the procurator for Granada in the Cortes, and only much later came to be applied to the art and literature of the time.

The broad outcome of the triumph of the landed magnates was a massive population flow to the cities, although for some the American empire

---

12   Aguinaga *et al.* 1981, p. 228.
13   *Ibid.*, p. 229.

permitted an escape route and a certain degree of freedom from the oppression and the tax burdens at home. (Cervantes himself was denied permission to emigrate). But Maravall stresses another, very significant aspect of this creation of the modern urban crowd, namely the emergence of a new form of self-awareness within the individual who knows that he can be anonymous within these urban crowds, and be largely unknown to others.[14] This is entirely unlike the form of self-awareness within an established rural community, where mutual recognition provides for both support and an informal but strong social control over the individual.[15] In the cities, at least, there was a new individual freedom and the potential to defy collective norms of thought and behaviour. These were the social conditions which saw the birth of the picaresque novel and its upwardly mobile hero. Far from being celebrated, however, this mobility aroused the anxiety and even outright hostility among the defenders of the old hierarchy like Mateo Alemán and Francisco de Quevedo, both of whom wrote picaresque novels to deplore this upsurge from below (Quevedo) or to lead it into moral reform (Alemán). For Maravall, the culture of the Baroque marks the first appearance in modern history of this "mass" society, of the alienated individual within the mass, and of the cultural productions principally intended for its control. He compares its extravagant mass spectacles to the Frankfurt School's version of the twentieth-century Culture Industry, seeing both as means of social stabilization through psychological control. This was a spectacular art addressed to the new dangerously mobile and volatile crowds of alienated individuals. To use Bakhtin's term, *addressivity* is what counts here, because this spectacular art was not simply the expression of a unified world-view or class ideology understood as a structure, even though Maravall uses the word "structure". Rather, even as described by Maravall himself, its verbal and visual forms deployed a would-be monological *addressivity*, very similar to Voloshinov's account of ideology as dialogical struggle. Bakhtin, as we have seen, formulates *addressivity* as that aspect of any utterance which anticipates its addressees' possible responses and is inwardly shaped by that anticipation: "from the very beginning, the utterance is constructed while taking into account the possible responsive reactions, for whose sake, in essence, it is actually created".[16] This account of *addressivity* fits exactly into the embattled culture of the Baroque described by Maravall. Its cultural hegemony

---

14 Maravall 1986, pp. 102–103.
15 From the Enlightenment onwards, the persistence of such social control in the countryside becomes a dominant metaphor for national backwardness and death-bound repression. It is common to such divergent works as Galdós' *Doña Perfecta* and García Lorca's Rural Tragedies.
16 Bakhtin 1986, p. 94.

was fissured inwardly by the very dynamic resistances which it anticipated and struggled to control or prevent from further development. The anxiety concealed within its apparently confident displays of power is its distinguishing, and actually rather modern, feature. Its preventive anticipation also made it covertly paranoid.

2   The Symbolic Divinisation of the State

In his *Society of the Spectacle*, Guy Debord wrote that the spectacle of power is the survival of an archaic reality into modernity:

> #23 The oldest social specialisation, the specialisation of power, is at the root of the spectacle. The spectacle is thus a specialised activity which speaks for all the others. It is the diplomatic representation of hierarchic society to itself, where all other expression is banned. Here the most modern is the most archaic.[17]

Debord's cryptic formulation is very incisive, but it elides the crucial point that the modern state is not actually archaic. The spectacles that it offers to its addressees should be understood as reaction formations within a modern or modernising political economy. Hobsbawm and Ranger make a similar point in their *Invention of Tradition*,[18] when they write of Royal processions and public appearances in 19th century imperial Britain as strategies of control, rather than as the true repositories of continuity from ancient origins which they claimed to be. Even in the present century they still make that emotional claim. The "archaic" nature of the spectacle of power noted by Debord, is not a real persistence of the archaic into the modern but a modern nostalgic reinvention. We should add that even in the early modern state, religious rituals such as coronations, which were originally performed by a small social elite in the presence of their peers and supposedly in the sight of God, became increasingly transformed into highly visible public displays, addressed to the spectating populace. Rituals became spectacular. It is therefore pertinent to ask what kind of gratification such spectacles offered, and continue to offer even nowadays, to their intended addressees. It may well be partly true that through them a "hierarchic society" addresses itself, as Debord states. His "diplomatic representation" of society to itself, by which he seems to mean a self-deceiving

---

17   Debord 1977.
18   Hobsbawm and Ranger 1983.

misrepresentation, would be a form of unconscious collective narcissism, seeking a reassuring image of its own stability through the repression of "all other expression". However, power is more than self-assured solipsism on the part of the power-holders, although that is undoubtedly a necessary part of the display. It is always power over someone else, and particularly over the many-headed Hydra of "the mob" (etymologically, the "mobile" *vulgus*). And that really means that Debord's specialists must also address those potentially dangerous subjects in order to control them. Any failure to control those others would rapidly bring about the collapse of the solipsist delusion too. Therefore this "diplomatic representation" is necessarily dialogical in Bakhtin's sense of being shaped by anticipation, and it conceals within its ostensibly monological display a secret anxious anticipation of its addressees' potential hostility, which it attempts to prevent from becoming conscious.

Maravall does not employ the Bakhtinian antithetical terms of monologism and dialogism, let alone *addressivity*, to describe the unavoidable engagement of the centralising and unifying discourses and visual displays of the state with all those disparate social forces which it sought to yoke emotionally and intellectually, to its own goals. This theoretical absence occasionally leads him to over-emphasise the effective power of his *dirigismo* in the embattled discourses of the time. But he very suggestively sees this engagement as the basis of a new kind of rational discourse, namely psychology. He argues that it is because of its embattled nature that this guided culture "dominated but did not annihilate the liberating forces of individual existence".[19] This is a sentence which Bakhtin or Voloshinov could have written. Consequently, he adds, there was a shift to psychological control entrusted to artists and writers, particularly those engaged in the visual and public arts. This did not preclude the resort to state violence whenever necessary, of course. But the truly suggestive point is that these unacknowledged legislators did not merely persuade; they helped to construct an area of "repression" in the addressees:

> The baroque monarchy made use of a large repertory of means [*medios*] to succeed in dominating the tension of adverse forces; this, along with the novelty of some of these means, revealed what was constitutive of baroque culture. It included aspects all the way from physical constraint, based on military force, which is the ultima ratio of political supremacy, to psychological expedients [*resortes*] that acted on consciousness and created within it a repressed psyche....[20]

---

19   Maravall 1986, p. 36.
20   *Ibid.*

It was perhaps because of the insufficiency of physical repression alone that throughout Europe in the Baroque epoch there was such an enormous growth of interest in this "science of the soul" which came to be called psychology. In English this term dates back to the late 17th century, but has earlier roots, according to the *OED*. In France, *Robert* dates it back to 1588, while its more modern usage as a "science de l'âme opposée à l'Anatomie" is attributed to the German Erasmian (and Lutheran) Melancthon. This was a new science, derived from rhetoric and aimed at understanding and mastering the hidden mainsprings [*resortes*] governing human behaviour. In the theoretical writings of the 16th and 17th centuries, human behaviour became increasingly conceptualised as a chaos ruled by the "passions"; but concealed within that chaos there were thought to be secret hidden mechanisms (an objective rationality concealed within the chaos) which had to be rationally studied by a superior intelligence, in order to be controlled by such understanding. This "science" which aimed at uncovering the hidden sources of order within the soul was in effect a rationalization of the more traditional theology for which the soul was a battleground between God and the Devil. In the next chapter on mysticism I will consider this rationality in Loyola's *Spiritual Exercises*.

In Maravall's view, this new "science", with its radical separation of the higher controlling mind from the body, which was conceptually mechanised as it was brought under the mind's control, is proto-rationalist. While being very characteristic of the embattled culture of the Baroque, it anticipated the radical mind/body dualism of Descartes. It aimed at control by reason, both externally over the physical universe or recalcitrant others in the social body, and also internally over the irrationality of bodily desires and their productions of erroneous fantasies in the mind. In this respect, the conceptual mechanisation was a secular supplement to ecclesiastical control and its confessional procedures. The desire to reduce both the mind and the world outside the mind to controllable mechanisms reveals the continuity between the Baroque fascination with magic and the neo-classical cult of Reason. Theodore Rabb, in *The Struggle for Stability in Early Modern Europe*, identifies this same historical continuity as the persistence of the desperate desire for control which arose as a response to the perceived threat of chaos and universal disintegration:

> All the themes and manifestations of the culture of the last two-thirds of the sixteenth century and the first third of the seventeenth that we have considered either as a means of escape from, or as an acceptance of, confusion, could also be regarded as desperate attempts to find a new order amidst disintegration. The witches, the astrologers, the alchemists, the hermeticists, the cabbalists, and even some of the neoplatonists,

hungered to find the key that could unlock some all-encompassing secret. They would have access to the true structure of the universe *if only they discovered the proper method*. For Kepler, the supreme magus of his generation, the hidden harmonies were a life-long goal. And the expectation of all who participated in the search was that magic, properly used, would be an instrument of control. Their ultimate aim was to alter or improve the course of nature. They would reveal *not only the order that had been lost but also the means of managing it* [emphases added].[21]

By including witches in this list of methodical searchers for order, Rabb is pointing to learned magus figures like Dee, or Shakespeare's Prospero in *The Tempest*, rather than to the damned (often feminine) causes of chaos to be found on gibbets and pyres, as well as figures like Caliban's mother Sycorax in *The Tempest* or the witches in *Macbeth* (or in learned treatises like King James 1st's *Demonologie*). The boundary between white and black magic was very uncertain, particularly for the marginalised. Still, the search for the "proper method" to discover "a new order amidst disintegration" points forward to its relationship with Descartes' *Discours de la Méthode*, where the methodical overcoming of his own doubt restores certainty and knowability to the universal order. Rabb quotes Bacon's *Advancement of Learning* and its call to "extend the bounds of human empire" over the "castles and strongholds" of nature, to argue that for these scientists and rationalists: "Control was the antidote to disarray".[22] Maravall likewise writes of the Baroque aspiration to "*univocal* science and *the passion to dominate technically* the surrounding world [emphases added]".[23]

3 Royal Charisma: a Concealed Contradiction in the Baroque Spectacle

In the socio-political sphere, this aspiration to "univocality" was a desire to dominate in order to overcome the threatening chaos of fragmentation. However, the dream of the secret keys to the magical or rational control over things is not quite the same as the attempt to maintain control over people. The theoretical or wishful re-imagination of people as things or bodies controlled by a superior rational mind does not resolve the problem of how to exercise actual

---

21 Rabb 1975, pp. 52–53.
22 *Ibid.*
23 Maravall 1986, p. 279 note 31.

control. In order to explain the *admiración* (wonderment or awe) aroused in the populace being addressed by the Baroque spectacle, Maravall employs the term "charismatic" to denote the subjects' perception of the king's divinely bestowed qualities, which is what the term "charisma" originally meant. He does not affirm that these displays always achieved their object. He is concerned rather with the modernity of the enterprise:

> Given the objectives of dissemination and effective action sought by baroque culture (though in saying this I am not irrevocably affirming that it succeeded), one can understand the interest in the manipulation of visual elements, the preponderant role granted to the optical function within the scope of the culture. On the other hand, appealing to the efficacy of the visual image is typical of societies where a guided mass culture develops.[24]

Maravall's argument that the "charismatic" element in Baroque culture consists in the "manipulation of visual elements" really entails what should be called a divinisation of the state made flesh in the visible body of the monarch. He gives a significant example of the verbal rhetoric which supplemented this visual construction of the monarch's "charismatic quality":

> In sermon literature, one can glean the program of encouraging the monarchy's charismatic quality (which in Spain had been hardly present before), now attempting to incorporate it, with its royal personages of flesh and bone, on the plane of supernatural existence. Paravicino, overlooking the dogma of the natural equality of human beings and even certain precise evangelical maxims, maintained that God particularly enjoys the worship and reverence rendered to a royal person, to the point that it seems "he brings the royal person near with a hidden bloodline of relation".[25]

---

24   Maravall 1986 p. 251.
25   *Ibid.*, p. 142. The divine bloodline of the Royal personage is central to Racine's biblical tragedy, *Athalie*. The tragic heroine Athaliah, who is the daughter of Jezabel, must be destroyed so that the bloodline of King David will triumph in the world, leading ultimately to Christ. In Racine's better known *Phèdre*, the eponymous heroine is directly descended from the Sun (the "brillant auteur d'une illustre famille"), the King and Father whom she has defiled because of the malign presence of Venus in her veins, inherited from Pasiphaë. In both plays, the divine bloodline is sullied by the mortal female line, and this brings down the divine curse upon those predestined sinners. But audience empathy runs counter to this patriarchal metaphysics.

Félix Hortensio Paravicino was a famous preacher whose portrait by El Greco now hangs in the Boston Museum of Fine Arts. As Maravall observes, his quasi-divinisation of the monarch's body "of flesh and bone" and the claim for a divine bloodline runs contrary to much in Christianity which insists on the equality of all in the sight and judgment of God. The monarch is exalted as a kind of second incarnation. But Maravall's argument, that the monarchy's relatively new "charismatic quality" could be made to indicate a divine presence, skirts around the buried contradiction noted by Max Weber in the very notion of "charisma" when it becomes "routinized" and is attached to an office or role. Weber's overall argument is that "charismatic authority" is not grounded in a bloodline but in the personal prestige of a leader. He was usually a warrior or a "charismatic" prophet, to whom that authority was delegated by his followers because they recognised his exceptional qualities. His qualities were indeed assumed to be God-given, but it is the social act of recognition by his followers (or occasionally hers, as in the case of Joan of Arc) that is important. In principle, a leader's reliance on his followers' recognition of these divinely bestowed qualities is actually the antithesis of both hereditary and modern bureaucratic authority:

> Charismatic authority is thus specifically outside the realm of everyday routine and the profane sphere. In this respect, it is sharply opposed both to rational, and particularly bureaucratic, authority, and to traditional authority, whether in its patriarchal, patrimonial, or any other form. Both rational and traditional authority are specifically forms of everyday routine control of action; while the charismatic type is the direct antithesis of this.[26]

Whether implicitly or explicitly, the collective recognition which sustains "charismatic authority" tends to question the sanctity of the bloodline by which feudal authority attempted to regulate the proper transmission of property, rights, status, and power. Charismatic authority was therefore a threat to the principle of monarchical inheritance too. So when Maravall refers to the attempt by Baroque Absolutism to construct a divine "charismatic" presence in the personage of the King, he illuminates a real symbolic practice, but he does not focus on the contradiction concealed within this address to the populace. I have called its goal "a kind of second incarnation", not to register any disagreement with Maravall's insight, but to point out that when the apologists

---

26   *Ibid.*, p. 361.

for Absolutism sought to deify the King (without saying so, of course), they were not making any political concessions to the need for collective recognition and consent which are the grounds for personal "charismatic authority". *And yet they were actively seeking to construct that collective recognition by spectacular means.* I will return to this issue of "charismatic authority" later, because Shakespeare's history plays reveal a concern with it as a threat which had to be encountered, in order for it to be mastered and controlled by the monarchical state.

4   The "Theatricality" of Power?

Maravall argues that the reliance on the visual image is "typical of societies where a guided mass culture develops".[27] But his theorisation of the emergent state's reliance on a new kind of appeal to the inwardness of its addressees raises the further question: how, and/or to what extent, did these symbolic practices of monarchical centralism achieve their aims? The standard answer, in the wake of the New Historians' adaptations of Foucault's arguments on the theatrical nature of pre-Enlightenment punishments, is summed up as "power on display".[28] But we may well question whether the spectacles of violence or of royal presence really were "power on display", or indeed whether power could ever be displayed unequivocally. Power is not a thing that can be shown, although it certainly may benefit from the illusion of its unchallengeable presence. It is better understood as a relationship of inequality, supported by a wide network of practices including violence or the threat of violence, but in the long run the consent of the ruled is crucial, and that recognition has to be won. It is not simply given. So the main question remains: how was that consent won? Stephen Greenblatt's analyses of the theatricality of Royal power in the early modern period are similar to Maravall's arguments on the culture of the Baroque. But he equates the displays too directly with effective power. For example, writing of Queen Elizabeth of England, he states that she was:

> a ruler without a standing army, without a highly developed bureaucracy, without an extensive police force, a ruler whose power is constituted in theatrical celebrations of royal glory and theatrical violence visited upon the enemies of that glory.[29]

---

27   *Ibid.*
28   Tennenhouse 1986.
29   Greenblatt 1988, p. 64.

Greenblatt's factual point on Tudor power is generally accepted: England at that time did not have a highly developed bureaucracy or the regular standing armies characteristic of later Absolutist rule on the Continent. But Francis Barker's critical response to this assimilation of power to cultural display through "a common logic of figuration" makes a strong point. He argues that Tudor power was enforced through an extremely widespread judicial apparatus for the application of large-scale hangings (introduced on Sundays for the first time by Henry VIII, together with the endorsement of capital punishment in the articles of the new national Church), and the vast expansion of torture which was continued under his daughters. Under Elizabeth 1st there was also a widespread surveillance network controlled by Walsingham. And, particularly in the latter part of her reign, the Queen often resorted to violent measures to put down riots and rebellions. So Royal authority actually did have a sufficiently developed repressive apparatus at its disposal, and it is not the business of the historian to forget it.[30] But that does not fully dispose of Greenblatt's Foucauldian view of the "theatrical" nature of the pre-modern display of power. After all, a number of those measures, such as Sunday hangings, were clearly designed to increase their visibility and enhance their meaning too. Henry's appropriation of sacred time was perhaps almost as significant as his seizure of holy sites. The violence of his justice would be seen to be done on holy days in accordance with God's retribution, like the Friday beheadings in modern Saudi Arabia.

Stephen Greenblatt cites the example of Queen Elizabeth I as a visible spectacle supporting the fiction of transhistorical permanence which had been elaborated theoretically in the medieval doctrine of the King's Two Bodies:

> Her visible being was a hieroglyphic of the timeless corporate being with its absolute perfection, just as, in the words of Coke, "a king's crown was a hieroglyphic of the laws". She was a living representation of the immutable within time, a fiction of permanence. Through her, society achieved symbolic immortality and acted out the myth of a perfectly stable world, a world which replaces the flux of history.[31]

He goes on to argue that "kingship always involves fictions, theatricalism, and the mystification of power", suggesting that the Queen herself seems to have

---

30 Barker 1993, pp. 163–164 *et passim*. Essentially, Francis Barker objects to the theoretical aestheticisation of judicial violence which downplays its physical reality.
31 Greenblatt 1988, pp. 166–167. I will return to this in Chapter 7, to argue that the metaphor of the Great Theatre of the World should not be seen as a structure of belief, but as a response to crisis and a symptom of anxiety.

believed in the myth of her divine *persona ficta*. In support of this he cites her own words on royal theatricality: "We Princes are set on stages, in the sight and view of all the world duly observed".[32] And in the concluding pages of the same book he argues further that this ideology was generally accepted as the truth, expressed through the widespread analogy of the Great Theater of the World:

> The theater is widely perceived in the period as the concrete manifestation of the histrionic quality of life, and, more specifically, of power – the power of the prince who stands as an actor upon a stage before the eyes of the nation, the power of God who enacts His will in the Theater of the World.[33]

The brilliance of Greenblatt's insights, and the lucidity of his exposition, nonetheless leaves something unattended to. Firstly, of course, the theatre was also "widely perceived" as a place of illusions and deceptions. Clearly, Puritan condemnations of visible displays of every sort took this to extremes. But, even leaving that aside, to say that the monarch's subjects simply accepted the homology of the prince as an actor on the national stage with God on the cosmic one, is not only to describe an ideological illusion, which Greenblatt himself rightly calls "the mystification of power"; it is also to confirm the fantasy of transcendence in the spectators' minds, as though this *goal* of the monarchical display were an always already achieved illusion. This could be called an ideology, which Greenblatt does not describe as a discursive or symbolic struggle, but as an established structure of belief.[34] This is Althusser's version of the *interpellation* of the subject, who is "always already" subjected by the Ideological State Apparatus. Greenblatt's theoretical shift from the affirmation of a widespread structure of belief to the concept of "mystification" signals only that his own demystifying stance has already accepted that what he identifies as false (for our retrospective gaze) has also to be understood as historically true for the mentality of the period. This is a familiar historicist move, and it is grounded in the concept of a single structure of consciousness, like Foucault's epochal *episteme*. If it were true that everyone, or nearly everyone, simply

---

32   *Ibid.* Greenblatt does not see this unavoidable exposure as an admission of vulnerability.
33   *Ibid.* p. 253.
34   Stephen Greenblatt and others like Louis Montrose state that there was considerable disbelief among the elite, especially in Court circles. There was even a degree of covert atheism too. These are important points, but the quality of the belief constructed by the address to the non-elite, is surely just as important. The elite may have had motive enough to believe, but how were the subordinated brought to "desire their own repression", as Deleuze and Guattari put it?

believed that life itself was theatrical (or "histrionic"),[35] then it would follow that the gap between the "Theatre of the World" and reality would disappear, as he says. But then his "mystification" would become a redundant term since this all-encompassing mental construct of the age, would be everyone's version of the real. But, *pace* Greenblatt, such a theory grants to the absolutist fantasy (the monarch as "a living representation of the immutable within time") the uncontested prior achievement of its monological goal. Against this view of ideology as an underlying structure, there is a need to re-affirm the ideas of Bakhtin and Voloshinov developed in Chapter 3, namely that a single ideology is an illusion pursued in a struggle against rival ideologies in a field of dialogical conflict. Therefore any established dominant ideology is always shaped inwardly by anticipation, which is a desire to control (or even to prevent) the anticipated responses of its addressees. Any actor, whether on a stage or in a public square, is always engaged dialogically with his/her audience or spectators, and if the monarch was in an analogous position, it was a precarious one. In order to understand the spectacular displays, and their attempt to construct the monarch as a quasi-divinity, it is necessary to understand them dialogically, as complex forms of *addressivity* shaped inwardly by the anticipated resistance of their addressees.

Stephen Greenblatt could have quoted King James I's *Basilikon Doron*, in which the King uses the same theatrical metaphor as Queen Elizabeth in order to express privately the anxiety concealed by the public display. He warns his son that the King is placed on a stage "where all the beholders' eyes are attentively bent to look and pry into the least circumstances of their secretest drifts".[36] Christopher Pye in an essay on this theatricality very perceptively notes that there is an admission here of the constitutive contradiction between the display of power and its vulnerability. He relates this to the need to rethink the issue of royal power in terms of "the subject's desire" (not just royal anxiety). But he does not quite explain it:

> [T]he vulnerability and the terrifying power of the king's visible presence are in fact inseparable – the subject's desire to reduce the sovereign presence to the fully exposed object of his sight lends the regal eye its penetrating, and impenetrable power.[37]

To point to the presence of a contradiction "in fact" is very useful but it is not an explanation. What remains unexplained is why the subject's desire "to

---

35   John of Salisbury's "Totus mundus agit histrionem" was current among the literate.
36   Pye 1988, p. 279.
37   *Ibid.*, p. 280.

reduce the sovereign presence to the fully exposed object of his sight" could have given rise to the opposite impulse of "lending the regal eye its penetrating, and impenetrable power". The suggestion seems to be that the subjects in question were already so in awe of the sacred, which Pye calls the "mysterious origins of power", that they welcomed the framing distance provided by the theatricality in order to protect themselves from the monarch's dreadful gaze. That is psychologically possible perhaps, but it does not quite explain the subjects' positive desire to "lend the regal eye" this unidirectional "penetrating and impenetrable" power which is the cause of their fear.[38] There is a contrary logic, though, which could explain why these subjects might desire to protect the mystery of the "origins of power" *from their own critical gaze and disbelief.* Why? Such an explanation would be concerned with how the subjects could be brought to identify with the sovereign's anxieties to the point of curbing their own desire to reduce him/her to the level of a "fully exposed object". The desire to reduce the monarch to the level of an object is in effect a regicidal desire. So the restraining force within the subject would not be terror in the face of divine majesty, or not that alone, but *loyalty*, which was commonly called "love" at the time. Loyalty calls for the subject's repressive denial of his own rebellious desires. Under normal conditions, loyalty must be supported by unconscious guilt (unconscious because regicidal desire must not even be acknowledged, to prevent the risk of its being enacted). The real issue, then, is how loyalty to the monarch, not mere legality and the threat of sanctions, was made central to the construction of the form of subjectivity required by the nation state.

In sum, if Royal power in the early modern period depended on spectacle, this brings up the question as to how its spectating subjects could have been persuaded to suspend their disbelief and, above all, to desire the proffered illusion. The spectacle has to engage with its spectators' or audience's potential resistances in order to construct a will to believe. How they could they have been brought to desire their own repression, as Deleuze and Guattari put it?[39]

5 Capturing the Will to Believe

The spectacle of power, which claimed to make the "glory" of the monarch manifest, is better described as a show of strength, whether to intimidate or to

---

38 Pye's all-seeing eye as the source of royal power seems to locate this unidirectional gaze as the precursor of Bentham's panoptical gaze.
39 Deleuze and Guattari 1972, pp. 124–125.

reassure its addressees. However, the spectacular strategy of constructing an illusion of the awesome "presence" of power might imply that any admission of vulnerability would destroy that illusion. Moreover, if the illusion of power depended on fear alone, it could last only as long as the fear lasted. That is why a suggestion of the ruler's vulnerability could also be evoked through an alternative mode of *addressivity* aimed at securing loyalty, not fear alone. A significant example of this is Queen Elizabeth's famous speech at Tilbury where, expressing her intention to fight like a man, and a warrior descended from English Kings in the face of the Armada, she chose to emphasise her vulnerability as a woman and a virgin, linked by a very strong metonymy to the realm itself in need of defense. Especially in a crisis, a ruler requires loyalty or "love", not mere acquiescence, and loyalty requires the subjects' identification with the ruler and his/her projects. That is why, in an epoch when belief in appearances was already becoming more than a little shaky, the "theatrical" address could be deployed to evoke an anxiety in the subject, and a consequent desire to defend a ruler who was felt to be threatened. This evocation of anxiety was not always so explicit, and was certainly not always successful (rebellions and street riots did happen). But capturing the will to believe, and to act accordingly, was the true goal of all such public displays in an epoch when disbelief could plausibly be linked to social mayhem, and even religious civil war. Under circumstances of heightened anxiety, the ruler's power could become an object of desire for those subjects who sought its presence in the spectacle. Roy Strong provides an example when he observes that the Queen's virtually religious feast of her Accession Day ("a day on which the imperial cause triumphed over the papal") was not just a triumphant display of power, but a powerful "reminder" which intensified loyalty through evoking a fear of returning chaos:

> [But] although it was a celebration of a deliverance from darkness, it was also constantly reiterated that the forces of evil still menaced England both within and without. The chaotic hordes of the Antichrist of Rome were only kept at bay while God's handmaiden ruled. Chaos would be let loose if ever she ceased to guide the realm of England. It was an atmosphere charged with these thoughts that generated the fervent cult of the Queen.[40]

Here it is clear that even though an intimation of the monarch's vulnerability might undermine the appearances of power, it could also function to elicit in its addressees a "fervent" compensatory desire to believe, and to affirm that

---

40   Strong 1987, p. 127.

belief. But this means that the nature of belief has undergone a change. Instead of being an acceptance of appearances as either a direct expression of reality or an indirect allegorical expression of a concealed reality, it becomes a solicitation involving an act of will in the would-be loyal believer.[41]

Capturing the will to believe required the opposite of distance and awe, namely identification with the monarch, or other central power-holder, by the dangerous sections of the population whose aspirations and interests were in many respects opposed to those of the elite. Paradoxical as it may seem, supplementing the awe-inspiring display of power, the threatened status of the monarchy could also be deployed, provided that the absence of effective monarchical power was represented, and accepted by the *addressees*, as a return to chaos. In such cases, the thesis of "power on display" should be seen as doubled by the more seductive covert strategy of "vulnerability on display". And, curiously enough, such intimations of vulnerability, even if touched with instrumental and manipulative cynical reason (as is almost certainly the case revealed by Shakespeare's history plays), also came close to the truth, since the reality of the matter was indeed the vulnerability of the "hollow Crown" and its consequent need for support from its subjects. Through intimations of the monarch's vulnerability, a fear of chaos, of monstrous anarchy, and even of universal collapse, could be instilled in a populace whose energies and rebellious discontents were precisely the problem for the ruling elite seeking to control them. This amounts to saying that royalist ideology was secured by the kind of *addressivity* which did not simply rely on the subjects' unquestioning belief in the divine nature of monarchical power but sought to construct it (or bolster it) by evoking their existing anxieties, thus opening the way to a "willing suspension of disbelief", to borrow Shelley's felicitous phrase. It is not unquestioning belief that is crucial in this *via negativa*, but anxiety, which is the precondition for arousing the will to believe and to defend that belief in action. The basis of this capture of the subjects' desire is not only their repudiation of their rational tendency to doubt the ideological fictions sustaining the social hierarchy but, above all, of their own potentially rebellious desires. These must

---

41 Even in the sphere which we would now consider purely religious, many thinkers in the sixteenth and seventeenth centuries recognised that "the will" was the road to (or back to) belief on the brink of being lost. Pascal is just the best known nowadays. Maravall, 1986 p. 75, quotes Descartes' view that judgments are based "on passions by means of which the will lets itself be convinced and seduced beforehand", and Gracián's *El Heroe*: "conquering understanding means little if the will is not also won over", *ibid.,* p. 77. In Chapter 6 I will argue that Loyola's *Spiritual Exercises* likewise puts the exercitant's will at the centre of their rational method for securing his inner persuasion.

be inwardly silenced (along with the critical doubt), because for the loyal subject they are "guilty" desires.

6   The Solar Theatricality of Absolutism in Shakespeare's Henriad

There is an important distinction to be drawn between the New Historians' version of theatricality and the real theatre. It is not just that the reality of power cannot be equated with its display. The further point is that, while the real theatre may well be an institution which relays and even reinforces a dominant ideology, it also stages it (quite literally) by constructing a position of potentially critical "outsideness" for its audiences. Shakespearean theatre, in particular, often puts royal theatricality itself on display. As for to the display of power outside the theatre, there were plenty of contemporary examples of anxious recognition that the physical appearance of the ruler before the people was an inescapable part of his/her "theatrical" role, but that it was reversible, and carried with it the risk of demystification through familiarity, and even the reduction of the ruler to the level of despised object in the eyes of the surveying crowd. Maravall mentions several writers who discussed this very danger. I would add that this same anxiety shaped the thought of Macchiavelli too, since for him the perception of the ruler's vulnerability by the ruled was the principal danger to be strategically prevented. He recommended the theatrical use of both extreme violence and unexpected mercy, arguing that the successful ruler needs to be simultaneously an actor and secretive director, or in his striking phrase: *simulatore e dissimulatore.* This theme is explored in Shakespeare's *Henry IV*, in terms of the recurrent solar symbolism of contemporary Absolutist theatricality. Henry IV anxiously expounds to Prince Hal the dangers to "sun-like majesty", because he fears its degradation through his son's "vile participation" with the social dregs and the grotesque body of Falstaff. In Henry's speech, the success of the King's solar theatricality depends upon sustaining what Lacan calls the "scopic drive", not on satisfying it. The danger to be avoided is unlimited seeing, because the satisfaction of that desire leads to its collapse into glutted appetite. Henry observes that Richard II, whose throne he had taken, had already lost the illusory "presence" necessary to "sun-like majesty" because he was "daily swallow'd by men's eyes". He concludes:

> So, when he had occasion to be seen,
> He was but as the cuckoo is in June,
> Heard but not regarded; seen, but with such eyes
> As, sick and blunted with community,

> Afford no extraordinary gaze,
> Such as is bent on sun-like majesty
> But rather drows'd and hung their eyelids down,
> Slept in his face, and render'd such aspect
> As cloudy men use to their adversaries,
> Being with his presence glutted, gorg'd, and full.
>   1 HENRY IV, 3.2.74–85

Henry IV tells his son that the eyes of the surveying crowd threaten to devour any ruler who fails to maintain the distance and rarity of appearance which stimulates and sustains appetite without satisfying it. According to this extended metaphor, any crowd that is not dazzled by the solar majesty of the king, will consume that king and become like sated cannibals, "gutted, gorg'd and full" with his "presence". Henry instructs his son onstage, and the audience offstage, that the desire of the crowd is sustained by the distant solar image, and must never be allowed to become sated through familiar "community".

However, in Shakespeare's dramatisation of English history, Prince Hal proves himself masterful in the control of appearances, but not from the Olympian heights required by the Absolutist solar spectacle. In Parts One and Two of *Henry IV* he engages in a skillful theatricalisation of himself even when he participates in carnivalesque transgressions in complicity with the lower social orders. By the end of this performance, the duplicitous Prince Hal banishes Falstaff from his presence on pain of death, to be remembered only in "a dream" of his former self. When he submits to the Law in the form of the Chief Justice as to a new "Father", the unrestrained lower appetites of Falstaff are banished from the realm by the new King who has also overcome the rebellious spontaneity of Hotspur and the other nobles.[42] This theatrical outcome is anticipated earlier when Prince Hal announces to the audience his secret plan to stage his own "reformation". Like his father, he too identifies royal power with the display of "sun-like" presence constructed by artful means. But there is a major difference. He refuses to be like Richard II who rode too high in the mental chariot of his solipsistic solar illusions and therefore came down "like glistering Phaeton", the classical usurper who stole the chariot of his father, the sun-god. What is required is not this self-destructive delusion on the part of the monarch, but a new kind of theatricalized engagement with his future subjects. Prince Hal still compares himself to the sun, but the power of the solar image is no longer dependent on the distanced spectacle recommended by his father. Instead there will be a theatrically contrived unveiling:

---

[42] This is a brief summary of Chapter 10 in my *Anxious Pleasures:* Hall 1995.

> I know you all, and will awhile uphold
> The unyoked humour of your idleness.
> Yet herein will I imitate the sun,
> Who doth permit the base contagious clouds
> To smother up his beauty from the world,
> That when he please again to be himself,
> Being wanted he may be more wondered at
> By breaking through the foul and ugly mists
> Of vapours that did seem to strangle him. (1.2.192 ff)

Prince Hal openly identifies his planned revelation as a strategy for captivating his subjects. It depends on provoking their desire for the imaginary absent object (himself as solar King) which, "being wanted [he] may be more wondered at". This desired appearance will not be a static and distanced spectacle but an act of appearance from behind a veil. The moment of unveiling will produce the same quasi-religious "wonder" or *admiratio* which Maravall locates at the centre of the dynamic Baroque struggle for psychological control:

> And like bright metal on a sullen ground
> My reformation, glitt'ring o'er my fault
> Shall show more goodly and attract more eyes
> Than that which hath no foil to set it off.
> I'll so offend as to make offence a skill,
> Redeeming time when men think least I will. (1.2.208 ff)

Prince Hal departs from his father's advice only in the manner of his reliance on the solar image. He even comments openly on the drama of its future unveiling, knowing that the power of the image to evoke "wonder" resides in its "being wanted". Moreover his royal *coup de théâtre* will be a "reformation", however hypocritical the "offence" of its skillful contrivance. He even says that he will appear as the desired Saviour, whose hour of arrival is unknown, therefore "redeeming time" at the moment of his unveiling (the literal meaning of the Apocalypse). This contrived Royal usurpation of a major religious narrative is powerful, even though it borders on blasphemy and would have shocked some.

But to whom is the Prince's "I know you all" addressed? Here Robert Weimann's analysis of theatrical discourse is very useful. He argues that the theatrical utterance combines a speech act addressed to the other protagonists within the upstage *locus* position, with a speech act addressed simultaneously to the audience from the downstage *platea* position.[43] Weimann gives an illuminating historical account of the origins and development of this divided discourse, as it progressively dissociated itself from the participatory speech of communal ceremony. (For him this was still partially retained in the intermediate voice of the chorus in Greek tragedy). With the historical emergence of theatres a new social space came into being, whether in ancient Greece or again with the emergence of drama through its expulsion from religious ritual (and from the churches themselves in the late Middle Ages). This new space enables a community to become a partially distanced observer of its own conflicts. Bakhtin calls this space "outsideness", and at first he attributed its critical capability to the novel. For Weimann, the theatrical utterance combines two different modes of speech which originally depended on whether the actor was speaking from within the upstage *locus* position or addressing the audience directly from the open frontstage *platea* position. But his main point is that *all* developed theatre deploys utterances which combine both *locus* and *platea* potentialities simultaneously. In this instance, the Prince is ostensibly addressing Falstaff, Poins and company, who have just left the stage. But if it is also understood as an address to the real audience (from the *platea* position or across the boundary later to be framed and then marked by footlights), it is an extraordinary anticipation of his own self-unveiling by the simulating Prince. As the Prince takes the audience into his confidence, he unmasks the theatricality which supports royal power. But at the same time there is a promise to that audience of a gratification to come.

This is a theatricality which does not conceal; but nor does it merely denounce the Prince's "hypocrisy" (as some commentators suggest). As a double-voiced address to the audience, this speech functions in a way which anticipates the distancing or "alienation-effect" of the theatre championed by Bertolt Brecht (but this is a matter of theatrical form, not of ideological agreement). Like Brecht's theatre, it demands a reflective response. The Prince's promise of a self-unveiling to come confronts at least some in the audience with their need to decide: Is the King-to-be displaying diabolical hypocrisy (which would make the future King a deceitful "Macchiavellian" actor); or is such Macchiavellian acting perhaps a new kind of desirable political intelligence which requires the virtues of anticipation, self-control, and the deferral of immediate satisfactions, of appetite or of revenge, in the ruler and his subjects? To many in the audience of the time this deferral of satisfaction under the rule of the Law represented by his "second father", the Chief Justice, must have appeared preferable to both the Carnival rule of unbridled appetite represented by Falstaff on the one hand, and the noble spontaneity of the

---

43   Weimann 1978.

rebellious Hotspur on the other. It would also have appealed to those middle-class addressees who felt threatened by the unrestrained divine pretensions of solar Absolutism. The bourgeois spectator who is enabled to see through Royalist theatricality is nonetheless captivated by it. This is not because he simply believes the transcendental metaphysics supporting royal power (as Stephen Greenblatt argues). Rather, he is captivated by its power to captivate the threatening lower orders, whom we might call the social "groundlings". That power is commonly known as "charismatic", but its origin is socio-historical and is not a direct effect of the exceptional personality.

7 From Solar Absolutism to "Charismatic" Seduction

When the former Henry Bolingbroke, who has made himself into Henry IV, refers to a king's need for sun-like distance to sustain the feeling of awe in his subjects, he also fleetingly invokes his need for "robes pontifical". But his son sets out to perform a staged "reformation", through a much closer engagement with his subjects' dangerous desires. The old King has expressed his anxiety over the dynastic succession and the future of the kingdom because he fears that his son's "vile participation" undermines the illusions which must be sustained by the controlled distance of a Sun King. But the new King Henry V, in a well-known speech to his followers, presents himself as a warrior leader of his "band of brothers". This is *charismatic* leadership. It depends on his follower's perception of immediate personal presence (however illusory its contrivance may be), not on hierarchical distance and awe alone. That form of leadership requires precisely the need for the "vile participation" so feared by his father. Henry V's words on the "band of brothers" are part of a famous speech which has echoed down the ages, for instance in "the few" of Churchill's Battle of Britain speech in 1940, and in the "Band of Brothers" of Stephen Spielberg's TV series (2001) based on a war novel of 1992 with the same title. Remarkably, this historical memory is foretold in the speech itself. The new King Henry V explicitly contrasts the egalitarian brotherhood, which is about to be forged in battle on Saint Crispin's day, with the settled hierarchical comfort of the "gentlemen abed" back in England who, he says, will remember it and come to envy it:

> And Crispin Crispian shall ne'er go by,
> From this day to the ending of the world,
> But we in it shall be remembered –
> We few, we happy few, we band of brothers;
> For he that sheds his blood with me
> Shall be my brother; be he ne'er so vile,

> This day shall gentle his condition;
> And gentlemen in England now a-bed
> Shall think themselves accurs'd they were not here,
> And hold their manhoods cheap whiles any speaks
> That fought with us upon Saint Crispin's day.
>   HENRY V, 4.3.57ff

In this speech the "vile participation" feared by Henry IV is rhetorically transformed by his son into a nobility of brotherhood ("be he ne'er so vile/ this day shall gentle his condition"). He promises that this condition of warrior brotherhood will become a memory (but only a memory), which will outshine and shame the actual hierarchy of gentlemen. He adds that in their "accurs'd" state of mind, these "gentlemen now abed" will feel emasculated and "hold their manhoods cheap" when they compare themselves with the "band of brothers". Max Weber's observations on "charismatic authority" sound drily theoretical by comparison, but they throw great light on Prince Hal's rhetoric and the emotional response which it still elicits in its offstage audiences. According to Weber, "The corporate group which is subject to charismatic authority is based on an emotional form of communal relationship [*Gemeinde*]". This means that, "Disciples or followers tend to live primarily in a communistic relationship with their leader".[44] Henry V appeals to the authority based on this emotional relationship between the "band of brothers" and their leader but, even amidst his verbal overturning of hierarchical values, the promised relationship is clearly distinguished from the political structure back in England. It is strictly extra-territorial, existing only as a memory for another future and imaginary scene.

Weber argues that "charismatic authority" is dangerous because it is in radical conflict with all established forms of power. For as long as it maintains its provisional sway, there can be no official positions or hierarchical organisation:

> Within the sphere of its claims, charismatic authority repudiates the past, and is in this sense a specifically revolutionary force. It recognises no appropriation of positions of power by virtue of the possession of property, either on the part of a chief or of socially privileged groups.[45]

Charismatic authority is "revolutionary" for Weber because it "repudiates the past" (which may be a questionable definition of the term). Consequently, "in its pure form charismatic authority may be said to exist only in the process

---

44   Weber 1964, pp. 361–362.
45   *Ibid.,* pp. 361–362.

of originating. It cannot remain stable, but becomes either traditionalized or rationalized, or a combination of both".[46] This restorative transition from "revolutionary" to "traditionalized" and/or "rationalized" charismatic authority guarantees the principle of inheritance which charismatic authority actually threatens:

> To a very large extent the transition to hereditary charisma or the charisma of office serves in this connexion as a means of legitimising existing or recently acquired powers of control over economic goods. *Along with the ideology of loyalty*, which is certainly by no means unimportant, allegiance to hereditary monarchy in particular is very strongly influenced by the consideration that all inherited property and all that which is legitimately acquired would be endangered *if subjective recognition of the sanctity of succession to the throne were eliminated*. It is by no means fortuitous that hereditary monarchy is more acceptable to the propertied classes than, for instance, to the proletariat [emphases added].[47]

First among the forms of "traditional authority" was the "sanctity" of the bloodline. To us "blood" may appear to be an arbitrary or empty signifier (except to racists and to aristocrats). But in the Middle Ages the bloodline was an indispensable form of social rationality, since it underwrote landownership, and the transmission of property and power across the generations, irrespective of any particular leader's "charismatic" or personal qualities. In that sense it was a social rationality which transcended time, no less than modern "bureaucratic" authority. But Weber's brief reference above to "the ideology of loyalty" is very important because it raises the question (which he himself does not raise) as to how even the non-propertied could be brought to support emotionally the hierarchical forms of their subordination. The monarchy's need to make an appeal to charismatic authority, despite the threat which it posed to the hierarchical social order, becomes clear here. The "ideology of loyalty" was required to sustain a feeling of solidarity or "brotherhood" within the "imagined community" of the nation state (Benedict Anderson), despite the normal everyday experience of the hierarchy maintained by that state. Moreover, it still enables most people's daily experience of that reality to be overlooked or set aside. Weber does not stress the duplicitous nature of this "charismatic authority" when it is reinvented amidst the apparatus of the modern state, although he does note its contradictory nature when he calls it "routinised charisma". In that modern context it is supported only by its spectacular address

---

46   *Ibid.* p. 364.
47   *Ibid.* pp. 372–3.

to potentially hostile audiences or spectators, whose loyalty has to be won over and over again. They have to be constantly persuaded to renounce their own discontents. Its remarkable success enables the nation state to be experienced as an "imagined community" persisting beyond the fearful state of emergency where charismatic authority may have once exercised a real if transient power.

8 Carnival and Charisma: the Concealed Connection

In Shakespeare's *Henry V* the new King's risky egalitarian appeal to the "band of brothers" is as skillfully manipulated as the dangerous equality represented by the Carnival body of Falstaff and his companions had been in the two parts of *Henry IV*. These history plays dealing with the emergence of the modern state in England, show remarkable insight into the monarchy's need to address, and eventually master, the rebellious social impulses of its subjects, if the modern state were to persist. The modern state's need to appropriate for itself the dangerous power of charismatic leadership is negotiated by Shakespeare's Prince Hal, as he duly becomes Henry V. This appropriation is normally concealed. But it is brought to light theoretically for us by Pierre Clastres' *Society against the State*.[48]

In this anthropological work, Clastres argues that the so-called primitive tribes, which coexisted alongside the great pre-Columbian empires in South America, were genuine examples of real and effective charismatic authority as it once existed nearly everywhere. He points out that the widespread tribal practices of bestowing sexual and other privileges and powers upon a charismatic leader for a limited period (usually for the purposes of war or other states of emergency) were always followed by his ritual dethronement, often by killing him. In his view, these rituals were tribal society's collective way of preventing the hereditary accumulation of power and property through lineal descent. Clearly, that power inherited through the sanctified bloodline is central to the form of authority which Weber calls "traditional" in the European context too. According to Clastres, it was precisely that accumulation of power beyond the life of a particular leader which the South American tribes had seen, even in pre-Columbian times, as supports for the oppressive imperial structures of the city-based empires in their vicinity. But, whether they were conscious of it or not, Clastres' key point is that the dethronement and murder of the leader was the only means available to the collective for preserving *the charismatic form of rule*. Through these culturally prescribed acts, the collective affirmed itself

---

48 Clastres 1974.

as the true source of the sovereign power and privileges which it bestowed on a particular leader in recognition of his special leadership qualities, but only for a limited period. For anyone who has considered Bakhtin's theories concerning Carnival laughter in his book on Rabelais, and especially the ritual elevation of *le roi pour rire* (the king for laughter's sake) followed by his laughing dethronement, Clastres' work is enormously suggestive. It is precisely this comic elevation of Falstaff as King in the Boar's Head Inn (*1 Henry IV*, 1.iv) followed by his anticipated dethronement and his final expulsion on pain of death at the end, which is incorporated into the two parts of Shakespeare's *Henry IV*. The appropriation of the Carnival-Lent cycle, followed by its suppression at the hands of the modernising state, has been noted and analysed by others.[49] But shadowing Bakhtin's analyses of this celebratory collective laughter, and his somewhat idealised "folk" memory which sustains the Carnival's repeated overturning of the oppressive social hierarchy, there is this underlying conflict between the rival versions of sovereign authority identified by Clastres. His theory enables us to see that the laughing elevation and the subsequent dethronement of the Carnival King, like the many other social inversions permitted by the Carnival festivities in general, was a symbolic affirmation of the sovereign authority of the oppressed in the face of their actual oppression and dispossession. It is this egalitarian "memory" which the warrior King Henry V confronts and reconciles rhetorically with the requirements of the new state. Critics who accuse him of hypocrisy are right but they miss the point; it is the emergent modern state itself which is duplicitous because it has to be. In order to come into being and to persist, the monarchy had to appropriate for itself the social forces which threatened its existence. They had to be to overcome and surpassed in the new state form. That is the dialectical drama enacted in the *Henriad*.

There may be a rather too rosy populism colouring Bakhtin's account of the Carnival and its origins in a millennial "folk" memory, but it raises a pertinent question: was the Carnival's purely symbolic overthrow of those in high places really the trace of a *longue durée* historical memory of far earlier social relations, as Bakhtin suggests (probably influenced by Cassirer)? If so, those relations would undoubtedly have been sorely missed in the face of the oppressive permanence of the social hierarchy and all the idealising sublimations mobilised by church and state to justify it. That, at least, is Bakhtin's version of the popular Carnival practices in the Middle Ages, which he traces back through an improbably long historical continuum to earlier times, and eventually to

---

49   Bristol 1985, p. 206 calls attention to the new King's institution of a "permanent Lenten policy"; Cf. Hall 1995, p. 215ff.

mankind's shared primal resistance to the terrors of nature.[50] But a far more probable account of this millennial "memory" of terror overcome by laughter is that it was engendered retroactively out of the actual historical experiences of oppression. This is not to reject Bakhtin but to re-read him. The retroactive production of a memory is the process which Freud calls *Nachträglichkeit,* or "retro-action". Freud has recourse to this concept to explain how a traumatic symptom has a dual source, both in an earlier shock whose memory has been repressed and in the subject's more recently experienced shock, which evokes the earlier one by repeating it.[51] Even as the earlier shock is recalled, its memory is still concealed behind a screen of misrecognition which protects the subject from becoming conscious of it, but it is also the source of his/her symptoms. However, in the context of the collective laughter of the Carnival, I am arguing for an inversion. The actual source of the collective shock concealed within its laughing recall, was never a single traumatic event in the remote past (which Freud in *Totem and Taboo* theorises as the primal murder of the Father) but the many events experienced in the real ongoing historical repetitions of social oppression. Accordingly, the laughter of the Carnival was the collective response to those shocks, and it constructed retroactively the pleasurable "memory" of the time of their overthrow. Such a memory is potentially a revolutionary anticipation of a deliverance yet to come.[52] That is why it could usually be enacted only on a special scene outside normal time, where it was shielded by laughter from conscious recognition, and therefore from acknowledgement of guilt by the "loyal" subject who could not laugh if his rebelliousness was too apparent.

In *Totem and Taboo* Freud treats the collective murder of the father by the "primal horde" as a matter of tragic horror arising from a repressed memory of parricidal guilt, which he later theorised as the basis of the Oedipus complex. For Freud this primal memory persists in the unconscious because the parricidal/regicidal desire and its imagined re-enactment have to be repudiated if civilisation is to continue. For Bakhtin, by contrast, its re-enactment in the

---

50 Bakhtin 1968, p. 335, interprets these primal terrors in the terms of the Romantic sublime. I will return to this at the beginning of Chapter 8.
51 Freud 2003.
52 Even in Christian texts this revolutionary "memory" can be found. The *locus classicus* is Mary's exultant joy at her pregnancy with the future Saviour: "He hath put down the mighty from their seats, and exalted them of low degree. He hath filled the hungry with good things; and the rich he hath sent empty away" (Luke 1, 52–53). This memory is a promise, which is central to Bertolt Brecht's *Caucasian Chalk Circle* set in a time of terror onstage and offstage. Against the narrative of that endlessly repeated terror there is a carnivalised narrative recalling "a time that was almost just". (Cf. Hall 1985, p. 127ff).

Carnival was a liberating "return of the repressed", but without guilt thanks to Carnival laughter. He quotes Goethe's positive report of the joyful parricidal cry in the Roman carnival: "Sia amazzato il signor padre!", accompanied by the significant gesture of snuffing out the paternal candle.[53] Bakhtin emphasises the leveling laughter of the Carnival crowds, their cancellation of all hierarchies, and their joyful overthrow of authority, rather than the repressed memory of parricide by the "primal horde". But this guilty "memory" is detectable within its laughing inversion. Bakhtin does not make explicit this connection between the joking by the Carnival crowd and the normally "unthinkable" (i.e unconsciously thought and desired) crimes of parricide and regicide, but he does hint at it:

> This admirable carnivalesque interjection of the boy merrily threatening his father with death and blowing out his candle *needs no further comment* [emphasis added].[54]

Towards the end of *Totem and Taboo*, Freud himself states that the primal murder of the father does not have to have been a historical event for it to be psychologically true. The concept of an originating historical event is likewise not necessary for Bakhtin's counter-narrative of the laughing symbolic overthrow of the socially constructed repression, which according to Freud is held in place by unconscious "Oedipal" guilt. Bakhtin writes of the laughter of the Carnival crowd as their overcoming of fear, but those subjects' inward rebellion was more significant than that supposedly conscious act. It was above all their rebellion against the unconscious anxiety which normally maintained their loyalty to the dominant order.

9   Carnival and Dialectics

The conflict of sovereignties barely concealed within the Carnival inversions has another aspect. The monarchy's reliance on the monarch's personal "charismatic authority" to control the mobile *vulgus* carried with it the tacit admission that the monarch's power depended upon capturing their loyalty. But at the same time, the centralising monarchy's aspiration to Absolute ("unbound") rule sought to deny the monarch's dependency upon his/her subjects' consent. Weber observes the contradictory nature of the "routinization of charisma":

---

53   Bakhtin 1968, p. 251.
54   *Ibid.*

As a rule the process of routinization is not free of conflict. In the early stages personal claims on the charisma of the chief are not easily forgotten and the conflict of the charisma of office or of hereditary status with personal charisma is a typical process in many historical situations.[55]

The point that this historical conflict is "not easily forgotten", either by the king or by his subjects, should be made more strongly and should not be relegated to "the early stages" alone. Any recourse to "charismatic" appeal by a ruler was troublingly close to the Carnival's covert reminder, through the laughing elevation and overthrow of its king or other office-holders, that the ultimate source of royal authority lay with the consent of the ruled. Weber noted explicitly that, "It is recognition on the part of those subject to authority that is decisive for the validity of charisma".[56] The important point is that the ultimate source of charismatic authority does not lie in the qualities of the leader (divinely bestowed or not) but in the social act of the recognition of those qualities by his followers, because that recognition makes them willing to be his subjects (for the time being, at least). Weber's observation seems to be indebted to Hegel's notion of the crucial role played by recognition in his Master and Slave dialectic. Slavoj Žižek makes a point close to this in his *Sublime Object of Ideology* when he picks up on Lacan's paradox that the madman who thinks he's a king is no madder than the king who thinks he's a King (the capital letter matters here because it denotes the illusion of an essential quality).[57] But Žižek is not theorizing the "mad" laughter of the Carnival celebrations. He glosses Lacan to show that there is no such thing as a king outside the social relations within which the identity of the King is actually constructed by the recognition of "his" subjects. He quotes Marx in *Capital*, who makes a general point on individual identity which Bakhtin could have made (as well as Lacan), concerning the perception of any self being dependent upon the gaze of another. Marx goes on to identify the significant misrecognition in this social establishment of the royal identity:

> Such expressions of relations in general, called by Hegel reflex categories, form a very curious class. For instance, one man is king only because other men stand in the relation of subjects to him. They, on the contrary, imagine that they are subjects because he is king.[58]

---

55   Weber 1964, p. 370.
56   *Op. cit.,* p. 359.
57   Lacan, *Ecrits* 1 (Collection Points) page 159, note 21. See also Wilden page 129, note 102.
58   Marx 1974, p. 63; Žižek 1989, pp. 24–25.

Marx focuses our attention on the assumed *a priori* identity of the King as a delusion in the subjects' imagination. This delusion arises from the subjects' failure to see that the royal identity is not the source but the consequence, of an unequal social relationship of power. More importantly for Marx, the delusion meant that the subjects have become blind, or rather have somehow been made blind, to the fact that they have the potential to reverse the relationship and revoke the royal identity. In Marx's version of this ideologically induced misrecognition, we can plainly see his reformulation of the Hegelian dialectic of the Master and Slave in order to explain a "political unconscious", even though he does not use that term. It is easy to see why the Absolute monarchs wished to deny their dependence upon the recognition of their subjects, even while paradoxically striving to gain it or retain it through theatricalised self-display. From the rulers' viewpoint, the Master-Slave dialectic amounted to a democratic threat, but it was a threat which had to be met with a measure of guile, if not by the ruler himself then by those specialists in charge of his public presentation. Hegel's dialectic which makes the Master dependent on recognition by the Slave or Bondsman is a theoretically formulated reminder which is remarkably close to the half-forgotten material practices of the Carnival's enthronements and dethronements of the King for laughter's sake (*le roi pour rire*).

Although Royal power may have refused to admit its need to appeal to the populace for its support, it did have to make such an appeal, just like any warrior leader of the early feudal epoch. But wherever the hereditary principle became securely established, the personal qualities of a monarch became merely accidental. In his *Elements of the Philosophy of Right*, Hegel sets out this logic when he argues that if the king's personal qualities mattered, hereditary monarchy would be the most irrational form of government possible; but since they do not matter, the hereditary principle in the modern monarchy is actually a guarantee of its rationality! All that is required is an office-holder to ratify the laws in a purely formal statement of will. Such emptiness at the centre could not have pleased the Hohenzollerns who, like all Absolutists, wished to retain the sanctity of the bloodline to underwrite personal rule. This is where the divinisation stressed by Maravall retains its importance, even though he does not explore the contradiction between "charisma" and "office", whose concealment meant that the monarch's need for recognition had to be denied even as it was actively sought. The monarch's denial of his dependency on his subjects' recognition developed to extremes in 17th century France under the Sun King. In England, where the power of the commons had to be more openly acknowledged and bargained with, this denial of reciprocity did not reach such monological extremes until Charles Stuart mistakenly attempted to eliminate that impediment to absolute rule.

10 Anticipation, Prevention, and Unconscious Guilt

Benedict Anderson's book on the origins of nationalism has made the concept of the "imagined community" quite familiar.[59] Briefly, he argues that the nation state was first brought into being linguistically, as a unifying project before becoming an established fact. In his historical argument the unifying standard language, promoted by the power of post-Gutenberg "print capitalism", was a major agency in building the consensual basis for the formation of the nation state. At the same time it downgraded the local non-privileged languages to the level of mere dialects. This argument is clearly derived from Gramsci's idea of linguistic hegemony and, as a historical thesis it has much to be said for it. But I have simply reintroduced a point not made by Anderson, namely that the "imagined community" also came into existence by virtue of the threatening fragmentation of the social order, and the consequent anxieties which it was called upon to overcome. The historical role of the monarchical state in overcoming that fragmentation and its attendant terrors, not only by coercion but also by capturing a consensual desire, cannot be set aside. Moreover, the nation state is still a field of stabilized conflict, and it continues to be "imagined" as a community in direct defiance of much of the evidence, including certain painful experiences of its real hierarchical divisions and exclusions. In short, the nation state is certainly a historical fact now, but the "imagined community" which sustains it functions as a wishful repair of its real inward rifts, and even as a strengthening consolation at times. In this respect it is very like the religious "heart of a heartless world" (Marx) which it partially replaced. It is also easily imagined as a community under threat from internal or external enemies, so that the desire for its protective order can rapidly become an anxious nostalgic demand for its defense or restoration. This reactive desire may take a socially aggressive direction, aimed either at a foreign enemy or a domestic scapegoat. That is all too familiar. But it also takes the form of an internalised aggression against the subject's own rebellious desires, in an act of internal policing to which Freud attributes the formation of the *super-ego*. That is to say, the aggression against the scapegoat (whether as mockery or as physical violence) and the repressive self-policing are two complementary forms of loyalty to the existing order.

There is a connection between this inward self-policing and social anxiety. Within the discursive strategies required to construct the secular "imagined community" around the figure of the monarch (or other figures like elected Presidents, unelected Generals, or even abstractions like the Republic, the

---

59   Anderson 1983.

Fatherland etc.) the more precarious that central figure is felt to be, the greater is the demand that the potentially rebellious forces should hold *themselves* in check. Subjectively, such identification with a vulnerable authority figure means accepting that one's own aspirations and desires are potentially disruptive, dangerous, and even monstrous. This self-condemnation, or fear of one's own desires, is what we call "guilt", and here Freud is right: it depends on the self's loving identification with an authority figure, and the loyal denial of the rebellious hatred which the imposition of authority provokes. In his family romance, the beloved and secretly hated authority figure is the Father, and in the anthropological perspectives of *Totem and Taboo* it is the already murdered Father of the "primal horde", who is suggestively close to the king in monarchical societies. The concept of identification carries with it this further ambiguity, to which Freudian psychoanalysis has alerted us: *viz.* to imagine oneself in the position of the ruler, or father figure, is at the same time to be in potential rivalry with him. Taken to extremes, it can amount to the quite common "mad" dream of being the King (or Napoleon, or Christ etc.). Seen in broader terms than the supposedly primary structure of the nuclear family, the installation of guilt to restrain this rebellious rivalry, which Freud attributes to the *super-ego*, is the key to the subject of the nation state. Through this agency, the modern subject is transformed into vigilant policeman and distorting censor of his own desires. This loyalty depends far less on the display of power on the part of an authority figure than on the more truthful, and perhaps therefore more cunning, intimation of the weakness at the centre (hence the increased social need for its confirmation within every individual). Anxiety and guilt secure individual and group loyalty far more effectively than state violence which, however necessary as the last resort, is a very temporary and unstable form of power.

Unconscious guilt does not necessarily denote an actual transgression subsequently repressed as a forgotten, unconscious memory. This act of forgetting by some individuals may sometimes be the case when there has been an actual rebellion or revolution which is subsequently repudiated. But unconscious guilt more commonly arises from an anticipated future act whose possibility as real act is denied (in psychoanalytical terms, negated or "foreclosed") by the very act of anticipation which prevents it. Despite the apparent paradox, the nature of unconscious guilt becomes clear here. It is the potential outcome of an act of transgression which is anticipated and therefore prevented in the thoughts/desires of the loyal subject him/herself (making it paradoxically unthinkable and yet thought). Moreover, this preventive avoidance of an act or a thought which could lead to a subject's consciousness of guilt, makes him/her responsible for upholding the forbidding law. Such a subject is not only answerable *to* the law, as in any system of criminal justice which specifies which acts are "guilty" in objective terms. In upholding the forbidding law against rival challenges even within the self, the subject assumes responsibility *for* its continuing existence as Law. The subject's moral "sense of responsibility", as it is usually called, rests upon the repudiation of "guilty" or irresponsible desires. The laughter of the Carnival festivities momentarily lifted that burden.

CHAPTER 6

Repairing the Universe: Mysticism as Loss and Longing

> Buscas a Roma en Roma, o peregrino,
> Y en Roma misma no la hallas ...
> (*You seek Rome in Rome, oh pilgrim/ And in Rome herself you do not find her*)
>   Francisco de Quevedo

∴

In the last chapter I discussed the construction of the nation state as an "imagined community" with the quasi-divine figure of the Monarch at its centre. This required its subjects' willing suspension of disbelief, which was achieved through various kinds of spectacular or "theatrical" *addressivity* (Bakhtin). But this in turn raises the problematic nature of belief, including religious belief, in an epoch when there was a widespread suspicion of all appearances. Belief no longer goes without saying. It becomes a matter of anxious affirmation, or desire to believe, in the face of contradictory experience.

In his study of mystical discourse in Spain and France, Michel de Certeau points out that the perception of a universal fragmentation in the early modern period called for repair. But however paradoxical it may seem, this desire for a single restored order engendered two distinct but interrelated aspirations: religious sectarianism and political rationalism, each with its now separated "frames of reference" and modes of discourse:

> To gain a perspective on the process which slowly replaced a divided Christianity with national *political* units, breaking down the social organization of universal belief into sects, "retreats", and "*spiritual*" communities, it is necessary to take a more general view that includes a recognition of the socio-political instability of the age and the fragmentation of its frames of reference. As a matter of fact, the "Macchiavellian moment" and the "mystic invasion" coincide. The project of constructing an order amid the contingencies of history (the problem of the reason of State)

and the quest to discern in our earthly, fallen language the now inaudible Word of God (the problem of the spiritual subject) arose simultaneously from the dissociation of cosmic language and the Divine Speaker. In addition, these two complementary restoration projects have recourse to the same "ecclesial" heritage of a unifying whole, although they express it henceforth in specialized modes: for one, the reason of State, for the other, the "community of saints".[1]

There is a political aspect to this argument about the psychological response within Christianity which sought to overcome "the fragmentation of its frames of reference". When he observes that "a multitude of microcosms appear, as reductions and replacements for the previous dismembered macrocosm", this means that not only the religious sects but also the monarchies could see themselves and strive to be seen by others, as agencies of rescue from universal collapse and as defenders of the otherwise lost transcendental connection. (This gives meaning to the later report, fictive or not, of Louis XVI's Apocalyptic cry: "Après moi, le Déluge"). De Certeau takes up Lacan's idea of the psychotic patient's terror of the "body in pieces" and applies it to the collective body. I would add that if there were countless representations of the territorial state as an integrated Royal body in this age of crisis (and there were), this visual organicism should be understood as an address to the beholder's underlying fear of fragmentation and the compensatory desire for its reassuring repair. De Certeau's reference to "these two complementary restoration projects" and their "shared 'ecclesial' heritage of a unifying whole" links the emergent rationalizing "Macchiavellian" State to the "community of saints", through their shared sense of crisis. At the same time, however, this emphasis on their shared response does not deny the well-known fact that they also tended to become rivals in their struggle to occupy the disappearing sacred centre. The struggle between them was sometimes overt, as in Henry VIII's England where the Monarch replaced the leader of the universal Church, and sometimes covert, as in most Catholic countries where the struggles between the universal claims of Ultramontanism and royal or princely interests ("regalian rights" in France and Spain) followed their own semi-concealed rhythms.

De Certeau argues that the "community of saints" became divided into sects, each of which was a fragment which aimed at restoring the universal whole with itself as the basis. The same could be said of the discourse of individual mystics like Saint Teresa of Avila or Saint John of the Cross, whose inward subjectivity became a scene of intimate dialogue with the otherwise absent

---

1   Certeau 1986, p. 87.

God. This "mystic speech" in dialogue with its absent Other made the subject's desire the scene of the discursive repair of the rift between the human and the divine. Such a turn towards inward subjectivity as the scene of universal repair is very important. It even anticipated Descartes' rational reconstruction of religious certainty on the basis of those inward "intuitions" which he held to be beyond doubt since they escaped the deceptions of sensual perception. This turn towards inward certainty also made the "mystics" and the Illuminists (*Alumbrados*) extremely suspect to the institutional defenders of universal Catholicism, particularly the Inquisition. It seemed to them to hover dangerously close to the Protestant heresy with its proclamation of the possibility of direct inward communication between the soul and God without the mediation of the Church. Moreover, the signs of this supposed inward encounter with the Holy Spirit were difficult to distinguish from witchcraft and possession by the Devil. Saint John, Saint Teresa, and even Loyola at times, fell under suspicion of heterodoxy, not so much for their projects of reform within the Church as for their suspect "Illuminist" basis.[2]

De Certeau includes the militant discourse of Ignatius of Loyola in this category of "mystic speech" [*mystique*] which grew out of a consciousness of loss and engendered the corresponding desire to overcome it:

> Sixteenth- and seventeenth-century *mystics* [*mystique*] proliferated about a loss. It is the historical figure of that loss, making readable an absence that has multiplied the productions of desire.... It is the ambition of a Christian radicalism traced on a background of decadence or "corruption", *within a universe that is falling apart and must be repaired*. It reiterates at the level of biographical experience all the vocabulary of the Church Reformation: division, wounds, sickness, lying, desolation, and so on. Individual bodies tell the story of the institutions of meaning.[emphasis added][3]

This shared response to disintegration explains how mystic speech "deconstructed from within the values which they held to be essential".[4] De Certeau even suggests that this pursuit of a lost or vanishing object constitutes the unwritten and unrecognised pre-history of the conception of desire to be found

---

2 Cf. Menéndez Pelayo 1956, pp. 180–8. This ultra-conservative historian fills several further pages justifying the Inquisition and relying on their judgments to distinguish between real and fake mysticism.
3 Certeau 1986, pp. 13–14.
4 *Ibid.*, p. 7.

later as the basis of Freudian and Lacanian psychoanalysis.[5] As for its historical conditions of possibility, he invokes Lucien Goldmann's reading of Jansenist spirituality in *The Hidden God* as the "product of a class which was in the process of losing its powers", in order to argue that the Spanish mystics were similarly displaced and marginalised. They too were bereft of status, identity, and a future, being largely from the *hidalguía*, the former knightly class doomed to loss of status (like Don Quijote), or else from *converso* origin like Saint Teresa of Ávila. The latter social group were suspected of maintaining a secret Jewish or Moorish identity, and so felt doubly excluded (or "exiled") from Spain's increasingly hierarchical and racist society.[6] But he adds that this particular social provenance of the Spanish and French mystics *sensitised them to the far more general sense of loss which afflicted the whole of Western Christendom in the early modern period*:

> That situation was intensified by another, which was, for believers of the period, indissolubly bound to the first: the humiliation of the Christian tradition. Within that tattered Christendom they experienced a fundamental defection, that of the institutions of meaning. They lived the decomposition of a cosmos and were exiled from it. They were driven out of their country by a history that degraded them. *Super flumina Babylonis*: a theme repeated indefinitely. They were filled with a mourning unmitigated by the rapture of new ambitions.[7]

Even the Scriptures, "that opaque reserve for believing and making others believe", gave no grounding for reassurance, having become as corrupt as the Churches:

> They obscured the spoken Word, the presence of which they were to have prolonged. To be sure, they still marked the spot, but in the form of "ruins" – a word that haunted the discourse of those who called for reform.[8]

De Certeau is careful in his formulations, because they have to cover the projects and language strategies of such diverse figures as Ignatius of Loyola, St Teresa of Avila, Saint John of the Cross, and the French mystic Surin. Nonetheless, in their very different ways they all shared the same drive to restore the

---

5   *Ibid.*, pp. 8–9.
6   *Ibid.*, pp. 22–23.
7   *Ibid.*, p. 25.
8   *Ibid.*

lost integration. De Certeau is close to Walter Benjamin's view of the Baroque imagination as a despairing response to a universe full of wounds,[9] when he refers to the mystics' response as an orthopedic restoration "of a universe that is falling apart *and must be repaired*". This compulsion, arising out of a perception of fragmentation which must be overcome, underpins De Certeau's recourse to the theory of desire arising from anxiety and "lack in being" (*manque à être*) which he takes from Lacan.

Perhaps because of his own membership of the Jesuit order, de Certeau's perspective as a historian is closely identified with his subjects' melancholic experience of the collapse and their response to the threat of fragmentation. But, seen from a dialogical standpoint, the absent cause of this "fragmentation of the frames of reference" was surely their multiplication, and the consequent competitive rivalry between their sources of authority. This expanded rivalry of discourses not only threatened the unquestioned nature or "givenness" of the single "frame of reference" (De Certeau) but made it an absent object of desire with an intensity that was not possible previously. The desired singularity emerged only at the moment of its eclipse, when this still unnamed "totality" became a lost object for the subject precisely because the new plurality or "diabolical" proliferation of discourses undermined its continuing unquestioned existence.

The compulsion to restore the universal integrity, whose loss could not be fully acknowledged, was entrusted to the intimations of the soul's desire for God, and these subjective experiences were uncovered as testimony to His concealed presence within every questing individual, *contemplative and militant alike*. There is a significant hint of Jewish mourning in De Certeau's reference to Psalm 137, *Super flumina Babylonis*, which for him obliquely refers to the "internal exile" experienced by these *conversos*. The key here is that while they wept "by the waters of Babylon", they "remembered Sion" which they vowed never to forget. Saint John of the Cross wrote his own Christianised version of this psalm in his *Cántico Espiritual*. But De Certeau's description of these mystics' melancholy as a "mourning unmitigated by the rapture of new ambitions" somewhat downplays the positive celebratory raptures in the writing of Saint Teresa, and in the feminine poetic voice of the otherwise ascetic Saint John of the Cross, to which I will return. De Certeau's general argument about all these mystics is that "their goal is to disappear into what they disclose". That is to say, their ultimate goal was not subjective self-expression, but to make the absent God reveal himself in the limited worldly language through which he was sought. But this also means that their goal was no longer just the

---

9   Benjamin 1977.

traditional one of the ultimate salvation of the soul of the individual pilgrim, or even the individual soul's ecstatic joy anticipated as the consummation of the union with God (which was already part of the Christian mystical tradition). Behind even these fulfillments was the intensified desire to repair the rift that was opening everywhere between the Word of God and the real, experienced world of his creation. This restorative goal is where the projects of active ascetic militants like Ignatius of Loyola and the sensuous contemplative mystics like Saint Teresa of Avila and Saint John of the Cross coincide (in the case of Saint Teresa, even within a single person) in a way which inevitably appears paradoxical to us.

1 The Reactionary Activist: a Serious Quijote?

In 1609 the former courtier and soldier, Iñigo López de Loyola, was beatified under the borrowed name of Ignatius. He had adopted this new name from an early Church father, when he had changed his life to become a soldier for Christ. The narration of that life, published under the title of *Reminiscences*, was dictated near its end (between 1553 and 1555) to a trusted member of his order, Luis Gonçalves da Câmara. It did not originally bear the title of *Autobiography*, which it now has, because it was not intended as the celebration of a particular individual but as a record and a testimony. Still, this particular protagonist and narrator could aptly be described as a "charismatic" figure whose recorded experience was intended to lend support to the continuing existence of the order which he had founded. So the document itself exemplifies Max Weber's view of the need for charismatic leadership to become "regularised" if it is to outlast its founder. Writing is the instrument of this regularisation, but this written record carefully establishes its own oral origins in the founder's words. His insistence that his words be transcribed by an amanuensis enables Loyola to eschew the vainglory which a heroic founding narrative inevitably invites. That is why he refers to himself throughout in the third person, as the Pilgrim. This exemplary modesty is particularly important because the narrative of the Pilgrim's conversion starts with his imitation of an epic hero, in a manner strikingly similar to the comic hero of Cervantes' famous novel. At this early point in his account, he relates an episode from his youth (March, 1522), when his devotion to the cause of Christ coexisted with his equally passionate imitation of the novels of chivalry:

> And he went on his way to Montserrat, thinking, as was always his habit, of the deeds he was to do for the love of God. And because he had his

whole mind full of those things from *Amadis of Gaul* and books of that sort, he was getting some thoughts in his head of a similar kind. Thus he decided to keep a vigil of arms for a whole night, without sitting or lying down, but sometimes standing up, sometimes on his knees, before the altar of Our Lady of Montserrat, where he had resolved to abandon his clothes and clothe himself in the armour of Christ.[10]

The similarity of this remembered act to the famous episode in Chapter 3 of the First Part of *Don Quijote*, published 50 years later (1605), is quite striking, although in the comic novel the changed setting of the vigil to an inn courtyard is a significant degradation. But this similarity is not as surprising as it might seem, since the remembered actions of the former Iñigo de Loyola and those of the fictional Don Quijote were both imitations of a vigil by Esplandián, the son of Amadís of Gaul, in *Las Sergas de Esplandián*, Montalvo's 1527 sequel to his better known *Amadís de Gaula*. There is no need to suppose that there was any intent on Cervantes' part to parody Loyola's text, even supposing that he knew it.[11] The important issue is that for Ignatius as retrospective narrator, no less than for Cervantes, there is a shared critical concern with the power over the imagination exercised through the widespread influence of the novels of chivalry. In its own way, Loyola's retrospective narration is as critical of this power as Cervantes' comic parody. Perhaps it is even more critical, since as retrospective narrator Loyola describes such novels as the illusory snares of the Devil from which he escaped after much spiritual struggle, whereas Cervantes' humour is more ambiguous. At all events, for Loyola there is a conflict between the novels of chivalry and the *imitatio Christi* to which he then turned in his life. But his narration of this spiritual development nonetheless shows how those novels laid the basis for the latter vocation in his mind. For example, he recounts an early inner spiritual stirring when he discovered that the pleasure which he derived from the worldly imaginings inspired by the novels did not outlast their immediate appeal, leaving him "dry and discontented", whereas the new intention to go as a pilgrim on foot to Jerusalem (which he never actually reached) produced a lasting happiness:

---

10   Loyola 1996, p. 20.
11   Cervantes' attitude to the Jesuits is open to debate. He has been considered favourably disposed, on the basis of some positive remarks in *El Coloquio de los Perros*, but, as P.E. Russell remarks, "his praise of the Jesuits is there so over-fulsome that one must suspect an inveterate ironist like Cervantes of indulging in tongue-in-cheek satire at the Jesuits' expense; in Part ll of *Don Quijote* he paints an unfavourable portrait of the kind of chaplain-confessor, usually by then a Jesuit, who was liable to be found exercising what many considered excessive authority in aristocratic palaces": Russell 1985, pp. 7–8.

> ... and he began to marvel at this difference in kind and to reflect on it, picking up from experience that from some thoughts he would be left sad and from others happy, and little by little coming to know the difference in kind of spirits that were stirring: the one from the devil, and the other from God.[12]

Loyola makes it clear that his new religious vocation arose from his contemplative reflections on the two kinds of subjective pleasure which at first appeared to him to be the same. An inserted note here, either from Da Câmara or from Ignatius himself, makes the further point that these reflections laid the basis for writing his *Spiritual Exercises*:

> This was the first reflection he made on the things of God; and later when he produced the *Exercises*, it was from here that he began to get clarity regarding the matter of the difference in kind of spirits.[13]

This connection between the subjective events being narrated and the later disciplinary procedures to which they gave rise is significant, and I will return to it. But it is also significant that his act of mental discrimination, which enables the divine source and the diabolical distortion to be separated and structured into a binary opposition, does not fully account for the inward processes which preceded it. Loyola's discussion of the subjective experience of confusion and struggle is far more interesting than this resolution, and far more characteristic of Baroque culture. The narrative deals with an ambiguity in the experience which cannot be fully clarified, because the very same illusions provided by the novels of chivalry contain the seeds of their own transcendence in the direction of the service of Christ. Loyola's narration of his own development is structured around this spiritual dialectic. That is to say, the well established opposition between worldly illusions and divine truth is complicated by the fact that the worldly illusions and desires (whose source is the Devil, we are told) turn out to be the vehicles through which the higher aspirations (whose soliciting source is God) first appeared on the scene of Loyola's own soul. And, as we will see, it is this dialectic which the *Spiritual Exercises* sets out to reproduce in the soul of each exercitant, but in a more systematic manner.

Ignatius' own retrospective self-narration may appear to us naive when compared with Cervantes' irony, but it is actually less naïve than the Pilgrim's reported responses within these early episodes. This is because the retrospective

---

12   Saint Ignatius of Loyola 1996, p. 15.
13   *Ibid.*

narration also imposes a double reading and a structure of "outsideness", albeit entirely without irony. Ignatius as Director of his Order and future Saint (not yet, but already blessed with a new sacred name, Ignatius) is engaged in narrating the process of his escape from imaginary delusions. Because it is a process marked by a conversion and new point of departure, it requires the earlier phase of confusion out of which the truth can be shown to emerge. As Maravall points out in his *Culture of the Baroque*, there was no longer a clear-cut distinction, along the lines of traditional Christian asceticism, between the deceptions of the world and the transcendent truths of religion. On the contrary, the truth always came veiled in the confusion of worldly appearances, so that these appearances were not simple deceptions, but were considered rather as labyrinthine or enigmatic vehicles within which the truth could be discerned. That is why "decipherment" became a key concept. The truth with which Ignatius as narrator is concerned is expressed in the Pilgrim's gesture of the assumption of the "armour of Christ". But this is not simply a replacement for the misleading secular armour of chivalric fantasy; it is a transitional moment in the dialectical process of coming to recognise the spiritual truth concealed within that worldly form of imaginary attachment.

Likewise, when Don Quijote reconstructs his precarious archaic armour out of some rubbish left over in his house by history (but being careful not to test it too much after his first all too destructive test!), this is also the means by which he constructs an identity and assumes a new name. My point is that the duplicity of appearances, and the consequent taking of the appearance for a veil over the real, is the common feature which links the embattled religious world view of the Counter Reformation to the comic madness of Cervantes' Knight. He too proclaims that the truth comes veiled, and that the worldly appearances of windmills, flocks, and other commonplace sights, require decipherment by an expert who has studied the wiles of the evil enchanters who control worldly appearances.

To appreciate the non-ironic doubleness of Ignatius' narration of the episode of the vigil, it is helpful to place it in its immediate context. Ignatius has just related his encounter on the road with a Moor who has said that he could accept the doctrine of the Immaculate Conception, but not that Mary could have remained a virgin after giving birth, "offering for this the natural reasons that were occurring to him". Ignatius goes on: "Despite the many arguments which the pilgrim gave him, he couldn't dislodge this opinion".[14] An apparently casual encounter here deals with some important issues. Meeting a Moor on the road is not a mere chance event, but a cultural encounter constructed in

---

14   Saint Ignatius of Loyola 1996, p. 19.

a text which links this reported dialogue to far more than the preoccupations of a private life. It is immediately loaded with an accumulated social history of ideological contestation and mortal combat. The reader is told that, in this instance, the conflict of ideas between Christianity and Islam did not issue into the victory of established Christian truth. Ignatius does not say what "the many arguments which the Pilgrim gave him" actually were. Instead, he narrates how the Moor rode ahead, leaving the Pilgrim subject to discontent with his own failure to persuade, and split by an emotional struggle in which the earlier forms of combat and their conventional literary idealisation sprang to his mind:

> And at this there came upon him some impulses creating disturbance in his soul; it seemed to him that he had not done his duty. And these caused him anger also against the Moor; it seemed to him that he had done wrong in allowing that a Moor should say such things of Our Lady, and that he was obliged to stand up for her honour. And thus there were coming upon him desires to go and find the Moor, and stab him for what he'd said.
>
> Carrying along a long time with the conflict aroused by these desires, in the end he remained doubtful, not knowing what his duty was.[15]

Ignatius' impulsive regression to violence in accordance with the code of honour demanded by the tales of chivalry was held in check by his reflective and uncomfortable awareness that the failure was his own, not the Moor's. The resulting inner conflict left him uncertain as to whether revenge should or should not be sought. As he knew where the Moor could be found, this psychological dilemma was inescapable. But its actual resolution took a practical form within his metaphysical presumption of a divinely ordered universe. Ignatius left the decision up to the mule which he was riding, and it was God who spoke through the mundane creature, because in the end:

> Our Lord willed that, though the town was little more than thirty or forty paces away, and the road leading to it very broad and very good, the mule took the main road, and left the one for the town behind.[16]

Again, this could remind the reader of the comic way in which the plot events of *Don Quijote* are frequently left to the random choices of Rocinante. But

---

15   *Ibid.*
16   *Ibid.*

Ignatius, as the sense-making retrospective narrator of his own life, transforms the decision of a mule into the guiding hand of God behind the plot, and this interpretation is more than a mere narrative device, because its transcendent meaning is made perfectly clear. The local details are emphasized because the mule, as a natural animal, would normally take the easy road but in fact took the more difficult one. This divine intervention occurred because the Pilgrim at the time was psychologically unable to exercise his free will (so important to the Jesuits), being torn between conflicting impulses and unable to distinguish between them. And this inability arose because what was for him at that time a properly violent defense of Mary's honour as Virgin Lady (we might say, a Dulcinea of his mind whose purity must be affirmed by deed) was still inseparable from his sense of being a Knight in the service of Christ. But for Ignatius as retrospective narrator, the exemplarity of such episodes consists in the way in which the narrative as a whole, including its attendant ambiguities and dilemmas, must be re-read *a lo divino* (that Counter-Reformation hermeneutics which transforms profane experience and written texts into vehicles of sacred truth). In this particular case, the profane worship and defense of a Lady becomes a step towards the spiritual arming of the warrior for Christ. The conflict of motives at the mundane psychological level is there to be transcended, but this transcendence is only psychologically possible, rather than being simply the outcome of miraculous intervention, because the cult of the Lady already had a semi-concealed religious content. So it was not *just* a snare or "diabolical" deceit but a step on the road to enlightenment. In the rationalised procedures of the *Spiritual Exercises*, this narrative device of placing the soul in suspense between alternatives, so that God will indicate His will, becomes the basis of its method.

The awkward marriage of profane and religious motives had always been a double thread of meaning running through all the epics of chivalrous Christian Knights. Indeed the "ideology of adventure", as Michael Nerlich has argued, was unknown in the ancient world and first came into existence in order to idealise, or at least justify, the activities of the violent class of warrior knights, both for that class itself and for others.[17] It also functioned as a myth in Lévi-Strauss' sense, namely that it negotiated a contradiction while partially concealing it, in this instance between warrior values and those proclaimed by the Church. Ignatius maintains this contradictory link but within the narrative

---

17   Nerlich 1987, Chapter 1. Nerlich also points out that the original chivalric epics emphasised the necessity of the Knights as a class to defend the otherwise defenceless King. This already archaic ideology is parodied in Don Quijote's argument for their return in order to strengthen the kingdom against the Ottoman Turks.

of its transcendence. Therefore the *divine* level appears in his narrative as the truth initially concealed within the profane illusions and deceits, but present within the desiring subjectivity of the protagonist. Furthermore, the narrative leading towards the revelation of this truth guides its development even before the protagonist comes to understand it consciously for himself. At that later point of his arrival at insight, the protagonist becomes the narrator, dictating from the perspective of the higher understanding which allows the narrative itself to be retrospectively written. Thus the life experience, inseparable from illusions and the deceits of the Devil, acquires meaning and order from the higher spiritual revelation implicit in it from the start. World and Spirit are held together, thanks to the narrator's testimony and retrospective narration. There seems to be a prefiguration of the Hegelian dialectic here, with the benevolent cunning of the Spirit operating initially behind the back of its unconscious agent in the world.

The testimonial quality of this text was intended to become the basis for the continuation of Loyola's charismatic authority after his approaching death. It authenticates his visions, such as seeing Christ in the rays of the sun, and all three personages of the Trinity, as well as the Virgin Mary and so on. The issue which this raises for a reader presumed to be of the faith, is not the skeptical one as to whether such visions are possible or not (all mystics had them), but rather whether such signs of apparently special favour by God might be vainglorious delusions, i.e. temptations from the great adversary himself.[18] Towards the end of his narration, when Loyola recounts his journey to Rome in the company of Favre and Laínez, he describes such a mystical experience when "he was very specially visited by God":

> And being one day in a church some miles before arrival in Rome, and making prayer, he sensed such a change in his soul, and he saw so clearly that God the Father was putting him with Christ, his Son, that he would not have the willfulness to have any doubt about this: it could only be God the Father that was putting him with his Son.[19]

Here the amanuensis, Gonçalves da Câmara intervenes in his own voice to lend support to Ignatius' assertion. He further bolsters this unusual intervention by introducing some earlier unspecified dialogues between himself and

---

18 Those claiming mystical experience were sometimes exposed to charges of witchcraft, e.g. Margery Kempe. Aldous Huxley in *The Devils of Loudun* explores how complex and politically involved such apparently private experiences could be: Huxley 1975.
19 Saint Ignatius of Loyola 1996, p. 60.

Laínez, whose testimony he reports as having been validated by Ignatius in yet another dialogue just prior to the act of writing:

> And I, who am writing these things, said to the pilgrim, when he was narrating this to me, that Laínez used to recount this with other details, as I had understood. And he told me that all that Laínez had said was the truth – it was because his own memory was not so detailed – but that he knew for certain that, at the time when he was narrating this, he had not said anything but the truth. He said the same as this to me on other things.[20]

These mutually implicated utterances are clearly intended to support the direct truth of the written testimony, but they are no less complex than the ironies of the emerging novel form. If they are read disrespectfully, they even verge on the comic.

2 Textual Authority: from Desire to Method

For Loyola and his companions in the Society of Jesus, founded by collective vow in Paris in 1534, the point was not just to understand the divine order obscured by worldly fragmentation, but to actively restore its presence in the world. That is the guiding intention behind both the *Reminiscences* and the *Spiritual Exercises*. In the former text, Loyola's narration of his own conversion starts with his being wounded at the siege of Pamplona in 1531, and the convalescence during which he could not find any of the "false books, which they normally call 'tales of chivalry'". He had been accustomed to reading such works, and wished to read some more to help his recovery.[21] Instead, he was given a *Life of Christ*, and a book of the lives of the saints. At this point in his life story, there has been an initiating traumatic assault on his body, which he has borne with the exemplary fortitude of the warrior. But as retrospective narrator, Ignatius now says that this kind of fortitude is also a form of deception. This is demonstrated by his decision "to make a martyr out of himself out of self-will", when he insisted on having his already re-set leg bones shattered again so that they could be more acceptably re-formed. Even the narrative order testifies to the transcendence of the mixed motives which he detects in his

---

20   *Ibid.*, pp. 60–61 footnote.
21   Saint Ignatius of Loyola 1996, p. 14.

soul, because without this worldly egocentric martyrdom "out of self-will" he could not have become later the peripatetic Pilgrim in the service of Christ.

There is a secret narrative force guiding his inward desires into a conflict with his worldly illusions. As retrospective narrator, Loyola clearly suggests that his dreams of devotion and service to an unspecified lady of his mind, in imitation of the novels of chivalry, were already secretly leading him in the direction of service to the Virgin Mary:

> And, out of the many vain things which had previously presented themselves to him, one held his heart in such deep possession that he was subsequently absorbed in thought for two and three and four hours without noticing it, imagining what he was to do in the service of a certain lady: the means he would take so as to be able to reach the country where she was, the witty love poems, the words he would say to her, the deeds of arms that he would do in her service. He was so carried away by all this that he had no consideration of how impossible it was to be able to attain it. For the lady was not of the ordinary nobility, nor a countess nor a duchess: rather her state was higher than any of these.[22]

Within the "many vain things which had previously presented themselves to him" fostered by his secular reading, there was a transformation waiting to be brought about by his new reading. And this joint convalescence of the body and the soul is where the reinvention of the chivalrous Knight as a soldier of Christ starts. For Don Quijote too, Dulcinea "was higher than any of these", although the real status of the peasant girl was far lower and, it must be said, somewhat closer to that of the biblical Mary. Loyola imagines Mary as the Queen of Heaven (*Regina Coeli*), higher than all mortal ranks but essentially in continuity with the hierarchy that is the Great Chain of Being. In his case, however, the felt need for the restoration of a Christian empire, at a time when the armed individual Knight could no longer make the truth appear in action (as in medieval combat or in a Crusade), becomes transformed into rationalised disciplinary procedures of a much more modern pragmatic sort. These procedures are not the subject of the *Reminiscences* but fall into the province of that more technical manual, aimed at the production of a new unified subject with the will to restore and defend the old universal order, namely the *Spiritual Exercises*.

In the *Spiritual Exercises*, there is also a conversion narrative which must be produced, or rather reproduced, in each individual addressee (the "exercitant"

---

22   *Ibid.*, pp. 14–15.

who submits willingly to the discipline of the exercises). But the exercises themselves are rationalized procedures which depend crucially on a calculated control over the narrative of the spiritual progress of the exercitant. This control could be described as a contrived theatricality. The narrative position of the Pilgrim in this progress is to be taken by the exercitant, while Ignatius retreats to a mediate position somewhere between the director actually in charge of the exercises, to whom the written text of the *Spiritual Exercises* is explicitly addressed, and the silent Divinity who is to be made manifest in the soul of the exercitant. This series of relays, shifting the ultimate source of textual authority, is worthy of Cervantes, or of the absent Arab historian Cide Hamete Benengeli to whom the ironic author, Cervantes, all too transparently submits as his mere relay. But in the case of the text written by Loyola's amanuensis, the modest intention is to obscure the author's own "illocutionary" role, so as to make the hidden God speak to the exercitant's as yet undecided soul.

The *Spiritual Exercises* place their contrived theatricality at the heart of the procedures for the revelation of truth in the individual soul of each exercitant. The *interpellation* exercised through a whole disciplinary discourse disappears into apparently technical procedures. Ignatius as author is effaced, so that the *addressivity* of the utterances (to use Bakhtin's terminology) originates from within these complex textual arrangements themselves, not from an individual author. It is perhaps worth remembering that the word "autor" in contemporary Spanish did not necessarily mean a writer who was the presumed origin and creator of the text, but was commonly the producer of theatrical performances on the basis of a written text or scenario. So, even to refer to Ignatius as an "autor" would not imply what we call authorship but rather the production, in the original sense of "bringing forward", of the work of its absent creator. Only in this sense is Ignatius to be recognised as the author-producer of the scenario which is the *Spiritual Exercises*, while the director of the exercises is, in the useful French word for this function, their "metteur-en-scène". Their joint productive activity is designed to be effaced behind the exercitant's practice of the spiritual exercises themselves, as he responds to their injunctions.

That is why the exercitant himself is assumed *not* to be the reader of the *Spiritual Exercises*. The text itself is cast as a set of precepts addressed by Ignatius to the director of the exercises and not to the exercitant, although the exercitant remains the ultimate addressee. Through this indirect address the exercitant is instructed to pursue the path of an inner crisis, by exploring the *pro et contra* of any question to be decided on mundane grounds. This strategy strikingly repeats the worldly training in rhetoric common in the courtly education of Renaissance Europe, namely an ability to argue from opposite viewpoints, and it reminds us that the Jesuits were renowned for the excellent education provided by their colleges. Usually this training ensured flexibility, coupled with a detachment from commitment to any specific point of view. Some critics have suggested that in the case of the Jesuits such apparent detachment actually contributed to a very worldly ability to manipulate others who were not so detached. But, at least in the case of the *Spiritual Exercises* this rhetorical strategy is organized for a different end. It confronts the exercitant with the undecidability to which human logic leads. This is a knowingly risky strategy because it employs the weapon of the lay opponent, or even of the diabolical adversary, namely the ungrounded skepticism threatening religious transcendence, in order to reach an *aporia* or impasse within the exercitant's individual subjectivity. The intention is to make the Divinity speak in the form of an inward persuasion or certainty at precisely that aporetic point of suspension when reason cannot decide. At the moment of indecision, the Divinity speaks inwardly, not to puzzled reason but to the will.

Such an equation of desire and revealed truth is extraordinarily close to Illuminism, of which the Inquisition did in fact suspect Ignatius along with contemplative mystics like Saint Teresa and Saint John of the Cross, since it makes God the internal voice of the true desire of the exercitant. This true desire then has to be distinguished from the delusions of the false desires or appetites. Such an internalization of the source of divine revelation in the practices of an order that was the scourge of Protestantism, provides an extremely interesting link between enemies, and it points to a general trend towards psychologisation and individuation. Despite the operations of this institutionalized Catholic discipline, the *Spiritual Exercises* hover close to making a claim for an unmediated relation between individual choice and the Divinity. But it is not really unmediated. When the exemplary narrative of the *Reminiscences* is transformed into the rationalised and repeatable techniques of the *Spiritual Exercises*, these techniques serve to resolve the divisions within each desiring soul, by resubmitting them to a unifying transcendent Direction. This is explicitly intended to be quite independent from the inclinations, personality, and intellectual interests of any particular director. The latter's role is not to preach and persuade but to ensure the proper conduct of the *Exercises*. In both the *Reminiscences* and the *Spiritual Exercises* there is a narrative which deals in fissures and contradictions, but always as a prelude to revelation of the truth concealed within them.

Loyola did not invent the practice of "spiritual exercises". They are part of the Christian tradition. He rationalises them, drawing up a set of procedures to be followed within specified time limits, in order to develop the soul's capacity for making the desired journey towards God. Underpinning the techniques of the exercises is a general theory of desire, modelled on the traditional narrative of life as a pilgrimage, which Loyola sets out in his section entitled "Principle and Foundation":

> The human person is created to praise, reverence and serve God Our Lord, and by so doing to save his or her soul. The other things on the face of the earth are created for human beings in order to help them pursue the end for which they are created. It follows from this that one must use other created things in so far as they help towards one's end, and free oneself from them in so far as they are obstacles to one's end. To do this we need to make ourselves indifferent to all created things, provided the matter is subject to our free choice and there is no prohibition. Thus as far as we are concerned, we should not want health more than illness, wealth more than poverty, fame more than disgrace, a long life more than a short one, and similarly for all the rest, but we should desire and choose only what helps us move towards the end for which we are created.[23]

The programme, then, is to train the soul to withdraw its affects from whatever objects it is tempted by, in order to permit the higher desire to attain its object. This higher desire is posited as common to all mankind, being actually God's purpose or desire, working within his creatures. It is single, but the distracting objects of lower desire are legion, like the Devil himself. Furthermore the tempter can attack from diametrically opposed positions. In view of this Loyola explicitly says that the director must arrange the successive order of the exercises, and of the supporting contemplations and scriptural readings, so as to suit the subjectivity of each person undergoing them. It should not be a question of imposing a single discipline, he writes, but of encountering the shifting enemy on the terrain of each subjectivity. Only such a flexibility in the contrived narrative will facilitate the desired encounter. This attention to individuality is repeatedly stressed by Loyola, and it involves a strategic silence on the part of the director of the exercises, in the sense that he must not explicitly instruct or exhort. This too is like the silence of the theatre director, aimed at allowing another voice to speak in the cosmic dialogue on the stage of the soul. It is suggestively similar to the equally strategic silence later recommended by Freud to make the soul/subject speak its hitherto silent other. The "other" being so solicited is of course completely different in the cases of Loyola and Freud, being for Loyola the aspiration to escape all bodily desires and other worldly temptations, in order to achieve its true goal of union with

---

23 Saint Ignatius of Loyola 1996, p. 289.

God, whereas for Freud the "other" is those very desires which are repressed in pursuit of such socially organized (i.e. discursively constructed) sublimation.

Stated baldly, this comparison of Loyola and Freud might seem perverse. But in addition to De Certeau's own reference to modern psychoanalysis it is helpful to invoke here Michel Foucault's comparison of its protocols with the older "confessional tradition" of which he considers psychoanalysis to be a modern variant. Foucault's point, in a nutshell, is that the concealed "truth" is made to reveal itself through a range of discursive practices which actually construct what they then proceed to "discover" in order to name, confess, and discipline them. For Loyola, who seeks to make the self-transcending desire appear from within the worldly desires which conceal and distort it, the strategic silence on the part of the director conducting the *Exercises* is as central to his discursive practice as it is to psychoanalysis. The aim of both disciplines is to make the truth appear without the intervention of the director's or analyst's personal views. It is the authority of a discourse which must prevail, not that of an individual, however charismatic.

There is an acknowledged control, then, but it takes the form of training the exercitant, still plunged in the darkness of his "lower" desires, in a certain dialectical capacity for discrimination and self-knowledge (*discreción*). The director's function is to instruct the subject in how to effect an initial detachment from the worldly objects of desire (which are not necessarily physical) by desiring the opposite. This focusing upon an opposite is to be merely preparatory, however, because the ultimate purpose of this flexible control of desire is its detachment from all objects through recognizing their nature as illusions. This moment of discarding illusions is the moment of *ascesis* or *desengaño* ("disillusionment") which enables the false or empty objects of desire to be replaced by a single focus on God, which we could anachronistically (but accurately) call the ultimate signified where desire comes to rest in fulfillment. Loyola explains this de-realisation of the mundane objects of desire, so as to enable the true object to emerge within the soul, where it has always lain concealed amidst the false attachments and secretly awaiting its recognition:

> For this, namely that the Creator and Lord may work more surely in His creature, if the soul in question happens to be attached or inclined to something in an ill-ordered way, it is very useful for her to do all in her power to bring herself round to the contrary of that wrong attachment. This would be the case, for example, if a person were bent on seeking to obtain an appointment or benefice, not for the honour and glory of God Our Lord, nor for the spiritual good of souls, but for one's own advancement and temporal interests. One must then set one's heart on what is

contrary to this, insisting upon it in prayers and other spiritual exercises, asking God Our Lord for the contrary, namely, not to want that appointment or benefice or anything else, unless the Divine Majesty gives a right direction to one's desires and changes the first attachment, so that the motive for desiring or keeping this or that thing be solely the service, honour and glory of the Divine Majesty.[24]

It is from this programme for the institutionalized direction of inner desire that the charge of hypocrisy against the Jesuits frequently found its ammunition in the incoming rationalistic age. Molière's Tartuffe, who attempts to acquire riches and to seduce daughters and wives precisely through piously claiming not to want what he is in fact trying to obtain, is a parodied product of these spiritual exercises. This comedy was considered particularly offensive by the *parti dévot* at the court of Louis XIV, because its serious implications went further than the grotesquerie of the vulgar deceiver.[25] If the director of the exercises is an instructor in a manipulative discourse, then Loyola might be considered the founder of a new psychological Macchiavellianism, as many still believe to this day. But if the director is indeed the intermediary for a God who manifests himself through subjective desire, as the *Spiritual Exercises* maintain, *or even if he genuinely takes himself as such*, then this inner theatre of the soul must be recognised as the scene of a struggle for the emergence of the truth, irrespective of whether we believe in its actual possibility.

3 Transverberation: the Divine Word Reincarnated

Loyola writes that the first stage in the exercitant's spiritual journey is to establish through the confessional dialogue the particular desires which the exercitant must then oppose in order to proceed towards the conversation or colloquy with God. The latter will then be able to "inflame" the already existing secret desire, which is the true desire of every creature:

> The one giving the Exercises ought not to move the one receiving them more to poverty or to any particular promise than to their contraries, nor

---

24 Saint Ignatius of Loyola 1996, p. 286.
25 In his *Caractères*, La Bruyère complains that Molière failed to portray a "real hypocrite" in the figure of Tartuffe, since he is far too obvious. Tartuffe is a conscious liar and deceiver who only fools those who wish to be deceived. A "real hypocrite" would perhaps be a self-deceiver who somehow achieves his desire to deceive himself. La Bruyère does not explore the unconscious duplicity behind such sincerity.

to one state or way of life than to another. Outside the Exercises it can indeed be lawful and meritorious for us to move all who seem suitable to choose continence, virginity, religious life and every form of evangelical perfection, but during these Spiritual Exercises it is more opportune and much better that the Creator and Lord communicate Himself to the faithful soul in search for the will of God, as He inflames her (*abrasándola*) in His love and praise, disposing her towards the way in which she will be better able to serve Him in the future.[26]

In talking here of the soul's true desire being inflamed by God himself, Loyola's language becomes less technical and far closer to that of Saint Teresa of Avila or Saint John of the Cross. The English translator's recurrent decision to emphasise the feminine gender of the soul may appear somewhat idiosyncratic (or even sexist, nowadays) since it is just grammatically normal in Spanish. In the original text, therefore, the gender might be considered "unmarked", as linguists say, meaning that it does not signify. However, this feminization of the soul is consistent with mystical discourse, for example in the writing of Saint Teresa or the poetry of Saint John of the Cross, to which I will now turn.

The *Spiritual Exercises* do not only enjoin the contemplation of carefully selected passages from the Scriptures. They give equal importance to the contemplation of holy images and meditations upon the sites of events in the Christian story. This is traditional enough, and it is also in conformity with the directive of the Council of Trent which insisted on the value of using images to maintain and propagate the faith. Protestant iconoclasm in reaction against such characteristically Catholic "idolatry" is well known. It has left its mark in the form of the vandalized/purified churches, and the colourless empty statue niches, to be found everywhere in Northern Europe. The roots of this violent reaction in favour of the Word alone can be traced back to a much older tradition which pitted the purity and spirituality of the Word against the corrupting or debasing power of sensual bodily imagery, which was often equated with femininity. Nonetheless, the insistence on the mediating power of the image, whether in the Catholic West or the Orthodox East, was inseparable from what remains a central paradox or "mystery" of Christian belief, namely the doctrine of the Word made flesh, its Incarnation. Marina Warner points out the struggle mediated by the paradox:

> The ascetic strain in Catholic doctrine has struggled with its incarnational and life-affirming aspects for centuries marked by Pyrrhic victories

---

26 Saint Ignatius of Loyola 1996, p. 286.

on both sides. The Word made flesh was a positive and joyous statement on humanity's behalf, although Mary's virginity – the unnaturalness of Christ's birth – undermined it.[27]

The Baroque art of the Counter-Reformation holds the two sides of this paradox together, sensual worldly "appearances" and transcendental meaning, but now in a tension exacerbated by anxiety over the loss of their connection. This was in some ways quite traditional, but it had also become a militant insistence on their unbroken continuity in the face of the despairing sense of breakdown and dissociation noted by Michel de Certeau. When Loyola insists on the importance of meditating on the representations of the sufferings of the wounded body of Christ and similar scenes, he intends this to be a means of knowing God and His love as an enduring presence in the world, in a way that is supposed to complement the knowledge gained through reading the holy texts. Whatever the tensions between the sensual image and the mode of knowing that it enabled on the one hand, and the more abstract knowledge gained from the holy texts on the other, the sense of their ultimate unity was as essential to Catholic orthodoxy as it was to the mystics of the time. That explains why the Baroque epoch in Spain is still remarkable for the extreme realism of the statuary produced for the purposes of contemplation in specific sites. It is a realism which insists on the continuing presence of the numinous "aura", whose destruction is celebrated by Walter Benjamin, somewhat ambiguously to be sure, at the hands of the desacralizing mechanical reproduction of images in the nineteenth century.[28] When the Council of Trent reaffirmed the value of sacred images, it was no doubt combating the iconoclastic charge of idolatry from the Protestant camp, but this defense of the sacred nature of images can now be understood (thanks to Benjamin) as a resistance to the emergent threat of their loss of *aura*. The title of an exhibition in 2010 (in London and Washington) of this painstakingly realistic religious art, "The Sacred Made Real", expresses exactly the meaning of this joint activity of artists and contemplators. Significantly, the final polychrome finishing of these extraordinary statues was known as their *encarnación*.[29] The Counter-Reformation vigorously reasserted the value of their contemplation as a way to truth, and Saint Teresa of

---

27 Warner 1976, p. 236.
28 Benjamin 1977.
29 National Gallery Catalogue 2010. The mode of production of this Baroque statuary was artisanal, being entrusted to the various guilds of carvers, painters etc, who fiercely defended their different roles in the production of the unique sacred object. These objects were only intended for specific sites, which is why their exhibition in 2010 in another space was unprecedented.

Avila herself states in her autobiography that she had difficulty in praying and understanding except through the sensory medium of the image.[30] This reliance on external scenes and images continued to be a necessary part of her inner life, because she says that she was unable to imagine divine or lofty matters except through the intermediary of natural scenes. She writes that these scenes reminded her of the Creator, awoke her awareness and functioned "like a book" addressed to her as a reader. Nature is for her of the same order as language. It is this need for a sensory presence, experienced as a mediator promising access to higher spiritual things, which explains her strong attachment to imagery. And yet in her account there is a clear indication that the images are insufficient. The presence which they re-present is only seen as from within the Pauline blindness or darkness central to Baroque anxiety:

> I was so lacking in the skills of understanding to represent things that, if it was not what I saw my imagination was of no use to me, while others can form representations wherever they withdraw alone. I could only think of Christ as a man; but the fact is that I could never represent him within myself, however much I read of his beauty and saw his images, but like one who is blind and in darkness (*como quien está ciego u ascuras*) who, although she speaks with a person and sees that he is with her because she knows for certain that he is there (I mean that she understands and believes that the person is there, but cannot see him), that is what happened to me when I thought about our Lord. For that reason I was so fond of images. How unlucky are those who through their fault lose that blessing! Clearly they do not love our Lord because, if they loved him, they would find delight in seeing his portrait, just as in life it even gives pleasure to see the image of the one whom you love.[31]

She says that her imagination by itself is inadequate for understanding, so that is why she needs images. This modest disclaimer of an ability to think abstractly like the learned men of the Church, was not unknown among women mystics. Hildegard of Bingen much earlier used it to claim an alternative kind of authority, distinct from the formal training in bookish knowledge from which she as a woman had been excluded.[32] For her part, Saint Teresa emphatically affirms

---

30   Saint Teresa of Ávila 1986, p. 169: "Tenía este modo de oración: que, como no podía discurrir con el entendimiento, procurava representar a Cristo dentro de mí, y hallávame mijor – a mi parecer – de las partes a donde le vía más solo".
31   Saint Teresa of Ávila 1986, p. 170 (my translation).
32   This contrast between male bookish learning and the feminine sensual and visionary imagination, relegated to the ancillary role (*ancilla*: handmaiden) by the abstract theology

the value of the image, against those who would deny it, probably the Protestants who show thereby that "they do not love our Lord". Her language expresses this love as a longing which, echoing Saint Paul, sees him only "as through a glass darkly" prior to seeing him "face to face" in the hereafter. The certainties of belief which she affirms in this passage are not sufficient to assuage her longing for his full presence, stimulated but not satisfied by the image which replaces it. It is in this context that the famous episode of the "Transverberation" (Penetration by the Word) should be understood. Her statement that she is incapable of imagination, except in the presence of what she actually sees, supports her affirmation of the reality of this vision and the physical experience of the visitation by the angel. She could not have imagined it, she says, and she even spends a few words on her inability to know what category of angel he actually belonged to! Saint Teresa's account of this episode, which is still celebrated as an optional Festival of the Transverberation by some Carmelites, provides the basis for Bernini's sculpture and its theatrical setting, more widely known as the Ecstasy of Saint Teresa, in the Church of Santa Maria della Vittoria in Rome. While it is understandable that even at the time there were many who, in defense of pious decency, affirmed that the bodily representation is just a metaphor for spiritual experience, such a defense does no service to either Bernini or Santa Teresa herself. Jacques Lacan observes:

> You need but to go to Rome and see the statue by Bernini to understand that she's coming. There's no doubt about it. What is she getting off on? It is clear that the essential testimony of the mystics consists in saying that they experience it, but know nothing about it.[33]

Despite the uncharacteristic bluntness with which Lacan deflates any purely spiritual reading and denies the mystics' own explanations, he immediately adds: "these mystical jaculations are neither idle chatter nor empty verbiage", and he sharply criticises Charcot and others for trying "to reduce mysticism to questions of cum (*affaires de foutre*)". For him, the divine explanations derive from feminine discourse: "And why not interpret one face of the Other, the God face, as based on feminine jouissance?" He includes Saint John of the Cross in this feminine discourse, to make the point that it has nothing to do with

---

of the male establishment, is intriguingly repeated in George Eliot's *Middlemarch*. In her preface, Eliot explicitly identifies her dynamic heroine Dorothea Brooks with Saint Teresa of Avila. It is not difficult to see the contrast between this heroine's questing desire for the truth, and the empty research of Casaubon, as he futilely seeks its origins in Rome where nothing is to be found any more, like Quevedo's pilgrim in my epitaph to this chapter.

33 Lacan 1999, pp. 76–77.

biological gender.³⁴ But perhaps the most striking feature of Lacan's use of Bernini's representation is not his crude language (which he then withdraws) but the equally uncharacteristic naïve realism with which he discusses its self-evident quality (just go and look!). Actually Bernini's work brings about a typically Baroque merging of sculpture, architecture, and theatricality which blurs the distinction between spectatorship and participation.

Bernini's statue representing the Saint's "ecstasy" is placed in the middle of the Cornaro chapel transformed by Bernini himself into the representation of a Baroque theatre, which Lacan does not discuss. The members of the patron's family are represented as her spectators, although some are discussing among themselves, and one is reading a book, probably Saint Teresa's *Vida*. The visitor witnesses them too, as they in turn witness the transverberation indirectly through the gestures and facial expression of the Saint, and through the agitated folds of the dress concealing her body. Of course, she is not performing for them, but in this theatrical setting something is being performed (expressed through a form) for all of the participants including the Saint herself. Bernini's statue, bathed in an unseen source of natural light, is placed within a sculptured theatre with the Cornaro family represented as distracted spectators occupying a space shared by the real spectators (the visitors or congregation). This work is a representation of the Baroque "theatre of the world". It unites the world and its spectators, both the represented ones and the real ones, in a single space, which is both real and imaginary. Moreover, the frame which usually distances the position of the spectators from the performance is removed for the real spectators as they enter the shared space. It is not that these real spectators are meant to believe that they are in a real theatre. The intended effect is rather a persuasion that it is only within the world reimagined as a theatre of appearances that the presence of the living truth can be detected beneath its veils. Saint Teresa's voluminous and agitated clothing is the most sensuously striking image of such a veil. To the worldly gaze it reveals what it covers. Likewise, the expression on her face, her bodily gestures, and especially her naked (discalced) feet, are all images functioning as veils, that is, as signs testifying to the unrepresentable presence of the divinity.

In her autobiography, written and rewritten at the urging of her confessor to account for her life and experiences up to that point, Santa Teresa begins the account which inspired Bernini's theatrical representation, by saying that she saw a little angel on her left side "in a bodily form, which I do not usually see except by miracle" (*en forma corporal; lo que no suelo ver sino por maravilla*). She explains, or seeks to explain, that this was therefore an exceptional vision.

---

34   *Ibid.*

She writes that although angels were often represented to her (intellectually, as it were), they were not usually so visibly and physically present to her as on that occasion:[35]

> I saw in his hands a long golden spear, and at its iron point there appeared to be a small fire; this seemed to me to go through my heart several times, even reaching my entrails. As he withdrew it, he seemed to pull them out with it, leaving me completely on fire with a great love of God. The pain was so great that it made me utter those moans, and the softness so extreme that it gave me great pain, for there is no desire for it to stop and the soul is not satisfied with anything less than God. This is not bodily but spiritual pain, but the body does not refrain from participating, and even to a great extent. It is such a loving caress (*requiebro*) passing between the soul and God that I beg him in his goodness to bestow its pleasures on anyone who might think that I am lying.[36]

Saint Teresa insists on the spiritual meaning of this ecstasy, but she also makes the participation of her body absolutely explicit (the pain, the moans, the softness of the shared caress) just as she affirms that the "bodily" form of the angel in her vision is unlike the usual way that angels are "represented" to her, and this is what makes it a special vision given to her by the Lord. Here "ecstasy" does not mean that the soul is outside the body, like a disembodied spirit or abstract mind. Neither she nor Bernini prudishly deny the orgasmic aspect of the experience of suffering and delight. But this is in both cases an orgasm with transcendental meanings within the shared Baroque imaginary of reconciled opposites: the wound that is a caress, the pain that is a delight, and ultimately the body that is at last one with spirit. As the Word penetrates the flesh, becoming one with it, it seems no exaggeration to say that it is experienced as the long-promised redemption ("paying all debts", as Saint John says in a poem to be discussed below), and that the wound is also the orthopedic cure, repairing the "universe that is falling apart" described by Michel de Certeau.

This is not a matter of some surreptitious satisfaction of bodily desire furtively clothed in rhetoric, but nor is the body excluded from the spiritual "ecstasy" (a misnomer since it is not outside the body) even if we can now knowingly describe it as "sublimated" sexuality. Such an inversion simply maintains the hierarchical separation of spirit and flesh (or mind and body), against which

---

35 Saint Teresa of Ávila 1986, p. 383 : "Aunque muchas veces se me representan ángeles, es sin verlos, sino como la visión pasada que dije primero".
36 Saint Teresa of Ávila 1996, p. 384 (my translation).

all "mystical" discourse is actually a protest. These moments are for Saint Teresa both visionary and bodily, when Word and flesh are one, and representation becomes presentation so to speak, breaking all the barriers keeping them apart. They are moments of redemptive repair, promising to overcome the disaster of universal disintegration and loss which Michel de Certeau perceptively names as the cause of the desire. The ecstasy has a cosmic significance, even though the scene of this visionary repair may be just an individual soul in one of the "retreats" which De Certeau sees as both a consequence of the fragmentation and a basis for the intended restoration of the whole disappearing cosmic order. Saint Teresa's ecstasy is an intense experience of the restoration of the fullness of meaning, promised by texts and images but always as an absent or lost object except at those rare moments of ecstasy which transcend their limits.

The same could be said of the erotic-spiritual poetry of Saint John of the Cross, who was Saint Teresa's younger protégé and confessor to the nuns of the reformed Discalced Carmelite order which she founded and tirelessly expanded. The best known of these poems narrates the passage of the soul, stealing out of the house into the "dark night" where union with the lover is achieved and celebrated in a rapturous address to the night itself in the fifth stanza. The title of this poem provides the spiritual gloss which is a summary guide to its "proper" ascetic reading: *"Songs of the soul in rapture at having arrived at the height of perfection, which is union with God by the road of spiritual negation"*. The curious use of the past tense in the title (the "rapture at having arrived") asks us to read the obscured meanings of the poem's opening narrative stanzas retrospectively from the moment of rapture. In the movement of the poem itself, this moment of encounter is the culmination of a journey of longing out of the imprisoning house. One of the difficulties (or, if one prefers, mysteries) in understanding the poem is that the night appears at first to be the condition of the soul's separation and imprisonment in darkness, causing its anguished longing close to despair, but also provoking the desire which will eventually be gratified and celebrated in the later joyful address to the night itself (not directly to the beloved). The poem opens with the famous stanza:

> En una noche oscura,
> Con ansias en amores inflamada,
> ¡Oh dichosa ventura!
> Salí sin ser notada,
> Estando ya mi casa sosegada.
> (*In a dark night/ with my longings inflamed into loves/ oh, happy venture! I went out unnoticed/ my house by now being calmed*)

This venture leads to the consummation which is the union with God. Prior to that, however, the night initiates the longings in the soul still enveloped in the darkness of the beloved's absence, in order to reward it (or her) later with bliss. Since the night of absence is the initiating cause of the desire, this means that it is also obscurely present as the solicitation to which the soul's desire is a response. In his commentary in *The Ascent of Mount Carmel*, Saint John makes the usual point reiterated by Loyola in his *Spiritual Exercises*, that God is the goal of every soul's aspiration, but that the opposing and obscuring worldly desires must be overcome or silenced in order for the divine presence to emerge. Accordingly, in his prose commentary to the first stanza, Saint John says that the darkness is the blindness from which the soul has to be free in order to leave the house, which he identifies as a metaphor for the imprisoning body. This interpretation of the darkness is entirely consistent with the strict ascetic monk whom Saint Teresa herself called her "little Seneca". But these clarifications do nothing for the poetic language, and its own way of understanding how desire is caused and intensified by absence (or "lack", to use Lacan's term). The darkness of absence may initially seem a preventive obstacle to desire, but the darkness of the house, and of the secret staircase through which the soul moves "sin otra luz ni guía/ sino la que en el corazón ardía" (*with no other light or guide/ but the one burning in the heart*), is not only an obstacle or a mere absence. It is also a solicitation because the longings (*ansias*) which it inspires, are an anticipation of that which is not yet present, and for whose presence to come there is longing but no guarantee. Here the double meaning of *ansia* as desire and anxiety is crucial. In the fifth stanza, after the longing soul has ascended the secret staircase, it is the darkness of the night of desire which achieves its goal, in the fusion of lover and beloved. This explains why, as the narrative ends, the poetic voice bursts out in praise of the night itself. The negative is transformed into positive:

¡Oh noche, que guiaste,
Oh noche amable más que la alborada:
Oh noche, que juntaste
Amado con amada,
Amada en el Amado transformada![37]
(*Oh night, who were the guide/Oh night, more adorable than the dawn;/Oh night, who joined/ The lover to the beloved/The beloved transformed into the lover!*)

---

37   Saint John of the Cross 1960, pp. 26–28.

With regard to the last two lines above, one of the most difficult points to translate into English is the simple one that neither the masculine Beloved "Amado" nor the feminine questing soul who is the Beloved "Amada" is more active than the other, while the night itself is now revealed as the active agent. The shift from narrative time to revelation is also significant for the meaning of the poem. The darkness may have signified absence, separation, and prevention of fulfilment, but this absence is now seen retrospectively as the agency which inflamed and guided the soul towards the fulfilment of the desire.

Another of Saint John's best known poems, "Songs of the soul in intimate communication and union of love with God", is not a narrative poem of quest and fulfillment, or of separation and loss, but consists entirely of a series of exclamations of delight addressed to the God who gives it in his presence. It begins:

> ¡Oh llama de amor viva
> Que tiernamente hieres
> De mi alma en el más profundo centro!
> Pues ya no eres esquiva,
> Acaba ya si quieres,
> Rompe la tela deste dulce encuentro.
> (*Oh, living flame of love/ Who tenderly wounds/ In the innermost centre of my soul!/ Since you are no longer fleeing/ Finish now, if you wish/ Break the web of this sweet encounter.*)

As in Saint Teresa's account of her Transverberation, body and soul are inseparable and the wound and the delight are one. The second stanza moves from these exclamations to include the redemptive paying of all debts, and the transformation of death into life:

> ¡Oh cauterio suave!
> ¡Oh regalada llaga!
> ¡Oh mano blanda! ¡Oh toque delicado,
> Que a vida eterna sabe,
> Y toda deuda paga!
> Matando, muerte en vida la has trocado.[38]
> (*Oh, gentle cautery!/ Oh, delicate wound!/ Oh, gentle hand! Oh, delicate touch!/ Which savours of eternal life/ And pays every debt!/ By killing, you have changed death into life*).

---

[38] *Ibid.*, p. 44.

In this poem, the erotic language of the desiring and then satisfied body, with its clear (to us) masochistic traces, is often considered by the pious readers instructed by Saint John's own glosses, to be merely borrowed from a worldly discourse and redeployed *a lo divino* in the service of religious allegory. Certainly, the poet's own commentaries on the meaning of his poetry speak for just such a "divine" level, possibly to make sure that the Discalced Carmelite nuns, who were his acolytes and intended primary readers, should be able to discern its promise within the language of worldly desire. But to reverse this spiritual clarification, and to say in the language of easy post-Freudian demystification that the poems are *really* just about sexuality, "sublimated" in order to get past a censorship (either that of the authorities or his own internalised one) is to miss precisely the integrational function of this language, namely its Baroque articulation of desire as a refusal of metaphysical dualism. Some of his poems certainly run the risk of a debased reading, and the feminine persona of his desiring soul may perhaps have increased that risk along with its identificatory appeal to the sisters. It would also be foolish to ignore his need to offer explanations to the Inquisition and other authorities to safeguard a properly spiritual interpretation. But this poetry speaks a language where Word and Flesh are merged even more intimately than the Soul and the Beloved enacting the consummation, as in the dialogue of another poem: "Songs between the Soul [*Esposa*] and the Bridegroom [*Esposo*]".[39] In this poetic dialogue Saint John's lyricism has strong echoes of the pastoral eclogues of Garcilaso de la Vega and of the sensuality of the biblical Song of Songs, but the "clarifying" commentary again has recourse to the dualist metaphysics which the poetry actually refuses. Saint John's erotic poetry of the dark night of absence and desire partakes in a specifically Baroque imaginary, which makes it a discourse of passionate resistance to dissociation, whether religious or rationalist. It rescues a universe in which the Word would not be sundered from the world. Saint John's exploration and ecstatic celebration of desire, and its irreducibility to either the merely physical or to the disembodied version of the "spiritual", notwithstanding his own strict ascetic austerity, is still capable of exercising an appeal and fascination on modern readers, even on those for whom the "incarnation of the Word" has become yet another metaphysical abstraction.

Saint John's poetry represents a cosmic dialogue, but one played out in the most intimate longings of the body and soul and their imaginary reintegration. Reactive to a situation of fragmentation and collapse, and in many ways reactionary in its nostalgic drive to restore a lost "totality", it is nonetheless a resistance to the oncoming alienations, including the radical split of the body from the soul inherited from the ascetic traditions of Christianity by the Age of

---

39   *Ibid.*, pp. 30–42.

Reason, and reformulated abstractly as the problem of the relationship of the body to the Cartesian "thinking essence". Historically speaking, in his defense of an integral world (whose non-condemnation of the Flesh is totally alien to both Protestantism and his own Catholic asceticism) this "mystic" poet can be seen to be responding to a predicament shared with the militant activist Ignatius of Loyola, although the written record of the latter's response could hardly be described as beautiful, let alone erotic. Nor does Loyola suggestively transgress the established boundaries separating active masculinity from passive femininity. Despite these differences, the connection with Loyola's writing and his recommended practices for silently directing the desire of the soul, consists in the fact that Loyola too seeks to mend the rift between worldly rationality and the lost omnipresence and centrality of the Word. For him the scene of this repair is the soul of the exercitant. Whereas it is always possible to view his procedures as complicit with the most debased rationality in the service of power and self-interest masquerading within the very empty "appearances" which they piously renounce, it is also possible to understand the contrived theatre of the *Spiritual Exercises* as an apparatus which repairs a fundamental loss for its desiring addressee. But that is to read them through the far more radical poetry of Saint John, and through Saint Teresa's refusal of the separation of body and soul for which her own erotic experience stands as testimony.

This struggle against dissociation is also to be found in the Platonic aesthetics inherited from earlier Renaissance thought. In his *Individual and the Cosmos in Renaissance Philosophy*, Ernst Cassirer points out that for Plato "Eros ... stands between the divine and the human, between the intelligible and the sensible worlds, and he must relate and join them to each other".[40] He argues that in the Neo-Platonism of Ficino and Pico della Mirandola the cosmic reciprocity is restored:

> Man's striving towards God, represented in Eros, would not be possible without a counter-striving of God towards man. Thus, Ficino resuscitates the basic notion of *Christian mysticism* and thereby gives his Neo-Platonism a new stamp. God, the absolute objective being, is tied to subjectivity, and bound to it as a correlate and necessary counterpart; just as all subjectivity is related and directed towards him. Love itself cannot be realized in any but this double form. It is as much the drive of the higher for the lower, of the intelligible for the sensible, as it is the yearning of the lower for the higher.[41]

---

40   Cassirer 1963, p. 132.
41   *Ibid.*, pp. 132–133.

As Cassirer observes, this restoration of the cosmic dialogue was actually a restoration of the traditions of Christian mysticism. Even within the Universal Church, the mystical traditions had always resisted that absolute separation of the intelligible from the sensible. Against the powerful ascetic tendencies within Christianity to elevate the spiritual and to demonise or annihilate the world of the flesh, the mystical traditions insisted on the interpenetration of the Word and the created world through the "mystery" of the Incarnation, and this is reformulated theoretically in Ficino's dialogical Neo-Platonism. In Cassirer's words: "Eros has become in a true sense the 'bond of the world'".[42] But for those who do not believe in the objective reality of the reply elicited from the absent God, the specifically Christian content of this mysticism is not its main significance. The dialogical nature of the demand is more instructive. The subject's anxious desire for a response in the face of its absence (which is the cause of the desire) engenders the response which it anticipates. That experience confirms for the desiring subject that the loss of the connection between the world of flesh and the world of spirit is itself an illusion.

4   Conclusion: from Mysticism to "Modernity"

Earlier in this chapter I invoke Michel de Certeau's insistence that the discourses of mysticism in the sixteenth and seventeenth centuries were anxious responses to the perception of universal fragmentation and the consequent drive to repair that disaster. This compulsion to unify provides the link between the militant activist Loyola and the otherwise quite distinct erotic testimony of Saint John's poetry and Saint Teresa's autobiography. When de Certeau compares this mystical discourse with the secular drive to construct a rational order for the centralizing state, he points to the sense of fragmentation and the intense desire to overcome it as the shared condition of possibility which gave rise to these otherwise distinct discourses, religious and secular. The shared anxiety over the disappearing centre is overcome by the proclaimed triumph over the threatening emptiness, which is the underlying cause of the desire itself. Seen in a historical *longue durée* perspective, the integration of the Word and the World, which was sought by the mystics in the depths of the desiring soul in order to overcome its disappearance from the empirically and rationally apprehended "real" world, is an anticipation of the drive to grasp or construct the absent "totality" which Lukács and his Marxist or marxisant followers identify as the lost object of bourgeois culture. Starting with his Hegelian *Theory of*

42   *Ibid.*, p. 133.

the Novel, Lukács' locates the lost integrity in ancient Greece and the Homeric epic, rather than in Christendom prior to the disastrous "dissociation of sensibility" (T.S. Eliot) or the "disenchantment of the world" brought on by scientific rationalism (Max Weber, echoing Schiller). But these differences in locating the historical moment of the loss of the hitherto unquestioned connection seem relatively unimportant. The shared feature, inherited from Renaissance Neo-Platonism and Baroque anxiety, is the "totalizing" drive to repair through aesthetic form what history has put asunder.

CHAPTER 7

Baroque Incompletion, the Captivated Subject, and the Humour of *Don Quijote*

The metaphor of the Great Theatre of the World was extremely widespread in the early modern period, and is familiar to anyone acquainted with Shakespeare or Calderón. But our over-familiarity with this metaphor tends to obscure its function as a paradox mediating an ideological crisis. On the one hand it evoked the contemporary anxiety over the possibility of a "disenchanted" world of empty appearances; but at the same time, if the world could be understood as a theatre there must be an author behind the appearances through which he still addresses at least some of his audience. Those appearances may be deceptive, but if they are communicative signs they contain a concealed truth which can be deciphered, and that means that they are not merely empty. That is how the metaphor of the Great Theatre of the World became central to the dominant ideology of the Baroque period. It held out the promise that the transient and deceptive worldly appearances were material signs, which could be deciphered to unveil the true being concealed within them. In conferring the ambiguity of signs, and therefore decipherability, upon the world of sensually perceptible phenomena, this imaginary theatricalisation of the material world enabled the threatening emptiness of the Baroque *horror vacui* to be overcome by a metaphysics of concealment, with its promise of an unveiling to come. What matters here is not so much the doctrinaire neo-Platonist separation of essential being (*ser*) from inessential worldly appearances (*parecer*) as their reconnection through the desiring subject's act of interpretation. This mental act repaired the universe for the subject in much the same way as the discourses of mysticism, which I have considered in Chapter 6. It was a collective response to melancholia, which it overcame, or in psychoanalytic parlance "negated", by symbolic means.

Antonio Maravall's analysis of Baroque culture explains why the painting and the literature of the time made use of difficulty in order to lure its addressees into a process of decipherment. For him obscurity is the key to this lure, whether it is the obscurity of the content or of its expression:

> I believe that in both instances these two modes of obscurity .... operated on the public in the same way: attracting the public, holding its attention,

making it participate in the work and use its forces in deciphering that work, thereby guaranteeing the work's influence on the reader.[1]

He quotes Pellicer de Tovar as a representative of these norms, "Being hidden is a condition of what has value".[2] Moreover, obscurity is the key incitement towards greater understanding in all areas of knowledge, and here Maravall quotes another commentator on the beneficial effects of a difficult book on its reader:

> [But] if its style is difficult and extraordinary, this itself incites him to understand it; we are naturally inclined towards understanding and knowing it, and one contrary expends its force on another – thereby with difficulty the appetite for knowledge increases.[3]

This struggle by readers to unveil hidden textual meanings was characteristic of the whole epoch:

> This is not a solitary reference. Decades later, Gracián would analogously maintain that "when the meaning is more obscure, the greater difficulty gives greater satisfaction to the reason [*discurso*] in finding it.[4]

Maravall's general conclusion is:

> Above all, however, the art and politics of the baroque were a *decipherment*, which evidently presupposed an interplay with difficulty and obscurity.[5]

His examples point to the broad assumption that the truth always comes veiled in obscurity, not only in written texts but in the material world too. This obscurity reveals to the diligent interpreter what it conceals from those deceived by appearances, which in Gracián's case, meant the uninitiated despised *vulgus*. Maravall is not concerned with Cervantes' humour in *Don Quijote*, but nonetheless his observations shed a good deal of light on Cervantes' comic treatment of the way in which the fictional Knight-to-be is first lured into the

---

[1] Maravall 1986, p. 221.
[2] *Ibid.*, p. 220.
[3] *Ibid.*, p. 221; the source is Luís Alfonso de Carvallo's *Cisne de Apolo*.
[4] *Ibid.* The source is Baltasar Gracián's *Agudeza y arte de ingenio*, 40.
[5] *Ibid.*, p. 224.

imaginary world of the novels of chivalry. It is precisely because the fascinated hidalgo takes their impenetrable verbal obscurity to be a display of signs veiling an inner truth that he is drawn into his tireless efforts to decipher them. The activity of textual decipherment parodied by Cervantes is continuous with the Baroque metaphor of the Great Theatre of the World, which likewise affirmed that there was a truth waiting to be deciphered from the obscurity of its material signs.

When Don Quijote tries to explain to Sancho Panza that the windmills, the flocks of sheep, and the barber's basin only appear to be those mundane things because of the influence of the malign enchanters who persecute him, he is initiating Sancho into the duplicitous reality of the Great Theatre of the World. This comic instruction is generally seen as a symptom of his madness, sometimes even identified as paranoia,[6] but it should also be seen as a characteristic symptom of the contemporary dialectic of anxiety and desire, which negated the inadmissible fear of universal emptiness and "disenchantment". Darian Leader's comments on the nature of the symptom, broadly Lacanian in inspiration, are very helpful here:

> Discussing the Schreber case, Freud observed that what we take to be the defining features of madness – delusions, hallucinations etc. – are in fact not primary but secondary symptoms. They are less constitutive of madness than responses *to* madness, attempts at self-cure, as Bleuler, Jung, Lacan, and Winnicott would also argue.[7]

Symptomatic delusions are reassuring in their own way because they are the subject's means of remedying (but not curing) the underlying cause, without becoming too conscious of it. If Don Quijote's delusions are to be taken as palliative "secondary symptoms" in this sense, not as a direct or "primary" expression of his madness but as a defense against it, their concealed underlying cause must be sought elsewhere, most plausibly in the melancholy to which these delusions are a response. Moreover, if these "secondary symptoms" are to be understood as "attempts at self-cure" which prevent a complete breakdown, we can see that they were characteristic of a whole contemporary discourse and not just that of an exceptional or deviant "mad" individual. But Don Quijote's typicality is not immediately apparent because, instead of the normal revelation of a reassuring divine presence behind the appearances of

---

6 Farrell 2006. But Farrell considers the "paranoid personality" of Don Quijote to be a deviant exception to the normality of his time. My argument is that he is representative.
7 Leader 2011, p. 17.

the world, his "mad" inversion uncovers a persecuting multiform malevolence. The important point here is that his active attempts to unveil the malevolence within the ordinary become an object of laughter for the reader of Cervantes' novel. In laughing at them, the reader's attention is distracted from acknowledging their normality.

In the culture of early modern Europe, the detection of the presence of diabolical forces actually served to re-enchant the world, perhaps even more effectively than the positive affirmations of belief in the concealed presence of the divine order. The detection of the diabolical within the proliferating uncontrollable heterogeneity of the known world was central to re-establishing the reassuring binary opposition of Good and Evil. This familiar binary is reassuring to the would-be believer who confronts the possibility of chaos or mere emptiness. The concept of Evil at least imposes unity on the multiform, which is the paradoxical reassurance provided by paranoia. We may not burn witches, heretics, or other deviants nowadays (although we have our own equivalent procedures), but the restoration of the old binary structure is still a powerful agency for defending whatever passes for the true and proper order of things. The self-styled good can always find an "axis of evil" to support their bipolar worldview. To grasp the full measure of Cervantes' humour in *Don Quijote* is to understand that it is not aimed exclusively at the Knight's "mad" deviancy from the normality of his time, or of our own later times, but at his covert conformity with a whole contemporary discourse. Cervantes' hero is the supreme comic version of this compulsion to repair the universe.

The desire to restore a disappearing certainty could rightly be described as nostalgic. But this nostalgia needs to be located, both historically and psychologically, within the modernising dynamic to which it was a reaction. The anxiety over the threatening emptiness, for which the symptomatic *theatrum mundi* provided its remedy, was produced by the threat to the sustaining beliefs or illusions which Max Weber later called the "disenchantment" of the world. Of course, Weber himself did not believe that there ever was a prior "enchanted" state of affairs, and it is fairly obvious to most of us that it was produced retrospectively. The imaginary object of this reactive desire was the numinous and integrated world, which could never be completely lost (being an object of desire) but was now felt to be obscured behind the deceptive appearances of the world. Nonetheless, it was still decipherable amidst the triumphantly proliferating "deceptions". This obscure object of nostalgic desire therefore had its dynamic origin in the changing and developing contemporary world, because it arose as a reaction against the plurality of discourses brought into being by the expansion of understanding which we know as the Renaissance. Without that proliferation, and the consequent conflicts between its incompatible discourses, the reactive desire for restored singularity could not have arisen with such murderous intensity.

To clarify this concealed negative dialectics more concretely: the expansion of knowledge in the Renaissance was pluralistic and decentring. It divided up the knowable world of experience and understanding into newly separated discursive realms: rational, experimental, aesthetic, theological, political, proto-psychological etc., each of which appealed for validation to its own forms of authority, but these were not easily reconcilable with each other. Certainly, we can rightly celebrate this expansive proliferation of incompatible and occasionally contradictory discourses as the source of Bakhtin's liberating "polyphony" of emergent modernity, on the grounds that it contested the previously unquestionable authorities of Church and State along with the supposed transcendental hierarchy supporting them. In Bakhtin's account those authorities were the objects of the "relativizing" laughter of the Carnival, which was incorporated into the emergent novel form, and more broadly into the new critical consciousness which novelistic discourse made possible.[8] But by the same token, that liberating expansion of possibilities was necessarily experienced by many (and sometimes by the same individuals) as a threatening loss of the singularity and "givenness" of formerly unquestioned certainties. At its extremes this loss could even be experienced as universal fragmentation calling for "orthopaedic" repair (Michel de Certeau), whether contemplatively in the body and soul of the desiring subject or actively and militantly in the external world. The discourses of mysticism (Certeau's *mystique*) discussed in the previous chapter were a major example of this anxious drive to restore the universe to its "real" but absent unity by transcending the universal fragmentation experienced at the mundane level. Similarly, the metaphor of the Great Theatre of the World promised a transcendence of worldly appearances, which explains why Bernini chose to represent Saint Teresa's Transverberation in a Baroque theatre (see Chapter 6).

1   **Theatrical Addressivity**

The theatre provided a convenient metaphor for the conservative (or more precisely, reactive) desire to overcome the threatening plurality of discourses because the ambiguity of its signs actually provokes the desire to decipher them. The theatre does not demand that its audience take its appearances for realities (which would be naïve, or mad), but neither does it demand that they

---

8   Bakhtin 1968.

knowingly watch an empty display (which would be pointless). Taken together, all its signs, whether verbal, gestural, or visual, constitute a complex *addressivity* (Bakhtin) which plays on the fact that the audience knows that its signs *are* signs, in order to provoke a desire to decipher what its verbal and visual signs might be simultaneously communicating and concealing (or deferring, since the temporal process is inseparable from the desire for final clarification). To believe in those signs as real presences would be simply foolish. But to see them as mere deceptions, not believing in their decipherability, would be to abandon one's own interpreting intelligence whose activity is an anticipatory desire for a truth not immediately given. So, insofar as theatrical signs are addressed to the subject's desire for a unifying, completed and authoritative meaning to emerge, they are apprehended as vehicles for a truth waiting to be revealed retrospectively at that moment of closure which Aristotelian dramatic theory calls recognition (*anagnorisis*), and which Bakhtin calls "finalisation". But since the signs in real theatres are organised around dialogues and conflicts, with the audience located in a position of potentially critical "outsideness" (Bakhtin's *vnenakhodimost*'), they can also function to provoke a questioning by that audience of the values affirmed by the characters onstage, or implied by the outcome of the dramatic action. The real theatres, which developed rapidly from the late sixteenth century onwards, offered their new audiences a multiplicity of different conflicting attitudes, ideas, and emotional responses, with which they could identify (or reject) to varying extents. In this respect, they were an important agency for the expansion of understanding and self-understanding which Bakhtin, following Cassirer, calls "becoming". Perhaps they were even more important than the emergent novel championed by Bakhtin for its creative incorporation of multiple and sometimes incompatible discourses. For the audiences of the time this emergent multiplicity of different possible positions introduced a hitherto unprecedented split between their previously unquestioned beliefs and the new potential for becoming other through "self-fashioning".[9]

2   The Comic Counter-discourse

Like the real theatres themselves, the metaphor of the world as a theatre was not entirely submissive to the Counter-Reformation's demands for ideological closure. A well-known counter-example is to be found in a passage from Erasmus' *Praise of Folly* (1508), where Folly's words seem to anticipate Jaques'

---

9   Greenblatt 1980.

famous speech in Shakespeare's *As You Like It*: "All the world's a stage/ and all the men and women merely players".[10] But in Folly's jocular speech, which may well have influenced Shakespeare, there is no trace of Jaques' melancholic lament over the emptiness of the theatre of life:

> Now what else is the life of mortal men but a kind of fable in which the actors appear on stage under the guise of different masks? Each plays his assigned part till the stage manager comes forth and takes them off stage. Indeed, he often assigns one actor several roles, so the performer who just now acted a king in purple majesty presently comes back a humble servant in rags. They are all but the shadows of real persons, yet there's no other way to put on the show.[11]

The reference to the actors as "shadows of real persons" is clearly drawn from Plato's argument in Book VII of *The Republic*, but the witty ambiguity of Erasmus' humour lies in Folly's assertion of the multiple possibilities which each "performer" might enact (or have "thrust upon him" like Malvolio's covert fantasy of greatness in *Twelfth Night*). Folly's jocular proclamation of multiple roles is apparently untroubled by the absence of any defining essence ("they are all but the shadows of real persons"), while the serious satirist who insists on trying to reveal the hidden reality is denounced as a lunatic:

> Well, someone will ask, So what? What's the point? Let me make my case. If someone in a theatre should try to strip the mask off the actors in the middle of the play, and show the actors' actual faces, wouldn't he be destroying the entire illusion, and wouldn't he deserve to be pitched out of the theatre by the entire audience as a troublesome lunatic?[12]

This could be laughed off as an inconsequential play with a familiar concept. Folly's words are surely not to be taken too seriously. But nor are they to be dismissed when this theme is developed in the following passage into a denunciation of the misanthropic "lofty moralist" who criticises everyone whom he considers beneath his own ethical level. Erasmus' Folly defends both sensual existence and the social necessity of acting against those who "despise and ridicule as madness whatever life has to offer". The targets here are those philosophers who maintain that the only truth is to be found in their own mental

---

10   *As You Like It*, 2. 7. 139–140.
11   Erasmus 1989, p. 28.
12   *Ibid.*

abstractions, because their ideal is "a marble statue of a man" who would rightly be taken by most as "a spook or monster".[13] Through the figure of Folly Erasmus gives a voice to the Carnival body, and here she protests against the elevation of abstract Truth (the Word) and its alienation from the flesh which it equates with illusion and deceit.

Later the passionate psychology underlying the fierce denunciations of all social acting (i.e."hypocrisy") became the principle target of mockery in one of the greatest comedies of the seventeenth century, Molière's *Le Misanthrope ou l'Atrabilaire*. This play provokes audience laughter at the ego-centric gratifications afforded to its hero, Alceste, by his "virtuous" misanthropic rage at the false pretences of the whole world, attributed to the "black bile" of melancholy in the title. This angry melancholic is even comic in the contradictory passions which lead him to destroy his own prospects for happiness by attacking his beloved social butterfly, Célimène. He attacks her for her hypocritical worldliness, but cannot tear himself away from her. He laments this weakness in lofty speeches which give him a spurious tragic grandeur, and when Célimène resists his imperious demand for her to abandon the world in order to live with him alone in the "desert" outside Paris, she comments with effortless wit on the fierce joy which he derives from his ego-centric anger. Now Erasmus' "troublesome lunatic" has become the main comic protagonist, but behind him there is a whole discourse being comically unveiled in its turn. "His majesty the ego" has a hard time in this play, and later Jean-Jacques Rousseau, who considered all the arts as corrupting, but especially the theatre, clearly felt targeted. In his *Lettre à M. D'Alembert sur les spectacles* (1758), he argues that its undoubted greatness as a comedy is inseparable from its moral depravity. By provoking laughter at his hero's intransigent virtue, Molière makes Alceste's virtue itself a duplicitous veil: if all his targets are hypocritical, as he virtuously proclaims, what is to be said of his own self-glorification in the name of truth, of which he appears to be unconscious?

Erasmus' irony is double-edged, mediated as it is through the voice of Folly. But it is not hard to see in his comic equivocation the seeds of his growing distance from the intransigent moralism of Luther (even when he agrees with the latter's denunciation of Church abuses) and from the hardening defensiveness on the part of Rome. That hardening would soon shape the ideology of the Counter-Reformation, and even see Erasmus' own works condemned by the Inquisition. The argument behind Folly's joking use of the metaphor of life as a theatre (John of Salisbury's *totus mundus agit histrionem* was often quoted)[14]

---

13   *Ibid.*, pp. 29–30.
14   John of Salisbury, "Policraticus" (1159), see West 2008.

is that the moralist's desire to lay bare the underlying truth of all the other "actors" is the desire of a misanthropic lunatic hostile to "the entire illusion" of human life itself. It too participates in the universal histrionic role-playing but it is an inquisitorial desire, and the implications may not have been lost on some of the inquisitors themselves. Later I will consider this fierce desire to unmask in the context of Cervantes' ironic treatment of Sansón Carrasco. He "cures" Don Quijote by destroying his illusions and engineering the *desengaño* which brings the novel to its conclusion. There are still many who take this closure and its exemplary death seriously because it restores the hero to his truth.

3 Capturing the Spectator's Desire

The idea of spectatorship as an activity of decipherment, dependent upon the evocation of a spectator's desire to unveil what is not immediately seen, is quite familiar nowadays, particularly under the influence of Lacan. This is also where the spectacle as provocation can be usefully correlated with Bakhtin's *addressivity*. Since looking is a desiring activity, not a passive reception, that desire is intensified by the subject's perception of incompletion, whether in the representation or in the subject him/herself. Lacan makes the point that the object of this desire is an absent object, which is sought by the gazing subject.[15] He finds a model in Pliny's story of the competition between Zeuxis and Parrhasios, and it is worth noting that this story was well known among Spanish painters of the Baroque period through Gerónimo de la Huerta's translation.[16] Pliny reports that Zeuxis painted the grapes so faithfully that the birds tried to eat them, but in reply Parrhasios painted a veil, which prompted Zeuxis to ask what it concealed. Lacan comments:

> [But] the opposite example of Parrhasios makes it clear that if one wishes to deceive a man, what one presents to him is the painting of a veil, that is to say, something that incites him to ask what is behind it.[17]

The deceptive representation of an object might be sufficient to activate the appetite of birds, because they would simply "think" (for want of a better word) that the object is present, there being no distinction for them between the

---

15   The usual English translation of Lacan's *le regard* (the look) is "the gaze". This is confusing because the French has none of the English term's connotations of fixity or steadiness.
16   De la Flor 2002, p. 108.
17   Lacan 1979, p. 112.

object and its skilful representation. But Lacan questions the kind of verisimilitude implied by Pliny's story: "There would have to be something more reduced, something closer to the sign, in something representing grapes for the birds".[18] In his *Iconology*, W.J.T. Michell does not follow Lacan's argument on the proximity of the image to the sign, but he makes a similar point on the duplicity of the image, namely that it could only exist for human consciousness:

> ...an image cannot be seen *as such* without a paradoxical trick of consciousness, an ability to see something as "there" and "not there" at the same time. When a duck responds to a decoy, or when the birds peck at the grapes in the legendary paintings of Zeuxis, they are not seeing images: they are seeing other ducks, or real grapes – the things themselves, and not the images of things.[19]

This human ability to "see something as 'there' and 'not there' at the same time" would also explain why there is a concealed normality within Don Quijote's "mad" coining of the hybrid term *baciyelmo* to name a barber's basin which is simultaneously Mambrino's helmet. In the case of the image made by Parrhasios, the object seen by Zeuxis is a veil, whose function is to conceal something. Parrhasios' painted veil is, in one register, a realistically represented object no different from Zeuxis' painted grapes. The difference noted by Lacan does not lie in the quality of the representation itself but in the viewer's expectation, since a veil exists in order to conceal something while also indicating the place of the absent object. For Lacan this means that, although the viewer may not know it, every image is always a sort of veil functioning like "something closer to the sign". The key issue is that the seduction of human beings requires an address to their desire for an absent object, and this desire must also be provoked. For Mitchell, the moment of the subject's capture by the image is the moment when the image is "seen as such", bringing with it an ability to see something as "there" and "not there" simultaneously. Later in his book, Mitchell writes that there is always a link between the image and the language through which the image is interpreted. He adds:

> This notion of "picturing the invisible" may seem a bit less paradoxical if we remind ourselves that painters have always claimed to present us with "more than meets the eye", generally under the rubric of terms like

---

18   *Ibid.*
19   Mitchell 1986, p. 17.

"expression". And as we have seen in our brief look at the ancient concept of the image as a spiritual "likeness" that there was always a sense, a primary sense in fact, in which images were to be understood as something inward and invisible. Part of the power of perspectival illusionism was that it seemed to reveal not just the outward, visible world but the very nature of the rational soul whose vision is represented.[20]

Mitchell's argument is that the representation of the external world is also a revelation of the inner world, whether of the artist or of the whole culture informing his technique (in this instance, Renaissance perspectivism). But, whatever the culturally specific nature of the image in question, that invisible "more than meets the eye" has to be pursued by the viewer. The latter encounters the image as an address to his/her own inward subjectivity, and in this essentially dialogical encounter, the viewer's experience gives rise to a response which interprets the image by seeking in it "more than meets the eye".[21] These arguments, by Mitchell or Lacan, are fully consonant with the dynamics of the theatre, in which all sensually apprehended appearances are known to be an address which must be provisionally completed by the audience's acts of responsive decipherment. But this applies to all signs, whether visual or verbal; they all participate in that complex *addressivity* (Bakhtin) which demands tentative completion through the response of the addressee, and at every moment that response is in effect a desire for meanings that are not immediately given. It is not exclusively confined to the theatre. Nor does it have to be confined to the satisfactions of closure. It may well open new pathways. That is why an old literary text, like an old painting, can become the occasion for the production of new meanings, while chronologically newer ones can sometimes seem to merely reiterate and reinforce the already known. That reassurance can itself provide the kind of gratification which Roland Barthes called *plaisir*, in contrast with the more productive openness which he called *jouissance*.

---

20 Mitchell 1986, p. 39.
21 Lacan's argument that the painting returns the gaze of the viewer from another position which fixes the viewer in that returning gaze, seems broadly compatible with Maravall's idea of Baroque art as an address to its subjects from a position of dominant power. But Lacan's analysis, possibly in polemic with Sartre's idea that subjective self-awareness is constituted by the reciprocity of the gaze (*le regard*), insists on its aggressivity. Therefore, in seeing the other as a completed and self-satisfied image, the subject's own gaze turns to violent envy (*invidia* being derived, as Lacan reminds us, from *videre*). Cf. Lacan 1977, p. 116.

4 Baroque Incompletion

The anti-realist techniques of incompletion are central to Maravall's view of some of the major paintings of the Baroque period. He theorises this incompletion as a specifically Baroque form of *addressivity* which implicates the viewers in the task of completion. These paintings are not even an attempt at the finished realism of *trompe l'oeil*, but almost the opposite. This is how he discusses the "unfinished" or "careless" appearance of some works by Velázquez:

> Today it has become customary to remark upon its character of being unfinished, careless painting. Ortega greatly stressed this aspect of Velázquez's work. Keeping within the boundaries of biographical explanation, the attempt was made to see this as a loss of interest on the part of the painter, who was distracted from his task by preoccupations other than painting. ...[But] We are interested in its historical grounds. Formulating it in this way we find that Velázquez's procedure was not unique, but had a place among the general current of painters of his time (with cases as distinguished as Rembrandt's), who enthusiastically practiced the painting of "smears" or painting "boldly" [*a lo valiente*], which Gracián was representative in admiring. The most interesting facet for us has to do with what was seen during the epoch: when Gracián himself praised Velázquez in this sense, and when Quevedo viewed his work as praiseworthy, they did not see certain profiles or colours carefully and fully placed on the canvas, but rather discontinuous and incomplete "splotches". Quevedo thought that this was much more "true" in the picture than a refined finish.[22]

Having established that these techniques of incompletion were not only intentional but widely appreciated for their "truth" (incidentally, by two figures also known for their satirical denunciations of the worldly "appearances" of the time), he gives us an interpretation which makes the incomplete painted surface a provocation to desire in the viewing subject:

> The receivers of the baroque work, being surprised at finding it incomplete or so irregularly constructed, remained a few instants in suspense; then, feeling compelled *to thrust themselves forward and take part in it*, they ended up feeling themselves more strongly affected by the work, held by it. In this way they experienced an incomparably more dynamic

---

22 Maravall 1986, p. 219.

influence of the work being presented, with a much greater intensity than when other tacks were taken. It is not a matter of ultimately obtaining the public's intellectual adherence so much as moving it; therefore this state of suspension was used to serve as the expedient to launch a more firmly sustained movement. And that was the question: to move [emphasis added].[23]

Lacan likewise attributes to Holbein's use of anamorphosis in *The Ambassadors* the effect of drawing the viewer into the picture, which he describes as a "trap". He argues that the famous distorted projection of a floating skull is only visible at the instant when the viewer's gaze turns away. So, for Lacan the way in which the skull catches the viewer's distracted attention is "the painter's way of showing us that as subjects we are literally called into the picture; and represented here as caught".[24] He bases these observations on Jurgis Baltrusaitis' *Anamorphoses*,[25] which examines several examples of the perspective distortions of anamorphosis as an artistic strategy specific to Baroque culture. Their aim is to involve the spectator in actively composing the image as he moves in relation to it in real space and time. The effects produced by anamorphosis are almost the opposite of those of the widespread *trompe l'oeil* representations, but for Lacan both were aimed at drawing the viewer into active participation.

When Maravall attributes the dynamic involvement of the viewer of Baroque paintings *a lo valiente* to a momentary mental "suspension" brought about by the use of obscurity and discontinuity, he too sees the temporal delay as a lure for eliciting the viewer's intensified participation. He insists that the technique of incompletion, intended to make the "the recipient" (the addressee) fill in the gaps, can be seen not only in painting but in literary works too, including those of Quevedo and Gracián. He also suggests, a bit more tentatively, that the apparent carelessness of Shakespeare's late plays puts them in the same category. The views of the Baroque theorists concerning the need for difficulty and delayed response in both painting *and* literary language,[26] are remarkably similar to those of the later, and currently still influential Russian Formalists like Viktor Shklovsky and Boris Eichenbaum. They argued that linguistic difficulties and discontinuities are necessary in order to slow the reader's attention and to focus it on the disparate discourses out of which the work is made. This mode of literary construction was noted by Shklovsky himself

---

23 *Ibid.*, p. 220.
24 Lacan 1987, p. 92.
25 Baltrusaitis 1976.
26 Maravall 1986, p. 220ff.

in his discussion of Don Quijote in his *Theory of Prose*, which identifies the shifts in Cervantes' style and register as "estrangement" devices for slowing the reader's reception.[27] Now, neither the Baroque theorists quoted by Maravall nor the later Russian Formalists theorise the discontinuities as a provocation of the reader's or viewer's desire for the absent coherence. But, if we recognize that the reader's attempt to overcome the textual discontinuities is a desire to make a hidden or implicit coherence appear (which goes beyond the Russian Formalist theories of the text), we can see how close this is to the temporal dynamics of the theatre.

5 The Aesthetics of "Becoming" versus Timeless Form

When he discusses Baroque painting, Maravall gives us the clearest expression of his view of Baroque culture as even more inwardly dynamic than the culture of the Renaissance because of its embattled management of the contradictory nature of modern experience. He sees in this painting a "greater antinomy between the struggle to grasp living reality and the weight that the aesthetic placed on ideal representations based on an abstract conception of the social hierarchies".[28] Maravall's thought is dialectical here, because the dynamic counter-truth of the "living reality" is artfully revealed both within and against the "ideal representations" which seek to stifle it. In his discussion of the "distant splotches" and the "thick brush strokes" employed by Titian, which were so appreciated in 17th century Spain, he provides an interpretation in which stasis and conformity to the deadening established hierarchy is not the dominant force. At least within this aesthetic space, the forces of transformation are allowed to make themselves felt:

> We ask ourselves what reasons sustained the general opinion in the seventeenth century towards this Titianesque manner of painting: it was judged that this way alone gave an authentic rendering of the living. It was a painting of what was incomplete, shifting, and unstable, a painting adequate for grasping the human being and life. Such an adaptation

---

27 Viktor Shklovsky 1929, pp. 91–124. Shklovsky's insistence on the reader's experience of temporal process means that the work's difficulty is increased in order to prolong the process of its reception: "Art is a means of experiencing the making of the object (*perezhit' delanie veshchi*), while the made in art is not important (*a sdelannoe v iskusstve ne vazhno*)", *op. cit.*, p. 13. Conceptually this is similar to Boris Eichenbaum's better-known essay: "How Gogol's Overcoat Is Made": Eichenbaum 1974, pp. 267–294.

28 Maravall 1986, p. 257.

is explained by saying that the human does not possess a being that has become, but a being becoming – a *fieri*, not a *factum*; consequently a being incomplete and in continuous change.[29]

It is the modernity of this mode of representing the normally repressed movement of "becoming" (*fieri*), which Maravall detects within the culture of the Baroque in general, but particularly in the painting. Maravall is probably influenced by Cassirer too. But for him the temporal movement is grasped by the spectator or the reader in response to the intentional incompletion of the work. At the same time, however, even his own descriptive terms like "shifting and unstable" seem to name an anxiety, not just a positive desire for change.

Similarly, in his significantly named *Cervantes and the Mystery of Lawlessness*, in which he discusses Cervantes' "Colloquy of the Dogs", Alban Forcione also argues that the "gaps" in Cervantes' style make the reader "resolve, tentatively, and always on his own, the apparent contradictions or to sanction their irreduceability".[30] Like Maravall he detects a similar contrast between the dynamic, changing nature of the real and the increasingly repressive "abstract" timeless forms demanded by the established order. It is particularly suggestive that he relates this dynamic Baroque style to Schlegel's definition of Romantic poetry in 1798, as the art of the "unfinished". So the later struggle between neo-Classical restraint and the rebellious energy of Romantic "becoming" is said to be prefigured in Cervantes' style. Forcione's argument is historical but not historicist, because for him there is no anachronism in seeing Cervantes' language retrospectively through its later development. He adds, in a very rich passage:

> It is a difficult style "asserting" nothing but its own freedom and demanding no less from its addressee, but, in its cultivation of ambiguity for provocation and illumination rather than for obscurity, it can reward the responsive reader with an experience of what Friedrich Schlegel referred to as the most profound activity of the human consciousness as reflective entity – its basic dialectic and dialogic movement as it passes through thought and counterthought, construction and deconstruction, in a restless drama, ever toward a fuller comprehension of truth and an awareness of its ultimate incompleteness.[31]

---

29 Maravall 1986, pp. 259–260. His emphasis on the semi-deponent verb *fieri* (which means either "becoming" or "being made") in contrast with *factum* (the "made" thing, or "that which has become") makes Maravall's observation very close to Shklovsky's insistence on process.
30 Forcione 1984, p. 178.
31 *Ibid.*, pp. 178–179.

This sense of unfinalised process, and the shift of authority to the individual reader's interpretation "on his own" (a response provoked by the very incompletion of the work), appealed later to the Romantics and their modern successors. The defence of freedom and the virtues of incompletion as aspects of a never-ending temporal process, are linked here with the idea that the gaps set up by literary ambiguity make for "provocation and illumination rather than obscurity". This could have come from Bakhtin or from Roland Barthes on the nature of the text. But there is also more than a hint of a counter-pressure exercised on the same reader, making him synthesise or "resolve ... apparent contradictions". This is actually quite different from his/her capacity "to sanction their irreconcilability". The two impulses can certainly co-exist in tension with each other, and Forcione's detection of this inner tension in Cervantes is admirable, but the first operation, which makes the individual reader an agent who dissolves appearances ("apparent contradictions") in order to reach a resolution, is more in tune with the reactive ideological demands in Baroque culture. Here the contradictions are not in the text to be "sanctioned" by a reader whose "fuller comprehension of the truth" involves "an awareness of its ultimate incompleteness"; on the contrary, they are to be "resolved" because, if properly grasped, they are only "apparent" not real. This means that the temporality of the process of understanding (which for Roland Barthes enables a text to be re-read differently and ensures its inexhaustible *jouissance*)[32] is nothing more than an "appearance" to be left behind by the emergence of the finalizing resolution.

What this must mean from a historical point of view is that when the heterogeneity of discourses comes to be experienced by many as a threat of fragmentation rather than as a liberating expansion of alternative possibilities, the desired reintegration is evoked as an absent or lost object for the interpreting subject to discover or construct for him/herself out of the patent signs of discord, incoherence, or (more benignly) incompletion. This is where the notion of the whole world as a divinely organised theatre of appearances became important for the dominant ideology of the time. The fragmentation could be overcome in a gratifying act of decipherment, but the scene for the recovery of this coherence would be henceforth the inward subjectivity of the addressee (viewer or reader). The truly significant aspect of Maravall's argument is that this shift to the inward subjectivity of the viewer makes the paintings and the literary works of the Baroque period distinctively modern. They were not merely representations of an outdated world view, but scenes of the unresolved struggle between the dynamic expansion introduced by the

---

32 Barthes 1977.

Renaissance (and early capitalism) and the anxious desire to rediscover the timeless sacred truth amidst the new destructive multiple discourses which threatened to obliterate it.

6   A Comic Great Theatre of the World

This detection of the internal mental and emotional dynamic within the apparently static contemplation of the image points to the way in which it captivated its addressees. Maravall's account of their reception of the works in question, like Forcione's account of the response of Cervantes' readers, focuses on those readers' and/or spectators' expectation of completion. When that completion is patently absent, they are drawn into making it for themselves. I will argue that their momentary mental suspension, followed by their compulsion "to thrust themselves forward and take part in it [the image]" as Maravall puts it, has a very significant resemblance to the episode in Part 2 of *Don Quijote*, in which Cervantes closely follows the development of his hero's response to Master Peter's puppet show.[33] However, unlike those spectators or readers who transform their impulse towards participation into a purely inward psychological movement, Don Quijote externalises it and acts it out. That externalisation marks him out as mad, and that overt madness serves to conceal his resemblance to the normality of Maravall's spectators or Forcione's readers of Cervantes. But this resemblance raises the wider question: do the readers of *Don Quijote* laugh at the mad exception or at his concealed resemblance to themselves?

Cervantes' typically complex and witty narration of this episode shows how, after a preparatory delay, this little puppet theatre becomes for his hero a scene in the Great Theatre of the World which draws him to "thrust [himself] forward and participate". It is important that the reader easily recognises in this episode a repetitive pattern of behaviour which characterises the Knight's comic madness throughout the novel. His reactions to the spectacle also resemble those reported in the case of so-called "primitive" peoples who, being unacquainted with the cinema, physically attack the villains on the screen. Therefore, his madness could be seen as evidence of a regression to a "primitive" or child-like simplicity. But we need to beware of such dismissive superiority on the part of the "civilised" (us), because the detection of a "primitive" mentality is a way of refusing to acknowledge a shared response. After all, some modern audiences

---

33   Cervantes 1985 (Penguin); 1978 (Ediciones Castalia), 2. xxvi.

have been known to shoot at screen villains, and the reactions of twentieth-century French audiences to the first moving pictures, such as the Lumière brothers' film of a train arriving at La Ciotat, were equally conditioned by participatory responses (although the participation in that case was expressed through flight rather than fight, unlike Don Quijote). The following close reading of Cervantes' narration will show that Don Quijote is not simply deceived by the spectacle, like the birds in Pliny's story, or the reactions attributed to primitives at a time closer to our own. However mad Don Quijote's responses may be judged by us, they are not a simple matter of his taking appearances for reality. Rather, he too responds to what Lacan calls the "invocatory drives" of speech and sight (and which Bakhtin calls *addressivity*), after an extended moment of aesthetic suspense.

Don Quijote's intervention in Master Peter's puppet representation of a tale of chivalry may appear at first sight to be just an example of a foolish bird-like response. When the reader easily recognises in it yet another "mad" repetition of the Knight's behaviour throughout the novel, this easy recognition of madness appears to make it the cause of the reader's laughter; so this episode could be cited as an example of Cervantes' comic mockery of the foolish Knight deceived by appearances. But actually Cervantes does not simply reduce his hero to the level of a mere object of the reader's superior mocking laughter. Cervantes' subtle narration of the developing outburst quietly refers the reader to the process which captures the Knight's desire but *fails to satisfy it*. Here the reader's posture of distance and mockery is more subtly accompanied and countered by a process of recognition and partial identification with this object of their laughter. Our modern term for this partial identification is "empathy", coined in 1903 as the English equivalent for Lipps' German psychological term *Einfühlung*. This measure of recognition is constructed by the developing narration, but it is withdrawn at the moment of the Knight's ecstatic *furor*. At that moment, the distancing which triggers the reader's laughter distracts his attention from what he and the Knight have in common. Yet it remains available for reflection.

Cervantes' narration shows how Don Quijote's ecstatic *furor*, when he leaves his normal "sane" self and fully enters into his imagined theatre of the world (laying the real theatre to waste), is a delayed response to a complex address, in which the visual representation is supplemented by a verbal commentary. At first the Knight is comfortably placed outside the frame set up by the puppet theatre, sanely accepting that he is watching a fiction in which the visual spectacle is simply supported and supplemented by the verbal commentary from the puppeteer's assistant. To that extent, the reader's viewpoint coincides with that of Don Quijote himself. The latter's first response to this oral commentary on the tale of chivalry (which he knows well) is to criticise it for being too flowery and loaded with excessive diversions and comments. Even within this negative aesthetic judgement, however, something else is stirring. His criticisms show that he *wants* the unvarnished truth, demanding that it be separated from the rhetoric which he considers superfluous. That is why he openly objects when the lad wanders off into considerations of the legal differences between Moorish and Christian law:

> 'Boy, boy', interrupted Don Quixote in a loud voice, 'go straight ahead with your story, and do not go curving off at a tangent; for it requires much proof and corroboration to bring a truth to the light'.
>
> [– *Niño, niño – dijo con voz alta a esta sazón don Quijote, seguid vuestra historia línea recta, y no os metáis en las curvas y transversales; que para sacar una verdad en limpio menester son muchas pruebas y repruebas*].[34]

At this point Don Quijote objects because digressions into legal discourse mean that endless proofs and counterproofs are needed to bring out a truth clearly and conclusively [*para sacar una verdad en limpio*].[35] Master Peter intervenes to agree with him, but on aesthetic grounds rather than on grounds of truth, instructing the lad to be more straightforward.[36] The next stage in the Knight's developing response to the narration is marked by his criticism of the lad's reference to the ringing of bells (a Christian practice) in the minarets of the Moorish town later called Zaragoza. From the point of view of historical realism, this objection is perfectly correct, but now Master Peter intervenes to defend his show and to disagree with Don Quijote's insistence on the need for historical truth. Echoing Aristotle's *Poetics*, he argues that it is of no importance, since plays often contain historical inaccuracies and absurdities without being adversely affected. Don Quijote agrees and falls silent before this dismissal of the importance of the real, but it is the silence before the

---

34   Cervantes 1985, pp. 639–640 (Penguin); 1978 (Castalia 2) p. 242.
35   "*Sacar en limpio*" is virtually synonymous with "*poner en limpio*": to make a fair copy. There is an underlying comic play with the idea of writing as a quasi-legal attempt to arrive at a clear truth, and its failure to do so. This recurs in the discussion between Don Diego de Miranda and his son Don Lorenzo on the indeterminate nature of the Knight's madness. See *infra*.
36   He urges him to refrain from both excessive scene-drawing (*no te metas en dibujos*), and from musical excesses: "counterpoints which tend to break under the strain of their own subtleties": (*contrapuntos que se suelen quebrar de sotiles*), in favour of plainsong (*canto llano*); *ibid.* Master Peter's speech is witty and sophisticated, like his later deliberations over the damages payable by the Knight for wrecking his stall.

explosion. At this point, the Knight's complex dialogue with the two creators of the theatrical appearances has shifted away from a relatively detached concern with style to what he takes to be substance (the real which the appearances are supposed to represent), because when it comes to tales of chivalry, which for him are historical records, his concern for accuracy is that of an ultra-realist to the point of pedantry. This ultra-realism expresses a demand that appearance and reality must coincide.[37] Cervantes' comedy shows masterly insight here. Don Quijote's ecstatic *furor* is not the consequence of his being simply fooled by theatrical appearances. Rather, it is because the false notes in the elaborate verbal and visual representation have ruined the possibility of the desired illusion that he is momentarily frustrated and falls silent, in apparent acceptance of Master Peter's argument. But that is a passing moment. The next movement in the Knight's desire for the absent real is provoked by these obstacles to belief. He intervenes actively in order to complete the illusion which the spectacle has *failed* to achieve for him. Don Quijote's intervention in the spectacle is aimed less at rescuing the fictional hero and heroine, although that is his conscious intention, than at rescuing the illusion for himself. That is to say, he tries to sustain the imaginary universe which captivates him, by rescuing it from the insufficiency of its symbolic representation. And, just like his interventions to rectify the real world throughout the novel, the consequence is wreckage, for which on this occasion he has to pay the puppet master. He continues to blame the evil enchanters, but now it is for creating the false illusions in his own mind rather than for altering the appearances of the objective world.

For any theatre audience, crises in a plot are moments of anxious anticipation, that is to say, of a desire for a favourable resolution doubled by a fear of its opposite. This emotional combination of anxiety and desire requires a measure of identification with the character onstage, but it is normally held in check by the aesthetic restraint which distances the spectator from the spectacle. But the Knight abandons this restraint when he responds to that anxious desire by inserting himself into the scene in order to be the agent who resolves the crisis. This transformation of Don Quijote from distanced spectator capable of critical observation, to uncritical principal protagonist is familiar, since it repeats his activity as a reader of chivalric romances throughout both parts of the novel. As usual, the moment which transforms the Knight's desire into action is also the moment of the reader's detachment and laughter. The suspension of the reader's identification with the character, at the very moment when the latter crosses the boundary to become a participant, is necessary to

---

37 This demand informed the extreme realism of Baroque religious statuary in Spain. It testified to the auratic presence of the sacred in the real.

the laughter, but the reader's identification with the hero is back-grounded rather than annihilated. This is quite different from saying, like Anthony Close that the Knight is a "risible" object of the reader's mockery throughout: "Don Quijote is mad and Sancho simple-minded, mental conditions that render them risibly infrahuman".[38] Although he attenuates this judgment elsewhere in his book, his overall argument is that the relationship between the reader and the character is constant and is underwritten by the hierarchy of differences taken to be natural according to the prevailing Aristotelian theories of laughter at the time. According to those theories, comic figures are intrinsically lower, ugly, and "risible" in themselves. But, *pace* Close, the difference between this active madman and the *desocupado lector* (the "idle" or "unengaged reader" addressed by Cervantes' work) is considerably narrowed insofar as that reader recognises that the madman openly practices what we all do mentally. The Knight's active participation is certainly abnormal and laughable, but it is at the same time recognisably similar to the normally passive, or rather esthetically pacified, responses of the spectators or readers. So the reader's sense of distance and difference from the madman shifts towards an acknowledgement of a shared response, not only here but on many comparable occasions throughout the novel. The reader's vacillating identification with the comic character may not be fully acknowledged (and certainly not by every reader), but nonetheless, it prevents the reduction of the hero to being little more than a mere object of contemptuous laughter or mockery. Not only that, it is the key to understanding the reader's deeper laughter.

7 The Captivated Reader

In his *Psychocritique du Genre Comique*, Charles Mauron analyses the moment of mocking laughter as the outcome of a rapid dialectic in which the subject momentarily identifies with the object or butt, but this is swiftly followed by a distancing and inward disavowal which enables the laughter to occur. This dialectical movement within the subject is summed up by Mauron as "an identification rapidly admitted, then denied" (*une identification rapidement consentie puis niée*), and it is this rapid distancing which enables the subject to overturn the potential anxiety arising from the identification. It is as though the subject says to himself, "I could be that other, but I am not" (*je pourrais être cet autre, mais je ne le suis pas*).[39] In the next chapter I will return to this dialectic

---

38 Close 2000, p. 339.
39 Mauron 1985, p. 21.

within the divided subject, which Mauron derives from his reading of Hobbes, but here my point is that this almost instantaneous inner movement is slowed down by being included in the developing narrative. Then greater reflexivity on the reader's part becomes possible, because when the inward dialectical movement from identification to disavowal is delayed, it becomes reversible. Then the instantaneously reassuring "I could be that other, but I am not" becomes the more reflective "I am not that other, but I could be". This reverses the hierarchical nature of satirical laughter observed by Bakhtin: "The satirist whose laughter is negative places himself above the object of his mockery, he is opposed to it".[40] For Hobbes' theory, the momentary self-elevation above the object of mockery, which he calls "sudden glory", is the basis of *all* laughter. But a close reading of how the laughter is actually produced by *Don Quijote* reveals a dynamically shifting relationship, oscillating between the reader's recognition of a quality shared with the hero on the one hand, and the distancing which suspends that recognition on the other. This withdrawal of recognition triggers the laughter. However, the object of this laughter is not the inferior "madman", or not him alone, but the discourse which produces the symptoms of madness which are recognisable in the "sane" too.

Although he was committed to the rational values of the Enlightenment, Dr. Johnson was sensitive to the reader's identification elicited by the figure of Don Quijote, and even to a certain degree of empathy:

> Very few readers, amidst their mirth or their pity, can deny that they have admitted visions of the same kind, though they have not perhaps expected events equally strange, or by means equally inadequate.[41]

It is curious that this quotation is to be found in both of Anthony Close's books on Cervantes, although he insists on the lower "risible" status of the mad Knight in accordance with the prevailing Aristotelian ideas of the time. He rightly objects to the "Romantic" version which softens or even eliminates the comic nature of Cervantes' work, but in the name of historical fidelity he restricts his understanding of Cervantes' comic practice to the prevailing hierarchical theories of laughter at the time. However, theories and practices do not necessarily coincide harmoniously, and laughter does not have to objectify a character to the point of reinforcing the laughing subject's egocentric security and his sense of absolute difference from the inferior, deviant, or "mad" object of that laughter. It can turn the laugher's attention to the ways of thinking and

---

40 Bakhtin 1968, p. 12.
41 Quoted in Close 1978, p. 12, and in Close 2000, p. 335.

feeling (beliefs, responses etc.) which he shares with the mad character. Dr. Johnson's sensitivity to this alternative kind of laughter which he finds in Cervantes, can verge on anxiety, and it may perhaps be related to his own fear of insanity. But it also raises the much larger question of the function and value of such laughter.

I have argued above that Don Quijote's own responses to the incompleteness of the representation of the chivalric episode in Master Peter's puppet show make him similar to the captivated spectator of Baroque paintings according to Maravall (and to Lacan's theory of desire). His dissatisfaction over the incompletion in the spectacle stimulates his desire to make the elusive completion manifest here and now. But, picking up again on Shklovsky's Constructivist reading of Cervantes' *Don Quijote*, and its similarity with the Baroque use of incompletion noted by Maravall, it must be said that as a literary figure, Don Quijote too is constructed *a lo valiente*, that is, across contradictions and gaps which have provoked many readers and critics ever since to produce their own completed interpretations of his character.

This question of the readers' response to the fictional character, which is essentially a dialogical response to a complex literary *addressivity*, is itself made an object of reflection and comic treatment in Part 2, where Don Quijote encounters a number of people who have read Part 1. Among the most widely discussed of these readers are the Duke and Duchess who invite him into their real castle, not an inn imagined as a castle. This enables them to recreate and confirm his fantasies, which they have already enjoyed as readers of Part 1, in order to repeat their enjoyment of his madness, but now as a spectacle. In effect, they transform their castle into a theatre, and themselves as former readers into spectators and participants. The fictional Arab chronicler, Cide Hamete Benengeli, is reported as observing ironically that in his view this makes them as mad as the Knight. In his ironic comment, the comic motif of the reversibility of mockers (*burladores*) and mocked (*burlados*) becomes a reversibility of sanity and madness:

> In fact Cide Hamete says that he considers the mockers were as mad as their victims, and the Duke and Duchess within a hair's breadth of appearing fools themselves for taking such pains to play tricks on a pair of fools.
>
> [*Y dice más Cide Hamete: que tiene para sí ser tan locos los burladores como los burlados, y que no estaban los duques dos dedos de parecer tontos, pues tanto ahínco ponían en burlarse de dos tontos*].[42]

---

42 Cervantes 1985, p. 916; Cervantes 1978 vol. 2, pp. 564–565. The trickery in question is their theatricalised awakening of Altisidora from her fictional death out of love for the Knight.

Although the ducal pair take themselves to be detached observers, the theatricalisation of their palace transforms it into a scene of their desire. Moreover, their self-positioning as mocking spectators (*burladores*) means that they remain unaware of the concealed interchangeability between themselves and the objects of their laughter (*los burlados*). Their contrivance of the spectacle of madness for their own enjoyment is a form of desire, identified here as excessive eagerness or insistence (*ahínco*). It is aimed at incorporating the literary fiction into their lives, no less than Don Quijote's re-enactments of *his* reading matter. As they are readers too, their pursuit of pleasure obliquely raises the question as to why other readers likewise find pleasure in his madness (whether or not we find an aggressive or sadistic element in it like some critics). If our enjoyment is comparable to the ducal pair, perhaps we are not quite "sane" either. Clearly Don Quijote himself is trapped by the way his desires have been constructed by the novels of chivalry, but Cide Hamete's ironic remark suggests that he is not alone. Those who turn him into a spectacle for their own pleasure, laughing at him from a detached position of supposed superiority, are no less trapped by the recycled chivalric discourse than the actively engaged hero. Cide Hamete's ironic observation points to an unconscious in the apparently detached observer. Seen from a purely formal point of view, his quasi-authorial remark belongs to a "meta-discourse", breaking the fictional frame to comment on the narrative from an outside position. But this rather formalist critical terminology does not adequately describe its full effect. It enjoins the reader too to suspect that his own detached "aesthetic" enjoyment is as unexamined as that of the ducal pair.

The Duke and Duchess are former readers of Part 1 of Cervantes' novel. And so is Sansón Carrasco, whose captivation by the chivalric text I will discuss separately. But there is another important character, Don Diego de Miranda, who has not yet heard "the news of the first part of this history". He encounters the Knight's madness for the first time, and is therefore puzzled by his strange combination of madness with lucidity. Noting the contradiction between the Knight's mad actions and his words which, he says, "were consistent, elegant, and well put", he asks his son, Don Lorenzo, to resolve the question as to whether he is mad or sane. He himself is unable to do so:

> I can only tell you that I have seen him act like the greatest madman in the world, and yet make such wise speeches as to blot out and efface his deeds.
>
> [… *sólo te sabré decir que le he visto hacer cosas del mayor loco del mundo, y decir razones tan discretas, que borran y deshacen sus hechos*].[43]

---

43   Cervantes 1985, p. 581; Cervantes 1978 vol. 2, p. 170.

Don Diego relies on his son's judgment as a practising poet and student of letters to clarify and resolve this problem. Here Cervantes gives the readers' demand for clarification a voice in the text. But after a long speech from Don Quijote, who tries to demonstrate that knight errantry is a "science ... that comprises all or most of the sciences in the world", his son's judgement is that it is not only a matter of the gap between words and deeds but of gaps in his discourse too. Don Lorenzo has been consulted as a writer, and now he has recourse to a writerly metaphor for the Knight's ineradicable madness. He calls it a "rough copy" (*borrador*) from which no fair copy could be extracted:

> All the physicians and authors [?] in the world could not give a clear account of his madness. He is mad in patches, full of lucid streaks.
> [*No le sacarán del borrador de su locura cuántos médicos y buenos escribanos tiene el mundo; él es un entreverado loco, lleno de lúcidos intervalos*].[44]

Don Lorenzo's reply to his father contains the difficult, and perhaps untranslatable, play on *borrar* ("to erase" or "to blur") and *borrador*, the writer's provisional draft or "rough copy". This verbal play is a response to his father's earlier statement that the Knight's lucid words "blot out and efface" (*borran y deshacen*) the mad deeds. In his reply Don Lorenzo says that the Knight's madness, complete with its lucid intervals, is a textual rough copy (*borrador*) which could never be made whole or complete by any medical doctors or "good scriveners" (*buenos escribanos*). The latters' business, of course, is the production of fair copies (the translator's unfortunate decision to substitute "authors" for "scriveners" or "clerks" misses the point). This is a good comic example of Baroque *conceptismo*, the play with meanings which go far beyond the more obvious punning, with its dependence on acoustic similarities at the level of the signifier.[45] Don Lorenzo's witty reply to his father equates madness with the production of "rough drafts", and its cure with the production of "fair copy". Uttered by a writer himself, Don Lorenzo's equation of Don Quijote's madness with an incoherent and unfinalisable text might appear to be just an appropriate choice of metaphor for him to make. But the idea of Don Quijote as the product of an incurably incoherent or blurred piece of writing (*borrador*),

---

44 Cervantes 1985, p. 583; Cervantes 1978 vol. 2, pp. 172–173.
45 John Rutherford's translation partly clarifies this *conceptismo* by introducing the term "fair copy", which is implied in the Spanish, while the notion of the "rough copy" or "draft" (*borrador*) is covered by the word "blotches". (A further meaning of *borrador* is "blotter"): "All the doctors and fine clerks in the world couldn't make a fair copy of that man by eliminating his blotches of insanity: he's mad in streaks, complete with lucid intervals". (2000, p. 604).

irreducible to clarity and order by any readers or scriveners seeking to classify him (is he mad or sane?) and yet clearly provoking such a demand for clarification, constitutes a witty and ironic meta-commentary by Cervantes on the nature of his own literary creation.

Mediated through the voice of this fictional writer and student of letters, Cervantes' witty reference to the ambiguity of his own writing amounts to a humorous defence of the principle of textual "unfinalisability" (Bakhtin). This may appear far-fetched, but it is precisely that irreducible quality which draws everyone into the attempt to "read" the hero, that is, to make him a fully intelligible fair copy for their own understanding. Literary critics are still drawn by this desire to finalise. The incomplete openness of this "rough copy" corresponds very closely to the seductive incompletion of both painting and writing *a lo valiente* discussed by Maravall, and by Forcione in his discussion of Cervantes' "cultivation of ambiguity for provocation and illumination". It provokes the impulse to completion, but it also prevents it, and here there is an ironic meditation upon that impossibility. Moreover, there is the further suggestion that incompletion is, in a potentially disturbing sense, truer than the reassuring clarity which a certain mode of reading demands. If so, we too may be linguistically incoherent "rough copies" or, in Bakhtin's terms, "unfinalised".

It is not that there is any doubt that Don Quijote is mad. That is not the issue. The problem is the perplexing inability on the reader's part (expressed within the text by Don Diego as he questions his writer son) to separate clearly the Knight's madness from the extremely "consistent, elegant, and well put" language with which he expounds his views, his ethical judgments, and his reasons for acting as he does. Despite the repetitive recurrence of his obsessions, this *ingenioso hidalgo* is infinitely flexible and surprisingly original in his discourse. That is why he constantly provokes the combination of astonishment and wonder known as *admiración*. The problem, as Don Lorenzo observes, is not the madness in itself but the sanity which is inextricably combined with it. This "blurring" or "erasure" effaces the normally accepted boundary between sanity and madness, and it is this provocative irreducibility which constitutes the humour of the work, while at the same time it prevents the reduction of the hero to the level of satirised object within the reader's superior understanding. This particular form of Bakhtinian "unfinalisability" is the creation of Cervantes and it endows his novel with a similar truth to "life" which, in Maravall's account, Quevedo and Gracián found in the incompletion of the paintings *a lo valiente*. It is not the kind of truth sought by neo-classical clarity or realist representation, but rather a construction which calls upon the reader to respond to an unfinalisable text. As readers, we are provoked into a process of decipherment of a text, whose humour vacillates between the distance and boundaries required by mockery and the moments of identification which blur those boundaries. This makes it impossible for us to reach a conclusion which would finalise the character and transform him into a mere object for our superior understanding and dismissive laughter. It also makes it impossible to finalise Cervantes' text itself.

8　Competitive Desire

There is another captivated reader of Part 1, Sansón Carrasco. He is a student of letters who makes his first appearance as a protagonist in Part 2 of Cervantes' novel. There he plays a major role as the Knight's antagonist who eventually overthrows him, bringing the novel to its close. His name (Sampson) already suggests his role in bringing down the temple of false illusions. The narrator draws attention to this, but negatively, by pointing to a difference in both physique and motivation:

> The Bachelor was not very big in body, although his name was Sampson, but a great wag (*socarrón*), of poor colour though of great intelligence.
>
> [*Era el bachiller, aunque se llamaba Sansón, no muy grande de cuerpo, aunque muy gran socarrón, de color macilenta pero de muy buen entendimiento*].[46]

His appearance belies his name but displays his character. He is "round-faced, snub-nosed, big-mouthed, all of which are signs of a malicious nature, given to jests and mockery (*amigo de donaires y de burlas*)". This is immediately displayed as he kneels before Don Quijote and addresses him in the language of the novels of chivalry as a Knight whose famous deeds are known everywhere, thanks to the Arabic author and his Castilian translator. Through these words and gestures he enters fully into the fiction, and instead of laughing at it he literally enacts it. However, his motives for this role-playing are never fully clarified. What is certain is that he has a long discussion with the Knight about the events of Part 1, and the powers of authors and presses to make or break a hero's prestige, including the Knight's own renown. But he remains completely silent about the comic nature of that renown. At first he encourages Don Quijote in his illusions by telling him that he has already become famous as the protagonist of Cide Hamete Benegeli's published record of his true exploits (i.e. Cervantes' Part 1). As Sansón continues in this vein, Don Quijote's niece

---

46　Cervantes 1985, p. 486; Cervantes 1978 vol. 2, p. 59.

and housekeeper are outraged at his betrayal of their trust, but we learn that he has concluded, together with the barber and the priest, that this collusion with Don Quijote's fantasy offers the only way to cure him. Nonetheless, there is already an opaque aspect to his concealed motives. This opacity is not dispelled by his stated intention to enter into the Knight's fantasy world as a therapist, in order to defeat him in combat and extract a penitential vow to renounce errantry for a year.

Towards the end of the novel, this intended cure finally works. After a short but significant onset of melancholy which the cure itself has precipitated, and a consequent brief flirtation with the idea of recasting himself as a melancholic poet from the pastoral tradition (leading Sansón to propose to become his melancholic double, Sansonino), Don Quijote resumes his former identity, and returns home to make a proper and exemplary Christian death. There is no reason to doubt Cervantes' own support for this Christian normality. But he is also a comic writer, and Sansón plays the role of the agelast, like Erasmus' "troublesome lunatic who deserves to be thrown out of the theatre". One figure, Don Antonio, protests that the cure has robbed the world of a source of infinite harmless pleasure. But there is another irony at the notion of the cure, although it remains largely unvoiced. Don Quijote's madness, it turns out, is a symptom which has held his melancholy at bay. So its rather violent cure precipitates the return of its underlying cause, for which the only available remedy now is his "enlightened" return to normal life to prepare for a good death.

Sansón Carrasco's mode of participation in the theatrical illusion staged by himself consists in his desire to destroy it in the name of the truth. His motivation for breaking into Don Quijote's imagined world contrasts with that of the Duke and Duchess. They desire to prolong it as a source of theatrical pleasure, while he desires to end it by destroying the hero's delusions. But both Sansón and the ducal pair are captivated where they think that they are in control. If we disregard the rather formulaic morality of the ending, when the Knight's *desengaño* leads him to accept the truth (and many critics take this finalising closure as Cervantes' last word), there is a deeper ironic suggestion that the madness and its deceptions have been a source of gratification, not only for the protagonist but also for the spectators and readers (including ourselves). Even his antagonist and therapeutical destroyer of illusions, is captivated (albeit differently) by the desire which draws him into the plot and then traps him like the spectators discussed by Lacan.

Sansón Carrasco's stated intention to cure the Knight is the goal of the desire which implicates him in the plot, but it is deferred and the novel is prolonged when, in the guise of the Knight of the Mirrors, he is accidentally unhorsed. Through this unexpected event he finds himself badly bruised and threatened

BAROQUE INCOMPLETION, THE CAPTIVATED SUBJECT 227

with death at the hands of Don Quijote, unless he agrees that Dulcinea del Toboso is more beautiful and gracious than his own fictional Lady and consents to go and present himself to Dulcinea as required by the laws of chivalry. He is quite literally trapped by the very fiction which he has sought to terminate by controlling it from within. His angry response to this reversal is in complete contrast with that of Tomé Cecial, Sancho Panza's neighbour who has played the role of his squire in this episode. In the dialogue between them, Cecial observes philosophically that it is easier to get into a situation than to get out of it, which is what he proposes to do by simply going home. But he goes further, making the same ironic point as the quasi-authorial Cide Hamete on the interchangeability of sanity and madness in the case of the Duke and Duchess. Cecial puts it as a rhetorical question:

> Don Quixote's mad and we're sane. Yet he gets off sound and smiling, while your worship comes out bruised and sorrowful. So, let's consider now which is the madder, the man who's mad because he can't help it, or the man who's mad by choice?
>
> [*Don Quijote loco, nosotros cuerdos, él se va sano y riendo: vuestra merced queda molido y triste. Sepamos, pues, ahora: ¿cuál es más loco: el que lo es por no poder menos, o el que lo es por su voluntad?*].[47]

Sansón's reply is that there is a difference between his own intentional madness and that of the Knight, because he can stop being mad when he wants:

> The difference between these two is that the madman of necessity will be so for ever, but the madman by choice will cease to be so when he will.
>
> [*La diferencia entre esos dos locos es que el que lo es por fuerza lo será siempre, y el que lo es de grado lo dejará de ser cuando quisiere*].[48]

The view that Don Quijote's madness is permanent and incurable because he is determined by it is perhaps arguable (his books have totally captured his will), although it must mean that Carrasco accepts the futility of his stated desire to cure him. But when he claims to be different from the real madman because he is sane and free to choose not to be mad, he immediately contradicts himself, by admitting that he is actually as trapped as the Knight. Whereas Tomé Cecial announces his free choice to cease being mad, by leaving for his home, Sansón replies that in his own case the earlier desire to cure the

---

47 Cervantes 1985, p. 561; Cervantes 1978 vol. 2, p. 147.
48 *Ibid.*

Knight has now become a desire for vengeance. There may be a measure of self-knowledge in this speech, but nonetheless he is trapped emotionally by his continuing participation in the fiction (not unlike Don Quijote, actually) in a way that Cecial is not:

> 'That is all right for you', replied Sampson, 'but it would be folly to suppose that I shall go back home till I have thrashed Don Quixote. And it will not be the desire to restore him to his senses that will drive me after him, but the desire for revenge; for the pain in my ribs will not allow me to entertain a more charitable purpose'.
>
> [- *Eso os cumple – respondió Sansón – porque pensar que yo he de volver a la mía hasta haber molido a palos a Don Quijote es pensar en lo escusado; y no me llevará ahora a buscarle el deseo que cobre su juicio, sino el de la venganza; que el dolor grande de mis costillas no me deja hacer más piadosos discursos*].[49]

The reader is never told explicitly whether his entrapment by this desire for revenge, is indeed what underlies Sansón's persistence. At the end there is no mention of it, but it has already been introduced by the narrator for the reader to infer later or to overlook. This chapter ends:

> Then Thomas Cecial went home, and left the Bachelor behind brooding on his vengeance. Our history will speak of him again when the time comes, but now it must make merry with Don Quixote.
>
> [*Tomé Cecial se volvió y le dejó, y él quedó imaginando su venganza, y la historia vuelve a hablar dél a su tiempo, por no dejar de regocijarse ahora con don Quijote*].[50]

The question still remains: what is it which continues to trap Carrasco, even when his stated intention to cure the Knight is defeated? Within the staged combats which he contrives to produce for the ostensible purpose of curing Don Quijote, there is a competitiveness which defeat has turned into a conscious desire for vengeance. Does Cervantes' novel throw any light on the sources of this competitiveness? This question points beyond the character of Carrasco himself.

The novel of 1605, later known as Part 1, criticises the deceptions of the novels of chivalry and the interpellative power of their discourse. But the

---

49   Ibid.
50   Cervantes 1985, p. 562; Cervantes 1978 vol. 2, p. 147.

reproducers of these illusions in Part 2 (1615) seek a gratification in which they would be the *autores*, in the seventeenth-century sense of producers, not necessarily original creators. Their enjoyment of the spectacle is a gratification which depends on their own sense of mastery, as they produce Don Quijote and Sancho Panza as *their* dupes, not the dupes of the chivalric discourse alone. They knowingly recycle the chivalric discourse parodied by Cervantes' novel in a fashion which can only be described as theatrical, with themselves in authorial control. But in Carrasco's case, this goes awry when he loses that control by being accidentally unhorsed, and this reversal brings about his shift to resentment and a desire for vengeance. For him, unlike Cecial (who is not a would-be controller), the reversal is not just an accidental event. He is now driven by a competitive desire to overthrow Don Quijote, still ostensibly for his own good, because his failure to be master of the plot does not appear to him as an accident but as a reversal which makes Don Quijote the triumphant party. In other words, as Cecial's ironic question suggests, Carrasco's defeat traps him and draws him even more completely into the desire for mastery which he has sought through the theatrical illusion. As he loses control over his plot, it acquires a new reality for him, controlling him through his desire for revenge.

9 Charisma and Competitive Envy

George Mariscal, in his *Contradictory Subjects*, argues that Carrasco is intensely attracted to the "charismatic" quality in Don Quijote. At the same time he is equally envious of him. The secret rivalry within this duplicitous acolyte is the basis of his covert motivation to destroy the Knight despite his admiration. Carrasco shares with the other characters the sense of wonderment (*admiración*) inspired by the Knight, and in his case it has originated in his reading of Part 1. Mariscal cites Maravall to make the point that the sense of wonder was the effect which the "diverse cultural practices" of the absolute monarchy and the church sought to inspire in the spectating populace:

> Spectacle, then, became a mass form of wonder insofar as it sought to astonish large groups of people, reduce them to momentary passivity, and ultimately subjugate them (that is, make them subjects).[51]

Mariscal's argument is that Carrasco's secret desire is aimed at appropriating the Knight's "charisma" for himself. He also emphasises its modernity. But he

---

51 Mariscal 1991, pp. 192–193.

does not point out that the source of this charisma is the power of the presses to make or break their heroes' prestige, even though that topic occupies the discussions between both of them throughout the whole of the chapter when Carrasco first appears (2:iii). However, he is right to see Carrasco as a resentful subject who desires to take for himself this power to captivate others.

Mariscal's observation on Cervantes' repeated use of the term *socarrón* supports his argument for the "repressed resentment" in the student himself:

> Indeed, the word *socarrón* connotes negative qualities and the kind of repressed resentment that will motivate Carrasco later in the novel. According to Covarrubias, the *socarrón* is "the dissembling scoundrel who only feigns interest [?] and when speaking with you *is secretly raging against you*".[52]

These observations on the dissimulation of motives by the *socarrón* are very suggestive, but the term itself is not limited to Sansón Carrasco's dissimulation. For example, the innkeeper in Chapter 3 of Part 1 is described as a *socarrón* when he plays along with Don Quijote's fantasy that his inn is a castle.[53] And in Part 2, when Sancho Panza, to his own surprise, manages to convince Don Quijote that he has been talking with Dulcinea herself, he too is described as a *socarrón*:

> And that rascal (*socarrón*) Sancho had all he could do to hide his amusement (*risa*: "laughter") on hearing this crazy talk from his master, whom he had so beautifully deceived.
> [*Harto tenía que hacer el socarrón de Sancho en disimular la risa, oyendo las sandeces de su amo, tan delicadamente engañado*].[54]

The feature common to all three examples, but passed over by Mariscal, is the suppression of laughter. This silencing enables the *socarrón* to "play along", that is to sustain the fantasy by participating in it, which open laughter would rule out.

---

52 Mariscal 1991, pp. 181–182. Mariscal quotes Covarrubias' definition of the *socarrón* as "el bellaco dissimulado, *que sólo pretende su interés*, y quando habla con vos está secretamente abrasando": Covarrubias [1611] 1977. Mariscal translates the highlighted clause as "who only feigns interest". But *pretender* is usually distinct from *fingir* in Spanish, unlike "pretend" in modern English. So perhaps "who only pursues his own interest" might be more accurate.
53 Cervantes 1985, p. 41 (here *socarrón* is translated as "crafty"); Cervantes 1978 vol. 1, p. 88.
54 Cervantes 1985, p. 532; Cervantes 1978 vol 2, p. 113.

The starting point for Mariscal's analysis of Carrasco's "repressed resentment" is that he is already an enthusiastic reader of Don Quijote's published exploits before he arrives belatedly on the scene in Part 2. But the significant omission in Mariscal's own argument is his inattention to Carrasco's silence about the comic nature of the published historical record which is Part 1. He rightly points to Carrasco's belief that Don Quijote possesses this "charisma", because he will be able to say that he has taken it from him in combat: "since I have conquered him, his glory, his fame, and his honour are transferred to my person".[55] But then, curiously like Carrasco himself, Mariscal assigns to it a substantial reality located in Don Quijote's person. He does not recognise that the competitive envy, which is Carrasco's desire to take the charisma from the adored one, does not depend upon the reality of that object of desire. For him, the object of Carrasco's envy is the "charisma" actually possessed by the Knight. And this "extraordinary quality of such an individual" is a positive historical development portending modern subjectivity.[56] If so, in desiring it for himself, Carrasco would not be deceived. But as he restages the fantasised chivalric world of Don Quijote in order to participate in it as a rival, Cervantes shows that Carrasco is captivated by the lure of a purely imaginary object whose only reality consists in that it seems to be possessed by another. His continuing captivation by this lure is only possible because he disregards the demystifying comic aspect of the published exploits of Part 1.

Carrasco's capture by a plot which he claims to control is essential to Cervantes' humour. In that respect he is no different from the Duke and Duchess. Although he is witty and intelligent, as befits the *socarrón*, instead of laughing he participates in the same fantasy as Don Quijote himself, and the lure which draws him into this participation is the purely imaginary object which Don Quijote seems to him to possess. This is where Lacan's analysis of the image is again very helpful. Carrasco seeks to obtain from his envied rival precisely that imaginary completion which he lacks, and which Lacan calls the *objet petit a* (the "little other object"):

> Such is true envy – the envy that makes the subject pale before the image of a completeness closed upon itself, before the idea that the *petit a*, the separated *a* from which he is hanging, may be for another the possession that gives satisfaction, *Befriedigung*.[57]

---

55 Mariscal 1991, p. 185.
56 *Ibid.*, p. 186.
57 Lacan 1987, p. 116.

The *objet petit a* is Lacan's term for that imaginary part of the self which is lacking but which seems to be located in the Other and is the cause of the subject's narcissistic and envious desire for completion. In this instance, Sansón Carrasco's aggressive desire to "cure" the Knight, by depriving him of his mode of being, his name, and his unearned title as Knight, has been shaped by his competitive desire dating back to his (mis)reading of Part 1. Here Mariscal's argument that Carrasco is motivated by his envy of the Knight's "charisma" is very persuasive. There is even a persuasive force in his in his observation that the potentially murderous rivalry underlying the acolyte's admiration is rather modern:

> The uncanny parallels between Sansón's behaviour and certain events in our own recent history (the celebrity-fan-assassination nexus) should not be discounted out of hand – the acolyte's obsession to be near (to become?) the object of his desire leads to the unavoidable moment when he must kill that object-person.[58]

But the imaginary "charisma" driving Carrasco's competitive rivalry with the Knight, captivates him because he fails to laugh at it. For all his mocking intelligence, Sansón Carrasco is captivated by the same discourse as Don Quijote himself. And, like the Duke and Duchess, he is not in control even when he thinks he is. Here again Cervantes' humour goes far beyond satirical mockery. He shows how the subject's ability to see through appearances, and even to manipulate them theatrically, by no means breaks their power to captivate him.

In discussing ideology as *adressivity* (Bakhtin) or *interpellation* (Althusser) by the market in Chapter 4, I point out that the construction of the modern consumer's desire for self-completion through the commodity being advertised, does not really depend on the real object but on that other "obscure object of desire" (Luís Buñuel) which, being imaginary, is completely unobtainable and is therefore infinitely renewable. Likewise, the object of Sansón Carrasco's fascinated desire is not an object which might be possessed, but the social prestige identified by Mariscal as the "charisma" whose possession promises to transform him into an object of others' *admiración*. Such is Sansón Carrasco's very modern form of competitive desire. But I would add that the competitive rivalry which sustains his desire is also central to Don Quijote's own imitative self-fashioning as a rival to the other chivalric heroes. Like

---

58 Mariscal 1991, p. 189.

Carrasco, he too is captivated by the power of publication.[59] For example, early in Part 1, when he returns in defeat from his first sally and a neighbour greets him as "señor Quijana", the neighbour's greeting is an unintended additional humiliation, because it reminds him of his real name and status. His angry response is that he knows who he is, but that he can be what he makes of himself by surpassing all his models:

> 'I know who I am', replied Don Quixote, 'and I know too that I am capable of being not only the characters I have named, but all the Twelve Peers of France and all the Nine Worthies as well, for my exploits are [or rather, 'will be'] far greater than all the deeds they have done, all together and each by himself'.
>
> [- *Yo sé quién soy* – *respondió don Quijote* –, *y sé que puedo ser no sólo los que he dicho, sino todos los doce Pares de Francia, y aun todos los nueve de la Fama, pues a todas las hazañas que ellos todos juntos y cada uno por sí hicieron, se aventajarán las mías*].[60]

Given the way in which all the other readers in Don Quijote's village excitedly compare the relative worth of the various heroes of the novels of chivalry (i.e. their "charisma"), as does the future Don Quijote himself, it is clear that Cervantes' novel identifies his self-proclaimed Knight's competitive relationship with his ideal models as yet another example of the competition between those fictional heroes themselves. Here an extra-textual social reality intrudes, and its effects are registered in Cervantes' comic text, precisely through the debates between the readers in Don Quijote's village over the relative worth of the various chivalric heroes. That competition between fictional heroes was actually a real driving force sustaining the mass production of chivalric novels, as it recycled the old epics in this new form for the new consumer market. Competition between the heroes of the various heroic narratives had been unknown to the earlier, largely oral epic traditions. It was brought into existence by the competition between the new presses in order to attract and retain

---

59   Cf. Girard 1976, pp. 1–10 *et passim*. Girard's analyses are brilliant but nostalgic. For him all desire is imitative, and he even identifies Don Quijote's imitation of Amadís as an *imitatio Christi* (p. 2). He argues that modern competitive individualism, which engenders murderous envy and its desire to become the envied rival (echoed by Mariscal), arises from the collapse of the hierarchical distance separating the acolyte from his revered model: "The imitation of Christ becomes the imitation of one's neighbour" (p. 59). He calls this collapse of hierarchical distance, which for him is disastrous, the "approach of the mediator".

60   Cervantes 1985, p. 54; Cervantes 1978 vol. 1, p. 106.

readership loyalty, and to profit from their capital investments in their respective heroes. In short, these heroes' "charisma" was absolutely essential to the new capitalist mode of production for the mass market.

This cultural development soon saw the birth of the literary sequel, in order to prolong the profitability of the "charismatic" hero. An early example was the writing of Feliciano da Silva, whose inflated prose style is mocked by Cervantes in Chapter 1 of *Don Quijote*, where it is the direct cause of the fascinated hidalgo's madness as he struggles to decipher its meanings. He is trapped by the Baroque desire to reach the truth presumed to be concealed within a difficult text. To borrow Walter Benjamin's terminology, Cervantes' humour registers the disappearance of the "aura" of the epic hero in the age of mechanical reproduction, but it returns as an endlessly reproduced object of nostalgic desire.

Da Silva's verbosity was in principle endless, and later Don Quijote displays his acquired skill in reproducing the very discourse which captivates him (for example when he mentally composes how his future historian will describe his dawn departure as he sets out on his adventures). This verbal expansiveness was not just a matter of stylistic inflation. Da Silva was an early innovator of the literary sequel, which is why Luís Andrés Murillo, the Cervantes scholar and editor of the Castalia edition, describes him very tellingly as the creator of "a kind of industrial literary production in the age of Charles v".[61] The competition between presses was between authors too, and Cervantes was as implicated in these commercial rivalries as any of the writers whom he parodies. We are even told that the *hidalgo*'s first response to Da Silva's style was his intention to imitate it, by taking up a pen to write a sequel himself. But he is lured into participation by his long discussions and ruminations on the relative merits of the different chivalric heroes, and this finally leads him to decide to enter the competitive fray himself, not just as an author but as a hero modelled on Amadís of Gaul. He will recreate himself as one of them, in order to outshine them all. He is so captivated by the competition that he literally becomes the hero of the sequel which he had intended to write.

The reliance of this commercially driven competition on the heroes' "charisma" lived on. An early twentieth-century example of the proliferation of chivalric heroes can be found in the mass production in the United States of the so-called "dime novels" from the 1880s onwards, and their investments in the Wild West heroes of the already faded past, which they reinvented as timeless myths. For a large part of the twentieth century, Hollywood expanded this appropriation to new levels, along with the remarkably similar male warrior fantasies of the charismatic Saviour on horseback, quixotically righting the

---

61 Cervantes 1978 vol. 1, p. 72, footnote 8.

wrongs of the world and saving whole communities with his miraculously accurate six-guns.[62] The spectators' identification with the images of the charismatic cowboy even outlived the films themselves in the famous Marlborough cigarette advertisements. These images were successful because they continued to provoke the desire to possess the imaginary charisma which promises to complete the gazing subject.[63] This commercial construction of the otherwise absent charismatic "presence" is still a potent ideological force and, as Mariscal's analysis shows, it conceals a potential for murderous violence directed at any rival who seems to possess that imaginary object of desire. Whatever its limitations, laughter is still our best protection against this captivating form of modern power. Laughter at least gives the laughing subject the potential to take a position outside its ability to colonize the imagination, and to resist it.

10 The Captivated Quixotic Critic

In his *Subject of Modernity*, Anthony Cascardi places Cervantes' *Don Quijote* at the origins of modernity. In itself this is not contentious. But Cascardi's distinctive contribution is that he focuses less on the psychological motivation of the protagonist and far more on the position constructed for the reader as the interpreter of a disparate text. He argues that this position anticipates the rational subject of modernity, which only appears later on the historical scene with Descartes. In his view, the fragmented and heterogeneous world of the Renaissance proliferation of discourses demanded an integration which only a specifically modern subjectivity could provide. Instead of making Don Quijote himself the hero of this struggle to recover a vanishing order, he entrusts this task to the reader and critic:

> But since the modern novel emerges, with Cervantes' *Don Quixote*, at a moment when the world has been carved up into a variety of independent discourses that are subject to no controlling authority or master code, it follows that neither the subject of the novel nor the novelistic world can be taken as given or simply reflected as a whole. Indeed the plurality of discourses in a work like *Don Quixote* shows us that the historical world can no longer be subsumed under the image of a social or

---

62 Cf. Wright 1977.
63 Cf. my discussion of Bernays' *Propaganda* in Chapter 4 of this book.

aesthetic whole. Rather the subject and the world must be fashioned by the synthesis of separate and sometimes incompatible parts.[64]

In effect, Cascardi's description of a world fragmented through the proliferation of incompatible discourses restates the crisis discussed by Michel de Certeau, for which "mystical discourse" (*la mystique*) provided the orthopedic remedy (See Chapter 6). But for Cascardi the fragmentation is repaired through the rationality of the reader, who recreates a unity which has ceased to exist. The final sentence in the above passage is particularly significant because of the imperative within the apparently factual statement that "the subject and the world *must* be fashioned by the synthesis of separate ... parts". He not only asserts that there is a new reading competence brought into existence through Cervantes' *Don Quijote* but also, and above all, that this new competence is necessarily a synthesising activity, in which the self and the world are at stake. This demand for a unifying synthesis enables the historical emergence of the "transcendental subject" of modern rationality and judgement, which anticipates Descartes and reaches its plenitude with Kant. Cascardi's point, in a nutshell, is that the world, as given in the proliferation of disparate discourses from the Renaissance onwards, has become irredeemably fragmented. Therefore, the function of the reader of the emergent novel is to supply the missing unity through the activity of reading. This activity raises the reader to a "transcendental" position where he has to supply the meanings which are no longer immanent in the world or the text, and which therefore must be supplied through his rational synthesizing as a reading subject. It is the reader, not the Knight who is the hero of this text.

Cascardi's idea that there is an implicit demand for synthesis in the act of reading associates this emergent subjectivity with what Bakhtin calls the pressure towards "monologism" within the centralising rationality of the nation state. It is not that Cascardi is simply wrong here. Far from it; he is illuminating. But he is not concerned with what is overlooked or even repressed within this emergent unifying subjectivity. He disregards the reading subject's capacity for laughter. That is perhaps why he cites Bakhtin only once, when he presents him as though he were in agreement with Lukács' nostalgic theses on the fallen and fragmented world which then must be overcome through the act of reading or interpretation:

> The *Quixote* is "modern" insofar as it shows us that the world cannot be understood through the principles of imitation and can no longer be

---

64   Cascardi 1992, p. 81.

subsumed under the image of any pre-existing social or aesthetic whole. The discursive heterogeneity of the novel, which Bakhtin described in terms of its "heteroglossia", corresponds to the discursive heterogeneity of the modern world. In response to this heterogeneity, the activity of reading becomes the process by which we may synthesize a (coherent) world, in Cartesian terms by representing that world, picturing it; in Kantian terms by bringing that world into agreement with the categories of our understanding.[65]

Although Cascardi's earlier imperative "must" is slightly moderated here to the permissive "may", this reading yokes Bakhtin to the need for a "monological" consciousness on the reader's part, which Bakhtin actually criticised and historicised as the negative achievement of the rationalistic culture of the centralising nation state. But given Cascardi's point of view, he is correct to point to Wolgang Iser as the contemporary phenomenological continuator of this Cartesian-Kantian tradition. Iser's *Act of Reading*[66] does indeed posit the reader as a phenomenological synthesiser who moves through the fictionalised time of the plot, negotiating its textual gaps and contradictions in order to reach the unrepresentable unity which is the ironic structure of the whole reading experience.

Because Cascardi is silent on the humour of *Don Quijote* and on the reader's capacity for laughter, his history does not go critically against the grain of the formation of the humourless transcendental subjectivity which it narrates. However, he touches on such a possibility earlier in his book, when he writes more dialectically of "the simultaneous increase in the mobility of the psyche and a heightening of the repressive powers of society".[67] This is perfectly consistent with the internal dynamics of Maravall's "culture of the Baroque". Reapplied to the proliferation of discourses in both the novel and the social order itself, this formulation could lead to a recognition of the reactionary nature of the demand for restored singularity. Bakhtin labels this demand the monological seriousness which is challenged by the social "heteroglossia" incorporated into the emergent novel.

For Cascardi, *e pluribus unum* is not just an ideal for states, but an imperative for coherence which the modern reader has to supply to a text. As an

---

65 Actually Cascardi marks a slight divergence from Lukács' thesis by saying that the modern novel is only "anticipated", not founded, by *Don Quijote*: "this is a text which projects at its limit, but does not itself contain, the position of 'transcendental' reflection associated with the subject's absolute claims to truth"; Cascardi 1992, p. 84.
66 Iser 1978.
67 Cascardi 1992, p. 25.

example he takes up the issue of the proliferation of available heroic models, which leads Don Quijote to say that he is capable of being any one of them.[68] Pointing out that many critics have said that this marks the end of a fixed world based on *mimesis*, Cascardi draws the conclusion that the emergent novel as *genre* corresponds to a new intellectual necessity:

> Phrased in terms of the requirements of genre, it can be said that the proliferation of models *demands* [my emphasis – JH] the stabilizing of identity in a way that can become institutionalized, fixed, and incorporated as a requirement for the comprehension of texts. This demand – which indicates a discursive possibility standing at the limit of the pre-novelistic framework of the *Quixote*, as of the works of Rabelais and Montaigne as well – consists in the formation of a governing point of view, one that relies on the separation of values from facts.[69]

When Bakhtin writes of the emergent modern novel as genre, with its own demands and requirements, it is in the opposite sense. The novel's incorporation of heterogeneous social discourses with their multiple and sometimes incompatible viewpoints and evaluations, is indissolubly linked to its resistance to unification and hierarchy, often in comic terms and sometimes in conflict with the author's own ideological commitments, as in the case of Dostoevsky. If this view is accepted, it undermines Cascardi view of the genre's "requirements for comprehension". The institutionalised stability of identity and meaning around a "governing point of view" is precisely what Bakhtin calls "monologism". He considers this singularity to be characteristic of the closed world of the epic as it was *reinvented* by the centralising cultures of Western Europe in the seventeenth and eighteenth centuries. Bakhtin's view of literary and cultural history does indeed coincide with that of Cascardi (and Lukács), but where Cascardi sees necessity and unifying transcendence, Bakhtin sees resistance to the attempted imposition of any "final word". For Bakhtin, the modern novel resists the reinvention of epic singularity, which is why the laughter of Rabelais became particularly important for him. This will be discussed in the next chapter.

---

68 Cervantes 1985, p. 54; Cervantes 1978 vol. 1, p. 106.
69 Cascardi 1992, p. 83.

CHAPTER 8

The Dialectics of Laughter and Anxiety

In his book on the art of Rabelais,[1] Bakhtin presents his view of Carnival laughter as a continuation of the millennial struggle against the ideological dominance of the ruling classes. These festivities temporarily overturned the self-idealising claims of the ruling class by inverting symbolically all the established forms of power and authority. Beggars were crowned as Kings, Servants became Masters, and many official ceremonies and modes of speech and behavior were travestied. Moreover, the materiality of the flesh was laughingly exalted above the dominant "spirituality" which normally denigrated it, and everyday mundane objects were given spiritual meanings which mocked the ideal transcendentalism of the established social order. This parodic festivity vindicated the "material principle" (Bakhtin) by placing it above the official spirituality which deprived the material world of meaning, reducing it to nothing. In its own way this levelling tradition which exalted the lowly was consistent with those aspects of Christianity which had always insisted on the presence of the divine within the lowly world, including the "word made flesh" of the Incarnation. Paradoxical as it may seem to our largely secular age, the laughing parodic inversions of the Carnival celebrations actually reaffirmed the presence of the spiritual within the material world, no less than the erotic intensities of Saint John of the Cross' poetry and Saint Teresa's "mystical ejaculations" (Lacan) discussed in Chapter 6. In effect Bakhtin's positive evaluation of this laughter which raised the lowly is an inversion of Hobbes' view of laughter as the moment of "sudden glory", which also elevated the lowly (the "pusillanimous"), but only in their own deluded self-estimation.

Bakhtin's reading of the carnivalesque language and imagery of François Rabelais is similar to that of his near-contemporary English literary critics like C.L. Barber and Northrop Frye. They too were influenced by historical anthropology when they interpreted the popular festive sources of Shakespearean comedy in terms of collective resistance.[2] Northrop Frye even saw this symbolic rebellion as a Freudian de-repression: "The action in comedy is intensely Freudian in shape: the erotic pleasure principle explodes underneath the social anxieties sitting on top of it and blows them sky-high".[3] The shared

---

1 Bakhtin 1968.
2 Barber 1965; Frye 1965.
3 Frye 1965, p. 75.

feature is the vindication of the desiring body and the overturning of the "social anxieties" which repress it. But Bakhtin also identified the resistance to fear within popular laughter as a primordial resistance, even prior to the symbolic struggles which mediated social conflicts. Bakhtin's argument shows the direct influence of Olga Freidenberg's anthropology. Her essay, "The Origin of Parody" (1926)[4] contains many examples of the parodic doubling of the sacred and the profane which are to be found in his book on Rabelais. She sees them as evidence of a trans-historical structure, whereas Bakhtin argues (somewhat unevenly) for popular struggle and resistance. There is a populist note here, because Bakhtin tends to idealize this millennial "folk resistance" through laughter, without paying sufficient attention to the proximity of the Carnival to the pogrom, and to its frequently misogynist manifestations. In such instances, the Carnival's mockery of society's marginalized or subordinate "others" reveals its provenance from within the hierarchical and patriarchal order. This form of mockery did not necessarily challenge the dominant ideology, let alone correct it. It might even be said to have reproduced it, sometimes violently, by raising the Carnival revelers to their imaginary position of Hobbesian "sudden glory" as temporary masters. However, despite this limitation, I will argue that Bakhtin's overall argument is more complex and more persuasive than it may appear.

To find a way of articulating the persistence of the primordial terror overcome by laughter within its later more "ambivalent" social forms, Bakhtin turns to the language of the Kantian sublime, which echoed Edmund Burke's earlier observation that "terror is in all cases whatsoever, either more openly or latently, the ruling principle of the sublime".[5] Bakhtin writes:

> We must take into consideration the importance of cosmic terror, the fear of the immeasurable, the infinitely powerful. The starry sky, the gigantic material masses of the mountains, the sea, the cosmic upheavals, elemental catastrophes – these constitute the terror that pervades ancient mythologies, philosophies, systems of images, and language itself with its semantics. An obscure memory of cosmic perturbations in the dim and distant past and the dim terror of future catastrophes form the very basis of human thought, speech, and images.[6]

For Bakhtin, the primordial resistance to this "cosmic terror" preceded the conflicts which arose later from the hierarchical differentiations of caste and

---

4 Freidenberg 1974.
5 Burke 1990.
6 Bakhtin 1968, p. 335.

class. But it still persisted as an "obscure memory" within the later symbolic forms of laughter which resisted *social* terror. The continuing influence of Cassirer's account of development on Bakhtin is evident here, because the earlier symbolic forms do not simply disappear historically but are modified as they are subsumed into the succeeding ones. So underlying all the Carnival forms, including Bakhtin's favourite "gay carnival monster", is the collective struggle of all human beings against primordial terrors, especially the terror of dimly remembered catastrophes and their anticipated return. Bakhtin makes this triumph over terror by collective laughter the key to all human culture because it lays the basis for "true human fearlessness".[7]

Bakhtin's language of the sublime may well appear overblown, but his main argument is that the symbolic struggle from below against the self-idealisation of the ruling classes was a continuation of the collective resistance to the primordial terrors which the ruling castes (or later classes) had commandeered symbolically to support their claims. In that sense the "sublime" served their interests. He even names religion as the main agency of the rulers' appropriation of this "obscure memory of terror" to impose awe and terror on their own behalf: "It is used by all religious systems to oppress man and his consciousness".[8] That is to say, festive laughter was a dialogical riposte to the ruling ideology, and it relied on the *desublimation* of its forms. Bakhtin is on empirically safer grounds here. There is plenty of evidence for the ruling castes' or classes' symbolic appropriation of the terrors of natural and/or supernatural powers, in order to justify and sustain the social hierarchy on the grounds of its continuity with the cosmic order. Indeed it would be difficult to think of any ancient empire (and perhaps modern ones too) which did not depend on this symbolic appropriation of natural or divine powers. But what is eluded by Bakhtin's invocation of the sublime terrors of nature is that even the supposedly primordial Chaos itself, including its monsters or its "monstrous" lack of form, were always retrospective inventions, wrapped in the timeless claims of myth to support whatever order had replaced the historically previous forms of social organisation. In short, the primordial powers themselves were always retroactively constructed "memories" which served to justify the current rulers as the legitimate inheritors of the heroic slayers and/or tamers of monsters, who had brought order and imposed form ("Apollonian" in Nietzsche's sense) upon the Chaos prior to their Olympian rule. One remarkable aspect of Athenian culture, if Nietzsche's *Birth of Tragedy* is to be given any credence, is that the primordial destructive energy was indeed an "obscure memory" preserved

---

7   *Ibid.* Some thinkers assign a similar prophylactic role to the monsters in children's nightmares: they enable future terrors to be faced and overcome.
8   *Ibid.*

by that culture. It was included within the symbolic order which assigned it a place, not only in the cultic celebrations of the creative destroyer Dionysos but also (*pace* Nietzsche!) of the Thesmophoria dedicated to the goddesses Demeter and Persephone. These ceremonies and sacred spaces show that although the patriarchal assumptions of the warrior aristocracy may have been dominant, they were not uncontested. Moreover, from the viewpoint of the subalterns within the continuing symbolic struggle, the earlier social forms were not only recalled as a time of primal terror and Chaos but also as a lost Golden Age. This counter-hegemonic "utopian" memory might explain why the comic theatre celebrated within the same festive celebrations as the tragedies, the very Dionysian or Thesmophorian "chaos" whose threat to return was a source of potential anxiety for the dominant ideology. The laughter of comedy should be seen as a way of overcoming that social anxiety, whether it was consciously acknowledged or not. In the extant literature of the ancient Mediterranean world, the "Old Comedies" of Aristophanes come closest to these festivities, because in them the heroes, and even the Gods themselves, suffer mocking degradation.

Bakhtin emphasises that the Carnival laughter of the Christian era continued the symbolic resistance of its festive pre-Christian antecedents, particularly the Roman Saturnalia. These festivities not only gave to the oppressed a momentary liberation from their normal fear of their overlords but also a release from their own internalised respect for the established order. The laughing inversions of the social and cosmic hierarchy served to question the transcendental claims which legitimated the dominance of the rulers. The Carnival practices reaffirmed the shared human condition by suspending all social differences and their supporting cosmology, in the name of the collective material body whose fleshly properties and fate are shared by all. The significant point in Bakhtin's argument is not really his affirmation of the "primordial" truths expressed by his rather uncritical use of the Kantian sublime, but the laughing *desublimation* of the ideological claims of the ruling castes or classes. This desublimation undid, however momentarily, the rulers' claim to divinely sanctioned powers which the dominant ideology imposed on the subjectivity of the subjugated. At such moments other possibilities are "obscurely remembered", and they constitute a dialogical riposte to the reigning ideology. The release of the laughing subject from the terrors of the sublime, which the ruling castes had appropriated as their own, was the momentary achievement of this mockery from below. It was a levelling negation of hierarchy and was potentially democratic. Moreover, the scene of this radical desublimation was not only the external space of the public square, where it was ritually enacted, but above all the inward subjectivity of the laughing participants in the collective celebrations. It could be said that for this laughter "all that was sacred was profaned" except for the important historical point that in the pre-modern world the profane did not yet exist outside the realm of the sacred.

1   Carnival Enters into History

Given the symbolic aspect of the real and violent struggles for hegemony in the feudal epoch in Western Europe, each successful warlord's appropriation of the mythical powers of the beasts and dragons to be found everywhere in their heraldic imagery, becomes perfectly comprehensible. Those imaginary powers were pressed symbolically into the service of the lineal descendants or followers of their alleged conquerors (like Saint George slaying the dragon). But equally comprehensible from a dialogical standpoint is the re-transformation of those symbolic feudal monsters into figures of laughter and mockery by the emergent city festivals from around the twelfth century onwards. The huge wickerwork representations of monsters and giants were not actually millennial "folk" creations (*pace* Bakhtin) but the products of a particular self-assertive activity on the part of the emergent cities and towns, where the new bourgeois-artisan alliance re-appropriated and reversed the symbolic powers of the terrifying monsters of feudal authority. The wickerwork giants rapidly became local patriotic emblems of their respective towns and cities, as their Carnivals re-appropriated for themselves the increasingly archaic images of feudal terror in order to mock them.[9] It is not difficult to see in these collective material practices the symbolic resistance underlying Rabelais' vast comic expansion of their range and meaning. To take a pertinent example: the feudal appropriation of the mythical powers of the monster can be seen in the various legends of Gargouille, the dragon said to have been subdued by the Merovingian king Clotaire when he became Bishop of Rouen (AD 631–641). The legends relate how the conquered dragon was led back into the city to be burned by this triumphant warrior King/Bishop, but its head and neck had too much fire of their own. As its power could not be destroyed, it was affixed to the church walls facing outwards to give protection against the other evil powers. So the conquered monster became the protective gargoyle, whose joking etymological proximity to Rabelais' Gargantua and Gargamelle is quite patent. Bakhtin's "gay carnival monster" at the centre of the Carnival celebrations, for which he cites many attested examples in addition to the literary giants of Rabelais' famous novel, clearly functioned in a similar way: the power of the terrifying monster

---

9   Cf. Bercé 1976, p. 99ff.

previously appropriated by the warrior class, is re-appropriated and inverted by the bourgeois-artisan alliance in the towns and cities, in order to enable its terrors be overcome by collective laughter.

Bakhtin himself seems to concede the limits to his own populist anthropology when he argues that the millennial repetition of the laughing counterclaims of the popular festivities could not become the basis of any conscious rebellion, supported by historical self-awareness, until there was a significant merging of their spontaneous resistance from below with the more reflexive consciousness to be found in those higher written traditions which we now call "literature". He writes that it was only when the millennial traditions of popular laughter were fused with the emergent literary discourses of the Renaissance that this culture of laughter was able to develop its inherent potential to become the basis of a new historical self-consciousness. Before that conjuncture, the potential for "becoming" remained isolated and therefore undeveloped:

> [And so] medieval culture of folk humor was fundamentally limited to these small islands of feasts and recreations. Official serious culture existed beside them but strictly divided them from the market place. The shoots of a new world outlook were sprouting, but they could not grow and flower as long as they were enclosed in the popular gaiety of recreation and banqueting or in the fluid realm of familiar speech. In order to achieve this growth and flowering, laughter had to enter the world of great literature. By the end of the Middle Ages a gradual disappearance of the dividing line between humor and great literature can be observed.[10]

A Marxist view of this would be that this ideological development marked the beginning of a new historically progressive alliance between popular aspirations and an emergent bourgeoisie, even if only at the level of temporary ideological concordance. In Bakhtin's dialogical account, the popular forms of laughter were not just passively appropriated by the "world of great literature". Rather, this conjunctural alliance enabled the culture of popular laughter itself to develop its hitherto unrealised capacity to break out of its former limitations:

> The culture of laughter begins to break through the narrow walls of festivities and to enter into all spheres of ideological life. Official fear and seriousness could be abandoned in everyday life. This process was completed during the Renaissance. Medieval laughter found its highest

---

10   Bakhtin 1968, pp. 96–97.

expression in Rabelais' novel. It became the form of a new free and critical historical consciousness.[11]

This could aptly be described as a "Gramscian" moment, when the spontaneous language (and images) of the popular masses enters into a new productive contact with the critical consciousness of the few but influential "organic intellectuals" of the time.[12] It also marks the moment of a Hegelian leap in consciousness, but it was a short-lived moment. In Bakhtin's overall historical argument, this breakthrough towards historical self-understanding was itself subjected to new discursive forms of reactive recontainment with the establishment of the Absolutist centralising nation state, and its neo-classical rationalist aesthetics:

> The seventeenth century was marked by the stabilization of the new order of the absolute monarchy. A relatively progressive "universally historic form" was created and was expressed in Descartes' rationalist philosophy and in the aesthetics of classicism. Rationalism and classicism clearly reflect the fundamental traits of the new official culture; it differed from the ecclesiastic feudal culture but was also authoritarian and serious, though less dogmatic. New prevailing concepts were established which, according to Marx, the new ruling class inevitably presented as eternal truths.[13]

For Bakhtin, this is not only a matter of new ideas, but above all of new forms of thinking and feeling, i.e. of aesthetic forms:

> In the new official culture there prevails a tendency toward the stability and completion of being, toward one single meaning, one single tone of seriousness.[14]

Bakhtin's aesthetic judgments on the monological limitations of neo-classicism are particularly pertinent because he relates them to a major historical shift in social relations, and the consequent "forgetting" of the earlier modes of understanding. He writes that in the period prior to the reign of

---

11 *Ibid.*
12 This perspective is suggested by Peter Ives, who writes that the differences between the "political" Gramsci and the "literary" Bakhtin should not be seen as exclusive. Cf. Ives 2004, p. 73.
13 Bakhtin 1968, p. 101.
14 *Ibid.*

Louis XIV, Rabelais had been understood unproblematically in the context of the still acceptable conventions of popular laughter:

> This is why Rabelais did not as yet appear exceptional, unlike everything else. Later the atmosphere in which Rabelais was understood vanished almost entirely, and he became a strange and solitary author who needed special interpretation and commentary.[15]

In the new situation, neither Boileau nor La Bruyère could understand Rabelais' pre-classical literary forms and their ambivalent humour, seeing in them only inexplicably "monstrous" combinations. To illustrate the neo-classicists' failure to understand the forms created in their recent historical past, Bakhtin quotes from the fifth edition of La Bruyère's *Caractères* (1690):

> Marot and Rabelais are inexcusable for scattering so much filth in their writings; they both had enough genius and originality to be able to do without it, even for those who seek rather what is comical than what is admirable in the author. Rabelais above all is incomprehensible: his book is a mystery [*une énigme*], a mere chimera; it has a lovely woman's face with the feet and tail of a serpent [*sic*] or of some more hideous animal [*quelque autre bête plus difforme*]. It is a monstrous jumble of delicate and ingenious morality and of filthy depravation. Where it is bad, it excels by far the worst, and is fit only to delight the rabble [*c'est le charme de la canaille*]; and when it is good, it is exquisite and excellent, and may entertain the most delicate.[16]

By now, according to Bakhtin: "the grotesque tradition peculiar to the marketplace and the academic literary tradition have parted ways and can no longer be brought together".[17] This dissociation of sensibility is extremely significant. Bakhtin is genuinely perceptive in relating the shift in style to the wider historical shift in ideology and emotional response. It amounted to an effect of the Absolutist revolution from above, as the dominant culture now repudiated "*le charme de la canaille*". The "Gramscian moment" was definitely over. But I would add that La Bruyère's "énigme" is not simply a sign of his failure to understand the "two-faced" nature of these now monstrous jumbles. Bakhtin

---

15   Bakhtin 1968, p. 107.
16   La Bruyère [1690], quoted in Bakhtin 1968, p.107–108. The English translation is in a footnote on p. 108.
17   Bakhtin 1968, p. 109.

does not investigate the nature of the forgetting when he writes that the leading neo-classical critics could no longer understand Rabelais and Marot. Arising out of the radical dissociation of sensibility noted by Bakhtin, La Bruyère's language is clearly symptomatic of the reactive anxiety expressed in his emphatic revulsion and repudiation of the lower undisciplined and almost formless body. His dismissive phrase, *le charme de la canaille*, should also be read symptomatically as an admission of a residual attraction to the repudiated "monstrous" lower body, amounting to a *nostalgie de la boue* amidst the emphatic repudiation.

In the light of the still recent historical background whose return in the seventeenth century remained a terrifying possibility, this repudiation of much sixteenth-century cultural production (routinely considered "barbaric" by the ideologists of the new official culture in France) should be seen as an oblique expression of deep anxieties. The neo-classicists' objections were not only made on the grounds of the indecency permitted in the recent past, but above all on the aesthetic grounds of its lack of order. That is why its relatively uncontrolled openness of form seemed to neo-classical aesthetics to border on the monstrous. Commenting on the way that heterogeneity appears to La Bruyère as a "monstrueux assemblage", Bakhtin writes:

> To characterise this strange combination, La Bruyère uses the image of the chimera – a significant symbol. The chimera is grotesque; in [neo] classical aesthetics there was no place for it. The combination of human and animal forms is one of the most ancient images, but it is completely alien to La Bruyère, the faithful spokesman of his time. He is used [sic] to conceive being as something finished, stable, completed, clear, and firm. He draws a dividing line between all bodies and objects. Even the moderate grotesque image of Melusine in popular legends appears to him a monstrous mixture.[18]

Bakhtin writes that this aesthetics was responsible for the narrowing of laughter towards purposive satire with the advent of the instrumental rationalism of the centralising state. But it is important to remember that the centralising state also came into being to overcome fierce internecine conflicts by imposing a unifying order. Certainly, this resolution of conflict operated in favour of the newly centralized power, but its suppression of mayhem explains why

---

18 *Ibid.*, p. 109. An earlier discussion of the monstrous "ugly" nature of loose open-ended forms is to be found in the literary judgments by the Canon of Toledo in *Don Quijote, Part One*.

it appeared desirable, or at least acceptable, to other classes too. The Crown was able to appeal to widespread anxieties over the possible return of chaos, in order to garner support for its centralizing policy. These anxieties had clearly been the case in Tudor and Stuart England too, and I have discussed them already in relation to Shakespeare's treatment of the ambivalent figure of Falstaff and the duplicities of Prince Hal. In France in the 1640s the example of the revolutionary wars in England and the execution of Charles I certainly reinforced those anxieties. But they had also been an important aspect of the wider support for the earlier centralizing ideology. Prior to Henry IV's proclamation of the Edict of Nantes (1598), France had been torn apart by the religious wars, and by the feudal interests taking advantage of them in order to reassert their independent powers. The revolt of the old warrior nobility (the *noblesse d'épée*) against the young Louis XIV in the 1640s, known as the "Fronde", served as a warning of their possible return.

2   Laughter and Religious Conflict

Bakhtin mentions the religious wars as one source of the terrors overcome by Rabelaisian laughter, but he does not focus on them as the active social force behind the narrowing of popular laughter to satire. In fact, a major force in the transformation of the popular scatological invective of the Carnival traditions into an instrument for the satirical degradation of opponents was not primarily the work of the rationalist champions of the new state hierarchy. They favoured courtly civility, politeness, and repressive restraint, later cultivated by the bourgeoisie too. Satirical degradation was far more characteristic of militant Protestantism and its Counter-Reformation opponents. Martin Luther in particular was a master of mocking scatological invective. But it is a mistake to regard him as just a Puritan agelast hostile to all laughter. In an illuminating article on the proximity of Luther's laughter to that of Rabelais, Hub Swart recounts Luther's own version of his sudden illumination and laughter in the monastery privy. It was the moment of his reconnection with his lower body, and of his release through laughter from his tormenting anxiety over God's Justice:

> Suddenly it dawned on him that, rather than being punished by God, it is God's justice by which we are *justified* or *rectified* (*gerecht* or *recht gemacht*) and saved from sin. This new translation contains the nucleus of Protestant theology. Indeed Luther's gigantic corpus of writing is simply the discursive echo of that tremendous roar of laughter that overtook

him "in that tower, in which the monk's 'secret place' was located ('in haec turri, in qua secretus locus erat monachorum')". It was a laugh that applied, not to a particular phrase or concept, but to a whole epoch, a whole world: laughter with historical generative force, a triumph of life over gloomy seriousness. The new art of reading was bestowed on him in a monk's privy. "This art [of reading] was bestowed unto me by the Holy Spirit in this cl[oaca] in the tower". (3232b) (*Diesse Kunst hatt mit mir der Heilige Geist auff diser cl[oaca] auff dem thorm gegeben*). It was an experience of relief and release. Luther was suddenly able to relieve himself of his burden, both mentally and physically.[19]

Hub Swart observes that Luther's narration actually compressed a longer process of reflection into a moment of sudden conversion which he calls a *Gestalt-switch*:

> ... the sudden transformation of a gloomy Catholic into a jolly Protestant [!], a sudden shift from gothic horror into Renaissance gaiety – thanks to the decisive experience of laughter. Two basic and relatively stable images of one and the same individual are separated from one another by a sudden metamorphosis. Young Luther, who devoted himself desperately to asceticism, had been suffering from melancholy and constipation. In his autobiographical account, the *Turm Erlebnis* is the turning point between the gloomy, inhibited monk he used to be and the jolly, highly productive ringleader of Protestantism he came to be.[20]

The suddenness of Luther's laughter and its transformative power suggests its proximity to Hobbes' account of laughter as "sudden glory", but Hub Swart's Bakhtinian view of this "Gestalt-switch" is that it was a revolutionary moment, not a passing delusion in the mind of the "pusillanimous" being derided by Hobbes. In an Afterword to his article, Hub Swart concedes the "demonic" other side to the triumphant laughter of this "jolly Protestant". Luther's purifying zeal was soon revealed in his fierce antisemitism and especially in his demand for the violent suppression of the rebellious German peasantry. This erstwhile revolutionary moved rapidly to normalization through counter-revolutionary violence, notwithstanding his down-to-earth homely *Table Talk*. Later, some pious Lutherans tried to spiritualise Luther's narrative by eliminating his scatological connection with the body, in a manner not entirely unlike the Catholic

---

19   Zwart 1999, p. 60.
20   *Ibid.*, p. 62.

commentaries on the eroticism of Saint Teresa and Saint John of the Cross (including his own). But Luther's self-proclaimed anal relief is distinct, and unavoidable. The famous incident when he hurled his inkpot at the Devil may have been a melancholic delusion (to which he was prone) or a legend propagated by the Grimm brothers, but it may also have been just an appropriate metaphor for his cleansing project through writing.

The English Puritans likewise made use of the popular language of the lower body for their own militant purposes. But once they were in power they abolished all the popular festivals, including the Christmas and Mayday celebrations, and they imposed a rigid repression on "indecent" discourse and behaviour too. It is not incidental that these arch-monologists and agelasts exterminated the incipient democracy of the Levellers and the Diggers. Under Puritan rule, the repression of the body and its sensual imagery in the name of the Word became absolute, which is why the restoration of the Monarchy was to a certain extent experienced by its subjects as a restoration of their traditional liberties. But the embattled narrowing of Carnival laughter towards satirical degradation was not exclusively Protestant. It was matched on the opposing side by the ideologues of the Catholic Counter-Reformation, which serves to explain why the humour of *Don Quijote*, while undoubtedly satirical in some ways, remains closer to the relativising inclusiveness of Erasmus than to the hardening fissure to come. The satirical writing of Quevedo is more representative of the satire which not only objectifies the alien other but also involves the abjection of all otherness, especially bodily desires, within the superior mocking subject. This kind of satire reinforces the principle of hierarchy because, whatever its targets might be, it raises the mocking subject above those "lower" objects of his mockery.

3   The "Risibility" of the Lower Other in Classical Aesthetics

The idea of the inherent risibility of the lower objects of laughter underpinned the hierarchy of styles and registers of speech which was imported into early modern Europe by the neo-classicism favoured by the centralising nation states. This aesthetics supported the principle of a single transcendental order which rooted the social hierarchy in the order of the universe. According to the theory derived from Aristotle, the tragic and epic registers were suitable for Kings and warrior heroes, while at the other end of the social and symbolic scale, the lower orders were fit only for the comic register, being inherently "ugly" and more likely to inspire revulsion or scorn. For Aristotelian aesthetics it was only the comic register which made their natural "ugliness" acceptable, by transforming it into a source of pleasure for the spectators. The latter could then laugh at them like the Homeric gods laughing at the debased spectacle of humanity. This transcendent hierarchy, coupled with the idea that it was only the appropriate comic style which could make the lower natural ugliness pleasing, is the doctrine which neo-classicism sought to reinforce as aesthetic practice. In France it was entrusted to the French Academy, founded by the King's minister, Cardinal Richelieu, in order to discipline and purify both the national language and its literature in the name of Reason. This disciplinary impulse put it in conflict with the still influential popular traditions of laughter with their incipient tendency towards levelling, as argued by Bakhtin in his book on Rabelais.

But this conflict of social values was itself dialogical, and in the seventeenth century it gave rise to a significant inner contradiction within the still predominantly aristocratic culture. This issue is addressed by Anthony Close in his *Cervantes and the Comic Mind of his Age* although he certainly does not interpret it in these Bakhtinian terms.[21] In Spain the members of the higher social orders felt authorised to mock their social inferiors, and they continued to do so in practice, thus reinforcing the social hierarchy (on the Homeric or Olympian pattern, so to speak). But by the late seventeenth century in France and England open mockery was no longer considered an appropriate response by the superior classes to their lower objects of derision. Perhaps the excessive affirmation of hierarchical distinctions was a threat to the new norms of politeness known in French as "le bon sens" which supported the recently achieved but still precarious national consensus following the religious wars. Another explanation is offered by Quentin Skinner, who observes that in the seventeenth and eighteenth centuries laughter itself was felt to be a threat to both the nobility and the emergent bourgeoisie (and to its womenfolk especially), if they gave way too much to this degrading bodily impulse.[22] That spontaneity would make them indistinguishable from the unruly lower orders. Ideally, every lower bodily impulse needed to be controlled, if it could not be entirely suppressed. This culture of self-restraint was a historically new development, and Skinner refers to Norbert Elias' *Civilising Process*[23] to support his argument on the new and increasing need for subjective self-control by the ruling class. In that earlier work Elias had theorised the emergence of courtly decorum and restraint

---

21   Close 2000. He sees no value in the popular traditions, which he labels "Aristophanic" and associates with mockery and aggressive cruelty, exemplified by the so-called *apodos* (mocking apothegms).
22   Skinner 2004, pp. 139–166.
23   Elias 1994.

as an ideal of control over all the urges of the body, including its tendency to laugh or to cry uncontrollably.[24] Skinner refers to certain English lords in the late seventeenth and eighteenth centuries, and particularly Lord Chesterfield who recommended in his *Letters to his Son* that the latter should not demean himself by laughing, whereas a restrained smile may be permitted. In the case of daughters, this self-restraint was even more urgent; to laugh was to give way to the dishonouring body.[25]

Skinner's observation suggests that the quasi-mandatory self-restraint on all bodily responses, including laughter and tears, came increasingly to depend on reinforcing the Cartesian mind/body distinction within the subjectivity of the dominant classes themselves. If so, individual conduct was no longer a matter of asserting the aristocratic individual's superiority but of sustaining the hierarchical order through self-restraint. In other words, aristocratic politeness was a matter of social responsibility. To depart from its norms was not merely to betray the self but also the social norms for which the aristocratic self was responsible. However, aristocratic self-restraint did not mean the repression of bodily appetites along traditional ascetic or contemporary Puritan lines. On the contrary, it is striking how aristocratic libertinism, which became fairly widespread among the aristocracy in France and England, scorned the moral restraints recommended by Calvin who coined the term "libertine" itself for religious and moral censure. Instead of morality, this transvalued libertinism put sexuality under the control of the free-thinking mind or wit (*esprit* in the happily ambiguous French term). For this still aristocratic culture, it was not the temptation of bodily appetite that was to be feared, but unrestrained spontaneity and the consequent "vile participation" (to quote Shakespeare's Henry IV, discussed earlier). That spontaneity would amount to the unthinking surrender to the lower body feared by Lord Chesterfield, and the consequent threat to social distinction.

For the courtly aristocracy of the seventeenth and eighteenth centuries it was not morality but wit which maintained the distinction between upper and lower, and wit demanded the subordination of the spontaneous emotions. This subordination of emotion to the supreme control of wit is central to the

---

24   In the second half of the eighteenth century, the anti-aristocratic cult of tears marked a totally different direction. A key text here is Goethe's *Sorrows of Young Werther*, in which tears and suicidal melancholy assume the attributes of uncompromising rebellion, not merely against the stifling aristocratic hierarchy of the German states but also against the restraints of rationality itself.

25   Chesterfield's book was a late example of the so-called "conduct books", intended to instruct the upper classes in proper decorum. The absence of laughter in Chesterfield's cold aristocratic wit is a major theme in Charles Dickens' *Barnaby Rudge*.

conflicts in Choderlos de Laclos' *Les Liaisons Dangereuses* (1782). In that novel the truly "dangerous liaisons" threatening the partnership of the rival dominant aristocrats, the Vicomte deValmont and the Marquise de Merteuil, are certainly not bodily appetites as such. As former lovers their mutual pleasure is now realized in their letters, where they recount their erotic conquests of others. This makes the reader of this epistolary novel the ultimate addressee of their witty and seductive language. In these letters they reveal how human beings can be seduced. But the mutual pleasure which they take in displaying their mastery over all others is also a rivalry which consists in demonstrating their superiority to each other. The immediate weakness in their joint dominance consists in the need for secrecy, and this is eventually broken when the letters are read by all. But the more fundamental threat to their dominance arises from the possibility of the spontaneous emotions which might escape from the Cartesian ideal of absolute control by their witty language. Early in the novel (Letter 81), the Marquise de Merteuil makes the diabolical proclamation that she has created herself through her studied command of literary language and moral deportment, including her imitations of the language of the sentimental novels of Rousseau and Richardson. She is the ultimate heroine of self-fashioning in the Age of Cartesian Reason, and she refuses to be a despised *machine à plaisir* like all the other "bourgeois" women whom she scorns for being subordinate to their bodies (and therefore to men). Eventually the triumph of uncontrolled spontaneity does occur, when Valmont's duplicitous discourse fails to conceal from the Marquise's sharp hermeneutics of suspicion that he has been captivated emotionally by his proclaimed victim, the Présidente de Tourvel. The Marquise's final revenge on Valmont for his attempted duplicity towards her, and the mutual destruction which ensues, is an act of passionate triumph over him but it is also an angry defense of the shared aristocratic values which he has betrayed. This remarkably witty novel, written on the eve of the French Revolution, charts the breakdown of aristocratic control and its mastery over passion exercised through the superiority of wit. That apparently self-assured superiority of a whole class was shortly to be swept aside.

4   Laughter and Unconscious Anxiety: the Emergent Modernity of Hobbes' Theory of Laughter

Bakhtin's idea of the dialogical nature of festive laughter, namely that the members of the *demos* might mock their superiors, was not acknowledged by the Aristotelian theory which was taken into the neo-classicism of the seventeenth century. That possibility was not even refuted. However, this theoretical absence does not necessarily mean that laughter from below was completely unthinkable, even for the Greeks of Aristotle's time. The fact that Aristotle did not express any anxiety over such rebellious uncontrollability on the part of the lower "risible" objects of mockery certainly does not mean that there was indeed no such anxiety. However, in writing about the "superiority theories" of Plato and Aristotle, Michael Billig argues in his admirable work on laughter and ridicule, that their sense of superiority was completely unchallenged. But he then concedes that such a view of laughter "falls short" in a very significant way:

> This superiority was not a sudden feeling that wells up, when a comic sight is viewed ... This superiority is more deep-seated. It is a form of life. The Athenian gentleman, making his ironic reflections in a limited democracy that permitted slavery and excluded women from public life, would be confident that he was superior from the moment of birth. These early superiority theories, falling short as they do in explaining the psychology of laughter, nevertheless succeed in illustrating how humour was bound up with an ideology of order, taste and superiority.[26]

Billig is right to insist that the humour of the ruling élite must have been "bound up" with its ideology. But when he maintains that this ruling ideology was a "deep-seated ... form of life", he does not mention the conflict between the old Athenian landed aristocracy with its warrior values and the despised subordinate majority whose rising influence was threatening those values.[27] However, the main issue here is theoretical. Like the New Historians' discussion of ideology in Tudor and Stuart England, Billig understands it as a single structure which characterises a historical epoch. In this instance ideology is taken to be completely at one with the lived experience of the "Athenian gentleman" who had unchallenged confidence in it. But there is a slippage in his argument when he concedes that the superiority theories of laughter fall short "in explaining the psychology of laughter", without clarifying what an adequate theory would be. Rather than seeing ideology as field of discursive struggles mediating social conflicts, he seamlessly identifies this "ideology of order, taste, and superiority" with the unchallenged mentality of the epoch. By contrast with such a unifying framework, a dialogical understanding of ideology permits a retrospective insistence that even in ancient Greece the laughter of apparently untroubled mockery must have involved an activity of psychological negation. In that

---

26 Billig 2005, p. 47.
27 Cf. Ismard 2017.

case, the assignment of a god-like superiority to the ruling caste would have allowed laughter to occur by overcoming their unacknowledged anxiety at the possibility of mockery (symbolic rebellion) from below. That unacknowledged anxiety might also account for Aristotle's hostility to the demotic comedies of Aristophanes with their festive carnivalesque inversions, and their displays of disrespect towards the gods, heroes, rulers – and, of course, philosophers.[28] Moreover, even the statement that "women [were] excluded from public life" needs to be measured against Aristophanes' *Lysistrata*, in which the women take over public life, defying their allotted sexual role in order to rescue society itself from male militarism and chaos. The problem raised by Billig's analysis can be resolved by turning to the unconscious anxiety produced by every dominant ideology as it struggles to negate its own conflicts with its subordinated, but not annihilated, others. I have made this argument in Chapter 3 where I discuss Voloshinov's version of ideology as a field of discursive conflict, rather than a containing structure. But Charles Mauron's definition of laughter as the moment of the subject's "overturning of an anxiety-producing situation" (*le renversement d'une situation angoissante*) is very helpful in its grasp of laughter as the subject's response to potential anxiety.

In his *Psychocritique du Genre Comique*,[29] Mauron is particularly interested in the genesis of the human capacity for laughter in childhood development, and he considers it a paradox that Freud did not perceive this important fact.[30] Mauron's main argument in this work of "psychocriticism" asserts the generic constancy of the Freudian family structure underlying the social production of laughter from the Greek "new comedies" of Menander and Terence, through the Roman comedies of Plautus, to the family-based comedies of Molière. This structural repetition turns on the young male interloper's successful bid to win the daughter away from her possession by her father or another *senex* figure. In Mauron's view, social anxiety is overcome in these comedies because exogamy becomes possible within patriarchy without recourse to Oedipal parricide. As a *longue durée* structural analysis of comedies based on the *familia*, this argument has much to be said for it. But this trans-historical Freudian structuralism is undermined when he turns to Hobbes as the theorist of a historically new dynamic theory of laughter, which he makes his own. Mauron's earliest historical model for his own theory of laughter is the argument first put forward by Hobbes, namely that laughter occurs at the moment of triumphant delusion when the subject's perception of his own weakness or "infirmity" is

---

28   *The Frogs*, for example.
29   Mauron 1985.
30   Mauron *op. cit.*, p. 19.

overcome by a compensatory feeling of "sudden glory". Mauron quotes in English the passage from Hobbes' essay *On Human Nature* (1650):

> "Laughter is nothing but the sudden glory arising from sudden conception of some eminence in ourselves; by comparison with the infirmity of others, or with our own formerly".[31]

He criticises Hobbes' theory for conceiving this transformation of anxiety into triumph as an event which occurs in full consciousness, albeit as a delusion, rather than as an unconscious "fantaisie de triomphe". But he adds that this idea of the "sudden" inward transformation was a major new insight. Hobbes' awareness of the importance of the suddenness of this mental event meant that he was able to discard the old idea of the "inherent risibility" of the object or butt of the laughter:

> Hobbes insisted on the suddenness of the triumph, and the importance of a rapid *tempo* was later to become increasingly acknowledged. In short, we seem to owe to him the idea that the risible is not a quality attached to the object of laughter (as the Ancients believed), but belongs to a relationship within the mind of the subject – which implies the relativity of laughter. In Hobbes' thinking, the theory of triumphant laughter was linked to the more general idea of a universal struggle: "The war of all against all".[32]

Mauron argues here that Hobbes' theoretical focus on the sudden inward movement in the laughing subject is recognisably modern, in contrast with the older focus on the fixed "risible" properties inherent in the object or butt of laughter. I would add that Hobbes reveals in their stead a new concern with the subjective experience of time, conflict, and instability. This makes him a characteristically Baroque figure as defined by Antonio Maravall, sensitive to the contemporary dynamics of change even though (or rather, *because*) this dynamic was threatening his own ideological commitment to the stable hierarchy which must be guaranteed by the Absolutist state.

Like Mauron, Michael Billig also sees Hobbes as a distant precursor of Freud, which he ascribes to their shared "psychology of suspicion". Rightly criticising the "ideological positivists" of Hobbes' time and ever since, who "claim that they feel no superiority to others when they laugh", Billig argues that

---

31 Mauron, *op. cit.*, p. 144, quotes the original English.
32 *Ibid.*, p. 145.

"Hobbes did not develop a psychology of self-deception, but the arguments of his psychology were pointing towards the need to understand the nature of self-deception".[33] Hobbes' "positivist" critics, both in his own time and in the following century, failed to see the genuine newness of his insights within what they took to be his faults. But our retrospective view remedies this:

> Hobbes had no readily available psychology of self-deception that he could use to argue that his critics were not pointing to flaws in his own arguments but to flaws in human nature. There would not be a systematic psychology of self-deception for another two and a half centuries, when Freud formulated his psychoanalytic theory. In many respects there are parallels between Hobbes and Freud. Like Freud, Hobbes was proposing a psychology of suspicion. Both thinkers were saying in effect: don't accept what people tell you about their desires, look for the inadmissible motives.[34]

Billig very persuasively sees this emergent "psychology of suspicion" as the exercise of the superior observer's penetration of others' moral or ethical "flaws". Actually, this assessment aligns Hobbes' theories with much seventeenth century wit, which likewise gave the witty observer a superior insight into others' motives. La Rochefoucauld is an eminent example of that generalising wit, but there were many others, including Laclos' fictional aristocratic heroes. Their wit provides most of the readers' pleasure in the novel (see above). However, Mauron takes Billig's thesis a step further because for him the truly new insight opened up for the first time by Hobbes was his account of the concealed psychological dynamics behind the moment of laughter.

Mauron quotes Hobbes' *On Human Nature* to show that the anxious awareness of weakness or vulnerability overcome by laughter is a universal human response which Hobbes was the first to consider significant. But in a better-known passage in *Leviathan* Hobbes does not write of "ourselves" or of our comparison with "our own" former infirmity. In this respect Hobbes is more typical of his time and class because he emphasises the inferiority and ignoble otherness of the one who laughs. Such people are inferior because they surrender to the "passion" of laughter precipitated by the delusion of "sudden glory". In the well-known passage below, the moralising Hobbes is certainly very apparent, and so is his aristocratic expression of contempt for those who elevate themselves by laughing. But for Mauron the key issue is nonetheless Hobbes'

---

33   Billig 2005, p. 55.
34   *Ibid.*

new insight into the suddenness of the self-glorification, which Hobbes himself emphasises by repeating it three times:

> *Sudden* glory, is the passion which maketh those Grimaces called Laughter; and is caused either by some *sudden* act of their own, that pleaseth them; or by the apprehension of some deformed thing in another, by comparison whereof they *suddenly* applaud themselves [emphases added]...It is incident most to them, that are conscious of the fewest abilities in themselves; who are forced to keep themselves in their own favour, by observing the imperfections of other men. And therefore much Laughter at the defects of others, is a sign of Pusillanimity. For of great minds, one of the proper works is to help and free others from scorn; and compare themselves only with the most able.[35]

Hobbes is often quoted as the theorist of laughter as an expression of superiority or dominance, although he condemns it on grounds which combine moral censure with aristocratic contempt. But actually, despite his aristocratic rejection of laughter as proper only to the ignoble "pusillanimous" beings who are all too aware of their own inabilities, he should be cited as the first to theorise the relationship of laughter to the prior inward state of anxiety which is overthrown in the euphoric moment of "sudden glory". Mauron locates this theoretical insight historically, by putting it in the context of Hobbes' broader argument concerning the levelling "war of all against all". In that context, each naturally competitive individual, irrespective of the merit conferred by rank or personal ability, aspires to that ego-centric dominance which is momentarily supplied by the illusion of "sudden glory". Hobbes was undoubtedly a thinker of his time and place, writing as a refugee from revolutionary England in Absolutist France. but as a truly original thinker, he was not just an anxious aristocratic defender of the threatened hierarchy. He was a dialectical thinker *avant la lettre*, sensitive to the contemporary threat to that order, which he theorised in terms of the natural "war of all against all".[36] Mauron's merit lies in seeing the dialectic of anxiety and its overcoming by laughter in *On Human Nature* and *Leviathan*, while disregarding the typically aristocratic contempt which led Hobbes to distinguish the superior status of those who do not laugh from those who do. Seen in this light, Hobbes' theory of laughter is not actually a theory of mastery which would be secure in its mockery of its lower targets, but

---

35   *Ibid.*, pp. 145–146.
36   See Chapter 4 for a fuller discussion of MacPherson's reading of Hobbes as a response to the destabilizing new power of the market.

a theory of insecurity overcome (like much of his political theory, in fact) and of the compensatory desire in the insecure individual to achieve mastery over the perceived weakness of the self in relation to others. That perception of weakness is negated in the triumphant moment of laughter. On this account, even the mockery of others' "defects" is the external, socially competitive manifestation of the unconscious anxiety overturned in laughter by the moment of "sudden glory".[37]

5   Modernising Hobbes' Dialectic

The passing detail in the 1650 essay, that when we laugh we not only compare ourselves with the weaknesses of others but also with "our own formerly", points to the developmental pattern which Charles Mauron makes central to his own theory of laughter as the *renversement d'une situation angoissante*. For him, laughter is an event which always occurs on the cusp or boundary (*lisière*) of anxiety, and it is in learning to laugh that the child learns how to overcome the "situation" which produces it. Here Mauron's developmental theory is compatible with the views of Vygotsky and Bakhtin. He outlines three phases in the child's development of this capacity to overcome potential anxiety through laughter, which are all carried over into adult life. The first is the child's ability to overcome the anxiety caused by the anticipated disappearance of the mother. The key idea here is not an actual traumatic disappearance but its anticipation in play. In effect this anticipation would be an active prevention of anxiety. He gives two examples typical of this first phase in childhood development. One is the game played by the mother herself when she stages her disappearance and sudden reappearance while exclaiming (in French) "coucou". Endlessly repeated, this play with a primary anxiety never fails to produce laughter in the child. The child even demands its pleasurable repetition. Mauron does not comment on the intersubjectivity of the game, or the essentially dialogical nature of the event and its repetition, which fulfils an expectation and satisfies the child's demand. The other example, taken directly from Freud's *Beyond the Pleasure Principle*, is that of Freud's grandchild playing alone, when he throws out a cotton reel and then recovers it, symbolically triumphing over the mother's disappearance. Again, Mauron does not comment on the child's alternating "fort/da" exclamations reported by Freud, which provide the verbal element for this

---

37 This dialectic makes the aristocratic Hobbes absolutely unlike the Nietzsche who wrote in the *Genealogy of Morals* that superiority and cruelty are the key to the genuine "healthy" laughter exemplified by Cervantes' humour in *Don Quijote*. Cf. Pérez 2015, pp. 168–175.

repeated symbolic departure and return of the substitute for the mother. Actually Mauron's analysis here is closer to Melanie Klein's reading of this famous scene than to that of Lacan.[38] But in either case, it brings out the relationship of the symbolic play to the potential anxiety being overcome by preventive anticipation.

The second phase identified by Mauron picks up on an observation by the comedian Max Eastman: that the child laughs at the ferocious grimaces and the roaring which would terrify it if it failed to recognise the aggression as a game. Here too the basis of laughter in symbolic play is important. The prior communication of non-aggressive intentions through play is a capacity which humans share with the higher primates and other animals, but the playful attack and defence (which provides the basis for later fight or flight decisions) is developed to an incomparably greater extent with the development of human language. It is also marked by a far higher degree of ambiguity over the boundary between the aggression which provokes the subject's defensive anxiety and the playful joking which overcomes it.

The third phase identified by Mauron deals with the child's overturning of the most complex and mature form of anxiety. This arises when the child desires to transgress an already acknowledged boundary. He/she has to solicit parental complicity in the transgression because, without the desired suspension of the parental prohibition, the child would incur the fear of reproof or punishment. Once again, Mauron's model is the game, clearly both inter-subjective and intra-subjective here. The child's anticipation borders on anxiety because the transgressive desire is directed against an acknowledged authority whose benevolent acquiescence is needed for the prohibition to be removed. The symbolic release from prohibition is the key to the explosion of laughter:

> [...] the infraction is followed by a pause [*une attente immobile*] which explodes into laughter as soon as the impunity is assured. The triumph is no longer a victory over the fear of being devoured (the grimaces) or abandoned (the "cuckoo" game) but already over the fear of punishment.[39]

---

38   Lacan's view is that the primary anxiety at stake here is not the loss of the mother but the infant's fear of engulfment by her excessive presence. For Lacan, the child must go through the phase of separation by realising that the mother has relations with the father. The child enters the Oedipal phase to escape from the primary narcissism in which he has seen himself as the centre of maternal attention; hence, in Lacan's argument, the need for the intervening phallic law of the Father to prevent a disastrous regression to maternal engulfment.

39   Mauron 1964, p. 20

If we accept that the anticipation of punishment is the basis of guilt, because the punishing agency has itself been internalised (Freud's theory of the super-ego), then the triumph of laughter is not only over the fear of an external agency but over the internalised prohibition whose defiance would normally engender guilt. This boundary is strongly defended, which is why in extreme cases even approaching it can provoke the anxious self-censure (guilt) which would make laughter impossible. For the same reason, when others tell jokes or relate comic episodes in order to solicit the subject's participation in a joint transgression, the subject often refuses to laugh if the joke "has gone too far". (Alternatively, he/she may immediately feel guilt at having given way to laughter). However, in Mauron's thinking on the dialectic of anxiety and laughter there is a regrettable absence, or at least an underdevelopment, of the role of language in the formation of the unconscious, whether on Lacanian lines or following the potential opened up by Bakhtinian dialogism. Laughter is actually central to Bakhtin's dialogism and its relationship to "becoming", because it is a response which affirms the subject's freedom to transgress the norms of his/her subjection. The potential anxiety which this transgression would normally incur is overcome by laughter, and therefore a new subject position becomes possible. This is a line of argument which I will explore below.

6 Playing with Breakdown: a Structural or a Dialogical Model of Laughter?

In *The Odd One In*,[40] the Lacanian theorist Alenka Zupančič, gives an illuminating account of the laughter produced by comedy based on the view (which is also Lacan's) that the pleasure of Freud's "innocent" or non-tendentious joke (dependent on purely verbal play), is actually the kind whose cause is the least accessible to either introspection or analysis. That is because the duplicity of the verbal form itself shields the subject from becoming conscious of the real source of his/her pleasure. By contrast, she argues, the "tendentious" sexual or aggressive jokes, which according to Freud's theory provide the greatest yield of pleasure through the lifting of repressive inhibitions, are actually the ones in which the unconscious seems to play hardly any role at all. And indeed, her point seems valid: there is very little that is surprising in Freud's analyses of the aggressive and/or sexual contents of these jokes, although they may have shocked some of his early readers. Freud argues that "tendentious" jokes permit the discharge in laughter of the psychic energy normally required to

---

40 Zupančič, 2008.

repress the aggressive and/or sexual drives. He downplays the significance of the purely verbal play of "innocent" jokes, and in the context of "tendentious" jokes he describes it as mere fore-pleasure, because the removal of inhibitions comes afterwards. But Alenka Zupančič suggests that this Freudian paradigm should be inverted:

> Should we not take a step further here, however, and ask .... to what extent the libidinal tendentiousness of jokes (their sexual and aggressive contents) are not already themselves a kind of smokescreen? A smokescreen that makes it possible for us to confront universal nonsense as the presupposition of all sense in a way that is not direct, but goes through the intermediary of the joke's content or butt that we laugh at? In this perspective, one would have to accept the possibility that the pleasure in obscenity and aggression, culturally admitted in the form of a joke, could itself have the effect of "lowering inhibitions" and making us more tolerant in accepting the real, paradoxical, and contingent constitution of our world, as well as its precariousness.[41]

She concludes that in the tendentious joke there is a combination of these two effects, which is quite similar to Freud's view. But the contentious point of her inversion of Freud's reasoning is her argument that through the linguistic play of the "innocent" joke we are brought to confront, and become more tolerant of, the precarious nature of the "contingent constitution of our world". Following Lacan, she argues that the coherence of our world is constituted by the signifiers of our language, and this linguistic coherence is precarious because it conceals the reality of "universal nonsense as the presupposition of all sense". The joke is therefore an occasion for a crisis in the structure of the "Symbolic Order". In support of her argument she quotes Lacan himself on "the signifying game" of the joke:

> All that Freud develops from there on consists in demonstrating the annihilating, the truly destroying, and disruptive character of the signifying game in relation to what we might call the existence of the real. In playing with the signifier man brings into question, at any moment, the world, all the way to its very roots. The value of the joke ... is its possibility to play on the fundamental non-sense of all usage of sense, as far as the latter is based on the usage of the signifier. As a matter of fact, this usage is itself

---

41 Zupančič *op.cit.*, p. 144.

profoundly paradoxical in relation to every possible signification, since it is this usage itself that creates that what [sic] it will have to support.[42]

Zupančič explores this Lacanian thinking on the constitutive but "profoundly paradoxical" power of the signifier. It is paradoxical for Lacan, because that power is revealed precisely at the moment when it undermines itself. So the joke takes us beyond its common sense mockery of objects into a far more radical encounter with its own signifying operation. For Zupančič, this is where the joke brings about a brief encounter with the unconscious:

> There is a level where we clearly laugh at the joke's butt, at person(s) or thing(s) that the joke makes fun of. Yet this is not the only level on which a joke functions. There is also the fact that each and every concrete joke (about this or that person or situation) is also a joke about the very functioning of our symbolic universe as constituted through signifiers and their specific, counterintuitive way of making sense. In other words, besides its story – and by the very "technical" means of constructing this story – a joke also brings to the fore something in which we are embedded deeply and permanently, without necessarily being aware of its functioning: the paradoxical, "illogical", non-linear and precarious constitution of our (symbolic) universe through speech.[43]

If we accepted Lacan's view that Freud's famous essay, *Wit and its Relation to the Unconscious* shows us "the annihilating, the truly destroying, and disruptive character of the signifying game in relation to what we might call the existence of the real", we would seem bound to accept that the innocent joke would precipitate a deep anxiety. That is why Zupančič is right to ask the most pressing question which it raises, whether we are persuaded by her tentative answer or not:

> How come we actually laugh at this? Should it not, rather, cause in us something like existential anxiety? In answer to this question, I am tempted to propose the following hypothesis: just as the narrative of the joke diverts our attention from the point where its twist will take place, the content-related butt of the joke diverts our attention from this other, more radical and more discomforting butt. Or, in other words: when we laugh at the butt, a certain amount of pleasure gets realized [through

---

42 *Ibid.*, p. 142; Lacan 1994, p. 294.
43 Zupančič *op. cit.*, p. 144.

aggression, presumably – J.H.] and makes it possible for us to laugh also in the face of this discomforting dimension (displaying the precariousness of our world and its dependence on contingent mechanisms of the production of sense) instead of being seized by anxiety in the face of it.[44]

The basis of her theoretical account of the joke is Lacan's affirmation that the coherence of the whole Symbolic Order is held in place by its key signifiers, and that to play with them is to reveal its radical unreliability. Her logical deduction from this is the "existential anxiety" which would result from the Lacanian premise that the Symbolic Order is destroyed when the power of the signifier is brought into question by "the annihilating, the truly destroying, and disruptive character of the signifying game" (Lacan). Her deduction seems unassailable, but her own question: "how come we actually laugh at this?" is unanswered, and is probably unanswerable within the Lacanian paradigm.

There is an even more striking example of this allegedly unchallengeable power of the signifier in Lacan's essay, "The Function of Language in Psychoanalysis", where he writes that Freud's account of wit (*esprit*) reveals the "regalian" dominance of the signifier at the very instant of the witticism (the *pointe*) when it undermines itself:

> For, however neglected by our interest – and for good reason – *le Mot d'Esprit et l'Inconscient* remains the most unchallengeable of his works because it is the most transparent, in which the effect of the unconscious is demonstrated to us in its most subtle confines. And the face which it reveals to us is that of the spirit [*l'esprit*] in the ambiguity conferred on it by Language [*le langage*], where the other side of its regalian power is the "*pointe*" by which the whole of its order is annihilated in an instant – the *pointe*, in fact, where its creativity reveals its absolute gratuitousness, where its domination over the Real is expressed in the challenge of non-sense, where humour, in the malicious grace of the *esprit libre*, symbolises a Truth that has not said [*qui ne dit pas*] its last word.[45]

Deciphering Lacan is always difficult, and the translations do not always help. The above translation of *esprit* as "spirit" rather than "wit" is an example. But here it seems clear that the unconscious is an "effect" of language which, however, is only revealed "to us" at the moment when the "creativity" of its

---

44 Zupančič *op. cit.*, p. 143.
45 Lacan 1968, p. 33; Lacan 1966, p. 148. The full title of Freud's work in French is *Le Mot d'Esprit et ses Rapports avec l'Inconscient*.

witticism (*pointe*) destroys the constitutive power of language ("its domination over the Real"). At that crucial moment of creative destruction it reveals the truth that it is essentially empty, "signifying nothing" so to speak, while it nonetheless continues to sustain the Symbolic Order. This is a remarkably Baroque theory, but without the comforting revelation of any "being" behind the display. The signifier's display of its power at the moment of its witty *pointe* is simultaneously an annihilating display of its own emptiness and, therefore, of the absolute gratuitousness of the Symbolic Order which it supports. This groundlessness is "a Truth which does not say its last word" because when wit (*esprit*) speaks as a free-thinking *esprit libre*, it is able to throw off its support for the Symbolic Order. This passing moment of "humour" is a rare moment of freedom, but Lacan calls its free "creativity" a "malicious grace" because of its destructive revelation of its own emptiness. But why would this moment of destruction be "creative" unless, instead of bringing about the destruction of all order, it is the moment when a new order becomes possible? The familiar conservative view of such moments is that they merely bring about a "return to order" after a momentary disruption. But, surely, the real point must be that, even at the micro level of the joke, a new order of coherence is created out of the breakdown. Lacan does not say this, however. His obscure reference to the "regalian power" conferred on the signifier by Language is a metaphor borrowed from the history of the conflictual relations in the Baroque period between the universal truth claims of the Catholic Church and the secondary "regalian" powers of the Kings or Princes. However much the latter powers may have disrupted the universal (Catholic) Symbolic Order, they were nonetheless dependent on its key signifiers.

Alenka Zupančič's searching question appears to be more of a challenge to Lacan than she intends. Lacan makes extensive use of Freud's famous essay but, strange as it may seem, not to formulate a theory of why the subject laughs. The active agency for Lacan is not the laughing subject responding to a disruption of the Symbolic Order, as it is in Zupančič's question ("How come we laugh at this?"), but the signifier and the slippery power of displacement and substitution through which it always already dominates the subject. In Lacan's account of Freud's joke work the subject is spared from Zupančič's "existential anxiety" by remaining unconscious of the destruction occasioned by the "creative" play of the signifier. Within this scenario, the subject would never be able to challenge the power exercised by language over his/her consciousness. In Bakhtin's terms, the subject would be unable to occupy a position of dialogical "outsideness" which is the source of the potential for creativity. The key issue is that in Lacan's theory, the subject has indeed no such capability. For Lacan the entire field of action is occupied by the signifier as it demonstrates its mastery "to us" (to the theorist or to the subject?) in the very act of undermining its own "regalian power" and thereby annihilating the Symbolic Order itself through the play of the witticism. This is not a theory of why the subject laughs but of the disastrous insight into the "existential" truth whose avoidance allows laughter to occur. If this disaster were to be apprehended by the subject, it could not result in laughter but inward collapse, as Zupancic's question makes clear. To that extent, laughter might be considered an unconscious therapy, but a therapy based on preventive avoidance.

My critique is not a simple dismissal. Lacan's account of the universal collapse that would result from the self-destructive power of the signifier may well be "unchallengeable" if it is taken as an account of the possible consequences of any subject's incapacity for laughter. The inability to laugh would be an indication of that subject's absolute reliance on the order sustained by certain key signifiers, which could only result in inner chaos, not creativity, if his/her confidence in them is broken. Perhaps this broken confidence is indeed a key to psychotic breakdown? But it does not provide an adequate account of laughter on the part of those subjects who are able to overturn their internalised authorities without having to undergo an anxiety crisis of existential proportions. The crucial point here is that the subject's discovery of the vulnerability of the authority of a particular discourse, whether "innocent" or "tendentious", is not the same as the overthrow of the authority of all language. That would be either impossible (according to the structural "prison house of language" paradigm) or catastrophic, as Alenka Zupancic's own searching question makes clear. So the psychoanalytical value of Lacan's theory would not consist in his exposition of a universal structure perpetually open to the potential failure of its signifiers to dominate "the Real", but rather in his revelation of the disastrous consequences for those subjects who cling to such a monological mental universe, for whatever reason. Such subjects would have to be in perpetual denial of their own experience of the multiplicity and flexibility of the languages in which they really exist. To them the revelation of their openness to change would necessarily appear as a threat of pure chaos, rather than a possibility for creativity and "becoming". This is where a dialogical account of the overthrow of a discursive authority through the joke differs from Lacan's theoretical account of wit as the occasion for crisis in the "Symbolic Order" brought about by the "annihilating" play of the signifier. So I would argue, on the basis of Bakhtin's dialogical account of language, that it is not a universal Symbolic Order that is overturned by the joke, but a particular discursive authority when it is transformed into a distanced object at which most subjects can laugh from their newly acquired position of "outsideness". A challenge to the authority implicit in any discursive order can certainly be a cause for anxiety, but that anxiety is not an absolute "existential anxiety", except for those subjects whose reliance on the particular authority being undermined is likewise absolute. For all others, that authority can be overcome without complete breakdown.

However, this argument brings up the whole relationship between laughter as a potential agency for social and intellectual change on the one hand (as a source of creative innovation),[46] and laughter as reactive resistance to change on the other. In order to defend the alternative possibilities provided by the dialogical model for understanding laughter, I need to revisit some of the arguments made earlier in this book. Bakhtin and his fellow thinkers insisted on the primacy of dialogical relations for the existence of human consciousness, and its capacity for development. This does not mean that linguistic structures are merely theoretical abstractions. The structures of language are real but they do not exist independently of the discourses which are plural and historical in nature, being produced, reproduced, and altered on the basis of dialogical communication, interaction, and occasional conflicts. Bakhtin argues in his late essay on *Speech Genres*, that the child assimilates the structures of his language along with the utterances addressed to him.[47] The child learns to make the "correct" abstractions from the utterances addressed to him, in order to understand and respond competently by formulating his own utterances in turn. It is a remarkable human ability, but it does not follow that these abstract structures can be traced back to a single *a priori* system, whether neurological or transcendental. In my earlier discussion of this plurality of social discourses, I added the comment that for the child there is initially no difference between the way things are (his version of "the real") and the utterances which "inform" him in the full sense of that word, i.e. form him inwardly in accordance with the historically developed consensual norms or *senso commune* (Gramsci) of his culture. This consensus corresponds to Freud's early concept of the "reality principle", but unfortunately Freud, like Lacan too, transformed its always provisional historical nature into an abstract universal ("the real").

The child's development through dialogical response to social *addressivity* means that s/he begins quite early to experience and to assert his/her own

---

46   Susan Purdie's concept of the joking subject's "mastery of discourse" comes close to this potential for innovation. She writes: "This is my claim that joking paradigmatically involves a discursive exchange whose distinctive operation involves the *marked* transgression of the Symbolic Law and whose effect thereby is to constitute jokers as 'masters' of discourse: as those able to break and to keep the basic rule of language, and consequently in controlling possession of full human subjectivity": Purdie 1995, p. 5. But her reliance on Lacan to argue for these "marked" infractions of the Symbolic Order begs the question as to whether such mastery is possible within the Lacanian paradigm.
47   Bakhtin 1986, p. 78.

relative autonomy (i.e. Bakhtinian *outsideness*) from the same authoritative utterances which s/he has previously assimilated without question. But the key theoretical issue is far wider than this thesis on childhood development. It is that at a certain point in *all* human development through multiple dialogical encounters (whether at the individual or the socio-historical level), the proliferation of discourses itself leads to tensions, contradictions, and sometimes even irreconcilable conflicts between their implicit authorities. Seen from the broader perspective of historical change, it is the increase in social differentiations and conflicts which introduces strains, and sometimes destructive clashes, between these discursive authorities. The Renaissance is the classic example of such development cited by Bakhtin, who also cites ancient Athens. Without this interactive development and its moments of conflict, the capacity for creativity and social change would remain merely potential. It is the dialogical encounter or event (*sobytie*) which enables the subject to actually become critical and self-conscious, thanks to the "outsideness" which dialogism makes possible.

However, the socially and historically variable degree of the subject's freedom from the authority of the prior utterances addressed to him/her, and of the creative openness to the possibilities of change or "becoming" which it brings with it, is not the only consequence of the constitutive "outsidedness" theorised by Bakhtin. The other consequence of this relative freedom is that the liberation and the expansion of possibilities are necessarily doubled at the same time by reactive anxiety. That is because the authoritative discourses being challenged from a newly won position of "outsidedness" must have already been internalised by the subjects themselves. So there is always a correlative anxiety, aroused simultaneously by the liberation from the authority of whatever discursive order is being made into an object of play. This reactive anxiety arises because it is only through the collectively shared discourses, previously installed in us by the authoritative utterances addressed to us, that we subjects have learnt to make sense of the world and of our own experiences within it. The discovery of the relative arbitrariness of this discursive order, which is the basis of the subject's freedom to question it and/or manipulate it from a position of "outsideness", is undoubtedly a moment of pleasurable release from its authoritative claims. But it must also be a moment of potential anxiety even at the very "boundary" or threshold of the triumphant liberation which overthrows it. So the other side of that liberation is a threatening sense of disappearing or lost certainties. That anxiety should be understood as a reactive desire to prevent the liberating disruption, in order to reaffirm the continuing reality of the particular discursive order in question. Consequently, if the subject (either an individual or a group) is to achieve any significant degree of autonomy from the already internalised authorities now being put into question, the reactive anxiety within the subject, which protects those authorities, must itself be overcome.

In the opening chapter of his *Book of Laughter and Forgetting* (1981) Milan Kundera makes a point similar to those who have criticised Bakhtin's rather one-sided account of Carnival laughter as levelling and socially liberating. Many have rightly pointed out that it could be extremely repressive in its production of butts for aggressive laughter, and even of scapegoats for real violence. These were often stereotypical women, witches, Jews, foreigners or other presumed deviants from the accepted dominant norms. Laughter in such all-too-common cases functioned then (and still does) to reaffirm the prevailing hierarchical norms themselves, along with the superiority of the laughing subject whose normality they appear to guarantee. In that respect the Carnival always had a reactionary underside. In Kundera's opening pages, the organised celebrations of collective joy in Stalinist Czechoslavakia functioned similarly, to distract criticism from the state persecutions of presumed outsiders such as poets and alleged deviants like Rudolf Slánský and his co-accused.[48] Nonetheless, Kundera affirms the existence of a primary liberation from the structures of repression (as does Bakhtin), but it is a liberation which in a second move is co-opted by the dominant "angels of order":

> Laughable laughter is cataclysmic. And even so, the angels have gained something by it. They have tricked us all with their semantic hoax. Their imitation laughter and its original (the Devil's) have the same name. People nowadays do not even realise that one and the same external phenomenon embraces two completely contradictory internal attitudes. There are two kinds of laughter, and we lack the words to distinguish them.[49]

The difference between the two "internal attitudes" is a real difference but it is concealed by "the same external phenomenon" which is the act of laughing. Kundera's insight is crucial but, *pace* Kundera, the link between the two opposing kinds of laughter is far more than a mere "semantic hoax". What they share is that in both cases a concealed or unconscious anxiety is overturned. But, as Kundera says, there is a very real "internal" difference between them.

---

48 These old Communists were arrested in 1951, charged with "Trotskyist-Titoist-Zionist" plotting in favour of American imperialism. Thirteen (ten of whom were Jewish) were executed in 1952. Slánský was publicly hanged.

49 Kundera 1981, p. 62.

Whenever the laughing subject is enabled to overturn the repressive hold of his internalised authorities, liberation into becoming other is made possible. In that sense, the capacity for laughter is the indispensable condition for all critical "outsidedness", and for all individual and/or collective transformation. But, on the other hand, if the laughing subject is successfully induced by the dominant discourse (Kundera's "angels of order") into mocking those which it designates as "other", the reassuring difference from those objectified "lower" or alien others actually functions to lock the laughing subject back into his ideological subordination and to persuade him unconsciously, not only of the truth of his "mind forg'd manacles" (William Blake) but of their desirability. Both kinds of laughter are responses which overcome the causes of anxiety, but only the first offers an effective liberation from the prevailing form of social repression which Gramsci calls "hegemony". Then Mauron's *renversement d'une situation angoissante* can even be therapeutic as well as revolutionary. In sum, laughter can foment dialogical critique and change, whether in the individual subject or in the social group, or else it can resist and prevent it. But it always arises on the boundary (Mauron's *lisière*) between those two potentialities. This psychological indeterminacy is not just "a semantic hoax". The most perplexing and revealing aspect of laughter is its irreducible duplicity, which Bakhtin calls "ambivalence". As a bodily response to an address to the subject, laughter is not merely natural, let alone neutral. It participates in the social production of meanings, either to extend them in new directions or to prevent those possibilities in the service of the existing order. Even at the micro level of the joke, laughter explodes at the moment when the contradictory demands for dialogical openness and "becoming" on the one hand, and for monological closure and reassuring permanence on the other, coincide.

Conclusion

A conclusion should be both a retrospective survey and a glance at possible future directions. This book has followed a trajectory pioneered by Bakhtin and Voloshinov from the potential opened up by the concept of linguistic dialogism to the apparently quite distinct possibility of understanding laughter dialogically in its different cultural contexts.

Bakhtin and Voloshinov were influenced by Ernst Cassirer's historical anthropology of symbolic forms and the inherent potential for "becoming" which underpinned his *longue durée* history. Cassirer identified the potential for change mediated by all symbolic forms, including language, but it was left to Bakhtin and Voloshinov to theorise that potential in terms of the multiple social dialogues which constitute human consciousness. This is where their theory coincided with the developmental psychology of their contemporary, Vygotsky. The critique of structuralism and its variants remains central to the dialogical project. The structures of language certainly exist and can be investigated, but they are historical creations brought into being by the dialogical encounters between the disparate discourses which have been internalised previously by communities and by individuals. There is no reason to suppose that they are grounded in a transcendental grammar or the biological structure of the brain.[1] Being historical outcomes, they are subject to further historical change, but the dialogical encounter which Bakhtin calls the "event" (*sobytie*) has not always led to positive development through benign collaboration.

As societies become more complex and hierarchically stratified along the lines of caste, gender, class or other historically created forms of identity, their different discourses also develop in dialogical tension with each other. Moreover, along with the multiple discourses themselves, the tensions between them are also internalised by the subjects of the shared but diversifying national languages. Such internalised conflicts are inseparable from all social development, especially when societies develop into increasingly complex wholes. But development is not mere change; it always involves a surpassing of its own earlier phases. For the beneficiaries of those earlier phases of social development, or for those who simply feel relatively secure within them, further change tends to appear threatening and even destructive. ("Things have gone too far"). This anxious response to the threat of "becoming" gives rise to the reaction formations which are the topic of this book. They became particularly

---

1 The resort to transhistorical structures suggests that the "hidden God" of Baroque culture is still a potent but unacknowledged deity in our ideological universe.

acute with the emergence of capitalism, which universalised the competitive market and the economic compulsion to perpetual change, but combined in a symbiosis with the territorial nation state and its counter-demand for stasis and unified control. Since capitalist ideology is inwardly divided, so are the subjects addressed by its split *interpellations*.

The subjective internalisation of these discursive conflicts has another very significant aspect. Writing about the subject's capacity for "becoming" through his/her dialogical encounters with the speech of others, Bakhtin introduced a temporal concept into that process, namely anticipation. As the subject forms his "own" thought prior to its utterance, he anticipates the possible responses of his addressees (whether they are actual addressees of a speech act or purely imaginary, hypothetical ones). Anticipation continued to play an important role in Bakhtin's theory of development through dialogism, but it also introduced that concept's negative corollary which Bakhtin did not identify (although it influenced his critical practice), namely prevention. Understood dialogically, prevention is an attempt (in psychological terms, a desire) to resist the anticipated change. That is to say, when an alien discourse is felt to threaten the subject's previously formed sense of order, it is repudiated, which means that it is prevented from entering into the subject's consciousness in order to protect that order and the subject's position within it. This internalised activity of preventive anticipation produces the unconscious. The unconscious is not simply the unknown; nor is it a mental activity that has become routine and is no longer an object of the subject's conscious attention. Still less is it an invasive remnant of primitive origins. It is rather the alien discourse which has become knowable but, instead of being assimilated in a process of dialogical "becoming" it is repudiated or "forgotten" (repressed) because it is a potential disruption. Although it is debarred from conscious acknowledgement it remains potentially knowable and is therefore a threat to the consciously known order of things and the subject's own self-positioning within that order. Bakhtin himself did not theorise the unconscious as the outcome of repudiated dialogical encounters, but to the theorist of "becoming" the Lacanian or Freudian statement that the unconscious knows no time should not be surprising, since the unconscious only comes into existence through the anxious prevention of the very possibility of change.

This is where the capacity for laughter testifies to every human being's capacity for escaping from the timeless structural imprisonments of the unconscious. It is a capacity whose existence depends upon the "outsideness" which Bakhtin and Voloshinov attributed to the dialogical nature of all consciousness. There is no discourse whose authority is not subject to potential overthrow from another position, which dialogism makes possible. The infraction of the subject's otherwise unquestioned internalised authorities is certainly a cause for anxiety. It can sometimes be acute, even though it is often not consciously experienced as anxiety at all (for example in verbal play). But the release from unconscious anxiety, which Charles Mauron called the *renversement d'une situation angoissante,* can be a therapeutic resolution. It can also be a source of intense pleasure when it is experienced as a liberating expansion of the subject's self-understanding in terms of its relationship with others in a new way. This potentially revolutionary power is what Milan Kundera, quoted in the last chapter, called the "cataclysmic" power of the Devil's laughter. It also explains why his "angels of order" always combine in a holy alliance to prevent it. Revolutionary laughter is a "spectre" which, to cite an infamous text, has to be exorcised by the righteous angels. They are the restorative agents who defend whatever ruling order is in place. Their "overpowering conformism", as Walter Benjamin put it, has to be confronted anew in every generation.[2]

2 Benjamin 1977, p. 257.

Bibliography

Aguinaga Carlos Blanco, Puértolas, Julio Rodríguez, and Zavala, Iris M., *Historia Social de la Literatura Española (en lengua castellana)*, vol. 1, Castalia, Madrid 1981.
Althusser, Louis *Lenin and Philosophy* 1971.
Anderson, Benedict, *Imagined Communities: Reflections on the Origins and Spread of Nationalism*, London, Verso 1983.
Anievas, Alexander and Nişancioğlu, Kerem *How the West Came to Rule: the geopolitical origins of capitalism*, Pluto 2015.
Bakhtin, Mikhaïl Mikhaïlovich, *Problemy poetiki Dostoevskogo*, Khudozhestvennaya Literatura, Moscow 1972.
Bakhtin, Mikhaïl Mikhaïlovich, *Estetika slovesnogo tvorchestva*, Iskusstvo, Moscow, 1979.
Bakhtin, Mikhaïl Mikhaïlovich, *Problems of Dostoevsky's Poetics*, translated by Caryl Emerson, University of Minnesota 1984.
Bakhtin, Mikhaïl Mikhaïlovich, "Towards a Reworking of the Dostoevsky Book" [1961], *Problems of Dostoevsky's Poetics*, Minnesota, 1984 Appendix 2.
Bakhtin, Mikhaïl Mikhaïlovich "Epic and Novel", *The Dialogic Imagination*, Holquist, Michael and Emerson Caryl (eds.), Texas University Press, 1981.
Bakhtin, Mikhaïl Mikhaïlovich, "Discourse in the Novel", *The Dialogic Imagination*, Holquist, Michael and Emerson Caryl (eds.), Texas University Press, 1981.
Bakhtin, Mikhaïl Mikhaïlovich, *Speech Genres & Other Late Essays*, (Caryl Emerson and Michael Holquist eds.), Austin, Texas University Press 1986.
Bakhtin, Mikhaïl Mikhaïlovich, "Toward a Methodology for the Human Sciences", *Speech Genres and Other Late Essays*, Austin 1986.
Bakhtin, Mikhaïl Mikhaïlovich, *Rabelais and his World* [*Tvorchestvo Fransua Rable*, Moscow, 1965] MIT Press 1968.
Baltrusaitis, Jurgis, *Anamorphic Art* [1969], New York, Abrams 1976.
Barber, C.L., *Shakespeare's Festive Comedy*, Princeton 1965.
Barker, Francis, *The Culture of Violence: Essays on Tragedy and History*, Manchester UP, 1993.
Barthes, Roland, *Mythologies*, London, Paladin 1973.
Barthes, Roland, "From Work to Text", *Image-Music-Text:* essays selected and translated by Stephen Heath, London, Fontana 1977.
Benjamin, Walter, "The Work of Art in the Age of Mechanical Reproduction", *Illuminations* Fontana/Collins, Glasgow 1977.
Benjamin, Walter *The Origin of German Tragic Drama*, New Left Books, 1977
Benjamin, Walter, Arcades Project, Cambridge, Mass. Belknap Press
Bercé, Yves-Marie, *Fête et révolte: des mentalités populaires du XVIe au XVIIIe siècle*, Paris, Hachette, 1976.

Berman, Marshall, *All that is solid melts into air: the experience of modernity*, London, Verso 1983.

Bernays, Edward *Propaganda* [1928, revised 1955], Ig Publishing, New York 2005.

Bernheimer, Charles and Kahane, Claire (eds.), *In Dora's Case*, Virago 1985

Billig, Michael *Laughter and Ridicule: Towards a Social Critique of Humour*, London, Sage Publications 2005.

Brandist, Craig, "Bakhtin, Cassirer and Symbolic Forms", *Radical Philosophy* 85, 1997 (p. 20–27).

Brandist, Craig, "Voloshinov's dilemma: on the philosophical roots of the dialogic theory of the utterance", *The Bakhtin Circle: in the Master's Absence*, Brandist C, Shepherd D, and Tihanov G (eds.), Manchester University Press, 2004.

Brandist, Craig, *The Bakhtin Circle: Philosophy, Culture and Politics*, Pluto 2002.

Braudel, Fernand, *L'Espagne sous Philippe II*, Paris, Hachette 1955.

Brecht, Bertolt, *The Caucasian Chalk Circle* translated by Frank McGuiness, London, Bloomsbury 2014.

Bristol, M.D., *Carnival and Theater: plebeian culture and the structure of authority in Renaissance England*, Methuen, 1985,

Burke, Edmund, *Philosophical Enquiry into the Origin of Our Ideas of the Sublime and the Beautiful* [1757] Oxford University Press 1990.

Butler, Judith, *The Psychic Life of Power: Theories in Subjection*, Stanford University Press 1997.

Casalduero, Joaquín, *Sentido y Forma del Quijote*, Insula, Madrid 1949.

Cascardi, Anthony J., *The Subject of Modernity*, Cambridge University Press, 1992.

Cassirer, Ernst, *The Individual and the Cosmos in Renaissance Philosophy*, Blackwells, Oxford 1963.

Cassirer, Ernst, *The Philosophy of Symbolic Forms* (translated by Ralph Mannheim), Yale University Press, vols 1 and 2, 1955; vol 3, 1957, vol 4 (posthumous) 1996.

Certeau, Michel de, *Heterologies*, University of Minnesota 1986.

Certeau, Michel de, *The Mystic Fable*, Chicago UP 1986.

Cervantes, Miguel de, *Don Quixote,* Penguin Classics, translated by J.M. Cohen [1950] 1985.

Cervantes, Miguel de, *El Ingenioso Hidalgo Don Quijote de la Mancha*, Madrid, Clásicos Castalia 1978.

Chesterfield, P, S., Earl of, *Letters to His Son*, Oxford World Classics 2008.

Chomsky, Noam *Reflections on Language*, Pantheon, NY 1975

Clastres, Pierre, *La Société contre l'État*, Paris, Minuit 1974.

Close, Anthony, *The Romantic Approach to 'Don Quixote': a critical history of the Romantic tradition in 'Quixote' criticism*, Cambridge UP, 1978.

Close, Anthony *Cervantes and the Comic Mind of his Age*, Oxford UP 2000.

Cohen, Walter, *Drama of a Nation: Public Theatre in Renaissance England and Spain*, Ithaca, Cornell University Press, 1985.

Covarrubias, Sebastián de, *Tesoro de la lengua castellana o española* [1611] Turner, Madrid 1977.
Debord, Guy, *Black and Red* [1967], Detroit 1977.
Deleuze, Gilles and Guattari, Félix, *L'Anti-Oedipe: capitalisme et schizophrénie*, Minuit, Paris 1972.
Deleuze, Gilles and Guattari, Félix, *Mille Plateaux*, Minuit, Paris 1980; [*A Thousand Plateaus*, Athlone, London 1988].
Dostoevsky, Fyodor, *Notes from Underground*, Penguin Classics 1972.
Eichenbaum, Boris "How Gogol's Overcoat Is Made", *Gogol from the Twentieth Century*, Robert A. Maguire (ed.) Princeton, 1974.
Elias, Norbert, *The Civilizing Process*, Volume 2: *State Formation and Civilization*, Oxford, Blackwell, 1982 [Basel 1939].
Eliot, Thomas Stearns, "The Metaphysical Poets", *Selected Essays*, London, Faber and Faber 1951.
Emerson, Caryl "The Outer Word and Inner Speech: Bakhtin, Vygotsky, and the Interpretation of Language", *Critical Inquiry* December 1983.
Erasmus, Desiderius, *Praise of Folly* [1504], Norton Critical Edition, 1989
Evans, Dylan, *An Introductory Dictionary of Lacanian Psychoanalysis*, London and New York, Routledge 1996.
Farrell, John, *Paranoia and Modernity: Cervantes to Rousseau*, Cornell U.P. 2006.
Flaubert, Gustave, *Oeuvres Romanesques Complètes*, Gallimard 2013.
Flor, Fernando R. de la, *Barroco: representación e ideología en el Mundo Hispánico (1580–1680)*, Cátedra, Madrid 2002.
Forcione, Alban, *Cervantes and the mystery of lawlessness: a study of El casamiento engañoso y El coloquio de los perros*, Princeton UP 1984.
Foucault, Michel, *The History of Sexuality*, (translated by Robert Hurley), Penguin 1978.
Frank, Joseph, *Dostoevsky: a writer in his time* (abridged), Princeton U.P. 2010.
Freidenberg, Olga M., "The Origin of Parody" (1926), *Semiotics and Structuralism: Readings from the Soviet Union*, International Arts and Sciences Press 1974, White Plains, N.Y.
Freud, Sigmund, *Beyond the Pleasure Principle,* Penguin 2003.
Freud, Sigmund, *The Unconscious* [1915], Penguin 2005a.
Freud, Sigmund, *Fragment of an Analysis of a Case of Hysteria*, 1905b, Penguin edition vol 8: *Case Histories I* 1977.
Freud, Sigmund, *Group Psychology and the Analysis of the Ego*, [1922] Standard Edition, Hogarth Press 1959.
Freud, Sigmund, *Totem and Taboo* [1912], Hogarth Press 1959.
Freud, Sigmund, *The Joke and its Relation to the Unconscious*, Penguin 2002.
Frye, Northrop *A Natural Perspective: the development of Shakespearean comedy and romance*, Columbia 1965.

Gardiner, Michael, *The Dialogics of Critique: M.M. Bakhtin and the Theory of Ideology*, Routledge 1992.

Girard, René, *Deceit, Desire, and the Novel: Self and Other in Literary Structure* [1961o] Johns Hopkins 1976

Greenblatt, Stephen, *Renaissance Self-Fashioning from More to Shakespeare*, Chicago University Press 1980.

Greenblatt, Stephen, "Invisible Bullets", *Shakepearean Negotiations*, Oxford, Clarendon Press, 1988.

Hall, Jonathan, *Anxious Pleasures: Shakespearean Comedy and the Nation State*, Associated University Presses 1995.

Hall, Jonathan, "Falstaff, Sancho Panza, and Azdak: Carnival and History", *Comparative Criticism* 7, 1985.

Hamlin C. and Krois J.M., *Symbolic Forms and Cultural Studies: Ernst Cassirer's Theory of Culture*, Yale University Press, 2004.

Hawkes, David, *Ideology*, Routledge, 1996.

Hazareesingh, Sudir, *Legend of Napoleon*, Granta, 2004.

Hegel, G.W.F., *Elements of the Philosophy of Right* translated by H.B. Nisbet, Cambridge University Press 1991.

Hill, Christopher, *Society and Puritanism in Pre-Revolutionary England*, Penguin 1964.

Hirschkop, Ken, *Mikhaïl Bakhtin: an Aesthetic for Democracy*, Oxford University Press 1999.

Hobbes, Thomas, *Leviathan*, Penguin 1968.

Hobbes, Thomas, *On Human Nature*, Oxford University Press 1994.

Hobsbawm, Eric and Ranger, Terence (eds.), *The Invention of Tradition*, Cambridge U.P. 1983.

Huxley, Aldous, *The Devils of Loudun* [1952], Penguin 1975

Iser, Wolfgang, *The Act of Reading*, Baltimore, Johns Hopkins University Press, 1978.

Ismard, Paulin, *Democracy's Slaves: a Political History of Ancient Greece*, (trans. Jane Marie Todd), Harvard 2017.

Ives, Peter, *Gramsci's Politics of Language: Engaging the Bakhtin Circle and the Frankfurt School*, Toronto UP, 2004.

Jameson, Fredric, *The Prison House of Language: A Critical Account of Structuralism and Russian Formalism*, Princeton, 1972.

Krois, John Michael, *Cassirer: Symbolic Forms and History*, Yale UP 1987.

Kundera, Milan, *The Book of Laughter and Forgetting*, Penguin 1981.

La Bruyère, Jean de, *Les Caractères, ou les moeurs de ce siècle*, ninth edition [1696], Paris, Union Générale d'Éditions 1980.

Lacan, Jacques, "The Function of Language in Psychoanalysis", [*Écrits 1*, Seuil 1966], *Speech and Language in Psychoanalysis*, Anthony Wilden (ed), Baltimore, Johns Hopkins University Press, 1968.

Lacan, Jacques, *Four Fundamental Concepts of Psycho-Analysis*, Penguin, Harmondsworth, 1987.
Lacan, Jacques, *Le Séminaire* – Livre IV, *La Relation d'Objet*, Paris Seuil, 1994
Lacan, Jacques, *Seminar XX*, [Seuil 1975]. Norton, New York and London 1999.
Laclos, Pierre Cholderlos de, *Les Liaisons Dangereuses* [1782], Penguin Classics 1961.
Lähtenmäki, Mika, "Voloshinov and Cassirer: On the Relation of Language and Reality", *Bakhtin and His Intellectual Ambience*, Zylko B. (ed.) University of Gdansk, 2002.
Leader, Darian, *What Is Madness?* Hamish Hamilton, 2011.
Lecercle, Jean-Jacques, *Une Philosophie Marxiste du Langage*, Paris, PUF 2004.
Lenin, V.I. "What is to be done?", *Collected Works* vol. 5, Foreign Languages Publishing House, Moscow 1961.
Lunacharsky, A.V. "Dostoevsky's 'Plurality of Voices'", *On Literature and Art*, Progress Publishers, Moscow 1965.
MacPherson, C.B. *Political Theory of Possessive Individualism* Oxford University Press, 1962.
Maravall, Antonio, *The Culture of the Baroque: analysis of a historical structure*, Minnesota and Manchester University Press 1986 [*La Cultura del Barroco*, Ariel 1975].
Mariscal, George, *Contradictory Subjects: Quevedo, Cervantes, and Seventeenth-Century Spanish Culture*, Cornell 1991.
Marx, Karl and Engels, Friedrich *The German Ideology*, Collected Works, vol. 5, Lawrence and Wishart 1975.
Marx, Karl, *Capital 1*, London 1974.
Marx, Karl, *Towards a Critique of Hegel's Philosophy of Right*, in *Selected Writings*, David McLellan (ed.),Oxford University Press 1977.
Mauron, Charles, *Psychocritique du Genre Comique*, Paris, José Corti, 1964.
Medina, José *Language*, Continuum, London 2005.
Menéndez Pelayo, Marcelino, *Historia de los Heterodoxos Españoles*, volume 2, Biblioteca de Autores Cristianos, Madrid 1956.
Mitchell, W.J.T., *Iconology: Image, Text, Ideology*, Chicago U.P. 1986.
Molière, Jean-Baptiste Poquelin, *Comedies* (*Le Misanthrope: ou l'atrabilaire* and *Le Tartuffe ou l'imposteur*) translated by Donald Frame, Oxford University Press 1968.
Morson, Gary Saul and Emerson Caryl, *Rethinking Bakhtin: Extensions and Challenges*, Northeastern U.P. 1989.
National Gallery Catalogue, *The Sacred Made Real*, National Gallery and Yale University Press 2010.
Nerlich, Michael, *The Ideology of Adventure*, University of Minnesota, 1987.
Nietzsche, Friedrich, *On the Genealogy of Morals*, (edited with commentary by Walter Kaufman) Vintage, New York 1989.
Nietzsche, Friedrich, *Twilight of the Idols* (translated and edited by Walter Kaufman), *The Portable Nietzsche* Viking Press 1973.

Parker, David (ed.), *Ideology, Absolutism, and the English Revolution: Debates of the British Communist Historians 1940–1956*, London, Lawrence and Wishart 2008.

Pêcheux, Michel, *Language, Semantics, and Ideology* [1975], Macmillan 1982.

Pérez, Rolando, "Nietzsche's Reading of Cervantes' 'Cruel' Humor in *Don Quijote*", in *el Humanista* 30 (2015).

Poole, Brian, "Bakhtin and Cassirer", *South Atlantic Quarterly*, 97, 1998.

Poole, Brian, "Bakhtin and Cassirer: the Philosophical Origins of Carnival Messianism", in Hamlin and Krois (eds.), Yale 2004.

Purdie, Susan, *Comedy: the mastery of discourse*, Harvester Wheatsheaf 1995.

Pye, Christopher, "The Sovereign, the Theater, and the Kingdome of Darknesse: Hobbes and the Spectacle of Power", *Representing the English Renaissance*, Stephen Greenblatt (ed.), Berkeley, University of California Press 1988.

Rabb, Theodore K., *The Struggle for Stability in Early Modern Europe*, New York, Oxford University Press, 1975.

Rousseau, Jean-Jacques, *Lettre à D'Alembert sur les Spectacles* [1758] Paris, Flammarion 2003.

Russell P.E., *Cervantes*, Oxford University Press 1985.

Saint Ignatius of Loyola, *Personal Writings*, Penguin 1996.

Saint John of the Cross (San Juan de la Cruz), *Poems*, Penguin 1960.

Saint Teresa of Ávila, (Santa Teresa de Jesús), *Libro de la Vida*, Madrid, Castalia 1986.

Sass, Louis: *The Paradoxes of Delusion: Wittgenstein, Schreber and the Schizophrenic Mind*, Cornell 1994.

Schalkwyk, David, *Shakespeare, Love and Service*, Cambridge 2008.

Sedgwick, Peter, *Psychopolitics*, Pluto 1982.

Shklovsky, Viktor, "Kak sdelan don Kikhot", *O Teorii Prozy*, Federatsiya Press, Moscow 1929.

Skidelsky, Edward, *Ernst Cassirer: the Last Philosopher of Culture*, Princeton UP 2008.

Skinner, Quentin, "Hobbes and the Classical Theory of Laughter", *Leviathan After 350 Years*, Tom Sorrell and Luc Foisneau (eds.) Oxford University Press 2004.

Strong, Roy, *The Cult of Elizabeth*, Thames and Hudson, London, [1977], 1987.

Sudir, Hazareesingh, *Legend of Napoleon*, Granta, 2004.

Tennenhouse, Leonard, *Power on Display: the Politics of Shakespeare's Genres*, Methuen, 1986.

Tihanov, Galin, "Bakhtin's Essays on the Novel (1935–41)", *Dialogism* 1, 1998.

Tihanov, Galin, *The Master and The Slave: Lukács, Bakhtin, and the Ideas of their Time*, Clarendon, Oxford 2000.

Tihanov, Galin, "Voloshinov, Ideology and Language: The Birth of Marxist Sociology from the Spirit of *Lebensphilosophie*, in "*Bakhtin/'Bakhtin': Studies in the Archive and Beyond*", Peter Hitchcock (ed.), *South Atlantic Quarterly* 3/4 1998 (pp. 596–621).

Todorov, Tsvetan, "Une explication du texte", *Dostoïevski: Notes d'un souterrain/ Zapiski iz podpol'ya*, bilingual edition, Aubier Montaigne, Paris 1972.

Volochinov, V.N., *Marxisme et Philosophie du Langage: les problèmes fondamentaux de la method sociologique dans la science du langage*, original Russian text [Priboi, Leningrad 1930] with translation into French by Patrick Sériot and Inna Tylkowski-Ageeva, Lambert-Lucas, Limoges, 2010.

Voloshinov, V.N., *Marxism and the Philosophy of Language*, Seminar Press, New York and London, 1973.

Vygotsky, L.S., *Thought and Language* [1956] M.I.T press 1962.

Warner, Marina, *Alone of all her Sex*, London, Pan 1976.

Weber, Max *The Sociology of Religion*, London, Methuen 1965.

Weber, Max, *The Theory of Social and Economic Organization*, Simon and Schuster, NY, 1964.

Weber, Sam, *The Legend of Freud*, Minnesota UP, 1982

Weimann, Robert, *Shakespeare and the Popular Tradition in the Theatre: studies in the social dimension of dramatic form and function*, Baltimore, Johns Hopkins University Press, 1978.

West, William N. "Knowledge and Performance in the Early Modern Theatrum Mundi", *metaphorik.de* 14/2008

Wood, Ellen Meiksins, *The Origins of Capitalism: a longer view*, [1999] Verso Publications, London 2017.

Wright, Will, *Six-Guns and Society: a structural study of the Western*, University of California 1977.

Zbinden and Henking (eds.), *La Quadrature du Cercle Bakhtine*, Lausanne, 2005.

Zizek, Slavoj, *The Sublime Object of Ideology*, Verso, London 1989.

Zupančič, Alenka, *The Odd One In: On Comedy*, MIT Press, Cambridge Mass, 2008.

Zwart, Hub, "The Truth of Laughter: Rereading Luther as a Contemporary of Rabelais", *Dialogism*, no. 3, 1999.

Name Index

Aguinaga, Carlos Blanco, *et al.* 134–136
Althusser, Louis 3, 98–101, 108, 113, 126, 146
Anderson, Benedict 5n8, 104, 115, 164
Anievas, Alexander and Kerem Nişancioğlu 130n5
Aristophanes 242, 255
Aristotle 8–10, 13–14, 17, 204, 250–251

Bakhtin, Mikhaïl Mikhaïlovich: Dialogism 1, 8–166 *passim*
   anticipation and prevention 27–33
   the authoritative utterance and dialogical conflict 85–90
   Carnival laughter 240–250, 267, 269
   dialogical *addressivity* and "becoming" 9–10, 19–21
   Dostoevsky and the prevention of "becoming" 35
   in literature and through *speech genres* 21–24
   versus systematicity 8–9
Baltrusaitis, Jurgis 211
Barber, C.L. 239–240
Barker, Francis 145
Barthes, Roland 108, 108n9, 209
Benjamin, Walter 62n51, 187, 234, 273
Bercé, Yves-Marie 243
Berman, Marshall 66–68, 73n71
Bernays, Edward 119–122
Bernheimer, Charles 51n33
Bernini 190, 203
Billig, Michael 245–255, 256–257
Brandist, Craig 2n2, 28–29
Braudel, Fernand 132–134
Brecht, Bertolt 154, 160n52
Bristol, M.D. 159n49
Burke, Edmund 240
Butler, Judith 99

Casalduero, Joaquín 39n7
Cascardi, Anthony J. 235–238
Cassirer, Ernst 2, 10–12, 17, 196–197, 271
Certeau, Michel de 5, 167–170, 203
Cervantes, Miguel de 6, 172–173, 173n11, 175, 201–202, 207, 215–219, 221–235

Chernyshevsky 60
Chesterfield, P, S., Earl of 252
Chomsky, Noam 9, 92
Clastres, Pierre 158–159
Close, Anthony 220, 251
Cohen, Walter 135

Debord, Guy 138–139
Deleuze, Gilles 88, 113–114
Descartes, René 140–141, 150n41
Dostoevsky, Fyodor 2–3, 21, 24, 31, 35, 37–39
   Brothers Karamazov 118n21
   Crime and Punishment 40, 42
   The Idiot 42n14

Eichenbaum, Boris 211
Elias, Norbert 105, 130, 251
Eliot, Thomas Stearns 118, 198
Emerson, Caryl 34–35, 48, 83
Erasmus, Desiderio 204–207
Evans, Dylan 127n1

Farrell, John 201n6
Flaubert, Gustave 62, 62n50
Flor, Fernando R. de la 133n8, 207n16
Forcione, Alban 213–214
Foucault, Michel 23, 123–124
Frank, Joseph 60–61, 73n72
Freidenberg, Olga M. 240
Freud, Sigmund 50–51
   anthropology 165, 259
   The Dora Case 95n23, 96–97, 116–117
   Freudian anthropology 119
   reactive thought 51n33
   Three Essays on Sexuality 126, 160–161
Frye, Northrop 239–240

Galdós, Benito 137n15
Gardiner, Michael 93n19
Girard, René 72, 76n80, 233n59
Goldmann, Lucien 170
Gramsci, Antonio 3, 16–17, 245, 270
Greenblatt, Stephen 4n7, 144–147

NAME INDEX

Hall, Jonathan 105n1, 152n42
Hamlin C. and Krois J.M. 2n2, 14n8
Hawkes, David 110n11
Hazareesingh, Sudir 59n44
Hegel 163
Hill, Christopher 90, 111–112
Hirschkop, Ken 85
Hobbes, Thomas 109–112, 117, 258–259
Hobsbawm Eric, and Ranger Terence 104, 138
Holquist, Michael 86n8
Humboldt, Wilhelm von 11–13

Iser, Wolgang 237n66
Ismard, Paulin 254n27
Ives, Peter 16n14, 93n19

Jameson, Fredric 9n3
Johnson, Samuel 220–221

Kaus, Otto 36
Kundera, Milan 269–270, 273

La Bruyère, Jean 246–247
Lacan, Jacques 17–19, 61n47, 122, 127n1, 189–190, 207–208, 231–232, 260n38, 262–265
Laclos, Pierre Cholderlos de 253
Lähteenmäki, Mika 2n2, 11
Laing R. D. 114–115
and Bateson 115n160
Leader, Darian 201
Lecercle, Jean-Jacques 88, 92
Lenin, V.I. 103
Lévi-Strauss, Claude 18–19
Lope de Vega 135–136
Lorca, Federico García 137n15
Lukács, Gyorgy 13–14, 197–198
Lunacharsky, A.V. 2, 36–37
Luther, Martin 248–250

Macchiavelli, Nicolò 151
MacPherson, C.B. 109–112
Maravall, Antonio 4n6, 127–130, 135, 139, 142–143, 199–200, 210–213
Mariscal, George 229–232
Marty, Anton 28–29
Marx, Karl 5, 95–96, 112, 114, 162–163, 245

Mauron, Charles 7, 255–257, 259–261, 270, 273
Medina, José 12
Menéndez Pelayo, Marcelino 169n2
Mitchell, W.J.T. 208–209
Molière, Jean-Baptiste Poquelin 185
 Le Misanthrope 206
 Tartuffe 206
Morson, Gary Saul 14n9

Nekrassov 72
Nerlich, Michael 177
Nietzsche, Friedrich 15, 54–55, 241–242, 259n37

Parker, David 91n16
Pêcheux, Michel 100n30
Pérez, Rolando 259n37
Poole, Brian 10n4
Purdie, Susan 267n46
Pye, Christopher 147–148

Quevedo, Francisco de 131, 137, 167, 250

Rabb, Theodore K. 140–141
Racine, Jean 142n25
 Athalie and Phèdre 142n25
Rousseau, Jean-Jacques 59, 109, 206
Russell P.E. 173n11

Saint Ignatius of Loyola 172–180
 Reminiscences 172–180
 Spiritual Exercises 179–186
Saint John of the Cross 171, 192–196
Saint Teresa of Ávila 188–192
Sass, Louis 23n22
Saussure, Ferdinand 8–9
Schalkwyk, David 110n12
Sedgwick, Peter 115n16
Sériot, Patrick 14, 93
Shakespeare, William 150–156
Shklovsky, Viktor 211–212, 212n27
Simmel 14
Skidelsky, Edward 14n8
Skinner, Quentin 251–252
Stendahl 59n44
Strong, Roy 149–150

Tennenhouse, Leonard 144
Tihanov, Galin 2n2, 15–16
Todorov, Tsvetan 42n16

Voloshinov, Valentin 1, 3n5, 8, 13–14, 17, 33, 83–84, 92–104
   dialogical conflict and repression 137, 271–273
Vygotsky, L.S. 1, 83–84

Warner, Marina 186–187

Weber, Max 5, 121–122, 131, 143, 155–158, 202
Weber, Sam 63
Weimann, Robert 153–154
Wood, Ellen Meiksins 106–107
Wright, Will 235

Žižek, Slavoj 162
Zupančič, Alenka 261–266
Zwart, Hub 248–249

Subject Index

Anticipation and Prevention   27–35, 43, 164–166
Antisemitism   115–116, 249
Authoritative utterances and internalised conflict   85–90

Baroque *addressivity*   133–141, 144–151, 153–157, 164–166
Becoming   2–3, 10–13, 20–24, 212–215
   laughter and   6
   the prevention of "becoming"   39–40, 42–45, 84, 134

Capitalism and "catastrophe" in Dostoevsky   36–37, 45–52
Captivation   127
   textual   199–201, 211–229
   visual   148–151, 207–212
Carnival laughter   6–7, 154, 158–162, 166, 203, 206, 239–241
   and history   243, 248, 269
Charismatic "presence"   141–144, 154–161
Christian Mysticism   5
   narrativised   168–172
   rationalised   172–180
   sensualised   187–196
Combined and uneven development   129, 130n5
Counter-Reformation ideology   133, 140–141

Decipherment and nostalgia   199–204
Desublimation   6, 240–248
Dialogism and dialectics   13, 101–104
Disenchantment   5, 104, 131, 198, 201–202
   and re-enchantment   5, 104
Divinisation of the state   104, 114, 131, 138, 142

Gramscian "hegemony"   3, 16, 21, 93, 100–101, 137, 164, 243, 270

Great Theatre of the World   133, 199, 204–207
Guilt   7, 73, 114–119, 121–122, 125, 148, 160–161, 164–165, 261

Ideology and *addressivity*   3, 98–101
Imagined Community   5, 144–166
Interpellations by market and state: the capitalist double-bind   105–126

Laughter and social hierarchy   250–253
   anxiety overcome   248–250, 255–259
   the potential for change   259–270, 272–273
Lebensphilosophie   14–16
"linguistic turn"   17–20
Loyalty   117–118, 118n18, 157

Marxism   2, 10, 13–17, 88, 90, 93–94, 109, 112, 114, 197, 244
Monetarisation and its cultural effects   130–136
Monologism and Dialogism   1–2

Narcissism   3, 4, 20, 139, 180, 260n38
Nature mythologised   107–110

Paradox as "frozen event"   52–54
production of the unconscious   21, 26–27, 48–51, 67–81, 92–98
Psychoanalysis   3, 5, 19, 109, 127, 165, 170, 184, 264

State theatricality   4, 127–130, 136–139, 144–155
Systemic and antisystemic accounts of language   8–10

www.ingramcontent.com/pod-product-compliance
Lightning Source LLC
Chambersburg PA
CBHW071151070526
44584CB00019B/2749